Library of
Davidson College

Village Viability in Contemporary Society

AAAS Selected Symposia Series

Published by Westview Press
5500 Central Avenue, Boulder, Colorado

for the

81-6083

American Association for the Advancement of Science
1776 Massachusetts Avenue, N.W., Washington, D.C.

Village Viability in Contemporary Society

Edited by
Priscilla Copeland Reining
and Barbara Lenkerd

AAAS Selected Symposium **34**

301.35
V7131

AAAS Selected Symposia Series

This book is based on a symposium which was held at the 1978 AAAS National Annual Meeting in Washington, D.C., February 12-17. The symposium was sponsored by the Anthropological Society of Washington, AAAS Section H (Anthropology) and the AAAS Office of International Science.

All rights reserved. No part of this publication may be reproduced or transmitted in any form or by any means, electronic or mechanical, including photocopy, recording, or any information storage and retrieval system, without permission in writing from the publisher.

Copyright © 1980 by the American Association for the Advancement of Science

Published in 1980 in the United States of America by
  Westview Press, Inc.
  5500 Central Avenue
  Boulder, Colorado 80301
  Frederick A. Praeger, Publisher

Library of Congress Cataloging in Publication Data
Main entry under title:
Village viability in contemporary society.
  (AAAS selected symposium ; 34)
  Includes bibliographies and index.
  1. Villages—Congresses. 2. Sociology, Rural—Congresses. I. Reining, Priscilla. II. Lenkerd, Barbara. III. Series: American Association for the Advancement of Science. AAAS selected symposium series ; 34.
HT407.V45   301.35'2   79-23565
ISBN 0-89158-472-2

Printed and bound in the United States of America

About the Book

The village is a ubiquitous form of human settlement that has housed the majority of the world's people for the past 10,000 years. Now, its viability is being threatened as villages worldwide are increasingly involved in national and international marketing networks and with new forms of technology. These papers by a notable group of anthropologists and economists offer a panoramic view of the village; its beginnings; present constraints; and future potential.

About the Series

The *AAAS Selected Symposia Series* was begun in 1977 to provide a means for more permanently recording and more widely disseminating some of the valuable material which is discussed at the AAAS Annual National Meetings. The volumes in this *Series* are based on symposia held at the Meetings which address topics of current and continuing significance, both within and among the sciences, and in the areas in which science and technology impact on public policy. The *Series* format is designed to provide for rapid dissemination of information, so the papers are not typeset but are reproduced directly from the camera-copy submitted by the authors, without copy editing. The papers are organized and edited by the symposium arrangers who then become the editors of the various volumes. Most papers published in this *Series* are original contributions which have not been previously published, although in some cases additional papers from other sources have been added by an editor to provide a more comprehensive view of a particular topic. Symposia may be reports of new research or reviews of established work, particularly work of an interdisciplinary nature, since the AAAS Annual Meetings typically embrace the full range of the sciences and their societal implications.

                                        WILLIAM D. CAREY
                                        Executive Officer
                                        American Association for
                                        the Advancement of Science

Contents

Figures and Tables xiii

About the Editors and Authors xvii

Preface xxiii

Introduction--*Priscilla Copeland Reining* 1

    The Village and Its Completeness   9
    Villagers and Their Cohesiveness 11
    Structural Inclusiveness   12
    The Whole and the Parts   14
    References   15

PART 1. THE VILLAGE DEFINED

1   On the Viability of Villages--*Margaret Mead* ...19

    References   32

PART 2. STUDIES OF THE VILLAGE

2   Millenium of Modernization: A Changing
    German Village--*Jack M. Weatherford* 35

    Pre-History   37
    Industrialization   45
    Post-Industrial Development   49
    The Changing Moral Community   54
        The Saxons,56; The Refugees,59;
        The Guest Workers,61

viii   Contents

       Conclusions   63
       References and Notes   66

3   Balancing on an Alp: Population Stability and Change in a Swiss Peasant Village—*Robert McC. Netting and Walter S. Elias* 69

       Peasant Population Equilibria   69
       Demographic History of an
          Alpine Community   71
       Total Population Dynamics   73
       Mortality   79
       The Constancy of Marriage   86
       Fertility and Fecundity   91
       The Fruitfulness of Potatoes   99
       Summary and Conclusions   101
       References and Notes   102

4   The Transformation of Hungarian Villages—*Conrad C. Reining* 109

       References and Notes   121

5   Time Perspectives in Village India—*Charlotte Wiser* 123

       References   159

6   The Middle Eastern Village in Regional Perspective—*Daniel G. Bates* 161

       Summary and Concluding Remarks   178
       References and Notes   180

7   Continuities and Discontinuities in China: The Natural Village and the Production Brigade—*Molly G. Schuchat and James D. Jordan*...185

       Introduction   185
       No One Typical Village   187
       Evolution of the Natural Village   188
         The Family Home,189; The Pao-Chia Control System,190; Public Works and Utilities,191; The Market Town and Village Industry,192; The Village and the State,193

Communes and the Production
    Brigade   195
    *Mutual Aid Teams and Agricultural
    Producers Cooperatives, 196*
Present-Day Observations   197
    *Population Movements, 197; Com-
    munication--Ties Between City and
    Countryside, 199; Effect of Self-
    Reliance, 200; Future of the Village
    in China, 202*
References and Notes   203

PART 3. DEVELOPMENT AND THE VILLAGE

8 The Future of Rice Monocultures in
   Malaysia--*Clive Bell*..........................207

   I.   Malaysia's Paddy Sector in
        Its National Setting   208
   II. The Economic and Social
        Organisation of Paddy
        Production   210
   III. The Sectoral Picture:
        Supply, Demand and Prices   217
   IV. The Economic and Social
        Organisation of Paddy
        Production in the Future   224
   V.   Some General Conclusions   230
   References and Notes   231

9 The Role of the Village in Sahelian
   Development--*David Shear* 235

   I.   Introduction and Overview   235
        *Background of the Drought,
        235; The Long-Term Response
        to the Sahelian Drought, 236;
        Village Emphasis, 238*
   II. Village and Underdevelopment
        in Historical Perspective   239
        *Examples of Permanence and
        Change, 239; Forced Migration
        and New Lands Settlement, 243;
        Other Historical Constraints, 244*

x   Contents

      III. Promoting Village Development through the Sahel Development Program   245
Using Basic Human Needs as an Approach to Integrated Rural Development, 249; Health, 251; Demographic and Health Planning, 252; Components of an Integrated Village-Based System, 253; Implementation: Timing and Decentralization, 257; Reinforcing the Village-Based Approach, 257; The Donor Community's Ability to Respond to Village-Based Activities, 259
    References and Notes   263
    Bibliography   265

10   New Village Uses of Renewable Energy Sources--*James W. Howe* 269

     I.   Current Energy Use in Developing Countries   269
A. Not Much Modern Energy is Used, 269; B. Most Modern Energy Use is Concentrated in Urban Areas, 271; C. Much Traditional Energy is Used in Rural Areas, 271
    II.   The Connection Between Energy and Development   272
    III.   Conventional Sources of Modern Energy   273
A. Petroleum, 273; B. Nuclear, 273; C. Other Site Specific Sources, 274
    IV.   Solar Energy Technology   275
A. Mini-Hydroelectric Generators, 275; B. Wind, 275; C. Generating Methane Gas from Organic Wastes, 276; D. Photovoltaic, or Solar Cells, 277; E. Simple Flat Plate Solar Collector, 277
    V.   Solar Energy Costs   277
    VI.   Testing Solar Energy Potential   279
A. The Need for Village Level Tests, 279; B. The Nature of the Tests, 280

	VII. Summary	284
	Notes	284

11 The Political Economy of Education for
   Village Development--*John Simmons* 287

	I. Types of Education	288
	II. Failure of Present System	289
	III. Solutions	292
	IV. "Expert Solutions"	294
	V. Conflicting Theories	295
	VI. Outlook	297
	VII. Strategy	299
	VIII. Illustrations of Education for Self-Reliance	300

The Problem-Posing Method: Brazil, 301; Reaching the Poor by Radio: Columbia, 301; Education through Rural Cooperatives: Bangladesh, 303; Barefoot Doctors: China, 304; Building Local Initiative: Senegal, 305; Self-Reliance for Community Needs: Sri Lanka, 306

	IX. Policy Issues	307
	Annex I	309

The Widening Gap: Literacy and Formal Education, 309

	References	313

12 Human Development in Traditional and
   Modernizing Villages--*Michael Maccoby*..........315

Psychosocial Needs	323
References and Notes	323

Comment--*Shahid Javed Burki*....................325
Reply--*Michael Maccoby*........................331

PART 4. DISCUSSION

13 A Concluding Comment--*Francis P. Conant*.......335

Universal Aspects of Villages	335
Field Studies	340
Viability	344

Index 345

Figures and Tables

Introduction

Table 1	Percentage of rural population by region and by overall state of development	2
Table 2	Components in the definition of village, villager and village structure	8

Chapter 3

Figure 1	Aggregate population estimates in Törbel	72
Figure 2a	Births, marriages and deaths in Törbel, 1685-1800	74
Figure 2b	Births, marriages and deaths in Törbel, 1800-1920	75
Figure 2c	Births, marriages and deaths in Törbel, 1920-1970	76
Figure 3	Emigration from Törbel by twenty-year periods	78
Table 1	Crude death rate estimates	80
Table 2	Adult age-specific mortality rates	82
Table 3	Infant and child mortality	84
Table 4	Adult life expectancy	85

xiv Figures and Tables

Table 5	Average total births by mother's age at marriage	87
Table 6	Age at first marriage	87
Table 7	Mean values for birth, survivorship, nuptiality and celibacy of children per family	88
Table 8	Negative evidence of family limitation	92
Figure 4	Comparative age-specific marital fertility rates	93
Table 9	Age-specific marital fertility rates	94
Figure 5a	Age-sex structure of Törbel population, 1750	96
Figure 5b	Age-sex structure of Törbel population, 1850	97
Table 10	Mean birth intervals for Törbel women	98

Chapter 8

Table 1	The salient characteristics of paddy farm households	212
Table 2	Growth rates of paddy production and net sown area in Peninsular Malaysia	217

Chapter 10

Table 1	Ratio of energy used in the United States compared to selected countries	269
Table 2	Energy use per hectare in rice production in various countries	270
Table 3	Comparison of fossil energy inputs for corn, rice and wheat	271
Table 4	Solar energy applicability matrix	278

Chapter 11

Table 1	Optimistic literacy projections	310
Table 2	Realistic literacy projections	310

| Table 3 | Functional literacy projections | 310 |
| Figure 1 | Illiteracy projections | 311 |

About the Editors and Authors

Priscilla Copeland Reining *is a project director in the Office of International Science, AAAS. A social anthropologist with field experience in African villages, she has studied land use/land tenure and population in Haya villages now known to have been continuously occupied over a 2000-year period. She has also carried out studies of renewable resources in villages and of the use of remote-sensing data sources for long-term, precise monitoring of the processes of desertification. Among her recent books are* Village Women, Their Changing Lives and Fertility *(AAAS, 1977) and* Challenging Desertification in West Africa *(Ohio University Press, in press). She is a member of the National Academy of Science's Board on Science and Technology for International Development.*

Barbara Lenkerd *is an anthropologist working with the Harvard Project on Technology, Work and Character. She is presently serving as researcher/educator for the ACTION agency's Work Improvement Program. She is the author of* "Mexico," *a case study in* Village Women, Their Changing Lives and Fertility,*(P.C. Reining et al.; AAAS, 1977).*

Daniel G. Bates, *associate professor of anthropology at Hunter College, City University of New York, has done extensive field research in the Middle East, studying nomadic pastoralism, demography, and rural land use. He is the author of* Nomads and Farmers: The Yoruk of Southeastern Turkey *(University of Michigan Museum of Anthropology, 1973);* Cultural Anthropology *(with F. Plog; Alfred Knopf, 1976); and* Anthropology: Decisions, Adaptation and Evolution *(with F. Plog and C. Jolly; Alfred Knopf, 1976). He is currently co-editor of the journal* Human Ecology, *and is a member of the Smithsonian Institution's Scientific Advisory Council for Archeology and Related Disciplines.*

About the Editors and Authors

Clive Bell, *senior ecomomist for the Development Research Center, World Bank, is a specialist in income distribution and resource allocation in peasant agriculture and in accumulation and income distribution in the development process. He is co-author (with H.B. Chenery et al.) of* Redistribution With Growth *(London: OUP, 1974), and has published articles on the theory of share tenancy, the political economy of agrarian reform, the effects of technical progress on peasant economies, and the long-term relationship between demographic and economic variables.*

Shahid Javed Burki *is chief of the Policy Planning Division for the World Bank. He is the author of* A Study of Chinese Communes *(Harvard, 1969) and of* Agricultural Growth in Punjab, Pakistan *(Cornell, 1974). His numerous articles on employment problems, institutional development and basic needs in developing countries have been published internationally in such journals as* Public Policy, The Middle East Journal, *and* World Development. *A former Rhodes Scholar, he served as the director of the Rural Works Program, as Deputy Secretary of Foreign Aid and as an economic advisor to the government of Pakistan.*

Francis P. Conant *is professor of anthropology at Hunter College, City University of New York and research associate at NASA Goddard Institute for Space Studies. He is active in the analysis and application of Landsat satellite data for African subsistence systems. His publications include,* "The Relationship of Contemporary Communities in Northern Nigeria to Abandoned Settlement Sites," (Annals 96, *New York Academy of Sciences, 1962),* "The Korok *in East Africa as a Unit of Physical and Social Space"* (American Anthropologist, *1965), and* "The Interpretation of East African Swiddening via Landsat Satellite Data" *(with T. Cary;* Proceedings, 4th Perdue Symposium on Machine Processing of Remote Sensed Data, *1977).*

Walter S. Elias *is research director of Project Well Aware at the University of Arizona. He has published on the topics of isonymy and inbreeding, late marriage, and genetics and migration in endogamous communities.*

James W. Howe, *currently a senior fellow at the Overseas Development Council, has served as director of the Program Office of the Latin American Bureau of the Agency for International Development (AID), as deputy director of the U.S. AID mission to Brazil, and as director of the AID operations mission to Vietnam. A former member of the Policy Planning Council for less-developed countries (Department of State), he is the author of numerous publications on world economic development, including* The Future of the International

Economic Order: An Agenda for Research, 1973 *for the Overseas Development Council. He also served as project director for the publications* The United States and World Development, Agenda for Action, 1975 *(Praeger) and* The United States and the Developing World: Agenda for Action, 1974 *(Praeger).*

James D. Jordan *is an author/editor for Defense and Foreign Affairs Quarterly Strategic Bibliography. He is the author of* Factors Influencing the Functions and Capabilities of the PLA *(Research Analysis Corp, 1970) and of papers on Chinese political theory, peasantry, women, and agriculture. He has been a Ford Far East Studies Fellow and is currently a member of the Association for Asian Studies and the National Committee on United States-China Relations.*

Michael Maccoby, *a psychoanalyst and social psychologist at the Washington School of Psychiatry, is also director of the Program on Technology, Policy, and Human Development of the Kennedy School of Government, Harvard University. He has assisted both industry and government in establishing social and human criteria for organizational improvement. He directed the Bolivar Project (for Harman International Industries and the United Automobile Workers) which applied principles of security, equity, democracy and individual development to the work environment. He has written many articles on the relationship between work and human development, and he is the author of* The Gamesman: The New Corporate Leaders *(Simon & Schuster, 1977) and coauthor of* Social Character in a Mexican Village *(with Erich Fromm; Prentice-Hall, 1970).*

Margaret Mead *(1901-1978) served as curator for more than fifty years at the American Museum of Natural History, taught and lectured at numerous universities and public forums, and was adjunct professor at Columbia University. She conducted field studies of tribal villages in Samoa, the Admiralty Islands, Bali, and New Guinea, and her books and articles describing these cultures received world-wide recognition. Her research interests centered on ethnology, personality and culture, child development, learning theory, and native languages and their applications to the fields of national character. The recipient of many honors and awards, she was a fellow of the National Academy of Sciences and was president of the AAAS, the American Anthropological Association, and the Society for Applied Anthropology.*

Robert McC. Netting *is professor of anthropology at the University of Arizona, specializing in cultural ecology, social organization, and historical demography. He has published articles on household composition, intensive agriculture, warfare, and local politics, and his books include*

Cultural Ecology *(Benjamin/Cummings, 1977) and* Hill Farmers of Nigeria: Cultural Ecology of the Kofyar of the Jos Plateau *(University of Washington, 1968). He is a member of the editorial board for the* Annual Review of Anthropology, *a fellow of the American Anthropological Association, and a councillor of the American Ethnological Society.*

Conrad C. Reining *is professor of anthropology at the Catholic University of America. His studies have focused on the German minority in southeastern Europe and on food production and economic development in tropical Africa. His book* The Zande Scheme *(Northwestern University, 1966) is an anthropological case study of economic development in Africa. A National Academy of Sciences/Hungarian Academy of Sciences exchange scholar, he has also served on the Board of Directors of the African Studies Association and is a fellow of numerous professional organizations, including AAAS, the American Anthropological Association, and the Royal Anthropological Institute.*

Molly G. Schuchat *is director of evaluation for Behavior Service Consultants, Inc. A social anthropologist by training, her research has focused on interrelations between cosmopolitanism and ethnicity in complex societies, especially in the United States, Hungary, and the People's Republic of China. Her current work involves youth services, mental health programs and community development in the United States. She is a fellow of the American Anthropological Association, the Society for Applied Anthropology and the AAAS.*

David Shear *is the incoming director, U.S. AID in Senegal, and former director of the Office of Sahel and Francophone West African Affairs, Agency for International Development. He was a visiting fellow at the Overseas Development Council and a senior fellow at the Institute for Advanced Studies, Princeton. His work is concerned with long-term planning and development, and in 1976 he received the Rockefeller Public Service Award for his work on Sahelian development. His publications include "Prospects for Long-Term Planning for Development" in* The Politics of Natural Disaster *(M.H. Glantz, ed.; Praeger, 1976).*

John Simmons, *a specialist in development economics, is with the Policy Planning Division of the World Bank. Among his recent publications are articles on education, rural development and popular participation, and various books, including* The Education Dilemma: Policy Issues in Developing Countries in the 1980s *(Pergamon, 1979);* Change in Tunisia: Essays in the Social Sciences *(with Russel A. Stone; SUNY, 1976); and* Cocoa Production: Economic and Botanical Perspectives *(Praeger, 1976).*

About the Editors and Authors

Jack M. Weatherford, *a research associate at the Center for the Study of Family and State, Duke University, and an anthropologist by training, is currently on the staff of the U.S. Senate as a AAAS Congressional Science Fellow. His areas of interest are aging, the family, and government policies. He is currently working on a book,* Nuclear Family Culture in Five Societies *(with M. Swartz et al.)*

Charlotte Wiser *has spent 50 years studying village life in India and was coauthor of one of the first Indian village studies. She has written four books documenting her observations of continuity and change in village life, including* Behind Mud Walls *(with W. Wiser; University of California, 1972, rev. ed.) and* Four Families of Karimpur *(Maxwell School of Citizenship and Public Affairs, Syracuse University, 1978), and has received the Qaiser-i-hind, an award for service to rural women in North India.*

Preface

This volume on the important question of village viability arose from several organizational innovations. The first innovation was the combining of the yearly program of the Anthropological Society of Washington, an affiliate of the American Association for the Advancement of Science (AAAS), with a AAAS panel in order to exploit the advantages of both types of meetings. The October through May monthly meetings of the ASW provide each speaker with almost two hours for presentation and questions--a wealth of time compared to the normal AAAS panel speaker's twenty minutes. Moreover, ASW has a long tradition of asking its speakers to prepare their papers for publication. The disadvantage of the ASW meeting schedule is that speakers, often from out of town, almost never have the opportunity to hear and question each other. At the AAAS panel, in February 1978, we reconvened most of the same speakers in a format ideal for such discussion.

Our ASW speakers were James Howe, Daniel Bates, David Shear, Conrad Reining, Charlotte Wiser, Molly Schuchat and James Jordan, Michael Maccoby and Shahid Javed Burki, and finally, Margaret Mead, who kept her commitment despite her then deteriorating health. In February, at the AAAS Annual meeting in Washington, D.C., our panelists were Daniel Bates, Charlotte Wiser, Clive Bell, Michael Maccoby, David Shear, Conrad Reining, James Howe and John Simmons. Francis Conant who had been scheduled as discussant for the morning's panel generously took on the afternoon set as well when Margaret Mead's illness did not permit her to attend the AAAS meeting. This format gave us some flexibility in planning and scheduling since not every speaker could appear at both AAAS and ASW.

We express our gratitude to these colleagues who joined us in this common effort, who gave doubly of their time and knowledge, and who examined combined programs as a means of strengthening the tie between the affiliates and the Association. However, we were not yet finished, for our AAAS-ASW panel was chosen for publication as a symposium volume. These contributors undertook the further task of reflection on others' points of view and of rewriting their chapters for publication. This was no small effort, and we truly wish to thank all of those who have stayed with us through the course to publication. We also want to express our gratitude to Rhoda Metraux who undertook a final extensive editing of Margaret Mead's ASW presentation after Dr. Mead's death in November of 1978.

The flexibility of the symposium publication program permitted yet another innovation--that of rounding out the volume with additional articles not presented at either ASW or AAAS. We were very pleased to be able to persuade Robert Netting, Walter Elias, and Jack Weatherford to add their articles to this volume.

The significance of the problem--the present status of villages and their probable future in a period of rapid change--led us from the beginning to view the problem in interdisciplinary terms. We attempted to capture the important experience of intensive village studies conducted by anthropologists and sociologists and combine it with the views of development economists and administrators. Such an approach is well suited to the interdisciplinary intent and platform available through AAAS. Among our contributors are six anthropologists, two historians, four specialists in development economics, two in political science, and one each in sociology, population genetics, and psychoanalysis/social psychology. Furthermore, a number of our contributors have the advantage of combining their principal discipline with use of a related methodology such as demography, history, archaeology, and political history, or have devised special approaches such as the long-term study and, even, ethnography at a distance--intensive interviewing of informants who are no longer resident in their natal village.

In acknowledging and thanking our contributors, we also wish to express our thanks for the steady support and interest in this volume shown by the AAAS Publications Office, its managing editor, Kathryn Wolff, and her staff.

Since villages occur in nearly every climate and on every continent except the Antarctic, their comparative study is, by definition, international in character. Therefore the sponsorship of the AAAS panel comes appropriately through the Office of International Science of AAAS, as well as the AAAS Section H, Anthropology. We are most grateful that not only did the Anthropological Society of Washington meet the expenses of its speakers, it is also arranging to distribute this volume to its membership.

> Priscilla Copeland Reining
> *Office of International Science*
> *AAAS*
>
> Barbara Lenkerd
> *Harvard Project on Technology,*
>   *Work and Character*
> *Washington, D.C.*

June 1979

Village Viability in Contemporary Society

Priscilla Copeland Reining

Introduction

Throughout the world, the single most frequent form of human settlement is almost certainly the village. Cities and towns are observably far fewer in number than villages, and isolated farmsteads or herding camps, though numerous (and difficult to count), are, we believe, less common than the larger and more permanent villages. Of the 4.3 billion people in the world in 1979, rural populations (villages, camps, etc.) accounted for more than two and a half billion; a conservative estimate puts the world's villagers at over two billion and the villages in which they live at about two million (1). (Percentage of rural population by region is shown in Table 1.)

In size, villages range from a low of perhaps a hundred permanent residents to a high of two or three thousand; thus close to a majority of the people in the world live in a situation in which they can develop extensive personal and frequently long-term contacts with a relatively large and stable group of people similar to themselves. The village-- the visible form of these invisible ties--is the subject of this volume.

In the voluminous literature about the important current topic of development there is a tendency to talk about rural populations as if they were collectivities of single individuals and to consider rural communities without taking into account their special characteristics. Here, however, we are talking about villagers and villages in terms of the characteristics which do make them more than simple collectivities, and we will attempt to examine some examples of this unique and varied type of human social organization. Our concern at this time is particularly appropriate, since, in the period since World War II, changes in the political and technical orders have been significant and pervasive, yet changes in the social order (the real increase in poverty, for example)

Table 1. Percentage of rural population by region and by overall state of development derived from the 1979 World Population Data Sheet. (1)

Region	Percent	Region	Percent
World	61	Latin America	39
More developed	32	Middle America	42
Less developed	72	Caribbean	51
Africa	75	Tropical S. America	40
Western Africa	80	Temperate S.A.	20
Eastern Africa	88	Europe	32
Middle Africa	72	Northern Europe	27
Southern Africa	56	Western Europe	20
Asia	73	Eastern Europe	42
Middle South Asia	79	Southern Europe	40
Southeast Asia	79	USSR	38
East Asia	69	Oceania	29
North America	26		

have often appeared almost inadvertent, while changes in the moral order ("what is right," to use Redfield's term) and their impact at the village level have too frequently been ignored.

While the village can be defined by enumeration of its many unique characteristics--which we will consider later--let us begin our discussion with Margaret Mead's statement (Chapter 1) that a village is "a human settlement that exists through time--a type of accessibility to the knowledge of each other which makes it possible to identify the people within the gates." That is, a village is a bounded group of people who know each other, and the constraints (and potential) of this personal knowledge may be one essential factor limiting the size of the village, determining its special characteristics, and shaping its future.

As a human invention, the village is associated with the beginning of the Neolitic, was independently derived in the Old World and the New, and continued and retained its position as the most common form of human settlement to the present. But villages have not been the dominant form of human settlement in terms of power, wealth, or other similar measures, for as towns and cities came into being, they always dominated the surrounding villages--as is clearly observable in those parts of the world where towns and cities have considerable historicity. This trend continues today, and this distinction is reflected in the terminology: we speak of "tribal" villages and "peasant" villages, but major centers of commerce, trade and political power are "cities" from the concept of citizenship in a formally constituted government or state. For much of the world's population, however, even in the face of the modernizing trends of today, trade, political activities and all other essential activities of living are still conducted in the unique, face-to-face milieu of the village.

If frequency of occurrence is a standard--and it is--villages are a very successful human invention which serve to organize a collection of individuals into a group with common goals, a commonly shared subsistence economy, and provisions for mutual support. If durability is a standard--and it is--villages at some particular sites are extraordinarily successful. Village site occupancy of one, two, or even three millenia is documented in this volume by Bates and Weatherford. That villages have been successful we need not doubt. But are they now and will they continue so?

We can gain some insight into the present status of the village by reviewing some recent studies, and we can look to its future as presaged by some recent formulations of policy.

We have seen the process of urbanization, especially in the last two centuries, accelerating the push out of villages of some of their best and brightest residents, who have been pulled into the market economy of the cities, which seem to offer a much wider range of individual options. Moreover, the process of commercialization--the demand for money income derived from the sale of crops, animals, or labor and the commercialization of energy sources has disrupted the subsistence economy of many villages. The social concomitants of commercialization have resulted in a division within villages, a threat to the continuity of their social networks, and thus, possibly, a threat to the continued existence of the village itself.

In undertaking this examination, however, we should also be aware that the past twenty-five years have seen the trend toward modernization slowed by the real and projected scarcity of fossil fuels and by reverse migration. Some of the world's cities are now losing population to rural areas and to villages. Nevertheless, trends toward industrial diversification and high technology have altered and continue to alter village, town, and city interrelationships. At this turning point in time, the authors in this volume are concerned with how successful and how useful have been the modernizing changes in the villages themselves, to what extent some villages have lost their distinctiveness and vitality, and what role can reasonably be projected for the village of the future.

Yet before we look to the future, we ought to be sure that the changes which result from the great transformation--to use Polanyi's term--are actually having a serious impact on the village. In many instances, as we see, for example, in the papers by Wiser, C. Reining, Schuchat and Jordan, Maccoby, and Bell, the answer is certainly yes. While the fabrication and distribution of material items through mass production holds potential for easing or altering some village tasks, it also threatens the internal division of labor within the village, since villagers participate in an intricate internal exchange of a wide variety of goods and services. In fact, industrialization can threaten the fundamental concept of "villager," since by definition villagers not only know each other personally, they know and are tied to each other through over-lapping economic as well as ritual, kin, and marriage roles. Will the village in this sense survive? Bell thinks not.

The basic question, whether the village will continue as a viable, recognizable, and functioning entity, is addressed either directly or by implication by all of the authors in this book. They consider "village viability" to be the capacity of the village to continue to be recognizable in its present form and for villagers to continue their face-to-face, multiple economic and social roles within and among other villagers, their families and their households, and to be adaptive to their immediate physical environment. Clearly, for villages to remain viable in this sense, villagers must maintain a balance between their vital relationships within the village.

Earlier studies of the village can help us clarify our understanding of villager, village, village structure, and inter-village networks. Since the 1920s, anthropologists have been concerned with the role of the village as the ultimate territorial unit combining residence, territorial placement, and social organization, and the work of Redfield and his students is notable in this regard (2, 3, 4, 5, 6). In the 1950s, Redfield brought field researchers together at many seminars to analyze and summarize their results from India and elsewhere (10). The seminar papers included in this book continue that concept of asking students of village society and development planners of rural programs to consider and reexamine the village and its multiple roles. In doing this, we recognize the significance of the Chicago tradition in highlighting the problem of the binding and pervasive relationships between village, town, and city, although we are not here attempting a scholarly update of the theoretical aspects of the folk-urban continuum. Rather, we are considering these problems because the past twenty-five years have seen the fabric of village life, its individual and village economic and social roles and expectations, severely stressed by worldwide industrialization, vastly enhanced communication, and radical changes in the worldwide technical and moral order (11, 12).

If there is a new threat to village viability, it is not in the mix between intra-village affairs and relationships and the wider world, which, as Wiser, Bates, and Schuchat and Jordan make clear, has always involved exploitation and control of villagers by city people and city institutions (to deliberately stress the bureaucratic nature of the city). Rather, it is the integrity, or wholeness, of the village which appears threatened, resulting in a more or less permanent separation of some roles on terms external to the village; and a polarization, potentially divisive, between the more successful and economically mobile villagers and the less successful and more vulnerable ones. Such a separation is now occurring through the working of land reforms, external credit arrangements, and new schools, crops, agricultural technologies, and means of communication.

The driving forces for such change are several, but two important ones are the overriding concern with agricultural productivity and the strohg trend toward bureaucratization, particularly in the developing countries, but also in the developed world. Belshaw sums up the assumption which drives much modernization in the agricultural sector: "Too many people on the land, and dependent on it, can stand in the way of its improved utilization." (13:253). Moreover, Fallers sees the substitution of specialization and bureaucratic methods for the multiple-roles, village-type organization as both a self-perpetuating force and an enabling mechanism for modernizing political structures (14).

The old-style village in the developing world should not, of course, be reified. Modernization can provide real potential and badly needed opportunities if the elemental reality of face-to-face relationships has such force that the new can be incorporated and adapted into village life, that is, if there can be a combination of old and new such that the material quality of life is enhanced without destroying the "moral order" of the village community. In Redfield's terms, both the technical and moral orders are interwoven in all societies at all levels, but the relative emphasis differs between village and city, and when this emphasis changes at the village level, it may be either traumatic or divisive, or internalized and accomodated (15, 16).

So far, we have said that the main attributes of the village which appear particularly vital are (i) villages are sufficiently small in size so that social interactions are characteristically face to face and (ii) these interactions involve villagers in more than one set of roles. We have also suggested that a chief source of strength of villages has been the derivation of their income from some mix of subsistence activities and commerce, and that that may become a source of weakness. Now let us define more precisely the village characteristics with which the contributors to this volume are concerned.

Village is that sedentary community for which the term "village" is the correct English gloss, even though, empirically, "village" subsumes a considerable range in size and variation in settlement type. The final test of village is, of course, the point of view of the villagers themselves (and marginally that of the observer). Four common types are nuclear, dispersed, linear and clustered farmsteads. Villages are commonly the smallest territorial unit of the society and are the essential components of the polity. Villages may also be defined with reference to their position in regionally organized sets of villages.

Introduction 7

While villages are also more or less permanent settlements, the degree of permanency varies. Some settlements are occupied during part of the year only, in others villagers abandon particular sites and build anew elsewhere in a process of predictable periodicity. These variants of "village" allow flexibility and match reality. There is a village domain or territory to which villagers have access through recognized usage rules. These vary with resources--arable land, pasture, trees, fishing grounds or ponds, and water supplies are all governed by usage rules. Kin relationships pertain and marriage rules nearly always are established and obeyed (whether exogamy or endogamy obtains).

In her contribution to this volume, Mead concentrates on the knowledge villagers have of each other's genealogies and experiences. The settlement must be named and understood to be a village by its inhabitants, and the villagers must span at least three generations--the full population pyramid-- and must have been born and reared in the village even though many may become migrants for part of their lives. Under her definition a village is "viable" if there is sufficient continuity of village membership so that children can be reared by adults who know and identify themselves with the village.

Implicit is the important factor of "collective memory," which, as Mead and Wiser both remind us, is extraordinarily complete concerning family histories and physical events of the village. Moreover, Netting documents the continuity of families which forms the basis for such collective memory; Schuchat and Jordan point out that, despite protracted periods of war and revolution beginning in the 1930s, the Li village in China still had 90 percent of its family units intact in the 1970s. The continuity of persons, families (and households) may provide the mechanism of memory, but the memory itself is a fundamental characteristic of villages, necessarily a part of the definition since the collective memory is village-specific.

Arensberg, writing in 1969, considered the fundamental nature of a community (villages being the most frequent type) as involving three generations and two sexes, and he set the community in theoretical context and provided tests for the identification of "viable" communities (17:248). His "viability" also concerned the selections of particular villages as <u>representative</u> communities for anthropological field study, but his other tests of village viability -- (i) completeness, (ii) inclusiveness, and (iii) cohesiveness-- are useful for helping us to define our focus on villages, villagers, and village structure.

Table 2. Components in the definition of village, villager and village structure.

Physical Attributes of the Village	Villager	Structure/ Organization
population size	face-to-face interactions	multiplex roles
composition	3 generations (both sexes)	marriage rules residential rules
houses	households	residential rules
bounded territory		access rules
resources	livelihood	subsistence/ market mix
name	identity for villager	
site permanence, degree of	shared experience/ collective memory	continuity of membership
completeness*	cohesiveness	inclusiveness

*Arensberg's "Test of viability" categories (19:247)

"Completeness" is concerned with whether or not a community is a geographically definable entity, a "whole," which is named and identified by that name. "Inclusiveness" is concerned with the degree to which a community contains in it the institutions, the culture, and the forces of the whole society of which it is a part. (The contributors to this volume deal with this characteristic in a variety of ways, but all consider it in studying various village situations.) "Cohesiveness" is concerned with the degree to which a community is integrated, common-minded, and cooperative. In our terms, agreement on the substance of the moral order would be a test of cohesiveness because shared experience of villagers is necessary if the moral order is to be maintained, grow, and change. Thus we have the regularities which are set out in Table 2: the village and its completeness, the villagers and their observed cohesiveness, and finally the status of the village structure and its institutional inclusiveness.

The Village and Its Completeness

The classic problems of our times--population growth, change in technology, and resource degradation--threaten the physical integrity of the village. Bates, Weatherford, C. Reining, Netting and Elias, Howe, Shear, Burki, and Bell are most concerned with the physical attributes of the village, its resources, and/or the ways in which village completeness have altered (Netting, C. Reining), can be expected to alter (Bell), or how plans can be made to achieve certain changes (Shear, Burki, and Howe). Howe focuses on technology change; the others consider also the relative proportion of village resources allocated to subsistence or to the market or commercial sector, whether material or human.

Some sites have a compelling combination of resources and other desirable characteristics for village establishment and continuation. Weatherford studied the long-time site of Kahl (near Frankfurt, Germany), on land at the juncture of a major river and a small tributary. Trans-Danubian villages in Hungary, sited on Neolithic foundations, are reported on by C. Reining and are millenia older than the present occupation. Site suitability would appear to be basic to the degree of permanence and hence to viability of these and of village communities studied by Netting and Elias, Schuchat and Jordan. Site considerations form the basis of the attraction of villages for planners (Shear, Simmons). But Bates, who has taken a regional look at village siting and continuity, points out that, in the area he surveyed in Southwestern Asia, few villages have actual physical continuity beyond about a hundred and fifty years.

When the village in the sense of continuity of a single cultural tradition and continuity of population line is considered, we find that some Swiss family lines go back five centuries (Chapter 3), although Turkmen village family lines appeared much shorter (Chapter 6). Villages such as that of the Li family in China can show decided durability during a period of radical change (Chapter 7), and Trans-Danubian villages were repopulated more or less from zero after the end of the Ottoman Empire (Chapter 4). In yet another variation, Sahelian settlement patterns changed strikingly from nucleated, palisaded villages to dispersed compounds after the imposition of colonial rule (Chapter 9). Clearly, villagers are vulnerable to war, military occupation (C. Reining), salinization of their farm lands (Bates), and many other factors, but still villages either continued or were reestablished, demonstrating their continued viability as human habitats.

As a given level of technology, the match between population size and village resource base, including a given set of crops, is vitally important to village viability. Netting and Elias demonstrate that the introduction of a new crop filling a previously unexploited niche resulted in a changed population trend for which the social mechanisms of marriage rules and celibacy were inadequate to maintain the balance between family resource and family size within the village context. This problem, which finally was manifest and solved through planned emigration of part of the village, did not destroy the continuity of Swiss village sites (Chapter 3). Their continuity may also have been influenced by their mountainous location, however; since both Maccoby and Bates show that highland sites are more viable and lowland ones are more vulnerable.

The complete village is one having resources within its territory adequate to its population; that is, of course, a junction not only of the technology but of the subsistence/market ratio. The relationship between village population size and resource base is altered by changing life style, as Reining discusses for Hungarian villages, and as Howe examines for the potential link between renewable resources within the village territory and their exploitation through new devices aimed at improving the utilization of the entire resource base.

Exploration of the potential of changing technology vis-à-vis the village is examined by Weatherford, who shows how industrial technology has altered employment patterns for Kahl villagers and also altered village size, shifting it from village size to town size. Yet Kahl, now larger than most villages, retains the basic village organization: "Kahl's primary organization and orientation is that of a village,... a community in which the majority of residents are connected by a web of multiplex relationships and frequent face-to-face interactions." (Chapter 2). Although as a site Kahl appears indestructible; yet in the experience of villagers, their lives and life-base have been vulnerable to destruction.

Village resources and population together are the area of concern, Burki suggests, of most developing countries, where basic needs of shelter, health, and education are the material aspects of development of highest priority. Maccoby stresses that many development planners try to deal with those basic needs in a material way without concern for the psychosocial life of villagers. The technical solutions to the need for food and shelter, while meant to increase villagers' security, may in fact decrease it by undermining culturally rooted ways of satisfying those needs. He stresses that while equitable access to food, shelter, and water is a basic aspect of physical security, the way such access is developed must include consideration of the organization of the village and the cultural values of those particular villagers.

Villagers and Their Cohesiveness

Assuming a village with an adequate site and safe resource base, villagers must also share some coherent and common sentiments. Mead and Maccoby are especially concerned with this aspect of the village community. Neither idealizes the village--Mead recognizes clearly that the more competent village residents may very well be pulled to the city and that the natal village can be a confining and mean place. Modernization may easily lead to inequities, as Maccoby's data on lowland Mexican villagers caught up in the course of modernization indicates: the village entrepreneurs may very well be exploitative of neighbors having different endowments and background. Arensberg would surely see the resulting inequities as a threat to cohesiveness, to cooperation, and hence to the village. Looking to the future, Mead predicts the "elective" village--one to which likeminded persons would choose to move--in which families could very directly and specifically fulfill the template of three generations by choice and not because they had no alternative.

Change may also lead to improved equity: Schuchat and Jordan point to a change, in their opinion for the better, in the production brigade (as the Chinese village is now called), since both the resource base and individual equity are improved. Wiser is also very attentive to villager cohesiveness, the cause of the invisible wall which villagers erect to keep strangers at arms' length and thus maintain village identity. Participation of villagers in planning, particularly in planning the education of their children can increase cohesiveness and cooperation among villagers. Simmons describes cases where villagers have increased their participation in planning for educational needs in their own village, and he shows how such participation can increase village cooperation in many aspects of life and does indeed strengthen the cohesiveness of those villages.

Structural Inclusiveness

For villages, this is the heart of the matter, and there has been much study of village structure to determine the articulation of institutional arrangements within the village and how it is changed by outside forces. Villages are not only controlled by cities, they are generated by them, says Bates, viewing the history of abandoned and newly formed villages in southwest Asia. The subsistence/market shift, most pronounced in lowland villages, is also taking place in highland villages as seasonal use of tractors, credit, and migrant labor also impinge in upland areas.

Of all our contributors, Bell is most certain in predicting major changes in the villages he studied. He argues that the Malaysan _kampong_ is not a convincing unit of aggregation and will change as boundaries, division of labor, and the commuting villager all erode the internal village structure in favor of participation of the villagers in the wider economy. As Bell points out, data on the subsistence sector is often lacking. Such lack hampers adequate planning for the subsistence/market ratio. In the Li village in China we learn that assumptions about malleability made in the 1960s concerning the subsistence/market ratio in that village were not substantiated, for in the 1970s the family-controlled subsistence plot has been re-established. At the same time, the basis of the multiplex roles--the dominant family and its gentry role--has changed, even with the substantial (90 percent) continuity in membership in the village and the collective memories of the village. On the other hand, many observers have affirmed and reaffirmed the strength of this village structure and the adaptive character of Han villagers-- in Irene Taeuber's words, "anything to survive!" (18). Moreover, the national policy on decentralization supports village organization.

Shear and Bates both look at the regional picture--Shear because the herder/farmer relationships are so basic to Sahelian society; Bates because population fluctuation, environmental degradation in a fragile environment, and political changes combine to make the fate of a single village understandable only in the context of the regional sweep. Shear also emphasizes the role of decentralization as the basis of policy and the obvious implications of decentralization for strengthening the subsistence sector while it alters the commercial sector.

Maccoby, noting the significance of "culturally rooted forms of satisfying social needs," goes on to state that the effectiveness of village development requires testing in terms of individual lives and cannot be measured by cash income alone, because the subsistence sector and the values of the affluent and progressive groups within a village can obscure the condition of poorer groups (within the village) and because "economic measures do not correlate in any single way with fulfilling the psychosocial needs for human development." It should be noted that there is a considerable degree of correspondence between Maccoby's categories—security, equity, individuation, and participation—and the three abstractions we are making from communities of the village type. Maccoby is working toward a systemic theory of the human community and any examination of its parts is necessarily analytical. However, security is principally based on resources, as noted; equity and individuation are aspects of villager role; and participation is basic to the village organization.

C. Wiser concludes that continuity of membership and self-sufficiency become measures of the soundness of Indian village structure (threatened by tractors, new forms of credit, and affluence for the few). The caste system in India orders relationships in a fixed division of labor and also specifies relative caste position in overall hierarchy. The jajmani system, first described for western scholars by William Wiser, is a system of contracts among villagers which provides a sensitive social/economic mechanism for adjustment of service to need (19). C. Wiser's long-term study recognizes the implications of caste, as qualified by the jajmani system's flexibility for reworking intra-village relationships. The Hungarian villages studied by C. Reining are clearly part of a planned economy, though some self-sufficiency and control may still be exercised at the household level. Many household members are, however, of the grandparental generation; the potential difficulty is lack of continuity of membership in households as the grandparents die and take their thrift, skills, and willingness to contribute to the productivity of the subsistence sector to their graves without having been able to teach their younger members who have become only part-time villagers.

The Whole and the Parts

In making the abstractions from the physical village, its inhabitants as a population, its resources, the shared experience of the villagers, and the analyses of how livelihood and social relations are ordered, we have boxed and categorized a whole. Among our contributors, the anthropologists analyze and demonstrate the relationship among the parts, and the social psychologist views the individual in a comprehensive context. The development planners take the village as a whole, are willing to take the "local condition and the general sociocultural tradition" into consideration, but are not themselves prepared to state what those conditions or traditions are. So it falls to the social scientists to specify and speak of such matters, and it is equally the responsibility of the development experts to listen. Thus, while our approach in this volume is pragmatic, we hope it will serve to inform, encourage, and assist both theoreticians and policy-makers.

We believe that many villages will almost certainly survive for the foreseeable future, for that is what our contributors are saying from their first-hand knowledge. Some villages and their inhabitants will almost certainly be destroyed, or will grow irrevocably beyond village size, and many a village's organization can be expected to change. But the village community, linked to but set apart from its neighbors, continues to offer an important means of organizing human activity at the local level, of giving shelter and the social substance of life to its inhabitants, and of providing the link between natural resources and productivity which is fundamental to life. We must remember however, as Margaret Mead said many times, change in village structure will come about naturally--if _villagers_ have continuity and control.

References

1. 1979 World Population Data Sheet of the Population Reference Bureau, Inc., Washington, D.C. 1979.
2. R. Redfield, *American Journal of Sociology* 52, 293-308 (1947).
3. R. Redfield, *Tepoztlan, A Mexican Village: A Study of Folk Life*, (University of Chicago Press, Chicago, 1930).
4. H. Miner, "The Folk-Urban Continuum," *American Sociologist Review* 17:529. Menasha, Wisconsin (1952).
5. O. Lewis, *Life in a Mexican Village: Tepoztlan Restudied*. (University of Illinois Press, Urbana, 1951).
6. R. Redfield, *The Folk Culture of Yucatan*, (University of Chicago Press, Chicago, 1941).
7. R. Redfield, *The Little Community*, (University of Chicago Press, Chicago, 1955).
8. R. Redfield, *The Primitive World and its Transformations*, (Cornell University Press, Ithaca, 1953).
9. R. Redfield, *Peasant Society and Culture*, (University of Chicago Press, Chicago, 1956).
10. M. Marriott, *Village India Studies in the Little Community*, (University of Chicago Press, Chicago, 1955).
11. K. Polanyi, *The Great Transformation*, (Farrar and Rinehart, New York, 1944).
12. R. Redfield, op. cit. (1953).
13. C. Belshaw, *The Sorcerer's Apprentice*, (Pergamon Press, Oxford, 1976).
14. L.A. Fallers, *Inequality, Social Stratification Reconsidered*, (University of Chicago Press, Chicago, 1973).
15. R. Redfield, op. cit. (1953).
16. R. Redfield, *A Village That Chose Progress. Chan Kom Revisited*, (University of Chicago Press, Chicago, 1950).
17. C. Arensberg, "The Community as Object and as a Sample," *American Anthropologist* 63, 241-264 (1961).
18. I. Taeuber, Personal Communication (1974).
19. W. Wiser, *The Hindu Jajmani System*, (Lucknow Publishing House, Lucknow, 1936).

Part 1

The Village Defined

Margaret Mead

1. On the Viability of Villages

Asked to give advice on the kinds of problems we believe in, in general, anthropologists have responsible advice to give. This is particularly the case with regard to questions having to do with villages. For example, what happens to villages as they become depopulated? Is the village a vanishing form or is it one that is still viable? And, of course, there is the basic question: What is a village?

As one step in arriving at a definition, I suggest that we consider different types of villages and their characteristics. At one end of the continuum there are the traditional villages with a culturally homogeneous population over many centuries; at the other end there are the new villages--recently formed in response to some developing economic activity or else as the outcome of migration or immigration. Today there are also both planned villages and elective villages.

Essentially I would define a village as a community in which it is possible for every resident to know every other person living there. I would also include having a name and some awareness of the settlement as a community, continuity over time, the presence of at least three living generations and a belief in the possibility of continuity of membership in the future. But some sort of knowledge about the members of the village community is an essential characteristic. Of course, this knowledge will vary in depth and detail in different age groups, among people of longer and shorter residence and by location within the village territory. But people will know--and know that others know, too.

It is about villages in this sense that I wish to speak here.

What it means to "know" everyone will itself vary in different kinds of community. It may include knowledge based on registers or photographs of earlier generations or of people who have moved away. It may depend in part on local television, used as one method of helping members of a new settlement to become known to one another. Or association with one another--and so knowing one another--may depend on the presence or absence of some central meeting place--a temple, a town hall, a place for laundering clothes on the bank of a river, a mill where women and children go daily to have their corn ground, a market in which almost everyone is both a vendor and a buyer.

As I see it, a useful definition of a village will show up the limitations of Marshall McLuhan's image of the "global village" (1). For he stresses only one characteristic of a village, the almost simultaneous access to information about any given member who may be involved in some newsworthy event. But he fails to include the decisive element--being _personally_ known to one another through time.

C. A. Doxiadis has pointed out that throughout the history of cities urban residents have been willing to spend about 45 minutes to get from one part of a city to another. What has changed is the distance involved as increasingly rapid means of transportation have come into use. I believe that we must visualize a village in much the same way. That is, we must expect the amount of territory that is included and the kinds of contact that are customary to alter with changes in technology and in settlement patterns.

Allowance always must be made for village residents' knowledge of the past and the reinforcement of traditional attitudes and beliefs about persons by reiterated comments, such as, "That is where Bangli had his old house; it burned down," or "That is where the first church stood; my grandfather helped to build it," or "That empty lot is where the house was torn down after John Smith hanged himself up in the attic." But one must also take into account the urge to escape from the bonds of fellow villagers' memories--and curiosity--that often drives more enterprising or imaginative residents away into larger, less intimate communities.

However, the village exists as a refuge from the city as well as the city as a refuge from the village. It is not enough to consider only those who are left behind as young and restless or ambitious community members move out; it is necessary also to include the less successful men and women who return because they have failed to adjust to the wider environment. And there is also the idea of the natal village, to which urbanized residents may return for holidays, in search of care when they fall ill or to live out a quiet and dignified old age. For all these the village is a refuge (2).

Given the great variety of forms a village can take and the different meanings that village life may have for its residents, I can see no reason why the village, as a face-to-face community of three or four generations of people known to one another, should not survive. It may exist within the kind of large city we foresee in the future; it may exist as a point of concentration for people who want a holistic style of living rather than one that is fragmented by extreme divisions of labor. The coming modern use of solar power, wind and water as sources of energy points today toward the localization of resources, and recognition of the need to conserve energy points toward village economic autonomy.

The idea of the village was developed in anthropology by anthropologists who went into the field, listened and observed ways of life in cultures that were, until then, unrecorded. Over time what they learned and newly understood contributed to the development of anthropological theory. So the fact is that anthropologists do know a lot about villages.

As anthropologists, we have worked in almost every existing kind of village, and we have worked in villages all around the world. Anthropologists have worked in mining villages without any place for a stranger to stay. We have worked in Spanish villages where there was no place for a Protestant or a Jew. We have worked in isolated, self-contained villages and in villages in continual communication with a network of other like--and sometimes unlike--village communities. Recently, anthropologists have worked in a large number of villages in India.

Anthropologists have made village studies because, for one reason, we have wanted to confine our research to communities small enough to be amenable to our specific techniques. For this reason, too, we know a lot about villages--even those anthropologists who have done no applied work and have not been concerned about the wider world, the activities of the United Nations and its agencies or the effects of foreign aid on small communities. What we do know about is the village as a whole system, because we work with whole systems. We also know what it is to study a living people. We do not think of people as "data-producing objects." Nor do we think of them as "subjects," in the sense of HEW guidelines against the misuse of human subjects in research.

In fact, we think of the people we work with as our collaborators. When we come into a village that is new to us, we know that we can succeed in our task only if the villagers trust us and that if we try to tell the truth eventually the villagers will respond with their truth. To start with they will tell some lies--a way of telling us what they would like us to hear or, alternatively, what they think we want to hear. And they may recommend a cookboy who is especially stupid or a thief--and a few other things of this sort. But as we prove to be trustworthy to them, they become trustworthy to us. This is a familiar way of working, one that any young anthropologist who has been adequately trained can acquire.

But once the field work has been done, it is necessary to work out definitions of the basic units of research, because if a mistake has been made in the nature of some unit, most subsequent research is likely to become distorted. That is why it is so important, now, to define correctly what a village is and, in terms of organization, what the social units are. Let me remind you, for example, that "family" and "household" should not be confused. The family is not the basic unit of society. The <u>couple</u> is the basic unit of parenthood, but the <u>household</u> is the basic unit of human society. It is the <u>combination</u> of kinship and common residence that makes this a unit, and the household is one unit in the community. The attempt to form a community that is primarily made up of families inevitably leads to many kinds of difficulties.

The point is that poor definition of a research field is serious and can result in confusion both among those who are carrying out research and among those others who are attempting to apply the new knowledge. Probably the principal confusion about the idea of the "village" in our generation was brought about by Marshall McLuhan through his image of the whole world as a global village.

Personally I am convinced that McLuhan has never spent any time in--or even seen--a village. The last time I challenged him on the subject, he said, "Well, I live in one." Whereas actually he is speaking of a small elite community of well-to-do people who live in expensive houses around a lake in an area that is very pleasant and highly zoned against intrusion. He calls that a village. Of course he is right in one respect, but only in that respect. One characteristic of a village is instant communication of significant events. This is a characteristic of a village that is small or logistically so organized that an event of importance can be communicated to everyone at once. People are not cut off from finding out that a house has burned down. But this is not universally the case.

Bali has villages that are dense to communication. In these villages there are individuals whose business it is to tell other individuals that they are to tell still others what is happening. There are also people who knock on the gateposts of other people to tell them it is their turn to do something. All this in connection with formal events in the village.

But accessibility of every member of a community to knowledge about every other member of that community is, I believe, a significant characteristic of any village. It will pay to study this, especially as forms of accessibility do vary. For example, there are villages where one can either see what people are doing or else hear what they are saying, but seldom can do both at once. On the island of Montserrat, in the West Indies, where Rhoda Metraux did field work, the village terrain has hills and deeply indented ravines, so that close neighbors often cannot see one another but hear every spoken word; at the same time they can watch people moving around their houses on a distant hillside but never hear what is said (3). Under these circumstances it is extremely difficult to make an accurate and intelligible map that indicates the sorts of knowledge people do have of one another.

Traditional villages in Iran present a different, but no less difficult problem. There houses are built of adobe and additions consist simply of knocking down a piece of wall and adding a bulge to the core of the house. So there is no way of mapping what goes on inside from the outside. The only way to show the interior is to open up a house like a cut honeycomb and construct a diorama. When a young American anthropologist who was working in such an Iranian village showed me these houses, I was in despair. How was she ever to map the village so that she could deal effectively with the problem of communication? However, an earthquake protection program has since removed the problem. The old adobe houses with their bulging rooms are being replaced with ugly square houses built of concrete blocks; they no longer have bulges.

Accessibility to knowledge about every member of a community includes, of course, knowing also who is a stranger. The dogs know it. The children know it too. And in a proper village the dogs learn in time that this person no longer is a stranger. When we first lived in Bali, I knew where my husband was walking around the village by the changing bark of the dogs. But when we came back after a year's absence, no dog barked and no child cried. When we first lived in Bajoeng Gede a woman would say, "Delighted to see you, come into my house," but the baby in her arms would scream with fright. When we returned, babies born in our absence did not cry. We were familiar, a part of the village (4).

Actual knowledge, of course, differs within the village. For example, old people may not know the names of the children. Although they know whose children they are, there is no good reason for learning their names. So a man who is a marvelous informant on everyone's ancestors is hopeless as an informant on the children. Often one must turn to a child to learn the names of children.

By the 1950s and 1960s a great many young American anthropologists had grown up in cities or the suburbs. That they did not even know what a village was like was made clear by the two questions they asked about my return to Manus in 1953, to Peri, a village I had studied first in 1928 (5). One question was: Did anyone remember you? The second was: Did you remember anyone?

Of course, the Peri village people not only remembered me, they knew what I had eaten for breakfast every single day. If I mentioned a name, I would be told, "Oh, you remember him. He was in the second canoe back of us the time we went to that wedding in Patusi!" Manus people have about nine names that are used differentially because of the many taboos. In 1928 I knew one name for for each person and perhaps two or three or four for some people, but never all nine. And so, in 1953, a name would crop up and I would say, "I don't remember him!" Invariably the reply would be, "Not by that name. You called him So-and-so." Perfectly accurately.

Before we came out, as a test to find out who remembered who, I made up a set of 1928 pictures of children, people who had since died and one ringer, a photograph of a person from the Solomon Islands, where everyone wore cloth laplaps just like the Manus. As a test it was a total failure because everyone remembered everyone and immediately identified the ringer and said, "That's not us." One man failed to identify his own tyrannical grandfather. And one picture showed a woman dressed in 1928 style; she was holding a baby. The viewers identified that baby as any one of the woman's five children until I said, "I took that picture." That settled it. "Oh, then it's Sophie." Just like that, without the slightest difficulty.

On the Viability of Villages

I remembered almost everything, too. I had been studying those people, looking at their pictures, writing about them and asking new questions of the material during all the intervening 25 years. As a result, the village and every person in it and their relationships to one another continued to exist in my mind as an ineradicable whole, just as I continued to exist in their minds as part of that chunk of their lives. In fact, they remembered everything about their lives in the same way up to a period of rapid, uncontrolled change. Then they tended to skip and falsify events. Our studies of memory showed that their memory for detail was accurate during stable periods and full of falsification and error during a time of rapid change. Later, as the situation stabilized, so did their ability to recall accurately.

There is something very disconcerting about going back. I have just returned to Bali and the village of Bajoeng Gede where once again I met Karba, one of the children we studied in the 1930s, about whom we made a film which I have used extensively in teaching and to which a large number of anthropology students have been exposed (6). Karba is still extremely real to me as a baby whom I carried around in my arms and who used to grab the pencil and scribble in my notebook. But today Karba is a priest in Bajoeng Gede, a great pompous man to whom I am not at all real; I am just someone he has heard about from his mother who remembers everything about me. And because he has only heard about me, Karba stares at me blankly, as he would stare at any stranger he had only heard about.

Earlier, in 1975, I visited a group of Arapesh whom we had studied in 1932 when they were living on the mainland, up in the mountains of the coastal range. After several moves they were now living in a new oil palm settlement on New Britain. Only two women, who had been very young when we worked in Alitoa, remembered that time and we recognized each other; the others had only heard about me. I was part of their past and well incorporated in it, but I was a "Missie," not someone familiar whom they could deal with easily. They received me with affection, but the kind of memory that goes with continunity was lacking.

These experiences made me realize in a new way the importance of stories that are told and retold in a village. Every time people pass a place where once a house burned down someone mentions it and they go on mentioning the event for 20 years or more. And this continuity of memory is an exceedingly important characteristic of village life.

As I said earlier, many American anthropologists never have lived in a village. When they go into the field they carry with them no experience of a village and do not record things about a village in the way a country person would have done. That is often called "middle class bias," but it is not bias, it is lack of experience. It is similar to what the Peace Corps made of culture shock. The Peace Corps organizers thought that "culture shock" is, for example, a response to seeing people urinate in the street--a negative response. Actually, of course, it is simply the response of middle class Americans who have never seen anybody urinate in the street. Nor have they ever seen a birth or a death or an open sore. Their response is not culture shock; it is life shock--the kind of shock any inexperienced person can get by going into the emergency room of a hospital in any American city.

I am not quite sure who invented the phrase "culture shock"--whether it was Ruth Benedict or I myself. But we thought of it as something positive, not negative, in the formation of an anthropologist--the intense experience of recognizing that everything in another, unfamiliar culture is different from one's own, that even those things that appear familiar are different because the context is different.

In the past our method of making an anthropologist was to take someone by the scruff of the neck and leave him (or her) alone in a community in a strange culture. If he (or she) survived the experience of culture shock one, twice, three times, then he (or she) was an anthropologist. We did not know of any other way to make an anthropologist. We still do not. Studying the Puerto Ricans down the street will not accomplish this. A people with whom one shares so many aspects of one's own culture cannot give one the experience of culture shock. But a person may well respond in this way to contemporary American Indians, who drive modern cars and wear modern clothes, when he discovers that they regard these clothes and cars very differently from the way contemporary Americans do.

The contemporary anthropologist who goes to study a village has to deal with a double problem--how to understand that culture and how to understand village life without ever having had experience of a village in one's own society. I am sure that many of the difficulties in arriving at a definition of a village that can be carried through time and into the future derive exactly from the lack of village experience.

This has been particularly true in India. There have been an extraordinary number and kind of distortions in studies of village life in India. For a long time the principal emphasis was on people leaving their village and going to the city, as if this were a one-way process. Eventually, however, a careful study showed that an individual who got into trouble in his own village moved to the city in order, as it were, to be come detoxified and then moved on to another village. For such persons the city was a kind of detoxification zone where a man could rid himself of an old quarrel and start anew.

In many other discussions the village has been treated as an historical form that is vanishing--that is diminishing as people leave for the city and never come back. Very little has been done to study the people who, having acquired some education, return to village life. In the developing world they may become important people in the villages because they can read and write and keep records. In a wider world they might well have been quite unsuccessful, but in the villages they are a success. Nor has very much been done with people like the Cook Islanders who spend their entire lives in Fiji or in New Zealand, but continue to send back taxes to their village council each year in order to maintain their position, in case they should want to return in their old age or decide to send their children home. And, of course, there is the outstanding example of the Swiss communes. Until recently a man--and his decendants in the male line--retained membership in his paternal commune even though neither he nor his father or even his grandfather had ever lived there.

A further complication in arriving at a viable definition of a village derives from the cultural evolutionary theory that the village is one stage in the development of types of social organization from the band to the modern megalopolis. It is of course exact that village living represents one stage in the formation of settlements. But this theory obscures the fact that village dwelling is a form that can recur, as far as we know, at any stage of history. For example, we know of nomadic peoples who have coalesced into villages; peoples living in such small, scattered hamlets that they can hardly be considered villages because there are not enough potential partners for the inhabitants to marry; and a community made up of small extended kinship groups that gradually grew together to form something, in New Guinea terms, almost like a town (8). We also know of village-like groups that are formed today because of a new industry or because an army of occupation brought its women folk with it. In fact, many new social groups are village-like in form, although they may not last long enough to have three living generations. It is, I think, legitimate to think in terms of an ideal form of any social unit--and in its ideal form a village contains at least three generations and has sufficient continuity through time so that its inhabitants know about the past of those with whom they are living. But there can be new as well as old villages, and when a new group forms its members have to get to know one another, intermarry and establish kinship ties and so, over time, acquire the characteristics of a village.

There are some anthropologists who deny that a particular social unit can at one and the same time be an historical and a general form. There are, for example, certain critics of the work of Alan Lomax, who has identified forms of music that are germane to historical developments in specific areas and also are associated with certain levels of technological development (9). These critics claim that "you can't have it both ways," but of course you can.

Based on a core definition, one can certainly say that the village as a form recurs over time and in different types of society. One can then speak of very old villages and new villages, villages that have remained remarkably stable over time and others--and we find many of these in the United States--that have gradually deteriorated as the more enterprising have gone away and only the unenterprising remain. There is, for example, a village in Ohio that was founded by two of my great, great, great grandfathers. It has remained about the same size for a century, but the people have become steadily less able to deal with the wider world. In such villages, where, over generations, the enterprising have left, one is likely to find such things as a high level of alcoholism or an unusual number of individuals with tics and other kinds of anomalies.

The pull toward cities and the push away from villages is a phenomenon that has been thoroughly identified and intensively studied almost everywhere in the modern world. Cities attract because they offer greater opportunities and, in some cases, more readily available food. On the whole, people do not starve as badly in cities as they do in rural areas. But people also are drawn to cities in search of anonymity and the chance to start over again. A man cannot make a new beginning in a village; everyone knows his family history and remembers that his forebearers "have always been like that." So a man or a woman who wants to start something new, who wants to be modern in a conservative village, will do better to leave. For example, the first man who wants to educate his daughters will not stay in the village where he--and they--will face continual criticism and attacks; he will pick up from his village in some remote part of Pakistan and will move with his children to Karachi where he can educate his daughters without the burden of criticism.

Wherever there are cities there is also a push away from the pressures of the village and the knowledge of the village; it is discouraging for everyone to have known you <u>when</u>. In some societies men in search of success only move to other villages, but the chances of success are so much greater in a large town or a city that enterprising individuals move into the city's orbit. This is a worldwide phenomenon, and the desire to succeed on a larger scale goes so deep that one is tempted to say that the village is a form of human settlement that, given the opportunity, almost everyone wants to leave.

In the ideal traditional village all one's relatives are there or in the next village--all of them, not just the ones you like but also the ones you cannot bear, for the point of the extended family is that one has to take relatives all alike. And the wish to get away from all of one's relatives is probably as deep and as widely shared a social tendency as is the desire of males to get away from the farm or the preference, given the opportunity, for monogamy over polygomy. It takes an almost cult-like belief in the values of rural life to take males back to small-scale farming, and this may not, in the long run, succeed any more than have attempts to reintroduce polygamy. It is equally probable, I think that we cannot reconstitute the older forms of the village. The older traditional village forms may continue to exist, unless they are totally destroyed by the spread of modern culture. But the villages of the future, which can still be called villages in terms of other characteristics I have outlined, will surely be different.

The new villages, as I see it, will be elective. They will be villages to which people move because they want to live there, not because their ancestors have always lived there. A next step in the formation of elective villages will permit people to bring with them, to live nearby, the relatives and friends they like and find congenial.

One example of this kind of thing has occurred in Puerto Rico; it is also an example of the extraordinary speed at which change can take place. In certain areas of Puerto Rico there is a very patriarchal style of living in which each man builds his own home and married women go out to church, to do a little shopping and otherwise hardly at all. The group that moves out from such a village is a female-oriented cluster consisting usually of a woman, her daughters and their husbands. At this stage there is an apparent matrilocal focus. But clusters remain together in this form only briefly. Soon the group moves to a town or city where men again build the houses--in what are known as slums--and the group again takes on a patrilocal cast. But then the housing project, which favors women and children over men, attracts slum dwellers and once more women become the center and men are pushed out. Such a cycle can take place in the history of a family in the short time of some 20 years.

In the contemporary world the ways in which groups of people select themselves to live together as a result of migration into a city or immigration across the sea or from one region to another becomes part of the style of the new village. And what we are now looking forward to, for the further development of new forms of village living, are new types of housing. There are some examples, but none is complete and all, so far, have defects.

Reston, Virginia, and Columbia, Maryland, are early examples of communities in which mixed generation, mixed class and mixed ethnicity are all deliberately built in. Such a community provides for diversity, for the presence of three generations and a place where, if you want to have her nearby, you can bring your grandmother or some other senior citizen relative. Reston has a small skyscraper--the only skyscraper in the village--designed for senior citizens. (Skyscrapers are, in fact, marvelous for elderly people who do not want to walk great distances and are happy to ride in elevators.) When I visited Reston two years ago, I was told that some 97 per cent of the senior citizens had younger relatives living there. And Jim Rouse, the builder of Columbia, Maryland, told me that fifteen of his relatives live in that community. They moved there individually because they wanted to be there, near relatives they like and, very probably, away from relatives of whom they are less fond.

This kind of selectivity also is characteristic of friends. Over and over again immigrants to America came as clusters of friends as well as in groups of relatives. They traveled together, formed the new communities and sent back home, in Europe, for others whom they had found congenial.

But at present we have developed no new way that makes it possible for people who are close friends or relatives to choose to live near one another for a lifetime. For example, there may be a community that is made up largely of well-to-do bankers and other businessmen. It may be village-size, but when the men retire, they must move away. There are no multi-dwelling apartments and they are no longer strong enough to deal with large lawns or snowy pavements in winter.

Similarly, the young must move away because they cannot afford to go on living in their parents' community. Since poor people are excluded from such a community, there is no one to cut the grass or shovel the snow, and the elderly must move to California, Texas or Florida where they live in communities where they do not have to cut the grass. They have exercised choice, but a kind of choice that is both restrictive and restricting.

There is, of course, a great deal more work that needs to be done on the village as a social form. However, I believe we know enough now so that we should put our understanding and ingenuity to work to devise new forms. It seems to me most likely that the village will survive as a chosen form, an _elective_ form, for people who choose to live a holistic kind of life--who like to know other people in diverse contexts, like to work near their neighbors, like to live near their in-laws, like to know their co-grandparents and the children's children of their friends. This is very different from the fragmented life of the city and the people who make this choice will be different from those who choose the city. They will also be very different from the inhabitants of traditional villages who have remained behind, without choice, or who have chosen to take refuge there.

Making this choice possible is a major challenge in our contemporary world.

References

1. M. McLuhan, personal communication.

2. Z. Eglar, <u>A Punjabi Village in Pakistan</u> (New York, Columbia University Press, 1960).

3. R. Metraux and T. M. Abel, "Normal and Deviant Behavior in a Peasant Community: Montserrat, B.W.I.," <u>American Journal of Orthopsychiatry</u>, Vol. 27, 1957, 167-84.

4. G. Bateson and M. Mead, <u>Balinese Character</u>, Special Publications of the New York Academy of Sciences, II (New York, New York Academy of Sciences, 1942.)

5. M. Mead, <u>Growing Up in New Guinea</u> (New York, Morrow, 1930); M. Mead, <u>New Lives for Old</u> (New York, Morrow, 1956).

6. <u>Karba's First Years</u>, 16 mm. black and white film produced by G. Bateson and M. Mead, 1952.

7. M. Mead, "The Mountain Arapesh, Part I: An Importing Culture and Part II: Supernaturalism," <u>Anthropological Papers of The American Museum of Natural History</u>, Vols. 36 and 37, parts 3, 1938 and 1940.

8. D. F. Tuzin, <u>The Ilahita Arapesh</u> (Berkeley, University of California Press, 1976).

9. A. Lomax, <u>Folk Song Style and Culture</u>, American Association for the Advancement of Science, Publication No. 88 (Washington, D.C. AAAS, 1968).

Part 2

Studies of the Village

Jack M. Weatherford

2. Millenium of Modernization: A Changing German Village

One of the smallest rivers in West Germany is the 23-kilometer long Kahl. It winds down the Spessart hills as barely more than a stream until it joins the Main river at the Bavarian-Hessian border. There posed in the corner made by the borders of the two states and the confluence of the two rivers is a community which also bears the name Kahl. Depending on whether one looks at this site as a community on the Kahl river or on the Main river, one has largely different perspectives on the community. The heart of the old village faces onto the smaller Kahl river, and along the banks of this river are rows of neatly planned vegetable gardens which are tended daily by the older citizens. Walking further out from these gardens, a visitor would be surrounded by one of Germany's largest forests, the Spessart. From its short run up in the mountains to the Main, the Kahl river is one of the rural pictures of Europe so favored by nineteenth century Romantics and twentieth century tourists alike.

If, however, one chose to look at Kahl from the vantage point of the Main river, the picture would be entirely different. Instead of thatched farmhouses, one would see a modern community of tract houses. Instead of decaying flour mills, one would see the imposing dome of West Germany's first atomic power plant. Walking along this side of the community, one would pass through the yards of a moderate-sized trucking company, and see cargo-ladden barges chugging up and down the Main. One could walk along the Main for kilometers and pass through the heartland of industrialized

Germany's Rhein-Main region. From this perspective Kahl resembles hundreds of other industrial towns in the modern world.

This duality of the community with fronts on the industrial Main river and the gardens on the bucolic Kahl river is more than a superficial description of appearances. Metaphorically, these two facades represent the deeper social and cultural divisions in a community going through the transition from village to town. Even though the community began undergoing industrialization in the mid-1800's and its population passed 8,000 in this decade (1), its primary organization and orientation is that of a village. It is still a community in which the majority of residents are connected by a web of multiplex relationships and frequent face-to-face interactions. Along with the traditional aspects of numerous extended-family households and family gardens (2), there are newer traits such as foreign workers, a traffic light, pollution, and a growing number of people who have moved to Kahl simply as a place to live. The newcomers are urban in orientation and do not participate in the traditional village networks; for them Kahl is a comfortable place to live not a complete life style. Kahl is today both a village and a town, or perhaps more accurately it is a village within a town.

A tourist or an historian in the district would find many more interesting places to visit. Kahl does not have a castle like the neighboring Alzenau. It did not enjoy market rights to have a market square like Hörstein. Unlike the town of Seligenstadt, it has no ancient abbey or Roman ruins. It produced no renowned men of letters like Hanau's brothers Grimm. It did not give the world any industrial inventors and famous magnates such as Steinheim's Kaiser Aluminum family; nor did it inspire any music such as Handel's "Dettingen Te Deum" named for another neighboring village.

Yet, Kahl is very much a part of the economic and political history and future of the area. Kahl's residents have been protected by and attacked by the inhabitants of the Alzenau castle. They bought and sold in the markets of Hörstein, paid tithes and taxes to the abbey. They suffered from the armies which fought at the Battle of Dettingen and attacked the Roman fortifications. During time of war, they found safety and food in the Spessart Forest and hills; in time of prosperity they exploited the lumber and peasants of the same area. Above all, Kahl survived as a community offering a home and livelihood to its inhabitants.

Probably the most remarkable thing about Kahl is that it is a constantly regenerating entity. Change, modernization, and development can be traced throughout the history of the village. Some centuries were more pronounced in either their growth or their destructiveness, but the village has adapted to each. There is no single factor which constantly provided support or sustenance to the community. The economic history of the village is a mix of agriculture, commerce, manufacturing, and mining. During some eras, one mode dominates over all the others, but changing conditions always bring about a shift within another generation or two. New modes are grafted onto existing structures and organization in the same way that old buildings are remodeled for new purposes. This process of changing lifestyles and changing institutions and buildings is the core of the history of Kahl.

Pre-History

For most purposes, European villages are "dated" from the time of a village or market charter or from the first official designation of the village as a fief or tax property. Usually this is the beginning of recorded civilization in the village and thus of the area's entry into history. For many villages, the historical period is only another phase, albeit the most recent one. According to this historical form of calculation, cities such as Mainz, Aachen, or Trier entered history early by virtue of the fact that they were in the Roman world and thus within the sphere of written records. More remote places such as Berlin or less significant places such as Kahl entered the picture much later.

As a continuously inhabited village under the same name, Kahl is probably a millenium old, dating from the Carolingian era (3). Archeologically, as

a community and a viable village, however, the
history of Kahl (under some possibly lost name)
stretches back several thousand years. Despite
some Stone Age finds in the village, habitation
on the present site dates from about 1500 B.C. (4).
Successive types of elaborate mound graves and
ceremonial complexes indicate that it was a community of constantly changing social and economic
organization between 1500 B.C. and 500 B.C. Who
these people were and whether or not they lived
there without interruption is not known, but it is
known that about 450 B.C. they were replaced by
invading Celts who were technically more sophisticated and probably better organized. These
Celts themselves were soon to fall prey to
successive waves of Germanic tribesmen (3).

   Kahl is almost directly on the line which
marked the border between the Germanic and the
Roman world. On the eastern bank of the Main
river were the German tribes; on the western bank
were Roman fortresses. Decades of strife were
interwoven with decades of peace and commerce
between the Romans and the Germans of the
Spessart area. Lines of trade would be established,
broken by war, and then reestablished. As the
Romans weakened, however, the Germanic tribes
penetrated the border and pushed back the Roman
lines just as one German tribe was itself being
pushed by another tribe behind it. This was the
age which is known as "The Wandering of the Tribes"
in German history (5).

   In Kahl, the Steuben tribe had been replaced
by the romanized Chatten who in turn were driven
back by the Alemannen. The Alemannen yielded to
the Burgundians in the fourth century, but they
reconquered the Burgundians in the following
century. The era of tribal conquests came to
a close in 496 when the Franks under King Choldwig
consolidated rule over a larger portion of western
Germany by the Battle of Zülpich. Even though the
Frankish court converted to Christianity at this
time, remote outposts such as the Spessart region
were essentially tribal and pagan. Even nominal
Christianity was several centuries away for these
people. The distant "rulers" did begin to send
missionaries. Following in the footsteps of the

Irish missionary St. Kilian and his brothers, Totnang and Kolonat, St. Boniface, the archbishop of Mainz, subdued the major centers of tribal religion (3).

It is from this point of Christianization that the name Kahl originates, but both membership in the Christian church and in the Frankish Kingdom was only a formality. The fact that Kahl was largely untouched by the growth of the Frankish Kingdom into the Holy Roman Empire and the subsequent division and redivision into smaller states is attested to in the fact that Kahl lacked a feudal overlord. It was so poor and so far removed from the centers of commercial and political power that no one claimed it as a fief. Instead, the tribal institutions were allowed to continue while urban Europe passed into medievalism and most of the rural areas were swallowed by great landowning lords. While other Frankish cities such as Nürnberg, Würzburg, and Frankfurt were ruled through guilds, city councils, and a hierarchy of aristocratic titles, villages such as Kahl were still electing tribal councils (3).

In Kahl all of the adult males were part of the council which met under a sacred tree every spring. The council called Märkerding, elected a leader and combined within it legislative as well as judicial powers. Tribal law was familial in orientation and followed traditional precepts of blood feuds and restitution. Only exceptional cases would be resolved by the Ding, or council (3,6). Because of this tribal autonomy from outside powers, this area was referred to as the Freigericht (or, free region), a name which is preserved to this day by the people, although not by the government.

Even after the crowning of the Frank Charlemange in 800, tribesmen lived by a combination of hunting and gathering, subsistence agriculture, and a few domestic animals. No one mode was sufficient to supply the population throughout the year. The land was too sandy for productive agriculture or for extensive grazing. The forest was not plentiful enough to support a hunting economy, but the sandy soil was suitable for a small rabbit called the "Sand Rabbit". A combination of gardening, hunting, and animal husbandry did suffice to support the community. This "barbaric" lifestyle and economic organization gave the villagers themselves the nickname of "Sand Rabbits", since the people, like the rabbits on which they preyed, had to eek out a livelihood in the desolate soil around Kahl.

The passage of the Middle Ages was not without its effect on Kahl. Having been located on one of the ancient trade routes connecting the Germanic tribes with the Romans, Kahl was on the fringes of commerce. Of particular importance to this time was the use of the route for salt caravans. This was not one of the major salt routes in medieval Europe, but it did supply part of the Rhein-Main area with salt taken from the higher areas in the Spessart hills. The importance of this route for Kahl was in the fact that it was a convenient and well-established conduit of produce. The connection with the agriculturally superior areas around Kahl was exploited by the building of mills in Kahl soon after the salt route opened. By using the water power which Kahl did have, the village specialized in the milling of grain which could be brought in over the salt route (3).

Secondary processing of agricultural produce is an early form of proto-industrialization, and it along with commerce represents one of the common forms of specialization in agricultural areas throughout the world. In return for milling, the miller is allowed to keep a part of the produce. Thus a village which was too poor and lacking in resources to be agricultural is able to perform a special service as a form of secondary agricultural production.

With improved access into the area by the salt route and with the new opportunities which the mills brought into the village, some degree of prosperity began to appear. Large mills were built and extended, but the same forces which enhanced the prosperity also whetted the interest of outside powers. In particular, the feudal lords on the edge of this Free Region began to

show interest in the barbarian Sand Rabbits. At
the same time, the trade route and the mills of
Kahl became easy prey for the "Robber Barons" who
roamed Germany during the 13th and 14th centuries.
Because the Free Region was a natural stronghold
for the Robber Barons, the Emperior of the Holy
Roman Empire finally authorized local lords to
move against them and in the process, to take
the village of Kahl as well as others as fiefs.

In the year 1500 Kahl became a joint fief co-
owned by the Archbishop of Mainz and by the Count
of Hanau (6,7). With this came the demise of the
tribal __Ding__. From thenceforth, the __Landrichter__
of the area was to be appointed by the lords
rather than elected by the people. The __Ding__ would
have an appointed membership, and it would be
concerned only with judicial powers, not with
making laws. It was given authority over civil
cases, and the older practices of family feuds
and restitutions were outlawed. Symbolic of
this demise of the tribal __Ding__, the court was
moved indoors (7).

For the first time the people were subject
not only to external laws, but to external taxation as well. In return for this the village was
supposed to be protected by the feudal lords. The
lords did manage to take their taxes and impose
their laws, but Kahl was too far from them and
too unimportant for them to offer real protection.
Both Hanau and Mainz demanded their feudal rights
but neither wanted to send in troops to protect
this still primitive village on the skirts of
their territory. The result was that Kahl was
still preyed on by robbers, the area was ravaged
in the Peasants Revolt, and to add to the external damages, the church decided to extend its
witch hunts into this primitive and still pagan
area. Between 1600 and 1605, there were 139
executions in the area of the Free Region (8).
This represented almost 5% of the population.
For better or worse, the area was being brought
into the modern world. Accompanying the new
technologies in milling and the improved trade
routes, religious orthodoxy was being imposed as
well.

The religious question was to plague Europe throughout the seventeenth century. In addition to witch trials, there was the growing split between Protestants and Catholics. Kahl had the misfortune of having its two feudal lords divide on the question. The Archbishop and Elector of Mainz remained loyal to the Catholic Church while the Count of Hanau embraced the Lutheran cause.

Being on the border between these two powers and being on a trade route of increasing importance, Kahl was fought over numerous times during the ensuing Thirty Years War (1618-1638). In the course of the war, Kahl was occupied eight different times by the troops of the Emperor, Spain, Mainz, Hanau, Sweden, and a host of other German states. Both the destruction to the village and the destruction to crops brought several years of continuous famine followed by the plague. Kahl had only a few dozen families at the beginning of the hostilities, but by the year of worst fighting in 1637, there was only a handful of people left (9). These few people sought refuge in the hills and forest of the Spessart. The village priest was dead, and every dwelling and mill was severely damaged.

Only after 1638 when the war began shifting to the north were the people able to return and to begin rebuilding the village. It was still to be another generation, however, before the church sent them another priest, despite the fact that Catholic Mainz became the sole lord of Kahl after the Treaty of Westphalia in 1648. When the next priest began keeping records in the 1660's, only three of the pre-war families were part of the new Kahl. The other residents were themselves refugees from the fighting in other parts of Germany and were peasants from the surrounding area.

On the ruins of the older mills, new ones rose up. As a prostrate Europe slowly recovered from the 3 decades of strife, prosperity returned to Kahl. New mills were built and the old ones expanded. In addition to making flour from grain, the mills were used to press oil. Additional processing of agricultural goods came in the form

of beer processing. Intermittent warfare did
occur in the following century, but for the most
part it was a century of prosperity for the
area (10). This grew with the wave of "enlight-
ened despotism" which was gaining momentum in
Europe. By the middle of the eighteenth century,
the Archbishop started a massive campaign of
modernization. In addition to building a new
church and several other buildings in the village,
he introduced manditory education in Kahl, built
new drinking fountains in place of the unsanitary
wells, ordered the baking of bread in a central
communal oven to avoid fire damage to individual
residences, and sent in trained teachers and
priests. He also fostered new crops such as
tobacco which did not grow in Kahl but was
cultivated in surrounding areas. The period was
also one of good weather and good harvests.
This spurred on the prosperity of Kahl.

    By the 1750's Kahl had grown to a population
of about 250 and in some respects was probably
a model of modernization. Ten separate mills
were in operation, literacy was increasing, and
building was booming. All of this, however, was
threatened severely by another reform which the
archbishop introduced. In addition to tobacco,
he compelled cultivation of another American
crop--the potato. After some initial resistance,
the cultivation of the potato spread. It was
simpler to grow, less susceptible to the variations in the weather, and easier to store. Of
grave importance to the people of Kahl, it
required no milling. Even though the peasants
of his area did not adopt the wholesale consumption of potato bread as advocated by the archbishop, the potato did assume an increased part
of daily food intake. Grain was still grown to
make bread, but the quantity declined severely
in the latter part of the eighteenth century.
The prosperity of Kahl declined in equal measure.

    The potato was not to be the only impact of
the Enlightenment on Kahl. By the close of the
century, Kahl was swept up in the paroxysms which
accompanied the French Revolution and the
Napoleonic era. The parade of armies passing
through Kahl was almost as severe as the Thirty
Years War a century and a half previously.

Repeated occupations by French, German, and Russian soldiers brought further ruination to the village. These occupations were inevitably followed by famine and the newer plaques of cholera, diptheria and typhoid.

In the process Napoleon abolished the Electorate of Mainz and gave Kahl to Hesse-Darmstadt. The victors over Napoleon then gave it to Bavaria. By the end of the war, the population of Kahl had declined to just over 300 people. In the winter of 1813-14 alone, 16% of the village population died from famine and epidemic (7). In addition, 14 Kahl families (over 50 people) had fled the area to settle in Rumania. A few richer families had been able to book passage to the Americas for settlement in Brazil and Argentina, despite stringent laws against emmigration.

The mills of Kahl survived the Napoleonic wars, but afterwards there was only enough grain to support the families of the millers. There was no added prosperity for the other residents. Once again, it was the presence of the ancient trade route which offered an alternative. At the close of the Congress of Vienna, the border separating the newly elevated Kingdom of Bavaria and the state of Hesse passed by the northern edge of Kahl. Located on the border and being a trade route, it was a natural customs station. The Bavarian bureaucracy built a large customs house in Kahl and sent in a small contingent of guards and officials to man it. This bureaucratic contingent and the accompanying repairs of the road and building of a new bridge across the Kahl river provided a margin of safety between poverty and real destitution. A few tradesmen were attracted to the area to participate in the building, and a few new homes were built for the customs officials.

In 1834, as quickly as it had been created, this margin against destitution collapsed: Bavaria moved to join the Zollverein (German Customs Union). The border was open to free trade and customs officials removed. The village sank deeper into poverty over the next two decades. Even the mills became idle when a

succession of poor harvests hit the area. With
the increased poverty and malnutrition, epidemics
returned to the area. What had been a model
village of the 1750's was a quagmire of disease
and poverty by the 1850's. The sanitary fountains
had given way to polluted wells which were
uncovered and disease-infested. The death rate
of Kahl was four times that of Lower Franconia,
the district of which Kahl was a part (4). It
was during this time that the Spessart became
known as one of the most primitive areas in the
German speaking world.

Industrialization

Even though the establishment of the
Zollverein had pulled the supports from under
the economy of Kahl, it also allowed for new
long-range developments which were to benefit
the village tremendously. With the free flow
of goods across the border, there was growing
demand for railroads connecting the various
nations. One major route was between Nürnberg
in Bavaria and Frankfurt in Hesse. In 1851
work began on this route paralleling the old trade
route which had passed through Kahl for over a
thousand years.

Well before the railroad was completed, its
impact was being felt. The work required laborers, and the laborers required lodging and food.
With the construction of the railway came new
homes, a food store was opened and a bakery was
needed to supply the needs of workers who had
no family to cook for them. An additional
aspect of the railroad boom was that the old
customs house was turned into a cigar factory
which employed 80 workers by the end of the
1850's (11).

Once the railroad opened, the town was
connected to a major trade route which encouraged
the development of manufacturing all along its
route. At first this manufacturing was in
larger towns, some of which were within reasonable distance to Kahl. When the building of
the railroad could no longer employ the population,
the new class of day-laborers found employment in

these plants. On Monday mornings before dawn large bands of young men and women would set out walking to these towns where they would spend the week working in the factories. Even though there were rail connections, the trains served commerce and richer passengers; not laborers. As rail prices declined over the next few decades, workers were able to commute on a daily basis.

Minor setbacks occurred during the 1860's brought on by smaller wars which eventually united all of Germany under the Kaiser. As ever, these wars and the movement of troops who now passed through the village by train brought new epidemics and new financial hardships. That combined with another year of poor tobacco harvests closed the small cigar plant. Emmigration to North and South America increased despite the fact that the United States itself was wracked by war and despite the heavy opposition of the King to emmigration. These economic set-backs were minor in the face of the introduction of railroads, the unification of Germany, and the push of the Imperial government for industry. As the push massed momentum, prosperity swept the nation. In addition to the resource of cheap labor, Kahl possessed the major ingredient for industrialization--water power. Not only was there the water power, but there already existed the in situ technology to use it--the mills. In 1879 one of these was converted from milling flour into a plant to make felt. At first it employed only 20 persons (barely more than the mill had done), but for the next 80 years, it was to be a growing and steady source of employment (3,11).

The success of the felt plant sparked the conversion of two other flour mills into saw mills to dress the lumber hauled down from the Kahl river valley. A fourth mill was transformed into a small factory to produce electrical fuses in 1888 before Kahl itself had been electrified. With the more sophisticated technology involved in manufacturing electrical equipment, there came a second generation of industrial production. One of the sawmills was specialized to make barrels. At the same time, the felt factory was successful enough that other manufacturers became interested in their machines. By 1900 the factory had shifted from the production of felt to the production of felt machines for other manufacturers.

Kahl was becoming a source of employment for the Kahl valley as well as a user of the lumber grown in the valley. In the late 1890's this prompted a private developer to propose construction of a 15-mile railroad into the valley. This allowed more of the peasants in the hills to come into the valley for employment (11). This increased impetus to manufacturing in the area also spurred on new building of homes as well as additions to the mills. Thus, a cement factory opened on the site of a sand pit in 1902, and this was followed by sheet-metal production four years later.

As the technology of industrialization progressed, water power was not enough for industry. Soon the small mills grew into factories, but they needed electricity. And growing factories needed coal. There was a small amount of coal in Kahl, but it was not of high enough quality to be used as a domestic product. With new techniques, however, it could be used by industry, and in 1900 the first open-pit for the mining of coal went into operation. To supply the needs of the pit, the owners built a small electric generator at the site. This, however, soon grew to supply the other manufacturers in the community and finally the homes as well.

The coal pits required new laborers. By now the workers of Kahl were accustomed to being factory workers with skills; they did not see themselves as manual laborers. Even the peasants who came in from the hills were more interested in working in the factory than in the labor-intensive coal pits. To work the coal pits, miners were brought from distant Saxony where industry was slower in developing. By 1911 there were over 80 "foreign workers" from Saxony working in Kahl. Not only were these laborers in the mines foreign, they were a lower class, and they were Protestants in a Catholic community. For the most part, these workers were excluded from

the village. They had to build their homes on
the far side of the Kahl river separate from the
traditional village. They slowly built up the
new area adding homes in between the small factories and the coal and sand pits. Within a
generation, this cluster of homes had grown into
a community even more modern than the old center
of the village and made the initial dichotomy of
Kahl into both an old and new village. The
Saxons were able to erect their own church in
1929, and with increased educational assistance
from the government, the children of the Saxon
miners were trained for craft occupations.

    In contrast to earlier wars, WWI was mini-
mal in direct impact on Kahl (12). Like other
communities, Kahl was taxed heavily and had to
supply men for the army, but there was no wholesale destruction of the village. Nor were there
the accompanying famines and epidemics; food
supplies were substantially reduced but not to
the levels of the previous century. Factors such
as the downfall of the Kaiser, the Treaty of
Versailles, and the devaluation of the Mark were
to have graver impact. Worker unrest grew in the
village, strikes intensified, and the economic
enterprises which supported the village began
to fail. At first, the Community Council tried
to check the economic collapse of the village
through direct involvement on its own. When the
coal mines were closed, the Council bought the
waterworks which the mining company had operated.
When one of the gravel and sand pits was forced
to close, the Council also bought it and sustained
it in operation. Eventually this was expanded
and under communal direction other sand pits
opened. This type of government involvement in
private enterprise was congruent with the
socialist aspect of National Socialism which was
emerging as an ever stronger philosophy. At the
same time, it was supported by ideologically more
leftist citizens who identified with the
traditional socialist and communist movements.

    As the community-owned gravel and sand pits
grew into ever larger craters, they began to fill
with water, creating small lakes surrounded, of
course, by sand. These natural-appearing lakes
were suitable for swimming and were quickly

A Changing German Village   49

exploited as communally sponsored recreational areas. The Council built up the beaches, installed diving and dressing facilities, and cordoned off boating sections. The first such lake was opened to the people of Kahl in 1934 (11). Even though the recreational facilities were destroyed in the wake of World War II, the lakes would later play a pivotal role in the economic direction which the village would take.

   Throughout the Nazi reign, prosperity grew in Kahl as throughout most of Germany. Even the first few years of the second world war did not interrupt this growth since workers who were conscripted to serve in the army were replaced by prisoners of war brought in from the east. In some respects the war was an economic boom to the village. It became a reasonably safe haven for a few smaller industries from the bombed cities. With the new industries, however, came new influxes of population. in the very first months of the war, the village, (like others) was forced to take in refugees from the Saar which was on the Western Front. As the war continued and the endangered areas grew to include all of urban Germany, more and more civilians were evacuated to remote regions like Kahl (11). By 1951 Kahl had been forced to accept close to a thousand refugees and thus pushed the population near 4,000. The village of Kahl was developing a town-size population and appearance.

Post-Industrial Development

   Small enterprises remained afloat throughout the war and were able to continue during the American occupation. Using both refugee labor as well as drawing the poor residents of the hills down by railway, the small plants remained viable. After the war, however, Kahl's greatest asset was the very sand that was the bane of the farmer's existence for so many centuries. A nation in ruins needed sand and cement to rebuild itself. The village-owned sand and gravel works expanded rapidly and was joined by several small private firms. Industrial production remained at its previous level, but the new growth centered around sand, gravel and cement. As pits were depleted and filled with water, new lakes were formed, and workers in the revived German economy began to have leisure time to enjoy them. In addition to remaking the original swimming area for local residents, the Community Council opened a new pit-lake as a camping ground which would attract people from other communities including Frankfurt. With the easy rail connections, workers from factories of Frankfurt could afford to bring their families on the 45-minute trip to Kahl, walk a few minutes to the camping ground, and spend the weekend. Other lakeside areas were opened where people could rent permanent campsites, and as German prosperity continued to increase these campsites gave way to small weekend homes. By the middle 1960's families from the larger cities were able to drive out in their own cars for weekends at these lakeside homes. As the building boom of the German economy subsided and the demand for cement and sand dwindled, the resulting slack in the economic development of Kahl was compensated by the growing business from the lakes (2,11).

Meanwhile the small industrial facilities of Kahl had difficulty competing with the larger industries of Germany. Because of communal growth restrictions on both industrial and residential increases, these facilities found it difficult to expand. Several of the smaller firms simply closed, unable to compete for land or for workers. The remaining firms had to rely increasingly upon the influx of foreign workers from southern Europe. The foreigners would work jobs which Germans would not and they lived in more cramped residences. As of the mid-1970's, industrial production in Kahl seemed to be declining.

The old sand and coal mines, however, left another legacy in addition to the lakes and building service employment in the area. From the early generator used to work the coal pits, an electric company had arisen and had endured long after the mines themselves were closed. Late in the 1950's a consortium of West Germany made plans to build the nation's first atomic power plant. In 1961 amidst much local excitement and national attention, the first atomic generator went into operation in Kahl.

Despite the initial enthusiasm and pride, the long-term economic effects of the nuclear power plant were not as significant as first anticipated. As a small, experimental facility, it did not readily improve the employment situation in Kahl which had a surfeit of workers. The effects of the plant were to be felt in other spheres of local life. Namely, it drew in a small community of highly trained professionals who needed a place to live. To these highly educated and urban-oriented people, Kahl was an attractive and rather bucolic village surrounded by trees and lakes at the bottom of the Spessart mountains. New homes were built, and by 1975 Kahl had grown to over 8,000 people including 600 foreign workers; this is almost triple the population of the pre-World War II community (2,11).

In total the industrial force of the village provided work for about 1,400 people, but most of these were either the foreigners or people commuting in from the mountains. Fewer and fewer residents of Kahl work in the village itself. For most of them, the higher paying industries of nearby towns offer them more financial advancement. For the residents, Kahl is becoming more and more of a commuter town with increasing employment in service jobs and decreasing employment in industry. There is little interest in the small electrical plant which employs 800 people, the majority of whom live in other communities. If anything, the plant with its foreign workers and "mountain peasants" is an eyesore to the residents; in the same way the atomic power plant has become an eyesore and a possible health hazard to the community in the opinion of many today. Still, the citizenry are dependent on these businesses as the source of community taxes. Without that tax base, it would not be possible to finance the public construction work which the city has initiated in the form of a new school, indoor swimming pool, increased sports facilities, street lights, sewage treatment plant, and a village library.

Possibly this dilemma between the financial contributions of the industries and their aesthetic liabilities will not be decided solely by the people of Kahl. Like so many other trends in the village's history, this too will probably be settled by outside influence. Already there is a new freeway under construction to parallel the old rail route. By the 1980's this should open and thereby cut in half the time it would take to commute between Frankfurt and Kahl. With its abundance of lakes, forest, and two rivers, those people who now have weekend homes and permanent camping spots in Kahl, may well become full-time inhabitants. Already the small number of professionals at the atomic plant indicate that life in a small community can be both enjoyable and as amenable as urban life. Even though Kahl will remain as an electrical equipment producer (as it was in the 1980's) and of electrical power, it seems to have moved beyond its industrial phase. Today its economy is based on a mixture of production and services, but the wave of the future seems to be in services--particularly in the exploitation of the image of the village as an ideal place to live.

The new social and economic organization of the village as a service-oriented rather than industry-oriented area is clearly evident in developments over the past decade. Both in the activities of private enterprises and in activities of the community government, there is increased concern with offering services to improve the quality of life. Cultural understandings about the quality of life have increased significantly. As more people share the understandings about the importance of services rather than just industrial output, the emphasis on existing industrial structures declines.

During the 1970's the village-owned-and-operated gravel and sand company has declined in production as old pits are exhausted and no new ones are opened. Instead, the new community enterprise is the operation and extension of the lakeside recreational facilities. In addition to developing areas for swimming, boating, and fishing, the Community Council has financed a jogging course through the forest and a gymnastics course for both team and individual sports(2). For wintertime activities, the schools have been adapted to communally financed athletic events, and a variety of educational and self-improvement courses. These classes vary from folk dance to modern math, from foreign languages to photo-safaris to East Africa. Community sponsored "cultural enrichment programs" include lecture series combined with excursions. This might be a one-hour lecture before boarding a bus to go to the opera in Frankfurt, or it might be a year-long lecture series on Iranian history in preparation for a community-sponsored charter trip.

The same trend toward community services is evidenced in the private sector of the village economy. In the face of stiff competition from large grocery stores, the older specialty shops owned by a single baker or butcher are changing the focus of their specialization. In addition to meat and sausage, the butcher now offers an array of pre-cooked dishes which the working wife can carry home at the end of the day. The butcher's wife centers her talents on catered dinners for special occasions. In a similar manner, the clothing stores which cannot compete with the department stores of the urban areas are being transformed into fashion boutiques which offer both advice and specialized clothing. Two of the traditional pubs in the village center have been transformed into restaurants which are oriented more toward visitors to the community than the local clientele. In a variety of ways, both the local government and private enterprise are responding to new demands and to a changing conception of what Kahl is and should be. As a small community it is less able to compete with urban areas as a source of industrial employment, but as a place to live it offers a variety of advantages over those same urban areas.

Kahl at present has a diversified and mixed economic base. in addition to the industries which have remained in the community and the new service oriented enterprises, even agriculture has persisted as an important economic variable. Kahl has no farmers; yet, gardening still plays a primary role in both the economic and social organization of the community. In addition to supplying produce for the families, the cultivation of gardens, fruit trees, and small vineyards is a mechanism which permits elderly citizens to play a contributing role in the kinship structures. As they retire from the industrial labor force, elderly citizens as well as some housewives who need to be near the home, manage family garden plots. These gardening activities along with the secondary activities of canning, and making wine are substantial contributions to household economy and insure the retired individuals productive positions in both kinship and community organization. These economic developments as much as the population growth indicate the extent to which the community has changed from a village into a town. With these changes, Kahl is becoming a convenient and attractive place for former urbanites to live, but this is done with profound effects on the traditional village organization.

The Changing Moral Community

There is another aspect of community life during this millenium of Kahl's history. In addition to the existence of the village as an economic and political entity interacting with the larger economic and political forces of Europe, there is the internal cultural organization of the village. This refers to the body of understandings shared by villagers as villagers. It includes what M.J. Swartz refers to as the existential understandings (which villagers share about each other) and the ideals or moral judgments which they utilize in daily interaction (13). On the day-to-day level, village life consists of diverse people interacting in a complex of social statuses and roles. These are the people who may be neighbors, kinsmen, colleagues at work, ex-school mates, members of the same political party, and fellow worshipers at the same church. This is what is called "the moral community" by

F. G. Bailey(14) since it is composed of those
people who know each other "in the round".
Their interactions are not limited to just one
role-pair; rather they have a choice of statuses
from which to choose one particular role in
any given interaction. Concomitantly, members
of this moral community do not judge one another
solely on performance in one role or even on one
status but on the totality of their reputation
in a variety of performances and on basic moral
values. These are moral judgments based on the
shared understandings of what it means to be
a decent and good person. These are understandings which transcend the expectations of
any particular role relationship. Other understandings are used to judge particular performances, but these are not the criteria for
membership in the moral community. Whether one
fails to meet expectations or one succeeds in
meeting them will determine the kind of reputation which the individual has, but it will
not bar an individual from membership.

People not included in the moral community
are those who are not known to the members
or who have only single role relationships with
community members. The boundaries of who it
is that is included and by what standards
their reputations are developed are likely to
change from one era to another. By definition,
knowing someone "in the round" cannot be
achieved quickly; nor can a multiplex set of
relationships with a variety of villagers be
established quickly. Nevertheless both the members of the community and the standards for
membership in the moral community do change
over time. Three such major changes have
occurred in Kahl since industrialization. These
are changes brought about by 1) the arrival of
Saxon laborers just before and after 1900,
2) the arrival of refugees during and after
World War II, and 3) the arrival of guest
workers in the 1960's and 1970's. Each of
these onslaughts of people into the community
had an impact on the moral boundaries of the
community. These mass movements of people into

the community were more than the traditional means of incorporating outsiders could handle. Consequently, tensions were created and the understandings about group membership were altered. Each of these three episodes is examined separately below.

The Saxons

From what evidence exists, it appears that for much of its history the definition of who fit into the moral community was determined by the limits of who lived in the village. These were the people who knew each other in the round and interacted in a multiplex of social relations. The non-members would be those people who were known in simplex relations; these included members of nearby villages, drivers of the salt carts who passed through the village, farmers who came to have their wheat milled, soldiers who were occasionally stationed there, and travelling journeymen who have roamed the area for several centuries. These outsiders did in some cases become members by settling in the village; this was usually accomplished by either marriage or adult adoption. The taking in of new members was slow, but there were shared understandings about how it was done. Consequently there was a steady flow of new members into the community, but this flow did not change the moral definitions associated with membership. That is to say that the physical boundaries might change, but the moral or cultural boundaries remained largely intact.

With the advent of industrialization, large numbers of outsiders began settling in the village. These new people were moving into Kahl in a single capacity as workers. This contrasts with the earlier in-migrants who came into the village as both workers (e.g., in the mill of a particular family) and as kinsmen (either by marriage or adoption). For the new influx of workers, there were no corresponding places in the social-kinship network of Kahl. To the factory owners the newcomers were employees. To shopkeepers they were customers.

But to the majority of Kahl residents the newcomers were not known as individuals but as members of a group variously referred to as "the Saxons" or "the gypsies". Incorporation into the moral community was limited by the fact that there was residential segregation of the migrants and that there were simply not enough "openings" in the traditional social organization as there were "openings" in the economic organization.

In recognition of some of the disparities, both the community council and the Bavarian government instituted programs to train the unskilled laborers for better jobs. An indirect outcome of these programs was that they also trained the people in how to be like the natives. This enculturation process was particularly marked in the second generation of Saxon children who attended the public school. Not only did school offer the children formal training in school subjects, but it tended to homogenize the children of older and newer residents both in terms of language and in terms of behaviors. It also gave the children prolonged personal exposure to one another. The school experience was able to modify educational-skill differences as well as behavioral and linguistic differences (15), but it was not able to alter the primary ideological difference--religion. The school imposed Catholic instruction on the Saxon children even though the Saxons were Lutherans, but this one aspect of enculturation was significantly resisted by the Saxons. Not only did they retain their Protestant religion, but they were able to start their own church in Kahl and eventually a network of church related organizations.

Religion represented the shared understandings about the most important moral topics, and so long as the differences existed between Lutherans and Catholics, it was not possible for the two groups to intermarry or to form a single, united moral community. Either the religion of one group had to change or else the understandings about membership in the moral community had to change, if the village were to remain one cultural and social entity. Despite historical precedents concerning the pivotal importance of religion, in the end it was those understandings which did change, i.e., the moral boundaries of the community were modified. The reasons for this change have as much to do with pan-Germanic trends as it does with the internal dynamics of Kahl itself.

During previous generations, religious and political systems had been interwoven so as to be largely indistinguishable. This was true formally in that the church and the state were interwoven bodies with churchmen being state officials and taxes going to support both institutions. It was also true ideologically in that being a good Bavarian was largely indistinguishable in most people's eyes from being a good Catholic. All Bavarians were Catholics living in an officially Catholic state under a Catholic king. In much the same way Lutheranism was interwoven with being a Prussian or a Saxon.

It was not until the unification of Germany that the separation of religious and political ideologies began. The process was accelerated during the nationalist era leading up to the first world war, as Hessians, Prussians, Saxons, and Bavarians all became Germans. The new Germany then had two state-supported churches, and one could just as easily be a good German in one as in the other.

This separation of the moral domains of politics and religion was carried even further in the Nazi era. Under the Nazis, not only were the two domains distinct, but the political one was more important than the religious. One of the primary understandings shared by Nazis (and imposed by them) was that the highest morality of all was that of the state-race. In Kahl this had the practical effect of destroying most of the church-oriented social clubs in preference to the new party-based organizations. The Nazis correctly perceived that one of the major obstacles to German unity under Nazism was the division of the population into two religious groups each with its own social and cultural organization. In communities throughout

Germany, the effort was undertaken to supercede these distinctions with a set of understandings which placed political morality and ideology above that of the churches. While the Nazis were never completely successful in making this ideological transition, they did lessen the distinctions between the two groups. In Kahl Lutherans and Catholics were now members of a single set of sports and leisure clubs under Nazi domination, rather than in religiously segregated clubs. The whole range of social activities and organizations under church control were passed to state and party control.

At the same time that Nazism fused the two communities, Nazism also forced out older segments of both communities. It was no longer important whether one was a Catholic or a Lutheran, but it was very important whether one was a Nazi or an anti-Nazi. Leaders of the old communist and socialist parties were physically excluded from the new community. Either they left through "voluntary" migration or they were taken away to concentration camps. By the end of the Nazi era not only had the demographic composition of Kahl been altered, but the boundaries of the moral community had been changed. Religious differences within the community have persisted with both social and symbolic significance attached to church membership, but today these distinctions are strictly _within_ the community. They do not preclude membership. The moral community was then composed of both Lutherans and Catholics. Many of the specific understandings about being Catholic or Lutheran continue, but their placement in the hierarchy of understandings has been altered.

The Refugees

Even though the Nazi era effectively left one moral community in Kahl composed of both Lutherans and Catholics, the Nazi era also left another legacy of newcomers in the village. These newcomers were at first evacuees from urban and combat areas, but by the end of the war they were simple refugees. These German refugees were joined in the years after the war by a flood of ethnic-Germans who were expelled from the Soviet-occupied countries of Eastern Europe, but all too often these ethnic Germans were as much Polish, Hungarian, or Czech as they were German. Between 1940 and 1950, the population of Kahl increased by 25% due to these new in-migrants.

Unlike the Saxons who had moved into economic openings in the village and from these eventually made a social place for themselves, the new refugees were coming into neither social or economic openings. The residents of Kahl did not want the newcomers in any capacity, economic or social. The newcomers were competition for everything including housing, food, and employment. The native residents, however, were forced to share their homes with the refugees as well as other resources. In addition the natives were subject to heavy taxes to pay for the resettlement of the refugees and to pay for part of the losses which the refugees experienced in being forced from their homes. The relations between the two groups was extremely bitter, but the bitterness was to be shortlived.

German economic recovery after the war was swift, and with it the economy of Kahl expanded rapidly. With their generally high industrial skills and high education levels, the refugees were able to contribute to the boom as much as benefit by it. The refugees were also politically astute and organized their own political party. This party gained enough seats on the village council to be the decisive group needed for any ruling coalition. The fact that this party was disbanded in 1966 represents not so much its failure as the complete success of the refugees in being incorporated into the community. By that time economic prosperity was far enough under way that the physical limits of the village had been extended to provide more housing, and almost all economic and political distinctions between refugees and natives had been overcome. Also by that time a new generation of refugee children and native children had been reared together and educated together.

Compared to the incorporation of the Saxons, the incorporation of the refugees was both quick and easy. The Saxons had brought about substantial changes in the understandings of what it meant to be a villager and a "moral" member of the community. In part because of the changes already made by the Saxons, the path for subsequent newcomers was much easier. The refugees had only to spend the time and effort necessary to fit into the existing social organization; they did not have to redefine it.

The refugees did not bring with them any moral or ideological understandings which were not already included within the existing body of shared understandings in the community. The earlier Saxons had brought both a separate religion and a separate "nationality", but by the 1940's when the refugees entered, the differences in these ideological systems had been reconciled enough that members of either could also be members of the moral community. This, however, was not to be the case with the next group of newcomers who began arriving early in the 1960's.

The Guest Workers

As the German economy continued to expand after the refugees had all been successfully integrated into the labor force, Germany began drawing in workers from southern Europe. The first guest workers in Kahl were from Italy. As isolated individuals coming into the community to find work, they were incorporated into the community despite the fact that their command of German was not very good. At that time the difference in the standard of living between the native Germans and the incoming Italians was not as extremely different as it was to be later. These first few guest workers were also Catholic, and because there were so few of them they were able to be absorbed by the community much like individual workers had been absorbed in earlier centuries.

Several of these earlier workers are still present in Kahl today. A few of them married local women and today live as Germans. They have usually come to claim that their own ancestry is in fact German because of some Tyrolian ancestor, and in this manner they have changed from guest workers to expatriated ethnics. In a similar manner some Italian families have been accepted into the community in toto. These families own their own homes, send their children to German school, have joined local clubs, and in general are indistinguishable from older residents except for the accents of the elder generation. These earlier families were aided by the fact that they arrived in time to take part in the extraordinary prosperity of the German economic boom. Today, the second generation of these guest workers is marrying with the children of native residents, and for all practical purposes they have been absorbed by the existing moral community.

After the initial ground was broken by these Italian guest workers in the 1960's, a host of other workers from Spain, Greece and Yugoslavia followed. These were in turn followed by Turks and Moroccans who numbered over 500 by the mid-1970's. Thus far, there is no sign that the Moslems are beginning to form any other relationships within the community than worker-employee and customer-shopkeeper. Once again both religion and nationality are interwoven in determining the moral boundaries of the community. The differences separating the Moslem workers and the native residents are more extreme and deep-rooted than the separation between native and Saxon (16).

One of the primary distinctions between Moslem workers and newcomers of earlier generations is that the Moslems are able to utilize improved communication and transportation networks to maintain their frequent interaction with their communities of origin. The children of Turks do not live in Kahl; they reside in Turkey where they go to school. They do come to Kahl for their vacations, or else the parents will return to Turkey for their vacation. Additionally, there are today both newspapers and

radio programs for Turks. The Turks living
in Kahl are strictly there in the capacity of
workers; as such they are treated collectively
as a group with few non-work relationships with
Germans. They are not neighbors to the German
residents, and they have no kin-ties. They do
not attend the same church, nor are the Turks
eligible to participate in the political process. Because of their own dietary restrict-
tions, the Turks do not eat with Germans or
participate in the festivals and celebrations which
revolve around food. Thus far, then there do
not appear to be any possible avenues for establishing the multiplex relations necessary for
extending the moral community of Kahl. As already shown in German history by the fate of the
Jews and gypsies, simple longevity and proximity
are not sufficient to erode those boundaries of
the moral community.

Conclusions

Because of the economic and demographic
changes in Kahl during the last century, the
community today possesses a combination of the
characteristics of village and town. One side of
the community faces the Kahl river and blends
into the Spessart forest; the other side faces
the atomic power plant on the Main and blends into
the industrialized Rhein-Main area. So too, the
organization of the community is divided between
a socio-cultural complex based on traditional
village forms and the more simplex relations of
heterogenous town dwellers (17). Just as
centuries-old timbered homes have had modern
facades of plaster added and tile roofs to replace
the thatch, so too has the traditional village
system been modernized with additional layers of
social organization and new moral understandings
to replace older ones. The primary supports
of the modernized farmhouses are still the older
timbers of the traditional design, and the primary
organization of the community is still based on a
village structure.

At the core of the community is the population which shares a common knowledge of one
another's reputations and a common set of shared

values and understandings. This moral community
has changed significantly as the population has
increased in the twentieth century, but it has
persisted. Those people who are not centrally
involved with this community are on the fringes
both socially and spatialy, and they do not form
a separate community. In this sense, there is
only one community in Kahl even though increasing
numbers of people do not belong it it; the non-
members are simply residents with simplex relations to each other (18).

Because of the economic and demographic
changes in Kahl during the last century, the
community today possesses both the characteristics
of a village and some of the signs of being a town.
One side of the community faces the Kahl river
and blends into the Spessart forest; the other
side faces onto the atomic power plant and leads
into Germanys' industrialized Rhein-Main area.
So too, the cultural and social organization of
the community is divided between a face-to-face
village and the more simplex relations of heterogenous town dwellers.

On the village end of the spectrum, the majority of the residents are still connected to
each other through the traditional networks.
They have kinship, religious, political, and
social ties. They may have gone to school together, they play cards together, possibly work
together, or have garden plots adjacent to one
another. Just as importantly, they share the
same basic understandings and values even though
they might belong to different churches or
different political parties.

At the town end of the spectrum, there is a
large community of foreigners who live in the
community without being a part of the primary
social relationships and without sharing in the
primary cultural understandings. In addition
there are increasing numbers of tourists and
weekend residents who spend time in the community
but who live primarily in urban areas and have
different understandings. In the same way the
residents of Kahl spend more time in other com-

munities where they go to visit, work, or shop. In the process they also develop relationships with other people who are not community residents.

There have been efforts to check the process of growth. Regulations on building severely limit the number of homes which can be built in the community and have long since brought industrial expansion to a halt. Even families which are given permits to build new homes must be town residents at least two-years before they may begin building. This allows the old residents and the newcomer time to adjust to one another. Despite these small efforts, however, Kahl has continued to grow and with the new freeway being built will probably grow even more.

There is no precise demographic point at which a community changes from a village to a town; rather there are a series of transformations in both the social and cultural spheres which contribute to the process. One of the important factors is population since there are physical limits to the number of people who can know each other on a personal basis. But of equal importance are the social networks connecting the individual members. In the late 19th century the village nature of the community was strained by the development of a Saxon community within it. Yet, with time a single, integrated community grew out of this. Thus, Kahl in 1930 with 3,000 people was probably more of a village than it had been in 1910 with 2,000 people. Even though it was larger in 1930, the population was socially and culturally more homogeneous and was all tied into a single social organization. This was in turn disrupted by the heterogenous newcomers after the Second World War, but again the community was able to incorporate them into the existing structure. This process of incorporation, however, could not go on forever. Even if the newcomers of the 1960's and 1970's had been German rather than foreign, it is doubtful that they could have been integrated into the community as effectively as the previous groups. The reason being that the community simply passed the size where everyone could know everyone.

References and Notes

1. The data for this study were gathered during fieldwork in West Germany between 1974 and 1976. Various parts were financed by the following agencies: The German Marshall Fund, NIMH (MH05209), The German Academic Exchange (DAAD), NSF (Soc75-18044), and the Council for European Studies.

2. J.M. Weatherford <u>Family Culture, Behavior and Emotion in a Working-Class German Town</u> (Ph.D dissertation, University of California, San Diego, 1977).

3. B. Scheuring, <u>Ortskunde von Kahl am Main</u> (Erziehungswissenschaftliche Fakultät, Würzburg, 1972).

4. H. Friedel, "Heimische Bodenfunde aus der Steinzeit" in <u>Unser Kahlgrund</u> 17 (1972).

5. N. Heimbücher "Die Schlact an der Kahlmund" in <u>Unser Kahlgrund</u> 12 (1967).

6. E. Rücker, <u>Markt Hörstein</u> (Gemeinde Hörstein, West Germany, (1973).

7. E. Rücker, <u>Grosswelzheim 1200 Jahre</u>. (Gemeinde Grosswelzheim/Karlstein (1974).

8. Christian Gräber, "Die Hexenprozesse im Freigericht in den Jahren 1601-1605" in Aschaffenburger Jahrbuch 6 (1976).

9. Church records were destroyed during the Thirty Years War.

10. K. Imgram, <u>Geschichte der Stadt Steinheim am Main</u>, Part I (Gemeinde Steinheim, West Germany (1973).

11. U. Bergman, <u>Siedlungsgeographische Untersuchung</u> in the files of Bürgermeister Oswald Will, Kahl am Main, West Germany (1974).

12. Georg Hubert, "Als die Amerikaner kamen" in <u>Unser Kahlgrund</u> 16 (1971).

13. M. Swartz, J. Akong'a, M. Murphy, G. Saunders, and J. Weatherford, <u>Family Goals and Culture in Five Societies</u> (expected publication in 1979).

14. F. G. Bailey, <u>Gifts and Poison</u> (Basil Balckwell, Oxford, 1971).

15. A detailed analysis of the importance of school in German towns is in R.L. Warren's <u>Education in Rebhausen</u>, (Holt, Rinehart, and Winston, New York, 1967).

16. J.M. Weatherford, "Deutsche kultur, amerikanisch betrachtet" in <u>Deutschland: Das Kind mit den zwei Köpfen</u>, H.C. Buch, Ed. (Verlag Klaus Wagenbach, Berlin, 1978).

17. A similar process is shown in G. Spindler's <u>Burgbach</u> (Holt, Rinehart, and Winston, 1973), but in Burgbach the changes occur because the community is incorporated into surrounding urban area and thus becomes a suburb.

18. The isolation of German family units in urban settings is analyzed in S. Salamon's "Family Bonds and Friendship Bonds", <u>Journal of Marriage and Family</u>, 1977.

Robert McC. Netting, Walter S. Elias

3. Balancing on an Alp: Population Stability and Change in a Swiss Peasant Village

Population growth has now become a familiar spectre, globally visible in the prevalence of people, the environmental changes they bring about, and the exponential curve that charts their increase. The generally accepted reasons for this rise have been the success of modern medicine, public health measures, and the technology of food production. As the Malthusian positive checks of starvation, illness, and war have loosened their hold, the proclivity to reproduce has powered astonishingly rapid growth. The possibility of control is seen only in modern methods of contraception, sterilization, and abortion. It is difficult to believe, however, that unchecked demographic increase or even short boom-and-bust cycles of growth and decline have normally characterized the human species. Self-regulating systems of population control have been documented for animals and often related directly to such social behavior as territoriality or dominance hierarchies [1]. There is evidence that hunter-gatherer groups tended to stabilize their numbers below the carrying capacities of their environments [2]. But the expansion of population since the agricultural revolution has convinced some biologists that former limitations are no longer effective.

> "No built-in (density dependent) mechanisms appear to curb our own population growth, or adjust our numbers to our resources. ...these mechanisms did exist in primitive man and have been lost, almost within historic times" [1].

Peasant Population Equilibria

The fact is that enduring, relatively stable communities of sedentary cultivators are a dominant feature of the cultural landscape in many parts of the world. The resilient peasant way of life, largely self-sufficient and with farming households exercising considerable control over necessary

local resources, has survived, even as cities have sprung up
and decayed and nation states have passed across the stage
(3). The peasant village often occupies the same site for
generations, and fixed territorial boundaries limit the
amounts of land, water, and wood which the inhabitants can
use (4). The technology of agricultural production is often
mechanically simple and relatively unchanging. With restricted resources and few improvements in the available tool-kit,
peasants may well be under some pressure to preserve a demographic equilibrium or risk a rapid deterioration in their
standard of living. But if numbers were regulated, we do not
know how this was done. Was peasant life indeed "nasty,
brutish, and short," with high mortality as the sure and ultimate control? Was migration the safety valve that prevented overcrowding and impoverishment? Were the same homeosta-
tic mechanisms present in different regions and at different
historical periods? Demographers and historians are now
suggesting that peasant population dynamics over time may be
observed with some precision, that their demographic characteristics distinguish them from other rural populations,
and that the significant regulatory mechanisms apparent in
Tokugawa Japan and medieval England may be quite different
(5-8). The possibility has been raised that

> "the European peasant household (or the peasant
> community, or both) operated as an effective pop-
> ulation-control mechanism, closely matching the
> opportunities for marriage and procreation to the
> number of persons the land could support" (7).

What Hajnal (9) has called the European marriage pattern
established potent social limitations on reproduction by
means of a high average age at marriage for both men and
women, along with a considerable frequency of celibacy.
Religious and legal sanctions against illegitimacy and premarital intercourse often bolstered the demographic influence of such practices. Perhaps the major factor governing
nuptiality among peasants, however, was the frequent requirement that land and the other goods needed to maintain
a viable household should be inherited or otherwise acquired
before marriage could take place (10-12). The sensitive
feedback loop from production to reproduction was the systematic connection of resource availability and legitimate
family formation (13).

The operation of both physiological and social regulators, the relative contribution of fertility, nuptiality,
migration, and mortality to the stability or change of a
village population, should be evident to the extent that
population size through several centuries can be reconstructed and vital rates inferred. In the absence of regular

dependable census counts, historical demography has developed the method of family reconstitution for combining data from parish registers of birth, marriage, and death to provide demographic profiles of related individuals (14). Though aggregative statistics may show secular trends in natality and mortality, only through the careful and often arduous recreation of the sequence of vital events in a number of families can indices of fertility, birth spacing, age at marriage, life expectancy, and infant mortality be tabulated (15).

Demographic History of an Alpine Community

The Swiss village of Törbel in the mountains of upper Valais offers a unique opportunity for investigating demographic processes (16). Its antiquity is indicated by documentary evidence of the village name in the 12th century and a local archive of parchments detailing events in the community's history from 1224 to the present. One house still in use bears the inscribed date 1483, but it is generally believed to be more recent than other extant buildings. The village territory stretching from the Visp River at 770 meters to Augstbordhorn peak at almost 3000 meters seems to have remained essentially unchanged for at least 700 years. The economy until recently was based on dairy cattle producing milk and cheese and on rye as the principal bread grain. Each household possessed sufficient irrigated hay meadows, vineyards, arable fields, gardens, and pastures to provide its own necessities (16). The alp for summer grazing and the forest for fuel were owned and administered communally. Tools and utensils such as the scythe, the metal-shod plow, the churn, the kettle, the spinning wheel, and the loom were of simple design and often local manufacture. Though cattle, sheep, and perhaps other farm products were sold in towns and some seasonal wage labor was undertaken, the community does not appear to have been dependent on the market economy in the past. In the medieval period, Törbel's feudal obligations to outside authorities were not great, and in recent centuries it has exhibited a large measure of political autonomy (17). By the fifteenth century, the community itself had established legal bars to granting citizenship to outsiders, and most of the surnames present in 1700 are still represented in the contemporary population. Since the mid-seventeenth century, the village has had a resident Roman Catholic priest, and a parish register of baptisms begins in 1665. Church records of marriages and deaths were kept from 1700, and these are supplemented by a genealogy book covering almost all families from the late seventeenth century on, a civil registry from 1885, and

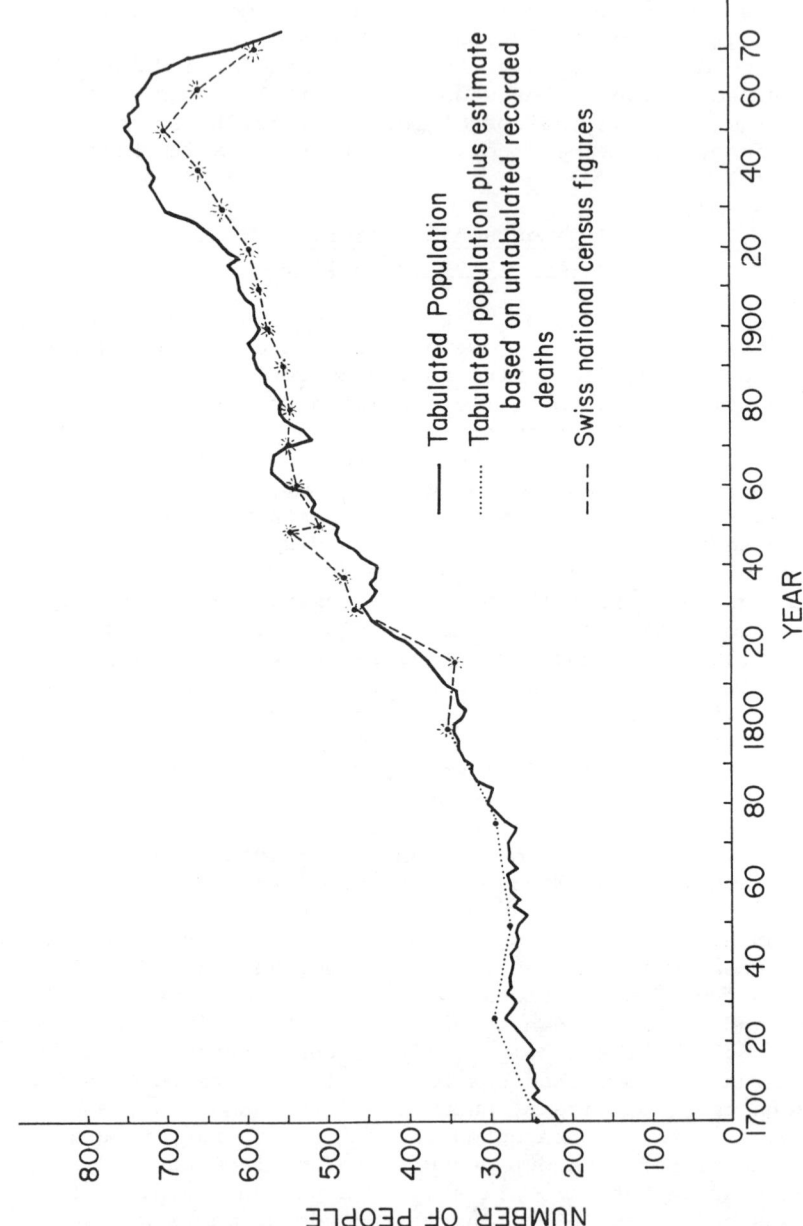

Figure 1. Aggregate population estimates in Törbel.

Population Stability and Change in a Swiss Village 73

various nineteenth century manuscript censuses and tax lists. The records are largely unbroken, undamaged by fire or war, and consistent in their chronicling of the remarkable continuity of a geographically isolated closed corporate community.

Total Population Dynamics

The time-consuming process of excerpting, collating, comparing, and eventually machine processing the data from the various available sources (18) resulted in a file of some 5500 individuals with vital statistics, names of primary relatives (father, mother, and spouse), family of origin and procreation, and migration information for each. Annual total village population could then be reconstructed by adding births and in-migrants to the previous year's population and subtracting deaths and out-migrants. Individuals for whom only birth dates existed and whose life span was unknown were not added to the aggregate totals. The resulting population curve (Figure 1) gives a reasonable approximation of trends within the village. The first Swiss national census took place in 1798, so all of our figures for the eighteenth century were developed solely from aggregating vital events of individuals including permanent shifts of residence into or out of the village. The curve probably somewhat underestimates the total number of residents for the first half of the seventeen hundreds because those born before 1665 and dying after 1700 lack birth records and so could not be included in the aggregate population. Using the number of such deaths, a slightly higher population has been estimated for 25 year intervals, but the total probably remained between 250 and 300. Official census figures for the nineteenth and twentieth centuries are marked by stars, indicating the close approximation of the derived population estimates to the federal counts. Where discrepancies occur, as in 1837 and 1846, the nominative census originals make clear that village citizens who had migrated to other villages or left the country were still being counted. Annual reconstruction also makes possible the charting of demographically significant short term fluctuations such as the dip of 1870-80 that completely escape decennial censuses. Our twentieth century estimates consistently exceed official enumerations that from 1850 on included only those physically present in the village on the day of the census. Over the last seventy-five years, the number of temporary migrants working outside the village but maintaining a permanent residence there has greatly increased. We have included such individuals in the local population, but they are not represented in the official totals.

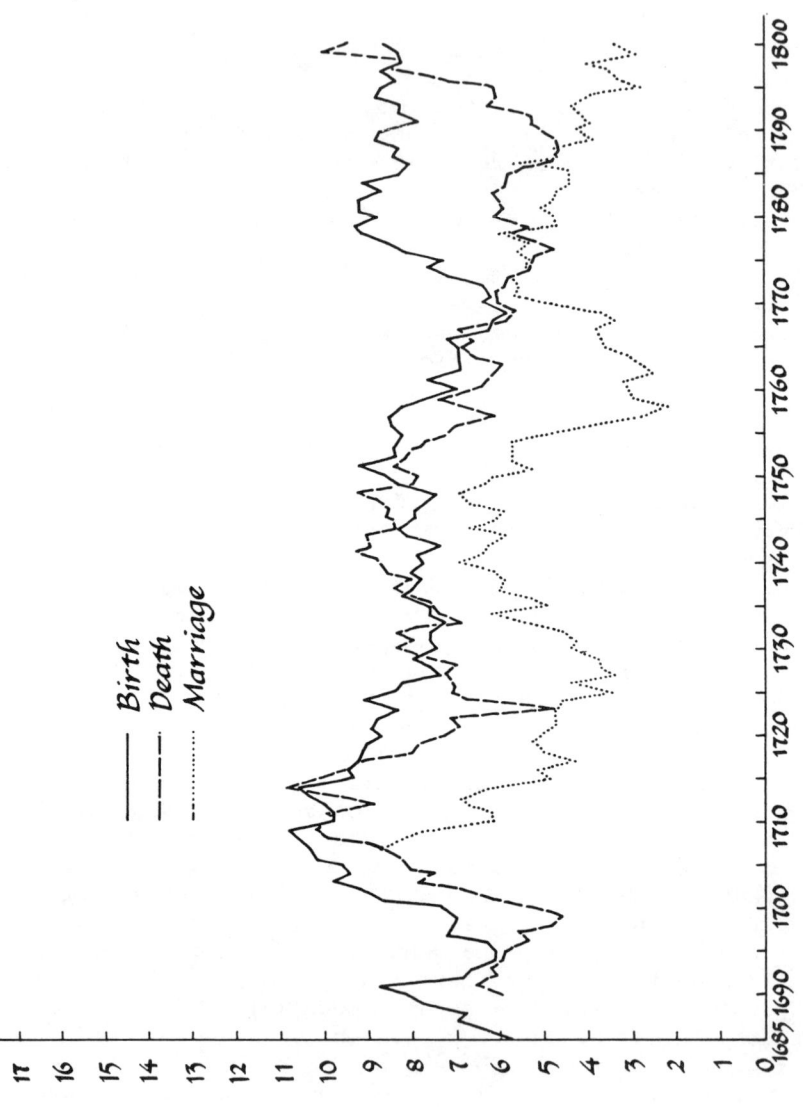

Figure 2a. Births, marriages and deaths in Törbel, 1685-1800 (nine-year moving averages).

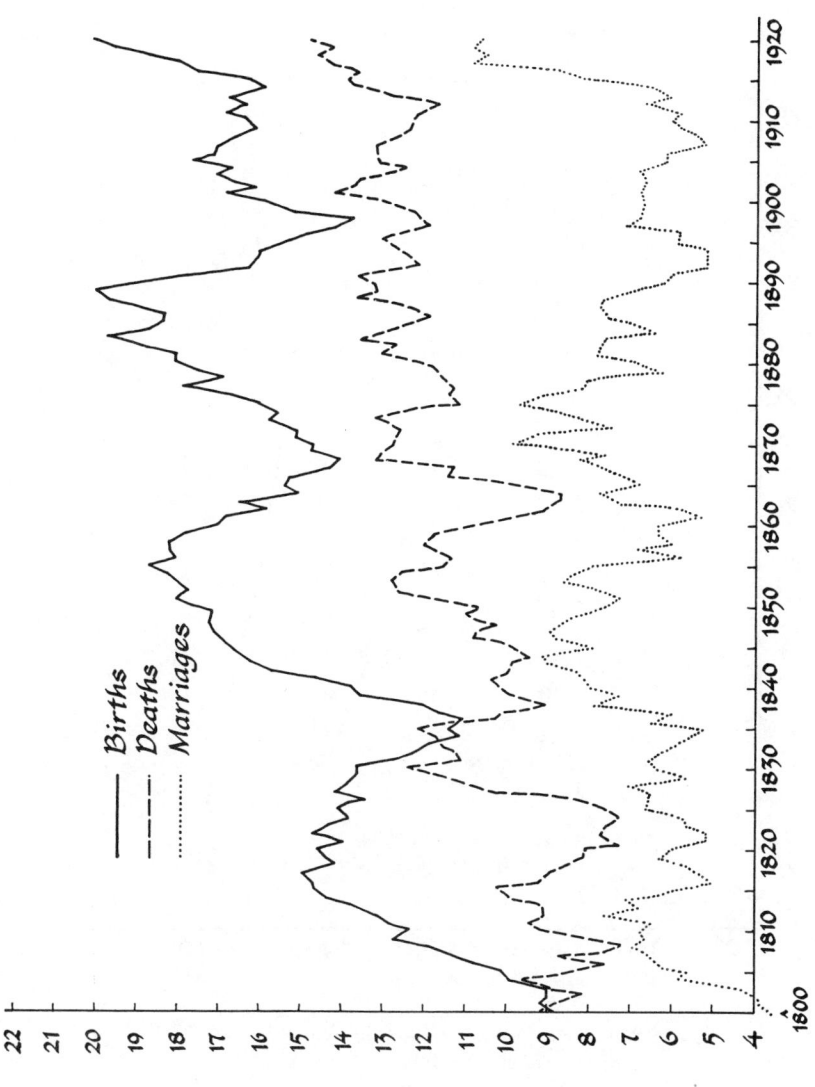

Figure 2b. Births, marriages and deaths in Törbel, 1800-1920 (nine-year moving averages).

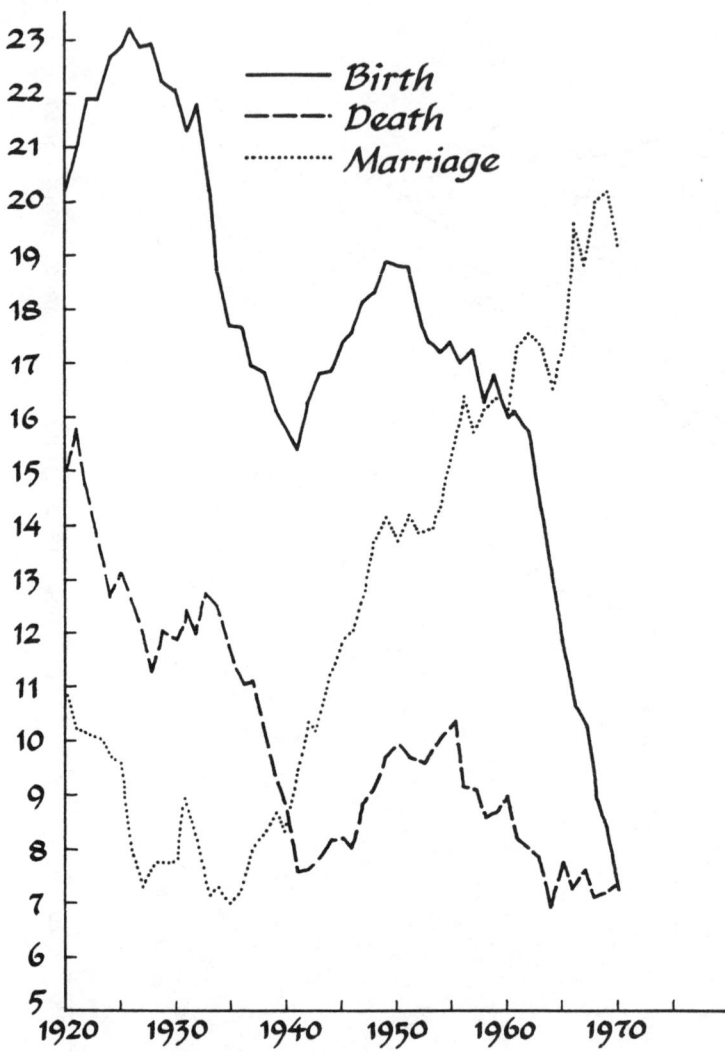

Figure 2c. Births, marriages and deaths in Törbel, 1920-1970 (nine-year moving averages).

The reconstructed population curve reveals several significant and previously unpredicted trends. For the first three-quarters of the eighteenth century, the population remained essentially static as one would expect if the local community had indeed arrived at a kind of equilibrium with its environment and limited productive resources. A nine-year moving average (Figure 2a) indicates a rough balance of births and deaths, and this was seemingly undisturbed by major immigration or emigration. This apparent demographic homeostasis ends in 1774 with the initiation of gradual growth (Figure 1). A more rapid increase begins in 1804 and continues with one ten-year hiatus until 1867. The entire period shows an average annual growth rate of 0.81 percent, a sustained though moderate increase that more than doubled the village population in the space of 93 years. The population loss of 1867-72 is directly attributable to the permanent migration of 63 individuals including seven complete families to South America. Though there had always been a trickle of single men from the village to mercenary service in the Vatican, elsewhere in Italy, and France, the wave of southern Swiss emigration, especially to the Santa Fe area of Argentina in the late nineteenth century, had a more pronounced impact on Törbel and neighboring communities. Migration, usually to other parts of the Valais, continued into the twentieth century (Figure 3), and the rise in population from 1919 to 1940 suggests in part the difficulty in finding permanent employment in the industrial sector of Switzerland during the Great Depression. The recent massive out-migration of village residents parallels the declining profitability of alpine farming, the availability of vocational education for the young, and the many opportunities for wage earning in the expanding Swiss economy.

Though migration has operated effectively to slow or even reverse the growth of village population in the last hundred years, there remains the more intractable problem of accounting for the marked growth in the period of agrarian self-sufficiency after 1774. Similar though often sharper increases are characteristic of many European countries during the same period, but the paucity of dependable eighteenth century national statistics has obscured both the beginning of the rise and the mechanisms by which it was effected. Though the Industrial Revolution influenced both fertility and mortality in a complex and significant manner (19), it came too late to bring about the entire change, and it does not explain major growth in rural areas and peasant communities. Törbel did not experience the florescence of cottage industry that dramatically increased the number of households and lowered the age of marriage in the hills above Zürich (20). Wage labor in the area did not become important

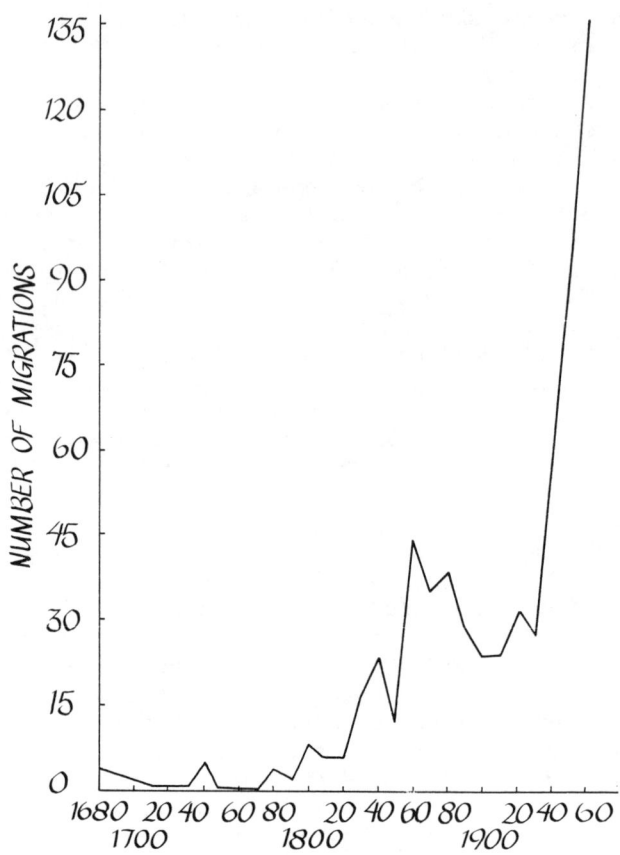

Figure 3. Törbel out-migration by twenty-year periods. Many cases of emigration, including those of mercenary soldiers and of many women who married out of the community, are explicitly mentioned in the parish records. Since citizenship in the community of origin is passed on in the male line according to Swiss law, it is possible to trace some migrants who left the village over 150 years ago. Women retain their surnames in the documents, so nonnative patrinyms mark almost all in-marrying females. For known in- or out-migrants, we used marriage dates to represent time of entry to or exit from the village population. If the individual did not marry, the date of departure was arbitrarily set at age 20. Because the duration of temporary migration was unknown, those who were absent as servants or seasonal laborers are not abstracted from our aggregate population, leading to obvious differences between the de facto national census figures and our de jure estimates for this century (Figure 1).

until the late 1800s when the tourist trade opened nearby
Zermatt and the building of railroads, tunnels, and a canalization of the Rhone offered seasonal jobs. As recently as
World War II, most families provided the bulk of their own
food; local mills ground flour, sawed lumber, and fulled
woolen cloth; village carpenters, shoemakers, and stone cut-
ters plied their crafts; and cash was not plentiful. It is
also unlikely that an improvement in hygiene or medicine decisively altered village population patterns. As McKeown
has demonstrated for the British Isles, the fall in mortality
due to infectious diseases began long before effective immun-
ization or therapy were available (21). Törbel has never
had a resident medical practitioner, and until the road to
the valley was finished in 1937, doctors had a ride of several hours on mule back to reach the village. Housing and
sanitary facilities had been little altered until the general installation of piped water and a sewage system in 1974.
A dramatic fall in the average number of deaths is seen only
after 1920 (Figure 2c), and the crude death rate declines
strongly in the period 1948-62 (Table 1).

Mortality

Is the earlier increase in population fully explained
by a drop in mortality? The theory of the demographic transition (22) predicts that a decline from traditionally high
levels of mortality precedes the corresponding fall in fertility, resulting in rapid population increase. The Törbel
averages of births and deaths do in fact begin to pull
apart after 1770, and during the nineteenth century a veri-
table mountain range of birth peaks at 30-year or genera-
tional intervals moves high above the average death graph
for the same period (Figure 2b). Several calculations of
crude death rate are possible, subject always to possible
inaccuracies in computing the base population and to decisions about whether to use recorded deaths only or include
all individuals with birth dates only as probable infant
deaths (Table 1). Yet regardless of the method, there appears to be a contrast between the high rates for periods
through 1750 and the lower but relatively stable rates from
1775 through 1850. Using a 25-year average of recorded
deaths and the mid-year (1700) total population, the period
from 1688 to 1712 appears to have had an incidence of death
above 40 while that for 1700 to 1750 averaged 33.5 per 1000
(Table 1, CDR III) or, if all uncomputable births are assumed to be early deaths, 40.6 per 1000 (Table 1, CDR III). The
following long period of 1775 to 1925 had either quite
stable rates averaging 21.9 (CDR II) or gradually declining
rates from 26 to 21 (CDR III). Only in the most recent
quarter century did mortality decisively drop to 13 per

Table 1. Crude death rate estimates

Year	Tabulated Population*	Tabulated Deaths in 25 Years†	CDR I π	Census or (Estimated) Population §	Recorded Deaths in 25 Years ∫	CDR II τ	Recorded Deaths plus Uncomputable Births Σ	CDR III Ψ
1700	219	179	33	(241)	255	42	305	51
1725	281	192	27	(294)	215	29	255	35
1750	266	200	30	(279)	194	28	255	37
1775	279	150	22	(292)	138	19	190	26
1800	340	188	22	350	185	21	219	25
1825	433	240	22	(450)	249	22	282	25
1850	481	277	23	508	304	24	338	27
1875	540	296	22	(546)	291	21	323	24
1900	580	322	22	571	312	22	327	23
1925	644	327	20	(610)	319	21	322	21
1950	746	218	12	693	219	13	221	13

Table 1. (continued)

*The tabulated population is created by incrementing annually the number of births and in-migrants to the population and subtracting the number of deaths and out-migrants.

†Deaths are tabulated for the listed year, for the 12 preceding years, and for 12 following years, and then summed to give a 25 year total. Thus the 179 deaths given in the 1700 row refer to all deaths tabulated in the period 1688-1712 inclusive.

πCrude death rate (CDR) I is obtained by dividing tabulated deaths by the average number of deaths per year and multiplying by 1000. The crude death rate per 1000 is rounded off to the nearest whole number.

§Total population is estimated in the eighteenth century by increasing tabulated population to take account of untabulated deaths (deaths of individuals lacking birth or marriage dates) during each 25 year period. In the nineteenth century, estimates are interpolated between known census figures.

∫Recorded deaths are all those mentioned in the parish burial register or civil register. It does not include certain deaths away from the village for which approximate dates of death have been tabulated.

¶Crude death rate II is based on the recorded deaths and the census or estimated population. It differs substantially from CDR I only in 1700 when the number of recorded but untabulated deaths was highest.

ΣUncomputable births are those for which no further vital statistics occur in the records. Treating all these as early deaths gives a maximum mortality estimate.

ΨCrude death rate III is based on recorded deaths plus uncomputable births regarded as deaths and on the census or estimated population.

Table 2. Adult age-specific mortality rates*

Age Group	1665-1789		1790-1914		1915-1974	
	Male	Female	Male	Female	Male	Female
25-29	10	12	7	12	3	3
30-34	6	11	2	10	8	6
35-39	5	12	6	12	4	6
40-44	9	16	7	13	10	8
45-49	15	16	13	13	13	10
50-54	25	24	18	18	21	13
55-59	38	26	24	18	25	15
60-64	51	46	18	37	35	24
65-69	60	64	43	59	55	35
70-74	59	77	81	92	74	60
75-79	128	100	101	95	104	90
80-84	177	184	187	158	144	137

*Rates per thousand were computed for the adult married population by the Cambridge Group. All known dates of death were tabulated and then optimistic and pessimistic assumptions are made about the mortality experience of those whose dates of death are unknown (25). The rates given are the average of optimistic and pessimistic estimates except for 1915-1974 when optimistic estimates are used because many members of the marriage cohort are still alive. Mortality rates were first calculated on 125 year periods (1665-1789 and 1790-1914) selected to approximate eras of premodern population stability and growth respectively. The modern period since 1915 is characterized by the breakdown of village isolation and economic autonomy as well as by major changes in demographic processes. Mortality rates calculated for 50 year periods show the same trends in finer detail.

thousand (Table 1). The general profile of the Törbel death rate is that of stair-steps, descending from fairly high levels with frequent bad years in the early eighteenth century to moderate levels for the following 175 years and a markedly lower rate, probably reflecting the advent of modern medicine, from the late 1930s.

Our confidence in the more general outlines of mortality change is increased by tabulations of adult age-specific mortality and the generation of life tables by the Cambridge Group for the Study of Population and Social Structure. The mortality rates show some improvement in the 1790-1914 period for males in the 40 to 60 year age bracket (Table 2). When males and females are compared, female mortality is markedly higher in the 15 to 44 age group, reflecting probably the health risks of child bearing before the advent of modern obstetrics. Perhaps for this reason, males outnumbered females in the village population until 1925. Age specific mortality rates for females before this century showed less change than those for males. The tabulation of infant and child mortality (Table 3) is somewhat less trustworthy than that for married adults because of a tendency especially in the latter part of the eighteenth century to under-report such early deaths. The more solid figures for the 1800s, however, are definitely high by modern standards, and although mortality from birth to age 15 may have declined somewhat, there are few grounds for suspecting a radical change in the life chances of infants until this century. The population crises in which epidemic disease or agricultural dearth severely pruned European peasant populations are neither especially frequent nor overwhelming in the Törbel records. Folktales remain of heavy mortality during a visitation of the Black Plague in the 1560s, and an obvious introduction of new family surnames took place in the succeeding years. Crisis mortality defined by a death toll of more than double the annual average (8) is seen in the years 1690, 1693, 1704, 1718, 1728, 1763, 1803, 1831, 1881, and 1918. The 1690s were certainly bad harvest years and 1918 shows the passage of the influenza pandemic. Even the most severe of these occurrences took no more than eight percent of the population, and nothing compares with the loss of one-fifth of the people in Colyton, Devon during 1648 (23).

Though average life expectancy at birth does improve through time in Törbel, the rise is irregular and not consistent for men and women. Fitting the Törbel data for ages 25 to 45 to model life tables (Table 4), the life expectancy for females increases by some 7.5 years from 1700-49 to 1750-99 and then remains constant in the 42.5 to 45 range

Table 3. Infant and child mortality (sexes combined)

Rates/1000

Ages	1700-49	1750-99*	1800-49	1850-99	1900-49
0	156	67	154	194	126
1- 4	107	48	75	66	32
5- 9	57	25	38	30	11
10-14	7	14	17	9	24

*The low rates for 1750-99 are based on obvious under-reporting of deaths during the first three months of life and probable failure to list many deaths of young children.

Table 4. Adult life expectancy

	Males					Females				
	At Birth*	25-9	30-4	35-9	40-4	At Birth*	25-9	30-4	35-9	40-4
1700-49	41.8-44.3	38.2	34.5	30.1	26.4	45 -32.5	33.7	30.6	27.6	24.1
1750-99	? -39.3	36.4	33.4	30.2	25.2	? -40.0	36.5	34.4	30.1	26.6
1800-49	45.5-47.9	40.8	36.4	31.6	27.5	45.0-42.5	35.7	32.3	29.6	26.2
1850-99	44.3-53.9	41.6	38.7	34.2	30.1	48.8-45.0	37.9	35.0	30.7	27.5
1900-49	49.6-51.8	39.3	35.3	32.0	27.4	52.5-55.0	41.8	38.1	34.5	30.7

*Figures for life expectancy at birth are arrived at by fitting Törbel mortality at the 0-14 and 25-44 age ranges to the model life tables in A. J. Coale and P. Demeny, Regional Model Life Tables and Stable Populations, (Princeton University Press, Princeton, 1966). Since infant-child mortality and the mortality of adult married people does not follow the same pattern, the two figures given are derived from the closest 0-14 table and the 25-44 table respectively. The actual life expectancy at birth should fall within this range. Note that female life expectancy estimated from 0-14 mortality (e.g. 45.0 in 1800-49) is higher than that based on the years of child bearing 25-44 (e.g. 42.5 in 1800-49). For males, the pattern is reversed, suggesting that infant-child mortality was a greater relative risk than that of adulthood.

until 1900. Males, on the other hand, show a downward trend in the eighteenth century. A pronounced increase of about ten years in the average life span of women in this century combined with a lowering of the age specific mortality rates in early adulthood suggests that the dangers of parturition had summarily declined. Men, on the other hand, may have undergone a slight decline in life expectancy since 1900 as they were subjected to the occupational hazards of new jobs such as tunnel building and heavy construction. In comparison with other preindustrial populations, Törbel longevity appears to have been within the range of variation but somewhat above the average due perhaps to its relative isolation and its high degree of local self-sufficiency. Estimates for later eighteenth century France give an expectation of life of 29 years, for Crulai in Normandy for 1675-1775 of about 30 (24), and for a sample of eight English parishes from 1550-1649 of 35 to 40 years, "an unusually high level by the general standards of early modern Europe" (25). Rural departments of late nineteenth century France ranged from 41 to 46 years for males and 43 to 50 years for females (26).

The Constancy of Marriage

Though the life chances of adults, if not necessarily of infants and children, were improving somewhat in this Swiss alpine commune, it is questionable whether mortality rate changes alone produced the population expansion of 1774-1867. Investigators have linked other demographic processes, particularly the falling age of marriage with its consequent increases in fertility, to the pan-European rise in numbers. For example, in the industrializing English village of Shepshed, the men and women of the second quarter of the nineteenth century "were both marrying about five and one-half years earlier than they had before 1700" (27). This largely accounted for an increase in the average number of children born per family from 4.38 to 6.16 (28), reflecting both the growing ease of marriage as cottage industry became the dominant occupation and the positive economic incentive of acquiring a wife and children for assistance in the work process and security during old age (29). Given the close linear relation of a Törbel woman's age at marriage to average number of births, any decline in age at first marriage would have substantially increased fertility (Table 5). The woman who began her childbearing between the ages of 30 and 34 had two fewer children than if she had married ten years earlier. But increased numbers of children cannot be traced to earlier marriage in Törbel. The high average age of marriage varied remarkably little for 250 years, hovering for females between 27 and 29 and for males in the range of 30 to 33 (Table 6). A slight relaxation of 1.2 years in the age

Table 5. Average total births by mother's age at marriage

Age	Births	N
15-19	6.58 ± 4.13	33
20-24	6.47 ± 3.72	171
25-29	5.62 ± 3.20	227
30-34	4.35 ± 2.47	122
35-39	2.48 ± 2.22	65
40-44	1.34 ± 2.64	35
45-49	.91 ± 2.39	11

of women marrying in the period 1750-99 may have given some impetus to the population growth beginning then, but the nineteenth century response was a return to earlier high levels, peaking at over 29 in 1850-99. The factors that imposed this preventive check on reproduction, presumably the need of both partners to inherit adequate agricultural resources to found a family, seemingly did not diminish during the entire period. The obligation to work for the family enterprise and to support aged parents who remained in control of the household persisted in the village value system. Long engagements and a premium on premarital chastity continued to be the rule. It was not incumbent on a household head to retire and divide his estate among offspring until he desired to do so, and children marrying before this formal division could not count on access to land (17).

Table 6. Age at first marriage

50-Year Period	Females' Average Age	Males' Average Age
1700-49	28.33 ± 7.05	30.85 ± 7.67
1750-99	27.11 ± 6.85	31.33 ± 8.34
1800-49	28.48 ± 7.21	30.05 ± 7.99
1850-99	29.10 ± 6.59	33.44 ± 10.14
1900-49	28.85 ± 6.82	32.55 ± 8.75
1950-74	27.13 ± 5.80	30.60 ± 5.37
TOTAL*	28.24 ± 7.10	31.49 ± 8.68

*Based on 734 families for males and 674 families for females.

Table 7. Mean values for birth, survivorship, nuptiality and celibacy of children per family

	1700-49	1750-99	1800-49	1850-99	1900-49
Number of families*	147	105	160	160	157
Births per family	3.84	4.69	4.88	5.07	5.66
Standard deviation	3.20	3.57	3.62	3.34	3.75
Uncomputable births†	0.76	0.83	0.43	0.27	0.12
Children reaching age 1π	2.44	3.49	3.62	3.71	4.75
Children reaching age 20	1.86	2.84	3.09	3.22	4.46
Children reaching age 20 as percent of births per family	48%	61%	63%	64%	79%
Gross replacement rate (Children marrying per family)	1.45	2.26	2.20	2.16	3.13
Net replacement rate	0.73	1.13	1.10	1.08	1.57
Celibate children	0.41	0.58	0.89	1.07	1.33
Celibates as percent of children reaching age 20	22%	20%	29%	33%	30%
Emigrating children§	0.06	0.28	0.79	0.92	2.38

Table 7. (continued)

*Families formed by marriages taking place during the specified 50 year periods and remaining resident in the village so that family reconstitution and reproductive histories are possible.

†Births for which no further dates of marriage, death, or presence in the population exist. Such cases appear to have an unpatterned distribution according to family size, birth order, and the presence of documented siblings in the same families. They may represent unreported infant and child deaths in large proportion, but some cases may be children who migrated permanently from the village before marriage. As documentation improves in the nineteenth century, the number of uncomputables declines.

πNumber of births minus those known to have died in the first year and uncomputables.

§Emigrants are those who settle permanently outside of the village. They include both married and celibate offspring. Labor migrants who seek temporary or seasonal work away from Törbel but maintain permanent residence there are not included.

Nuptiality was the socially defined strait gate which regulated who could reproduce and when. As Goubert (30) has noted, "marriage is the main act of demographic significance that depends on the human will..." Continuity of the family line, transmission of property, and the socioeconomic standing of succeeding generations depended upon marriage, and decisions concerning alliance furnished a crucial element in the peasant household's strategy of survival (31). Not only was marriage in Törbel delayed well beyond physical maturity but many adults never entered into matrimony at all. Table 7 indicates that though both the gross reproduction rate of children ever born per household and the number of children surviving to adulthood were increasing from 1700 to 1900, the number of those children who themselves married held constant at about 2.2 from 1750 to 1900. Once the need to subsist from local resources lessened and the pressure to find a mate from within the village relaxed, the average number of those marrying in this century jumped up.

Assuming that there is no difference in the sex of marrying children, the net replacement rate is found by dividing the number of marrying children by two (32). This suggests that the 1700-49 population was not replacing itself, and indeed there may have been a slight downturn in population during this time. Almost 80 percent of all surviving children in families formed during 1750-99 went on to marry, but this proportion slipped to 71 percent and then 67 percent in the following 50 year periods. A replacement rate near 1.1 was maintained and the proportion of eligible individuals marrying went down in inverse relation to population growth. Normally such a low replacement rate would have restrained the annual rate of population increase, but both the number of children born per family and the survival of these offspring were climbing. Clearly the average number of those remaining celibate was rising too (Table 7). Between 1700 and 1899, the actual number of surviving children per family who never married went up more than two and a half times. In relative terms the proportion of adult offspring who remained bachelors and spinsters went from approximately one out of five to a high of one out of every three. Celibacy without continence would naturally have exerted much weaker demographic control. In Törbel, there was an appreciable frequency of conception before marriage ranging from 8 to 25 percent (33), but these cases were judged somewhat shameful and the couple almost always married before the birth. Illegitimacy, though clearly marked in the records, is rare, and the strong social opprobrium it evoked is symbolized by the custom of baptizing such an infant under a black veil (34).

Fertility and Fecundity

The evidence appears very telling that the traditional north European mechanisms of late marriage and high celibacy not only continued to operate in Törbel but functioned in a density dependent manner, making marriage more difficult as a growing population competed for limited local resources. The annual crude birth rate responded predictably to these constraints, declining from an average 35.6 in the period 1688-1762 to 31.9 in the years of population growth 1763-1862. The almost constant number of children per family who married should have allowed replacement of the population in each generation and a bare minimum of growth. The crucial factor not fully governed by nuptiality is fecundity within marriage, and it was a major increase in reproductive potential that nudged population upward and countered the tightening restrictions on marriage. The sharp jump in the average number of children ever born per family took place in the period 1750-99 (Table 7), and it was accompanied by a 13 percent improvement in the survival rate to age 20. Thereafter, the average number of births continued to advance slowly, but survival chances increased very little until this century. The very real increase in fertility is obvious in the comparison of age-specific marital fertility rates of 1790-1914 with those of the preceding 125 years (Figure 4). Age specific rates for the eighteenth century are at the same general level as those of Crulai and Colyton, though Törbel had somewhat lower rates in the early years of marriage and higher rates at age 30 and above. A later age of marriage tended to concentrate Törbel fertility at the higher age ranges. The nineteenth century curve maintains the same general shape but exceeds earlier levels for all ages except 45 to 49.

One possible explanation of dampened fertility in the 1700s is the practice of conscious family limitation (15, 55). Evidence for abortion or mechanical means of contraception is entirely lacking, and informants consistently deny that members of a pious, staunchly Roman Catholic community would ever countenance such methods in the past (35). A series of demographic measures also give no hint of family limitation in Törbel (Table 8). The average size of completed families varied from 5.3 to 6.0, but did not fall sharply until this century. Many of these families were large, and the percentage with nine or more births has been quite constant with no visible tendency to decline in frequency. Completed families with no children are few and similarly constant at a level not far above that predictable on grounds of natural sterility. In many societies, fertility limitation can be detected in the declining age of the

Table 8. Negative evidence of family limitation*

	1700-49	1750-99	1800-49	1850-99	1900-49
Number of completed families†	30	45	87	103	57
Mean number of births	5.3	6.0	5.9	5.8	4.8
Standard deviation	3.4	3.6	3.7	3.6	3.7
Percent of completed families with nine or more births	28%	22%	24%	23%	21%
Percent of completed families with no births	13%	9%	13%	13%	19%
Average age of mother at birth of last child	42.39	42.74	41.69	42.24	42.18
Penultimate birth interval (months)	34.6	39.6	31.3	30.3	24.9
Ultimate birth interval (months)	40.7	44.7	38.5	38.0	31.9
Difference between ultimate and penultimate (months)	6.1	5.1	7.2	7.7	7.0

*The quantitative measures of family limitation in this table were applied and explained by Wrigley (23).

†Completed families are those in which the wife reaches age 45 in marriage or in which the marriage is known to have lasted 30 years or more.

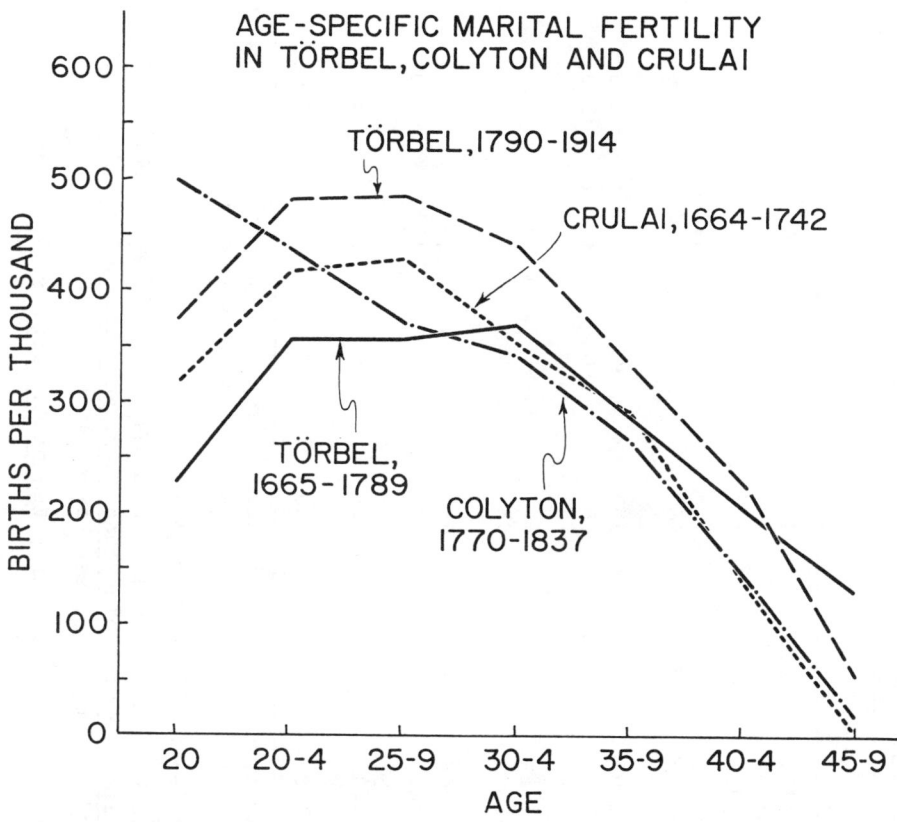

Figure 4. Comparative age-specific marital fertility rates.

Table 9. Age-specific marital fertility rates (by age group).

Group	Time Period	U20*	20-24	25-29	30-34	35-39	40-44	45-49
Törbel Swiss	1700-1749	250	403	358	390	392	224	131
	1750-1799	200	327	369	278	309	196	154
	1800-1849	400	475	458	407	356	205	66
	1850-1899	444	509	484	442	371	236	35
	1900-1949	556	566	551	487	418	219	20
Törbel Swiss	1665-1789	238	359	358	369	288	209	130
	1790-1914	375	483	486	442	373	230	53
Anhausen Germans†	1692-1799		472	496	450	355	173	37
	1800-1899		482	525	525	362	148	12
Colyton Englishπ	1720-1769	462	362	342	292	227	160	0
	1770-1837	500	441	361	347	270	152	22
Crulai Frenchπ	1674-1742	320	419	429	355	292	142	10
Hutterites∫	1921-1930		550	502	447	406	222	61

*Under 20 rates for the eighteenth century in Törbel are low, due both to the paucity of teenage marriages and possibly also to the presence of adolescent subfecundity.

†Rates from this Bavarian village are in Knodel (36).

πRates for Colyton are from Wrigley (23), and he takes the comparative figures for Crulai from E. Gautier and L. Henry, Crulai, Demographie d'une Paroisse Normande au XVIIe et an XVIIIe Siécles, (Institut National d'Estudes Démographiques, Paris, 1959).

∫Hutterite rates in Knodel (36) from L. Henry, Eugenics Quart. 8, 84 (1961).

Population Stability and Change in a Swiss Village   95

mother at the birth of her last child. Törbel shows a consistently high average age at last birth, suggesting that the approach of menopause rather than conscious choice caused the cessation of births. If a woman attempts to control her fertility after having some desired number of children, the difference between penultimate and ultimate birth intervals should go up (23). This effect is absent in Törbel, and the eighteenth century period where limitation might have taken place shows the smallest differences. The age-specific marital fertility curves show no concavity on their upper sides that would indicate restraints on conception. Indeed, the fertility rates for Törbel women from 1900-49 exceeds those documented for contemporary Hutterite populations (Table 9) which are generally accepted as showing natural fertility in the absence of family limitation. Rates for the eighteenth century are commensurable with those for a German rural village where Knodel sees "reduced fertility caused by postponed marriage rather than voluntary birth control" (36).

It does not seem likely that the members of the Törbel community were either consciously limiting or increasing their fertility. The changes taking place in average numbers of children, survival of children, and adult life expectancy were probably too gradual and too variable in the short term to be observed by other than statistical methods. The structure of the total population also changed very little. The age-sex pyramids (Figure 5a-b) continue through time to show the verticality characteristic of stationary or slowly growing populations. The proportion of those in the lowest age classes from 0 to 14 remained fixed at about 32.5 percent during the latter eighteenth century and rose to only 34.7 percent in 1850. Though the composition of the population showed no marked fluctuations, the total numbers expanded, indicating even, general growth.

If women were having more offspring without a lowered age of marriage or the relaxation of conscious restrictions on family size, births must necessarily have been coming closer together. Strong support for this hypothesis exists in a comparison of birth intervals in successive fifty year periods (Table 10). In every class, namely between marriage and first birth, first and second, etc., the birth intervals before 1800 were longer than those after that date. The differences between 1750-99 and 1800-49 levels are statistically significant in three cases. The unexpected appearance of birth spacing as the significant factor in increased fertility suggested to us that the conditions of the particular peasant community may not have been as stable and unchanging as we had thought. Some factor had altered the workings of the Törbel ecosystem in the late eighteenth century, inducing

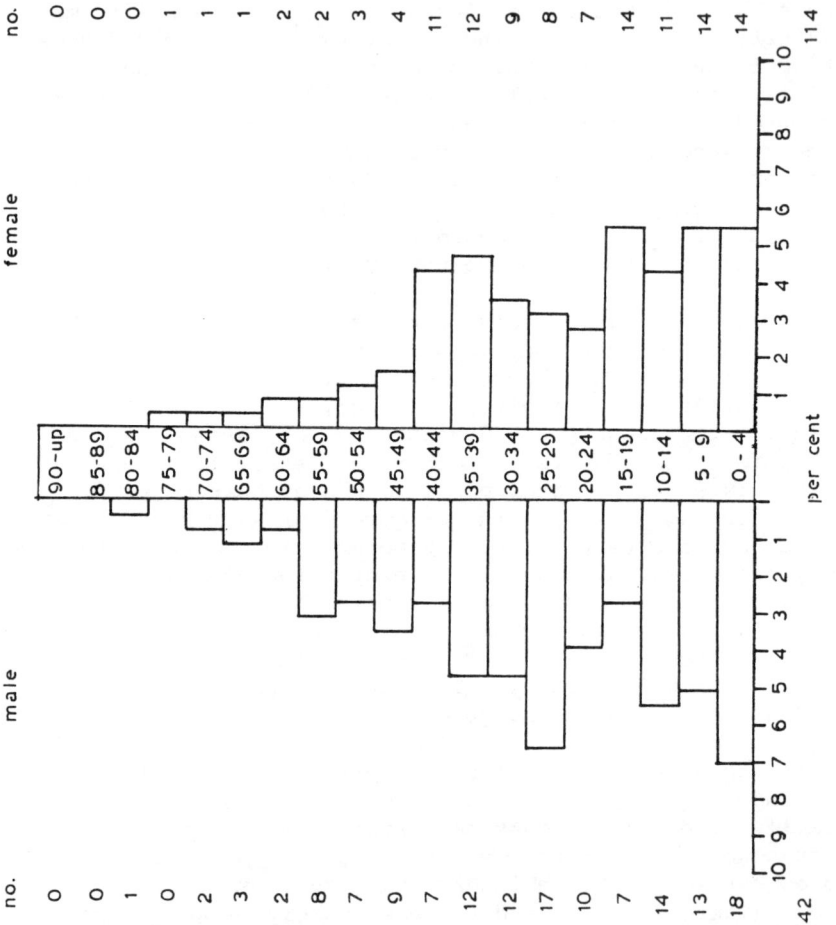

Figure 5a. Age-sex structure of Törbel population, 1750.

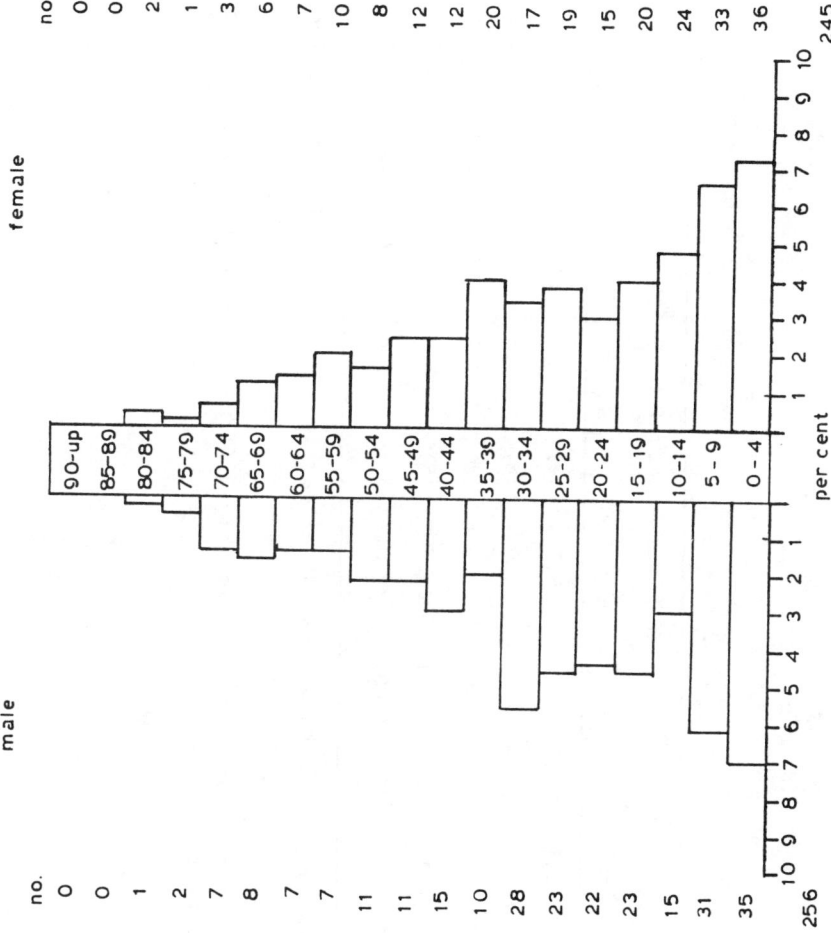

Figure 5b. Age-sex structure of Törbel population, 1850.

Table 10. Mean birth intervals (months) for Törbel women

Period	Marriage – 1*		Mean birth interval							All Intervals	
			1 – 2		2 – 3		3 – 4		5*		
1700-49	23.9	(41)†	27.9	(47)	29.2	(42)	30.4	(37)	32.5	(97)	29.3 (264)
1750-99	24.5	(60)	29.9	(58)	28.9	(48)	31.5	(38)	34.1	(135)	30.7 (339)
1800-49	15.3π	(99)	23.9π	(99)	25.9	(94)	29.1	(83)	29.9π	(275)	26.1 (650)
1850-99	15.8	(107)	25.8	(123)	25.7	(115)	27.3	(99)	29.2	(300)	25.9 (744)
1900-49	17.7	(136)	19.9	(148)	22.0	(133)	26.4	(117)	25.4	(401)	23.1 (935)

*Births occurring eight months or less after marriage not included in this calculation.
†Number of births.

π1800-1849 mean birth intervals significantly different from 1750-1799 intervals, p.<.001,<.02,<.01 respectively using the t test.

Population Stability and Change in a Swiss Village

population growth by simultaneously lower mortality and raising fertility. If there was no evidence for changing standards of health care or sexual practices, perhaps the observed differences were physiological and traceable to a nutritional change.

The Fruitfulness of Potatoes

The one item of Törbel subsistence technology that had been introduced during the period covered by our demographic records was the potato. This American import had probably reached Europe by 1570 (37), but its adoption as a major crop by peasant cultivators was both slow and irregular. Though it became widely spread in seventeenth century Ireland, the potato did not enter the staple economy of highland Scotland until after 1750 (37, p. 355). It failed to become a significant part of the diet in many parts of England until the 1790s (37, pp. 494-507), and its acceptance in Norway took place around 1800 (38). In Switzerland, potato cultivation spread from the Lake of Zürich area to the broad central plain in the mid-eighteenth century (39), and it completely replaced bread grains in the high, wet valleys of Canton Uri between 1750 and 1800 (40). No firm date has yet been fixed for the diffusion of the potato in Valais, though historical sources mention its adoption at Nyon on Lake Geneva after disastrous crop failures in the 1770s (37, p. 115). European peasants were loathe to grow tubers until bad weather spoiled their traditional cereals for several years in succession, and it is possible that the extraordinarily heavy precipitation and unseasonable cold of the years 1768-1771 (39, pp. 81-83) initiated this process in Valais. This mountain crop was, in any event, well adapted to the steep slopes and high altitudes of the Alps. In Törbel it flourishes in small plots up to 1900 meters. It could be grown on the plowed Ackerland in the formerly fallow years between crops of rye, but it also yields well in minuscule gardens worked with hand tools and fertilized with manure from the cow barns. In 1919 potatoes occupied 13.42 hectares within the village territory as opposed to 24.14 for grain (41), but their annual production can be estimated at about 255,000 kg. as against 31,400 kg. of rye (42). Within living memory, boiled salt potatoes were consumed practically every day, forming a mainstay of the diet that also included rye bread, milk, and cheese. Since potatoes did not replace cereal grains but were planted in both fallow fields and in gardens either too small, steep, or high for efficient rye production, they must have allowed a quantitative increase in the provision of carbohydrates from a fixed land area.

A direct connection between improved nutrition from new

food crops and European population increase has frequently been postulated (43). Usually, however, the potato is seen as ameliorating the recurrent demographic crises following poor grain harvests and thus lowering mortality (38). Less attention has been given to the effect of a larger and/or more dependable source of calories in raising the level of fertility. A variety of recent studies (44-48) now suggest a relationship between nutrition and birth interval. The resumption of ovulation following birth is influenced by the duration and intensity of breast feeding (49) and by the physical condition of the mother. A review of various lines of evidence suggests that "nutrition may be an important determinant of human ovulation," and that the duration of lactation as well as the absence of supplementary infant feeding are positively associated with the duration of postpartum amenorrhea (50). Nursing mothers among the well-nourished Hutterites have an average period of postpartum amenorrhea of six months, while investigations show that the period in Taiwan is 11 months (46) and in Bangladesh 16 months (47). Under-nutrition and "hard living" plus the estimated drain of 1000 calories per day on the nursing mother (45, 51) may delay conception even in the absence of marked clinical signs of malnutrition. In fact, the reproductive system appears to begin "shutting down" more rapidly than other physiological operations during times of nutritional stress. Wartime famine amenorrhea has been noted among modern European populations as when a third of all fertile Dutch women ceased ovulating during the food shortages of 1945 and among German city dwellers in 1916-17 when the potato ration was temporarily replaced by rutabagas (52). Women visited their physicians not because of illness but because the cessation of menstruation convinced them that they were pregnant. There is no reason to think that the eighteenth century Törbel diet was seriously deficient in either protein or calories, and in a generally healthy population, a lower caloric intake may result in lower body weight without restricting activity levels or producing permanent damage (53). If the nutritional level of eighteenth century Törbel mothers was somewhat below the level of 1800-99, it might account for the difference in average birth interval of 30.161 months as compared to 25.994 months (Table 10). These two figures yield estimates of the period of postpartum amenorrhea of 8.861 and 4.694 months respectively (54). Even the initial levels of nearly nine months do not approach the levels of 10.6 months for Punjab sample villages or 17.7 months for a presumably poorly nourished population in Zaire (49).

Longer birth spacing also appears to correlate with pronounced seasonality of conceptions and births (55). Strong seasonal swings are most apparent in the earlier periods in Törbel, and the fluctuations diminish with time. From 1665 to 1880, conceptions were lowest in July, August, September, and October when the outdoor labor of hay-making, irrigating, reaping, and tending of the vineyards was at its height. Some men were away from their families herding the cows and making cheese on the alp. August, September, and October were also months of very few marriages after the April-May-June peak in both marriages and conceptions. It may well be that the combination of somewhat restricted caloric nutrition and the seasonal demands of high agricultural work effort acted to prolong birth intervals and thus depress the potential fertility of a marriage.

The biochemical pathways by which nutrition interacts with fertility are beyond the scope of this essay. The role of a critical fatness ratio, the timing of the release and implantation of the ova, the effect of frequent and vigorous sucking by the infant on the secretion of prolactin, and the energy requirements of reproduction must be left to others. The Törbel data does make clear, however, that a change in fertility took place sometime around 1800 (56), that it resulted from shortened birth intervals, and that preceding periods of lower fertility showed no signs of conscious family limitation. Though both infants and adults may have experienced somewhat lower mortality during the same period, a drop in the death rate alone is not an adequate explanation of the demographic change. The potato had the potential to substantially increase the caloric resources of the local population without the addition of new land, investment in expensive technology, or major decline in the provision of dairy or cereal products. As a high-yielding, storable, easily prepared food crop, it increased the carrying capacity of the village territory. Women were better fed, and we hypothesize that their fecundity increased, quite apart from any change in age of marriage or less demonstrable alterations in pre- or post-marital sexual behavior. No radical shift in nursing patterns need be postulated, though it is possible that the soft mashed potato mixed with milk allowed earlier supplemental feeding of infants than did the dry, coarsely-ground rye bread (57).

Summary and Conclusions

The reconstruction of population levels and the dissection of demographic dynamics in an alpine community has both supported claims that social mechanisms may tend to restrain growth in a density dependent manner and substantiated the influence of exogenous factors that can decisively disturb this equilibrium. The Törbel evidence supports Wrigley's contention (23) that it was within the power of preindustrial communities to halt population growth and yet their powers of growth were also remarkable. A new crop added to the traditional subsistence repertoire in a long-established relationship with the environmental regime did not modify customary checks on population. Late marriage and high celibacy mediated by the need to inherit a viable economic base even increased the restraints they exerted on family formation. The uncontrolled variable and one that responded to the caloric gift was fecundity. The largely unperceived effects of nutrition on marital fertility and on mortality ran counter to the time-tested European peasant regulators and ultimately broke their constraints. The corporate community endured only by parting with its migrant offspring and sending its sons and daughters to work in the burgeoning urban economy. Unlike the proleterianization of cottage industry or landless agricultural labor (15), the Törbel farmers were not moved to marry young and sire large broods by economic opportunity and necessity. With self-denial and hard work and strong communal institutions, they maintained their independence and fended off poverty. But food supply and with it human physiology had left their accustomed tracks, and population grew. A delicate, systemic balance, perhaps only one of many that peasant peoples have negotiated with their environment, was struck, then wavered, and began the readjustments toward some problematic equilibrium in a world beyond the village.

References and Notes

1. V. C. Wynne-Edwards, Science 147, 1543 (1965).
2. R. B. Lee and I. DeVore, Eds. Man the Hunter, (Aldine, Chicago, 1968), pp. 241-243; R. B. Lee, in Population Growth: Anthropological Implications, (MIT, Cambridge, 1972), pp. 329-342; D. E. Dumond, Science 187, 713 (1975).
3. E. R. Wolf, Peasants, (Prentice Hall, Englewood Cliffs, 1966); D. J. Greenwood, Peasant Studies Newsletter 3, 3, 1 (1974).
4. Farming settlements on the Swedish island of Gotland have been shown archaeologically to occupy a constant area divided into similar field parcels and supporting the same number of households from approximately 700 A.D. to 1800. S. -O. Lindquist, Personal communication.
5. P. Laslett, The World We Have Lost, (Scribner, New York, 1965).
6. E. A. Wrigley, Population and History, (McGraw-Hill, New York, 1969).
7. C. Tilly, The Historical Study of Vital Processes, CRSO Working Paper #108 (Cent.Res.Soc.Org., Ann Arbor, 1974).

8. R. D. Lee, Ed., Population Patterns in the Past, (Academic Press, New York, 1977), pp. 2-11.
9. J. Hajnal, in Population in History, D. V. Glass and D. E. C. Eversley, Eds., (Aldine, Chicago, 1965).
10. G. C. Homans, English Villagers of the Thirteenth Century, (Russell and Russell, New York, 1960).
11. H. J. Habakkuk, J. of Econ. Hist. 15, 1 (1955).
12. L. K. Berkner, Am. Hist. Rev. 77, 398 (1972); in R. D. Lee, op. cit. pp. 53-69.
13. R. Schofield, in Sozialgeschichte der Familie in der Neuzeit Europas, W. Conze, Ed. (Klett, Stuttgart, 1977), pp. 147-160.
14. M. Fleury and L. Henry, Nouveau manuel de dépouillement et d'exploitation de l'état civil ancien, (Paris, 1965); E. A. Wrigley, An Introduction to English Historical Demography, (Basic Books, New York, 1966).
15. D. Levine, Family Formation in an Age of Nascent Capitalism, (Academic Press, New York, 1977), pp. 2-3.
16. R. M. Netting, Anthropol. Quart., 45, 132 (1972). R. M. Netting, in Irrigation's Impact on Society, T. E. Downing and M. Gibson, Eds., Univ. of Arizona Anthropological Papers 25, (Univ. of Ariz. Press, Tucson, 1974), pp. 67-75; R. M. Netting, Household Dynamics in a Nineteenth Century Swiss Village, (ms., n.d.); A useful illustrated description of Törbel ecology, subsistence methods, and social organization is given in F.G. Stebler, Die Vispertaler Sonnenberge, Jahrbuch des Schweizer Alpenclub (1921). Recent anthropological studies with demographic information on Valaisan communities include G. Berthoud, Changements Économiques et Sociaux de la Montagne, (Francke, Berne, 1967); J. Friedl, Kippel, A Changing Village in the Alps, (Holt, Rinehart, and Winston, New York, 1974); J. Friedl and W. S. Ellis, Human Biol. 48, 23 (1976); D. Weinberg, Peasant Wisdom; Cultural Adaptation in a Swiss Village, (Univ. of Calif. Press, Berkeley, 1975); E. B. Wiegandt, Communalism and Conflict in the Swiss Alps, (Ph.D. Diss. Michigan, 1977).
17. R. M. Netting, Hum. Ecol. 4, 135 (1976).
18. W. S. Elias and R. M. Netting, Methods in the Analysis of European Population History: The Case of Törbel, Canton Valais, Switzerland, paper presented at the Annual Meeting of the Amer. Anthropol. Assn., Nov. 1977. Computer processing of the Törbel demographic data was planned and organized by Larry Manire with the assistance of Carol Margolis and other members of the Dept. of Anthropology Research Support Section, University of Arizona. Roger Schofield kindly made available to us the unparalleled programs and tabulating facilities of the Cambridge Group for the History of Population and

Social Structure. The possibility of accurately reconstructing total population numbers for Törbel derives from both the high quality of the records and from socio-political factors that emphasized the stability of community membership. Inferences drawn from family reconstitution in the majority of European village studies are limited by the rapid turn-over of population. Adolescents leave their homes to become servants and adults migrate from one parish to another to marry or become tenants. Typically only 15 percent of all resident families can be reconstituted. J. H. Hollingsworth, Annales de Demographic Historique (1970). In a twelve-year period at the end of the seventeenth century, one Nottinghamshire village lost and replaced 40 percent of its population. R. S. Schofield, Annales de Demographic Historique (1970). A Swedish manor parish of the 1740s had more in- and out-migrants than births or deaths. D. Gaunt, Scand. J. His. 2, 183 (1977). In Törbel virtually all resident families since 1700 can be reconstituted and genealogically linked. No new male lines were successfully established by in-migrants after 1700, and in-migrant females, usually identified as such by surname and village of origin, figured in only 14 percent of 917 marriages. By contrast, the English agricultural community of Bottesford had less than 10 percent of all parochial marriages from 1610 to 1851 in which both bride and groom were natives (15, p. 39). Because of local citizenship rights, endogamy, and economic dependence on inherited resources, Törbel individuals tended to stay put. For demographic purposes they can be kept in observation more continuously and with fewer uncertainties than their counterparts in other European peasant areas.

19. Levine (15), pp. 58-87.
20. R. Braun, Industrialisierung und Volksleben, (Eugen Rentsch, Erlenbach-Zürich, 1960).
21. T. McKeown, The Modern Rise of Population, (Academic Press, New York, 1976).
22. For a brief outline of transition theory and the criticisms levelled against it, cf. Culture and Population Change, (Amer. Assoc. for the Advance. of Sci., Washington, 1974).
23. E. A. Wrigley, Econ. Hist. Rev. 19, 82 (1966).
24. Wrigley (6), p. 131.
25. R. Schofield and E. A. Wrigley, Infant and child mortality in England in the late Tudor and early Stuart period, (ms., n.d.).
26. Wrigley (6), p. 175.
27. Levine (15), p. 62.
28. Ibid., p. 74.

29. Ibid., p. 80.
30. P. Goubert, in The Family in History, T. K. Rabb and R. I. Rotberg, Eds., (Harper and Row, New York, 1971).
31. P. Bourdieu, in Family and Society, R. Forster and O. Ranum, eds., (John Hopkins Univ. Press, Baltimore, 1976), pp. 117-144.
32. Levine, (15), p. 75.
33. Cf. the frequency of 14 to 20 percent occurring over two and one-half centuries in a Bavarian village, J. Knodel, Pop. Stud., 24, 353 (1970). In Colyton, on the other hand, one-third of all first children were conceived before marriage according to Wrigley (6), p. 88.
34. J. Bellwald, Der Erlebnisraum des Gebirgskindes, (Universitätsverlag, Freiburg, 1960), p. 44.
35. It has been postulated that rural districts in southwestern France went from natural fertility to sporadic birth control by the practice of coitus interruptus in the eighteenth century, but the use of such conscious methods has not been demonstrated. J. Ganiage, Trois villages d'Ile-de-France au XVIIIe siecle, (Travaux et documents, I.N.E.D., No. 40, Paris, 1963); P. Goubert, Deadalus 97, 593 (1968). Another possible explanation of birth spacing is that the presence of an infant affects the sexual behavior of the parents in some unconscious way. Reduced frequency of intercourse, altered sleeping arrangements of the mother, or the increased burden of work on the mother may delay a new pregnancy. J. Knodel and E. Van de Waal, Popul. Stud. 21, 109 (1967). A significant change in sexual or residential patterns appears unlikely in late eighteenth century Törbel, but it cannot be conclusively ruled out as a cause of higher fecundity.
36. J. Knodel, Pop. Stud. 24, 353 (1970). The application of a measure developed by Coale and Trussell for indicating the level of fertility control implicit in an age schedule of marital fertility gives index values for Törbel that are consistent with natural fertility and show little or no fertility control at any period. J. Knodel, per. comm.; J. Knodel, Popul. Stud., 31, 219 (1977).
37. R. N. Salaman, The History and Social Influence of the Potato, (Cambridge University Press, Cambridge, 1949), p. 68.
38. M. Drake, Population and Society in Norway, 1735-1865, (Cambridge University Press, Cambridge, 1969), p. 157.
39. C. Pfister, Agrarkonjunktur und Witterungsverlauf im westlichen Schweizer Mittelland 1755-1797, (Geographisches Institut der Universität Bern, Bern, 1975).
40. J. Bielmann, Die Lebensverhältnisse im Urnerland während des 18. und zu Beginn des 19. Jahrhunderts,

(Helbing & Lichtenhahn, Basel, 1972), p. 179.
41. Stebler (12), p. 58.
42. 1950 figures for Embd, a village immediately adjoining Törbel with similar climate, show that rye was producing 12 to 15 kg. per ar (100 square meters), a yield just half that of the Swiss average. Potatoes in the same locale gave 150 to 180 kg. per ar, an amount not greatly under the national average. A. Imboden, Die Produktions und Lebensverhältnisse der Walliser Hochgebirgsgemeinde Embd und Möglichkeiten zur Verbesserung der gegenwärtigen Lage, (Schweizerische Arbeitsgemeinschaft der Bergbauern, Brugg, 1956), pp. 38 and 51. Whole grain rye provides 334 calories per 100 grams and raw potatoes have 76 calories. B. K. Watt and A. L. Merrill, Composition of Foods, (U.S. Department of Agriculture, Washington, 1975). Using the lower yield figures cited above, a plot of 100 square meters would produce 114,000 calories in potatoes or 40,080 calories in rye, giving potatoes a 2.8 to 1 advantage. Though potatoes indeed have only about one-sixth the protein of rye, it is probable that protein was not a nutritionally limiting factor where dairy products were consumed year round. Both peelings and small potatoes are usually given to pigs in Swiss villages, so that some of the new carbohydrate source was converted back into protein.
43. W. A. Langer, Amer. Hist. Rev. 49, 1, (1963); A. W. Crosby, The Columbian Exchange, (Greenwood, Westport, 1972); McKeown (21).
44. R. G. Potter, M. I. New, J. B. Wyon, J. B. Gordon, in Public Health and Population Change, M. C. Sheps and J. C. Ridley, Eds., (Univ. of Pittsburgh Press, Pittsburgh, 1965), pp. 377-399.
45. R. E. Frisch and R. Revelle, Science 169, 397 (1970); R. E. Frisch, Social Biol. 22, 17 (1975).
46. A. K. Jain, T. C. Hsu, R. Freedman, and M. C. Change, Demography 7, 255 (1970).
47. L. C. Chen, S. Ahmed, and W. H. Mosley, Pop. Stud. 28, 277 (1974).
48. G. B. Kolata, Science 185, 932 (1974).
49. J. Knodel, Science 198, 1111 (1977).
50. H. Delgado, A. Lechtig, R. Martorell, E. Brineman, and R. E. Klein, Amer. J. of Clinical Nutrition 31, 322 (1978).
51. R. E. Frisch, Science 199, 22 (1978).
52. E. LeRoy Ladurie, in Biology of Man in History, R. Forster and O. Ranum, Eds., (John Hopkins Univ. Press, Baltimore, 1975), pp. 163-178.
53. W. A. Stini, Ecology and Human Adaptation, (Wm. C. Brown, Dubuque, 1975), pp. 66-67.

54. Potter, cited by Knodel (49), estimates that under conditions of less than adequate nutrition, the menstruating interval lasts about ten months, gestation requires about nine months, and an additional two-three months on the average are taken up by pregnancy wastage. We subtracted the total of 21.3 months from the average birth intervals computed for 603 and 1394 births in the eighteenth and nineteenth centuries, respectively, to arrive at estimates of the duration of postpartum amenorrhea.
55. D. S. Smith in Population Patterns in the Past, R. D. Lee, Ed., (Academic Press, New York, 1977), pp. 40-42.
56. Numbers of births fell in the 1750s and rose after 1765 following an increase in marriages, but the nine-year moving average of births did not advance in a really substantial way until after 1800. (Figs. 2A, 2B). Short-term changes in fertility are smoothed in the age specific rates for 1750-99 (Table 9) but are clearly marked in the figures after 1800, at which time aggregate population also began to increase most steeply (Figure 1). Though the potato may have appeared in Törbel around 1770, its acceptance into an ancient and highly integrated subsistence system was probably gradual. An innovation that may begin with a few people planting tubers in a corner of a vegetable garden may spread by fits and starts as individual peasants learn techniques of propagation and cautiously evaluate the risks inherent in growing any new crop. Törbel folklore records the ridicule to which the first farmer producing two whole pack baskets of potatoes was subjected. That a major alteration in agriculture and food habits should require decades is both economically and psychologically creditable. Physiological effects on either fertility or mortality would in all likelihood only appear when the new food resource assumed major importance in the diet. The admittedly speculative relationship we offer between nutritional and demographic change is based on an interpretation of trends, not the identification of a revolution. The potato was no magic potion for population.
57. It is perhaps indicative that a further major increase in fertility and decline in birth interval became apparent in the twentieth century (Table 9). Though still largely self-sufficient in food, the Törbjers had begun to buy cheap corn meal imported from Italy for making polenta. White bread was still rare in the early 1900s, and the loaves specially purchased in valley towns were saved for consumption by sick people and by women who had recently been delivered. Infants were regularly given a pablum or Brei made from white

wheat flour cooked in butter, but nursing bottles were not introduced until the 1940s. Nonetheless, a sharp drop in the average birth interval points to the possibility of earlier weaning and the substitution of cereal and dairy foods for breast milk.

58. Our research has been supported by grants to Robert Netting from the John Simon Guggenheim Memorial Foundation, the University Museum of the University of Pennsylvania, the National Science Foundation (GS-3318), and the Center for Population Research, National Institutes of Health (5 R01 HD08587-02), and to Walter Elias and Robert Netting from the National Science Foundation (BNS 76-83118). We would like to thank the following for their careful reading and suggestions on earlier drafts of this manuscript: Ester Boserup, Rose Frisch, John Knodel, Steven Kunitz, Peter Laslett, and William Stini.

Conrad C. Reining

4. The Transformation of Hungarian Villages

This report is a byproduct of my primary work in Hungary which focuses upon the history of the German minority in southeastern Europe. I have combined historical research with participant observation (1). Material has been obtained from church and state archives, from publications as well as from firsthand observations during an 11 month stay in Hungary in 1974-75. Nine months of that time were devoted to field research in rural areas, seven of them in residence in a small village in the southwestern part of the country. I was not studying the current scene, but was collecting information from the remnant German population about their past. I learned a great deal about current life, however, by living in it. When this opportunity arose to comment upon the viability of villages in modern Hungary, it seemed that I could do something as a spinoff of my main work.

For my field research I chose the Tolna-Baranya region in the triangle formed by the Yugoslav border, the Danube, and Lake Balaton because it has had the greatest concentration of German speakers in modern Hungary. About one-third of the population of this area had been ethnic Germans until WW II. That minority was reduced to about 20 percent of its former numbers during and after the war, but this area still has the largest concentration of "Swabok", the Hungarian name for "our Germans". The villages upon which I focused include the remnants of their formerly dominant German-speaking populations.

Before World War I, there were about two million German speakers in the Hungarian kingdom, some had been there for more than five hundred years, but most were descended from the pioneers who reclaimed this favorable farmland after the recession of the Ottoman Empire. Most of the immigrants from the Germanies to the west came to the Hungarian territories during the 1700's. They were so well established by the 20th century that those who found themselves to be citizens of other countries, particularly Romania and Yugoslavia after the partition of Hungary after WW I, remained in their homes and continued their previous way of life with little change until WW II. Then catastrophe struck this group. It suffered great losses during and after the war, with considerable variation in the different countries (2). Most of the German Hungarians were expropriated and large numbers fled or were expelled. Furthermore, the German language was no longer permitted in the village schools and it was generally discouraged outside the home. Today there are few youngsters who will attempt to speak German and many reply in Hungarian when their parents speak to them in German. This contrasts strongly with the situation before WW II when much of the German-speaking population of this area could not speak Hungarian. Many of my friends told me that they had to learn or relearn Hungarian in the postwar years. We met one woman who had spent all of her 96 years in Hungary but who still spoke only the local German dialect.

There are 100,000 to 200,000 Hungarians who regard German as their home language, making them still the largest ethnic group in the country. Only the Gypsies rival them in numbers, although both groups are very difficult to count with any accuracy.

This brief history of the Germans in Hungary will suffice for the present purposes (3), since my comments apply to all Hungarians that I observed and the figures from the literature pertain to Hungarians in general. My narrow experience has been buttressed by use of a valuable collection of articles by a group of Hungarian economic geographers (4). Their regional and national statistics have been combined with my worm's eye view. There has been a great degree of homogenization within the Hungarian population since WW II, particularly of the younger generations. So, what I have to say about the viability of Hungarian villages is a national, pan-ethnic phenomenon.

Hungary was slow to industrialize and retained a strong emphasis on rural life, producing exports in meat, grain and wine until WW II. Serfdom was not abolished until 1848, Hungary being one of the last countries in Europe to do so. Much of the arable land was held by a small elite of wealthy estate owners who used the surplus labor of the villagers in addition to that of their tenants who lived on the estates. Important characteristics of rural life were retained long after they had disappeared from much of western Europe. Until WW II, the nucleated villages of Hungary had something of the character of those of western Europe of earlier centuries despite the beginnings of industrialization and the

sizeable migration out of the rural areas, particularly to
North America, from the end of the 19th century onward. Industrialization in Hungary, when it finally occurred, was
concentrated, along with transportation and other services,
in the capital city, leaving the countryside relatively unchanged, although an alternative livelihood was provided for
some of the surplus rural population. Budapest, which grew
rapidly over the turn of the 19th and 20th centuries, came
to have a disproportionate part of the population and all
of Hungary's medium and heavy industry except for mining. It
still has one-fifth of the nation's ten million people. Just
as significantly, the capital took on an aura of all things
urban and socially superior to the rural life.

Most villages were concentrated collections of habita-
tions, surrounded by their plowland, pastures, meadows,
vineyards, and forest lands (5). They were almost closed
systems, and usually at considerable distances from others.
They were large, most containing 150 to 1,500 or more houses,
with shops, church, school, craft facilities, mill, icehouse,
inn, administrative offices, along with other resources for
virtual self-sufficiency. All closure and self-sufficiency
of this kind is of course relative. Very few human communities have ever been completely self sufficient and certainly those of the large scale societies of Europe and elsewhere in more "advanced" regions have always been greatly influenced by the rules and actions of the macro-economic
systems in which they have been imbedded. The important
thing is that these relatively isolated and self sufficient
villages were the primary units of identification for their
inhabitants. The villagers felt unto themselves and
different from others. Marriage tended to be within the
village when possible and when it was not, each village had
certain other preferred villages for courtship and marriage
alliances. The strictness of adherence to these rules varied
among the three peasant social classes in the past: the landholders, the craftsmen cottagers, and the unpropertied laborers. The landholding peasants were more able to conform to
ideals of marriage within their class and in the interests of
maintaining and increasing family land holdings were the most
likely to intermarry. Members of the other classes of
peasants had to be more flexible as to marriage and they also
were more likely to migrate out of village and region than
the wealthier peasants.

Village land was intensively utilized. The meadows were
mowed for green fodder for stall-fed animals and hay for
winter feed, while the pastures were utilized directly by the
herds of sheep, pigs, horses, and cattle not being stall-fed.
Each village had specialized herdsmen to take care of each

kind of animal in the pastures and forests. Pigs were led into the forests in the fall to fatten on acorns and beechnuts. Even in hilly regions, up to 99 percent of the village lands were utilized, the waste area mainly steams, roads and pathways. Where it is possible to plow, fields went right up and over hills; where it was not possible, extensive vineyards and orchards were planted.

In the old days land was everything. Acquisition and holding of land was the key to rural existence. As it happens, the ethnic Germans in Hungary were particularly noted for their drive to acquire more and more land, but all peasants in the old system were generally oriented to the control over arable land. That has all changed.

In the last thirty-three years there have been two basic alterations in the system of landholding. In 1945 private ownership of more than 120 hectares was prohibited, and the large estates, comprising about 35 percent of the arable land, were distributed to the poorer of the peasants (4, pp. 17-18; 7, pp. 542-43). This was a move vividly remembered by my older friends as a great step in the right direction. They indicate, however, very soon thereafter there began the movement toward collectivization which vitiated the 1945 land reform. The former large estates were made into state farms and, more gradually, village lands were put under cooperative management. The "contributing" of land to the village cooperatives was often not voluntary from the viewpoint of the landholders. Although the rigidity of the early socialization of land has been modified a good deal, the collectization of agriculture has continued by stages until over 90 percent of arable land is under state control. The old style peasant, working on his own small farm, can hardly be found anymore. There are now only about 45,000 independent agricultural workers who are not members of some kind of collective project. They own about 25,000 small farms in remote areas not suitable for mechanization. These private farmers are less than two percent of the 2.6 million active agricultural "earners" (4, p. 16).

Aside from these small farms, private holdings are permitted only in very small plots. The limit per family is about two hectares and most do not have that much, half of the private plots being less than half a hectare. The total significance is great, however, because such a large portion of the population has something of a garden or vineyard or both. In 1972 there were 1,675,000 such plots. At least half of the country's families and 80 percent of the rural ones own some land. Even among non-agricultural workers, 40 percent have gardens (4, p. 20). Many of these private

The Transformation of Hungarian Villages

undertakings produce significant surpluses over household needs. These gardens and vineyards are extremely important to their owners and to the national economy. Altogether they produce more than half of the nation's fruit and eggs, as well as large portions of the wine, poultry, and vegetables (4, p. 21). Household plots provide about half of the agricultural income of the rural families, amounting in total to twice the value of the produce of the large, mechanized state farms and only one-third less than that of the cooperative farms which are also largely mechanized (4, p. 21-22).

Another extremely important feature of the domestic scene is the large number of privately reared domestic animals. Almost everyone in the rural areas keeps domestic fowl and pigs, some also have cows and there are still some horses. These are used mostly for private cartage and for tilling private plots. Many households keep more poultry and pigs than they can utilize and the surplus can be sold into the national market. Here there is another vital linkage with the centralized sector, because the private plots cannot produce sufficient feed for the large numbers of animals being raised by the rural households. Citizens have to buy feed to supplement what they can raise themselves for feeding their stock. About 40 percent of the fodder produced by the cooperative farms is consumed by privately reared stock (4, p. 21).

There is, therefore, in operation a combination of the old and new systems. Private plots and houseyards still produce considerable amounts of the national agricultural products despite the great changes that have taken place in the social and economic systems. These changes can be seen as a vast social experiment for testing the viability of the village which was the pattern of residence in the old system. Ownership of most of the land has been removed from families and centralized nationally in the form of state cooperative farms. This single fact has had profound effects on the attitudes of persons toward rural life. As we are wisely told elsewhere in this volume, at the bottom of all adaptive processes are decisions made by individuals. Often now, I am told, Hungarians feel that there is no point in living in the country if they cannot have more land, so they decide to move to the city. The fundamental attitude here is extremely important and has been basically affected. As always, human adaptive patterns are complex, however, and there are many families that are busily engaged in a combination of urban and rural, wage and private, labor. This often entails a great expenditure of time and energy. Most rural households contain members with industrial employees who also work long hours on the land, while urban dwellers have rural interests, too. Family organization is still important, as will be noted a number of times in this report. All manner of combinations are available for observation. Often the migration or restructuring of occupations, or combination of these modes, take place in two or more stages and are done in family terms rather than individual ones. It is not as easy to acquire capital in the city as in the country, but families see that the best way is to have a foot in both. This often takes a unit larger than the nuclear family.

The way of life of almost everyone in the rural areas has been sharply altered by the new system in a number of ways. The impact upon the old system of residence has been severe; the village is under great pressure to adapt to a radically different mode. First of all, there has been a shift of population from rural to urban settings. In 1973, only 52 percent of the population lived in rural areas as compared to 62 percent in 1930. The absolute number of rural inhabitants, it should be noted, has not decreased at the same rate. The increase in urban numbers is mostly in terms of the overall natural increase. The out-migration from the rural areas was heaviest between 1949 and 1960, but was more than made up by the relatively high birthrate at the time. Rural population increased by 2.5 percent despite the heavy outflow. Between 1960 and 1970 the rate of migration to urban centers moderated but the birthrate fell and the death rate increased, so that the rural areas lost 2.4 percent of their people in those ten years (8, p. 31).

The rate of village out-migration varies considerably throughout the country, for proximity to urban jobs means that commuting may be chosen over moving to the city (4, pp. 11-21). The shift in population from rural to urban does not represent the sharp increase in industrial workers, for there has not been urbanization commensurate with the increased industrialization. Only about 40 percent of those now living in villages are employed in agriculture as compared to 75 percent in 1945. The vast majority of the non-agrarian village dwellers commute to their work. One-tenth of the entire Hungarian population and one-fifth of the rural workers are commuters. A substantial number of these commute on the weekly or semiweekly basis. They have rooms in town or some kind of dormitory arrangement, returning home on the weekend or every other weekend (4, p. 15). There is even some "reverse commuting" of city dwellers to rural jobs, particularly white collar workers on state and cooperative farms. These are estimated to be 15 percent of the commuters in the country (4, p. 19). One out of every four wage earners works in a place other than that of his residence (9, p. 42).

It can be seen that there has been a deep shift in the occupational structure of the country. Even those persons engaged in agriculture work on a very different basis than before. As already indicated, there has been a great decrease in the proportion of agricultural workers among the nation's workers. In 1949, 55 percent of the labor force was in agriculture, as contrasted with 22 percent in 1973. It is estimated that only 15 percent of active population will be engaged in agricultural work by 1985 (4, p. 12). Furthermore, the vast majority of the active agricultural workers are hired wage earners on cooperative and state farms, in state forest projects, and the like. Their life styles are comparable to those employed in factories. Consessions have had to be made progressively in the direction of making hours and wages comparable between farm and factory jobs in order to keep workers on the farms.

Another striking effect of the great changes during the last 30-odd years has been to produce a different age distribution for rural and urban populations. The urban population is much younger than the rural one and much of the agricultural work is being carried on by persons near and past retirement age. Particularly noticeable is the paucity of young male agricultural workers. Most of those are engaged in operation or maintenance of the machinery which is so important in the operation of the state and cooperative farms. Forty percent of the agrarian population is over the retirement age (55 years for women and 60 for men). The entire Hungarian population is aging, but this does not create as much of a problem in the cities as it does in the rural areas, especially the sparsely populated ones, where there is no chance of the population replacing itself as the older persons die (8, p. 12). In some villages there have been no marriages or births for some years and in many others funerals are more common than weddings or births.

Important differences in goals and orientations exist between the generations. It is too early to be able to predict patterns for the future, but at this time there are vital linkages between city and village. There is a great deal of movement back and forth between city and country, not only in the commuting already noted, but also in the form of family visits and trips to sell surpluses in the city. For example, women in our village traveled by train to Budapest to sell eggs. One woman made this trip, which took about two and one-half hours each way, on a daily basis. Leaves were also taken from city jobs in order to help parents and other relatives with harvesting, butchering and the like. We have already noted that the surplus domestic goods can be sold into the national market system, but very often any extra animals raised for the use of children and other city-dwelling relatives. Most of this important subsistance activity is being carried on by the oldsters, often by those who are no longer in the official labor force. Adjustments will have to be made as these elders die off. Already there has been a significant reduction in the proportion of homegrown produce in supplying the rural population's needs (10, p. 91). The purchasing of more and more food in village shops is putting heavy pressure on the distribution system (10, p. 107).

Official policy appears to be clearly in favor of maintaining the viability of villages. The old ones had to be used after the war because they contained very significant capital investment in residence and other infrastructure. They have served as dormitory communities, in many cases, to house persons working elsewhere. In the early period of intensive development of industry, the villages received little state support. From 1950 to 1970 only six percent of state financed housing was built in rural areas, although 44 to 47 percent of all new homes were rural ones. The housing shortage has been much more severe in the cities than in villages, where there are empty houses and even demolition, with much regional variation. Now the policy is to develop the village system along new lines. Both for practical and ideological reasons, great efforts are being made to reduce the contrast between city and country life as well as regional differences.

By now almost every hamlet is accessible by road and all with over 200 persons are linked into the bus and rail system so important for the commuting patterns already noted. We visited one that previously had been reached only by wagon track and footpath. Ours was one of the first cars that was able to go up to the edge of the old settlement as the road was being finished. The village showed signs of loss of viability with empty houses and unused kilns for the pottery that had been the old village's main product. However, new life was obviously beginning since some of the houses were being reconstructed, including some as vacation houses for city dwellers. The improvement of existing roads is seen to be of prime importance in the development plans, but this is an expensive operation that will take a long time to accomplish.

Electricity had already been introduced in the countryside before World War II. But the postwar electrification program was given high priority so that all Hungarian settlements were linked to the electrical grid by 1963. Ninety percent of householders had chosen to pay for bringing electricity into their homes by 1970, as compared to 46 percent in

1949. In the rural areas the proportion of wired homes increased from 60 to 88 percent between 1960 and 1970. Most of the rural houses still without electricity are in the areas of dispersed settlements (10, p. 105).

Piped water is being installed in rural settlements as quickly as possible. In 1949 only one-fifth of all dwellings were connected to water mains. This figure remained virtually unchanged for 10 years but a new program resulted in an increase to 41 percent by 1970. The amenity has not, however, been standardized as can be seen by the lack of its installation into much new construction; only 62 percent of homes built between 1966 and 1970 have running water. Only 10 percent of villages had water systems in 1970. This was evidently largely accounted for by urban homes, since the proportion of village houses with such systems increased from 2.5 percent to only 5.4 percent in the same ten years (10, p. 106). Altering the old style of rural life in this respect meets the same constraints of limited resources as the improvement of the minor road network.

The use of gas for cooking has, by contrast, had a great rise in the rural areas. From 1960 to 1970 the national figure rose from 14 to 60 percent of homes using gas, both from mains and from propane tanks. In the rural areas the use of gas spread even more rapidly, largely through the distribution of portable propane cylinders, from 2 to 45 percent (10, p. 106).

Food shops exist in almost every village. The smaller shops do not have the range of choices found in larger ones and there have been distribution problems, complicated by the increased demand by villagers for foodstuffs as they grow less of their own. The most striking change from the old system is in the mass distribution of bread. One can still see brick bake ovens in the yards of many old homes, but very few households still bake their own bread. This is, we were told, because of the lack of availability of wheat. Each household previously had its own wheat ground at the local mill. Every family we knew bought bread distributed daily to village shops from a central bakery. This single item, very important in the national diet, appears at every meal regardless of the variety of other carbohydrates available. Bread is cheap, evidently being subsidized on a national scale.

The old one room village schools have been largely replaced by graded establishments. This has necessitated the combining of children from two or more smaller villages in some cases and, therefore, the busing of some to a school in a neighboring village.

Medical services have always been poor in rural Hungary, so efforts are being made to provide more for the modern villages. Clinics are held by travelling medical personnel in those villages without resident services. In 1972 there were still only 7.5 physicians for each 10,000 rural inhabitants as contrasted to 36 in the towns and 46.4 in Budapest (10, p. 107). Ambulance service is available, but the increasing numbers of private cars are often used in medical emergencies.

The advent of almost universal electricity has meant that the public media could spread over the entire country in a way never conceived of before. Radio and TV coverage is total and many rural homes display TV antennas even on the by now scarce thatched roofs. Along with the other media has come the establishment of movie theaters and the "culture houses". The later are centers for all manner of activities, such as club meetings, lectures and concerts, especially for the youth. Again, larger settlements have larger, and often impressive, newly constructed, cultural centers than do the smaller villages where older buildings are often converted to this use. Every settlement we saw had motion picture facilities of some sort, with a good deal of difference in frequency of showings (from daily to biweekly), according to size of population served.

Only the telephone system lags far behind in the communication and media scene. Our village had 3 telephones, one each in the store, the administrative office and the post office. There were no private telephones and when the post office was closed the public phone could be used only for emergencies by calling the operator in a larger village eight kilometers away.

Albeit unevenly, the total effect of these changes is to reduce the traditional sharp and often invidious distinction between urban and rural lifeways. Another facet of this policy is found in the decentralization of industry. Before WW II rural industry consisted mainly of mining, handicrafts and food processing. These are now only a small part of rural industry, partly because a number of worked out mines have been closed, but more importantly because of the decision to disperse industry as it was stimulated to grow (11, p. 71). As late as 1958, 46 percent of all industrial workers were still located in Budapest, 33 in country towns and 22 in villages. By 1973 the figure for the capital had diminished to 31 percent, for towns it had risen to 47 percent. The latter figure includes villages, however, that had been enlarged in the process to the category of towns. One-fifth of the nation's industry and one-third of provincial industry is now located in villages (11, p. 83-86).

Urban growth has been in the development of new centers rather than in enlarging old ones. Along with the policy to decentralize industry has been one to increase the number of economic centers and even to start completely new towns. In 30 years 33 new towns have developed mostly by enlarging and combining existing settlements. Ten of these exist solely because of the rapid growth of industry. Only three of the 33 have grown because of tourism, which is not without influences from industrial development since much tourism is internal (11, p. 73).

Linked to these developments is the concept of the "central settlement". Somewhat under one-third of the 3,150 villages of Hungary have been designated as nuclei for serving their surrounding villages. The majority of those designated as central settlements have not yet been able to begin to carry out their functions because of infrastructure deficiencies. Most counties have larger centers, however, and these have tended to expand as people have chosen to migrate beyond their designated center to larger ones (6, p. 68-69).

The forces shaping the residential problems of the future are complex. There are all sorts of variations from region to region and within regions. In general, smaller and more remote villages are having a relatively greater out-migration and some may well disappear. On the other hand, larger villages with good employment possibilities close at hand are being built up and are proving to have a combination of the attractions of both urban and rural life. The smaller settlements appear to be supplying people to the larger ones in a way that is not officially approved of and plans are being devised to arrest this tendency.

In summary, then, we have here a massive test of the viability of the village in a rapidly changing scene. It can be safely said that not a single hamlet in the entire country has been unaffected (8, p. 36) by the great movements in population, by the changes in occupational structure, by the altering of the basic relationship of people to their land, by rapid and dispersed industrialization, and by the blurring of the deep traditional distinction between urban and rural. The villages are no longer isolated, nor are they nearly as self-fufficient as before. The boundaries between classes, categories or workers, and ethnic groups are no longer operative as they were in the past. The supreme test is in the marriage patterns which show a much higher degree of intermarriage, according to any of the old distinctions.

There is a complex set of variations in the adaptations which still show a remarkable amount of family coordination and mix of the old and new systems. However, much of the subsistence pattern of the old system is being carried on by persons no longer in the official labor force. Their knowledge and interest in the old life ways are not being transmitted as completely as before. It cannot yet be predicted how the new system will substitute for their contribution to the national economy.

In retrospect it can be seen that the viewpoint of the survivors of the old system, who were my main sources of information, is quite different from that of their children and grandchildren. What was a shock to the landholders was evidently a release to at least some of their children. The old systems of inheritance of land and household meant that the inheritors had to wait for parents to die before full adult status could be achieved. The radical change in land holding patterns gave the inheritors alternative modes of behavior that were not available before.

Add to that the mobility, both socially and spatially, that was not possible before. People are free to move, to change jobs, and to marry in ways not available before. With still another ingredient, that of a period of time for getting accustomed to the changes, we have a deep difference between generations. The younger ones are income oriented rather than land oriented (12). All freedoms have their prices but the younger Hungarians appear to be much less resentful of the past changes than their parents are.

The reasons for living in rural settlements under these circumstances are complex (13). The older residents are there because they are accustomed to rural life; they have the knowledge of the previous subsistence methods and value them. The younger ones are more attracted by the resources of the cities. As living accommodations come under construction in urban centers, they are quickly taken up. We noted, however, that even among the young there are those who see advantages to the larger residences and gardens of the villages, as well as the greater quiet and cleaner air. Anyone who has been in the cities in winter when soft coal is the primary fuel will know that clean air is no mere slogan.

Villages--or rural settlements--will survive but with different social and economic functions. Some more will become towns and even those that remain about the same size will be different in operation, in significance to their inhabitants, and in the nature of relationships to other units of settlement, urban and rural.

References and Notes

1. The exploration for this research was done with the help of the Catholic University Research Fund. The American Council of Learned Societies provided a grant for a summer course in the Hungarian language. The main period of research was supported by the Hungarian Academy of Sciences (MTA) and the U.S. National Academy of Sciences.
2. PAIKERT, G.C., The Danube Swabians, Nijhoff, The Hague (1967).
3. REINING, C.C., The Rise and Demise of the Germans in Hungary, Folia Slavica. (in press)
4. ENYEDI, G., Rural Transformation in Hungary in Enyedi, G. (ed) Rural Transformation in Hungary, Akademiai Kiado, Budapest (1976).
5. Not all Hungarian villages were of the nucleated type. In the Great Plain east of the Danube, in some areas where herding had been the most important feature of life, homesteads tended to be on a dispersed pattern. Much of the change described here pertains also to the dispersed settlements, although they have proved to be less viable in the face of modern trends, and current policy is to try to consolidate the residents of dispersed settlements. (6).
6. LACKO, L., The Hamlet and Farmstead Regions of Hungary: Planning Problems in Enyedi, G.(ed) (1976).
7. PAMLENYI, E., A History of Hungary, Corvina, Budapest (ed) 1973 pp. 542-3.
8. VOROSMARTI, Mrs. and TAJTI, E., Demographic Characteristics of Rural Settlements in Enyedi, G. (ed) (1976).
9. BELUSZKY, P., Functional Types of Rural Settlement in Hungary in Enyedi, G. (ed) (1976).
10. BARTA, G., Changes in the Living Conditions of the Rural Population in Enyedi, G. (ed) (1976).
11. TATAI, A., The Growth of Rural Industry, in Enyedi, G. (ed) (1976).
12. ENYEDI, G., Personal communication (June, 1978).
13. MADAY, Bela, Urbanization and the Vanishing Peasantry in Hungary Annals New York Academy of Science 220:560-68 (1974).

Charlotte Wiser

5. Time Perspectives in Village India

I was introduced to "viability" and its meaning near the end of my 50 years of service in India. During those "pre-viability" years, I had to be satisfied with "security" to explain the barriers set up by villagers to discourage or exclude outsiders. Later, I added "tranquillity" and "peace of mind" to describe the benefits derived from their "security" measures. Now that I have found the word for which I had waited so long, I intend to use it.

My involvement with villages of North India has been intensive, rather than extensive, limited to four districts of Uttar Pradesh, the Northern State. I first became aware of the existence of villages in North India when my fiance and I were seniors in the School of Social Work at the University of Chicago. We were attending a series of lectures on people of cultures other than our own. The lectures which appealed to us most were by an American who had recently spent ten years among farm families of North India. He described vividly the farmers and their work. With worn-out soil, with oxen taking the place of our mechanized equipment, and with antiquated implements, they managed to produce enough food for their families. He was not critical, but respected them for making the most of what they had. For their benefit, he had built an Agricultural Institute in a town named Allahabad, on the bank of the Ganges River. The Institute was training young men to go out to villages of the area, to introduce ways of increasing production with simple implements that could be locally made.

At the close of his last lecture he announced that while traveling over the United States, he was looking for young people with training in social work. As the farmers increased their production, they would be able to raise their standards of living. At this point, social workers could help. The proposal attracted us. We were both preparing for urban social work somewhere in America; and the idea of social work among village people of North India was as far removed from urban work as could be. However, we were young, in our early twenties; we were romantic, recently engaged; and we were ready for adventure. What could be more of a venture than this? After several conferences with the lecturer, we volunteered.

Bill set out for India immediately after graduation, sailing on the last ship to go via the Mediterranean and the Suez. Shortly after that, the route was closed by the First World War. I delayed for a year, serving as a YWCA secretary, while trying to convince my family that I would not die during my first year in India. I already had shots for typhoid and a scar to prevent smallpox; cholera and plague were under control; and cobras were rare. Meanwhile, Bill was to send glowing letters about life in India. I was puzzled. He wrote about college students, not farmers. But he was in India, and this was all I wanted to know. My family remained adamant. So, at the end of a year, I said "goodbye" and left for San Francisco. I sailed by the Pacific on a ship of a Chinese line.

Bill met me in Calcutta. Six days later we were married in Allahabad, in a college chapel; and a bungalow, over one hundred years old, became our home. Then it was that Bill shared the fate of our plans. He had withheld the disappointment while we were on opposite sides of the world. It would have been difficult to explain in letters, and if I had known, I might not have come! When he had arrived in Allahabad, prepared for his role in the extension program, he was met with the devastating news that the program had not materialized. It was still a dream of the lecturer. In the light of the realistic present, it seems incredible that two graduates of a large university could have been so naive, or a man as internationally known as the lecturer, could have been so misled and misleading. When we had volunteered, America was riding high on a wave of optimism. Idealism was a favorite topic for graduation speeches, and ideals were acceptable to most thinking Americans. Ideals had a share in our choosing to go to a neglected part of the world rather than to some affluent American city. To Bill the disappointment presented a challenge. When he recovered from the shock, he accepted the post of supervisor of four hostels in a sister college of the Institute. Instead of working with illiterate farmers, he was surrounded by college students, ready to exchange their information on India for his on America.

There was still much to learn. Bill was already studying Hindi and I joined him. There were no crash courses offered then. Eventually, we set up our own routine, including college teaching, language study and village visits.

Indian college teachers our age offered to go with us to villages within bicycle reach of Allahabad. Villages and farm plots were small. This made it possible to visit several over a weekend. On our early visits we had no idea of what to expect. Neither did our teacher guides. They had never visited villages. They went now as friends, to help with the language. After a few village visits we were able to anticipate the attitude of the men who would come from fields or family enclosures to meet us. They were polite and at the same time discreet. Had we known then what we learned ten years later, we would have been more sympathetic towards them. When we had become part of a village which was striving to preserve its viability, we learned to regard strangers from the village point of view. Our farmer hosts in Allahabad District did not know us or why we had come. There were several counts against us. The teachers were definitely townsmen, in dress, in manners, and in speech. And villagers had learned from their own experience and from reports of others, that men who came from towns were looking for chances to take advantage of illiterate villagers. Bill and I, with our fair skin and khaki outfits, common among Britishers and other foreigners, must surely be associated with the government. And government officers were known to interfere with village affairs, especially in the enforcement of the law. Our hosts did not dare be outspoken, telling us to move on. It might be construed as an insult to an important person and open to punishment. So they were cautious and cool.

Learning the language was complicated by the existence of several variations. With our tutor in the college we were learning to read and speak Hindi. In the rural area we used colloquial, or rustic, Hindi. In my first, and Bill's second summer we spent our two-month vacation in a language school, just introduced. There we learned Urdu, a Muslim language. We wondered why a Muslim language was used in government circles. Two reasons were given: first, because it was the court language of the Moguls, predecessors of the British; and second, more Muslims than Hindus were ready to accept government posts and were prepared to go to England for training.

Language was the main drawback for us. In villages near Allahabad, we had reached the point where we could understand and be understood. But in the outlying hill regions, even in the same State our efforts at conversation were met by blank stares or muffled laughter, and nothing the hill people said was intelligible to us. Our viability suffered. We had long discussions on the divisive effect of languages within a nation like India.

Their customs were as diverse as their languages. They worshipped countless gods and goddesses, varying in different parts of the country. There were noticeable variations in their ritual, and yet they were all united as Hindus. There were smaller religious groups--Sikhs, Christians, Muslims, Buddhists, Parsees, and others, loyal to their religion, but they were overshadowed by the giant, Hinduism. There were reform movements within Hinduism, like the *Brahmo Samaj*, limited to Brahmins, and the *Arya Samaj*, and others appealing to the intelligentsia. But all of these were within the Hindu fold.

Once a year, in January and February, a large religious gathering, a *mela*, held at the *sangam*, the point where the Ganges and the Jumna River meet. A whole city is constructed, all of bamboo, on the sandy river bank. It remains for two months or more, as long as the *mela* continues. Then, it is washed away and replaced the next January. Every sixth year the *mela* becomes the *kumbh mela*, much larger. In the twelfth year it becomes greatest of all, the *magh* (great) *kumbh mela*. The *magh kumbh mela* occurred the winter after our vacation in the hills with Professor J. He had been granted permission to use the "lookout" on a particular day, and invited us to join his party from the University. The lookout was a wooden structure with a long uneven stairway leading to a wooden platform, high above the crowds. Official reports stated that there were more than a million pilgrams gathered at the *sangam* on that day, and there they were, on the sand beneath us. Some were submerging themselves in the icy cold water or coming out with teeth chattering. Others were following processions of priests. The rest were moving about in the mass of human beings, shouting and chanting. The religious fervor they engendered seemed to rise up and engulf us. It was intoxicating. I grasped the wooden railing around the lookout to steady my shaking knees. We made no effort to speak. Obviously, the others were as overwhelmed as we were. We finally climbed down the stairway, almost as shaky as our knees, and plunged into and through the mob. The roar of voices in a medley of tongues made it impossible to hear one's neighbor. If anyone needed evidence of the unifying power of Hinduism, this was it.

Our routine was wearing thin. We were wondering how we might move beyond our limited circle in Allahabad when a telegram arrived from Kanpur, the largest industrial center in the North. It was signed by a stranger representing a group of British owners of textile mills there. A few days later the representative came to interview us. He was surprised to find us so young but still made the offer. The mills needed two persons trained in urban social work. They were familiar with social welfare in Britain and were preparing to call a team from London when a member of their group heard about us. We had the required training and we were in Allahabad just one hundred miles away. In the beginning we declined the invitation for two reasons. First, our training was for urban work in America, far different from that in India. And secondly, our purpose in coming to India had been to help village people. The representative assured us that the mills were like an overgrown village. We would be in close touch with men and women coming directly from their village homes. Also, we would be working with more villagers in one day than we could in a month in an ordinary village. By the end of his two-day visit we agreed to attempt the venture.

For the next four years we worked in Kanpur and our education about village life continued by work with the villagers who had moved to the mills. Bill's chief concern was the development of cooperative purchasing societies especially for the workmen and their families. Everyone was involved in the project and its success was the talk of the mills, the streets and the council house. And it did succeed.

I worked especially with the mothers and children. Comparatively few women were employed in the mills, but I found many in the city who had come to make some sort of home for their families. They were living in dirty back lanes and were crowded into small rooms shared with other families. I learned from the women I visited how nostalgic they were of their village families and their own courtyards. Their days in the city were long and empty. Their viability was as low as that of their husbands was high. On my first visits I was horrified. The sickness among the children was appalling. The city doctors who held clinics in the mills attacked the city officials, aided by the mill owners. They finally succeeded in getting a decent sewage system along with housing laws.

Our first serious undertaking was an outdoor creche in two mills. At once, mothers living in the city began spending most of every day with their small children and babies in the fresh air and sunshine of a creche. The two public health nurses assigned to work with me looked after their small ailments. The effect was magic. The men had their work and their games and classes; and now, their wives and children, no longer cooped up in smelly quarters, walked to one of the creches. After the first few days, the women lost their fear of walking down a city street without a husband walking ahead. And they were not molested. Mothers working on the looms also found the creches a help. They could carry on their work knowing that someone was looking after their children.

Eventually our aim was to help each woman in small groups or individually to find her place, her role in the mill community as she might have done in her village. The experience for me was enlightening. A village woman could talk more freely with others outside of her village; and with Mrs. Allen or me, she felt free to share her intimate family relationships. I did not realize how much I was learning in preparation for life in a village. Later in Karimpur, I found a family courtyard not as easy a place for confidences as a big, impersonal city.

Suddenly our four years ended. We could have spent the rest of our lives here with congenial men and women on challenging projects. However, we still looked forward to living and working with people in their own villages. We returned to the needed discipline of study and classes at the University of Chicago, in what had become the Graduate School of Social Service Administration.

If we had left India directly from Allahabad, we might not have returned. We had come uninvited, except for one person who forgot us. We had come to Kanpur because we were wanted and were given a task for which we were prepared, and in which we could excel. We were the same persons in different situations. After the years in Kanpur, we thought only of returning, sure that the opportunity would come.

In the middle of our year of study a cable came bringing the hoped for opportunity. It urged Bill to come to the rescue of a number of rural cooperative loan societies which were threatened with liquidation. They were in Mainpuri District. The mention of Mainpuri was all that he needed for his acceptance. It was the district that had attracted us most when we had made the round of rural districts of Uttar Pradeser soon after our arrival in India.

Immediately after the university term ended, we sailed to Bombay and went directly to Mainpuri. As Bill studied reports of the ailing societies, he found their condition more serious than the cable had implied. In addition to straightening out garbled finances, he had the more complicated task of restoring normal relations between the embittered organizers on the one hand, and embittered members on the other. Organizers were professional men living in Mainpuri Town, the district headquarters. The members were extremely poor laborers living in scattered villages.

During the ordeal he had a wise, experienced guide, the district magistrate. Bill had consulted him on government regulations of cooperative societies and had been surprised to find him concerned for the welfare of the village people in his district. Others limited their interest to official duties and their rank. He was chief officer of the district, and the only Indian official. Other officers, all British, were under his jurisdiction. During his many years in office he had become increasingly interested in the life of villagers, he himself being an Indian, and he had found how different their thinking and their habits were from his own. He had to learn a great deal before he could advise or direct them effectively. And, as foreigners we had still more to learn in order to serve them effectively. If we honestly wanted to be social workers in rural North India, we must learn firsthand the reasons for a villager's point of view. And this knowledge could not come from occasional visits, but from living inside a village. We agreed.

When we made known our intention to live in a village, our friends in district headquarters, both Indians and foreigners disapproved. They thought it rash. It was a health hazard for us, and a great hazard for our two sons. The magistrate stood alone in his approval; and it was respect for him and his judgment that led the others to accept the idea. He suggested three villages with what he considered maximum possibilities for learning, while still being ordinary. We visited the three and chose Karimpur.

On village visits near Allahabad we had discovered that people did not rent or sell enclosures. Every enclosure was occupied by descendants of the men who had built them long ago from mud dug from the bottom of the nearest pond and smoothed by hand. Later came bricks of mud, pressed into molds and dried in the sun. All mud walls suffered from the heavy monsoon rains and had to be repaired each year. Small wonder that one of the first changes in village living for those who could afford it was to invest in kiln-baked bricks for house walls.

Knowing that we could not rent an enclosure, we settled for a tent home. We had been in tents of district officers when they toured the district. By the time we moved to

Karimpur, officers toured by car and tents were outmoded. We had three tents, loaned us by missionary friends. Like the officials, missionaries now toured by car. All three tents were liberally patched with large squares of canvas of different colors. The furniture was shabby and scratched from many seasons of touring. However, both furniture and tents were sturdy and carried us through all kinds of weather during the next five years.

On that eventful October morning when we drove into the mango grove beside Karimpur, we were elated. Bill had been in India for ten years and I for nine. And during those years we had looked forward to this moment. Our purpose in coming to India had been to serve in villages of the North, and Karimpur was one of them. It looked like the hundreds of villages we had passed along the dusty roads, but it was different. It was to be our home for the next five years. Tent raisers, six of them, were waiting for us. They had come the night before with three oxcarts loaded with canvas and camp furniture. The men looked frail, but when we saw them in action we found them sturdier than they appeared. For years they had raised and lowered tents for the magistrate who had sent them. They knew their job and were familiar with the grove. They refused our offer to help and went about their work shouting in rhythm as they hoisted a large pile of canvas and transformed it into a circular roof around a tall center pole. Not being wanted by the tent raisers, we tackled the car bulging with passengers and last minute odds and ends.

First to tumble out were our two sons. In seconds, Arthur Dana was swinging on the low limb of a large mango tree, and Alfred was tugging at Prem to lift him to another tree. Prem, a boy of thirteen, was the mainstay of his family in Mainpuri. His camp duty was to draw water for our household needs from an open well in the nearest lane. Because we were non Hindus, we were not allowed to touch the well. We knew that Prem was a *chamar*, a leather worker by birth. *Chamar*s handled the hides of dead animals which classified them as outcastes. Had our neighbors questioned his caste, he would have been ostracized as we were.

In what seemed a short time, the tent raisers called us to survey our tent home. Even though it was empty, it looked homelike. Outer walls had been secured. And inner walls divided the space into three rooms. Two smaller tents were soon up. One was to be our office and dispensary. The other, much smaller, would be the kitchen.

When the tents were up and the magistrate's men were ready to haul furniture, they accepted our help. Everything was folding if possible. Packing cases stood on end and fitted with shelves, became cupboards. An over-size, screened cupboard built on stilts was to protect our food from flies and hungry dogs who crept in under canvas walls in search of food. Beds were ordinary village *charpais*. The tent raisers, thinking us newcomers, commented frankly in Hindi on both the furniture and tents. Any official would have thrown them away long ago. We thought them unique. Every patch and every scratch could tell a story of past journeys or users.

Having finished their duty, they climbed into the empty carts and departed. We watched them leave with a sense of release. They were our last tie with town life. From now on we would be villagers. We were covered with dust, disheveled, exhausted, but jubilant. Bill leaned against the broad trunk of a mango tree, lifted his khaki topee and mopped his brow. I leaned against the nearest tree and used my cape as a fan. Our sons were fascinated with climbing such large trees and did not need us.

We walked over to the family tent, lifted the screen and dropped down on two folding chairs at the folding table. We were alone at last. At one time we had hoped to live in an enclosure. Since then we had found that voices carry over courtyard walls like the aroma of toasting wheat cakes. Privacy was a luxury villagers had never known. Right now we welcomed it in a tent in a grove. We were free from the anxiety of friends and the criticism of others over our present folly. We were making a fresh start and could begin plans for the future. We were viable.

Rustrum's polite cough outside the tent door jarred us back to the present. When we responded, he lifted the screen and came in, balancing a tray with everything needed for tea. On his heels came the boys, sniffing Rustrum's cookies. From that day on, rain or shine, Rustrum, our cook, reminded us that four o'clock was teatime.

We had been so occupied with setting our house in order, and so absorbed in our reminiscing and planning that we had not noticed the complete absence of a welcome.

When twilight fell, Rustrum reappeared carrying four lighted lanterns, with instructions to hang them on branches where light was most needed. He reminded us that they would provide the only light we would have while we were in the village. We had become used to oil lamps in Mainpuri.

Lanterns were another step toward simple living. As it grew darker, we were more aware of our isolation. We gathered in the family tent, except for the intrepid Rustrum. There was no answering light from village enclosures. Walls hid whatever light might be burning inside. The world around us grew black. The only sound was the wailing of jackals.

Our isolation continued through the next day and the next and the one after that until there was no doubt that we were deliberately shut out of the village. The boys were happy with a whole grove of mango trees to climb. But Bill and I were puzzled and hurt. We had come as friends, but were being treated like enemies. It had not occured to us that the goodwill was all on our side. The people of Karimpur had no reason to want us or to accept us. We were strangers to them, as we had once been to the villagers in Allahabad District.

Finally we took our problem to the magistrate. He had regarded us as fellow workers, and like others who had gone before us, he had given us the benefit of his years of experience. He was not surprised. He had been given the same cold reception when he had started out. With every thought he expressed, he added to our understanding of viability. Centuries earlier, groups of families had built protective earth walls around their settlements to keep out marauders. Now there were invisible walls around each village to protect it from modern invaders. Outsiders were regarded as dangerous until they proved themselves friends. Officials, by reason of their authority, could bypass the walls but could only go inside as far as the villagers chose.

We had worked with mill workers fresh from village homes and learned now about village life from them. But they lived in Kanpur District and had not come this far. Also, the villagers Bill helped out of their co-op troubles were extremely poor. No one in Karimpur would have been interested in them or listened to them.

Until we came, men and women of Karimpur were able to go about their daily routine free from strain. They were viable. When they found us sitting on their doorstep, with every indication of staying, they were disturbed and determined to keep us out. They were guarding their viability.

The magistrate advised us to remain alert to any opportunity to be of service to anyone in the village. Meanwhile, he would investigate. There might be some covert reason for our severe treatment. He consulted with Panditji who, in addition to being village priest, acted as liaison between district officials and the village. Together they tracked down a rumor that we were in the pay of the British government to assess their crops with a view to increasing taxes. Nothing could have been more damning. In the absence of newspapers or radios their news came via rumor. And it was accepted as we accept, without question, the news handed out to us. Panditji soon came to our tent as host to welcome us to Karimpur. Panditain, his wife, was the first woman to invite me to her courtyard. They remained our closest friends in Karimpur. News of Panditji's visit spread fast. And at last we were "in."

However, our full acceptance by the village did not come until we had found and filled our roles in village life. Every adult, we discovered, had his or her role. For a man, this was his share in the work performed by his family, whether farming or a trade, or hired as day laborers. Outcastes were included. Sweepers raised swine, the village sewage system. *Charmar*s removed dead animals and cured the hides. *Dhanuk*s were chiefly day laborers. They were regarded as outcastes because their wives were the midwives of village families and birth was considered unclean.

Word of our medicine cabinet soon spread. Our neighbors knew of medicines beyond their reach in the Mainpuri bazaar. When the first doors of the village enclosures were opened to us, the door of our family medicine cabinet flew open, and remained open during the next five years. My role was at once identified. When our supply of medicine ran out, I replenished it from a small chemist shop in Mainpuri. We had intended to charge a small price for the tablets. Free distribution might hurt the independence of village men and women. However, we soon learned of a government ruling that every tablet sold must be recorded in a special register. We gave up the idea. It would have taken time that could be more usefully spent. A woman doctor, an American, in a mission hospital about forty miles away came to my rescue. She was large and competent. Village people and also Americans had come to trust her, a giant in her field. She was one of the few professionals who believed that a lay person like me could learn to treat routine cases. There were not nearly enough trained doctors to meet the needs of the multitude. I needed her help. I was unprepared for the ailments and illnesses of village children. There were varieties of diarrhea that I learned to identify, and fever from different causes. Still more disturbing were festering sores, worse than any I had seen. Distended abdomens I had observed in Kanpur. But they had been treated in a mill clinic. Most distressing were the children screaming with pain when brought by mothers. Their eyes were swollen beyond recognition, some bleeding, and lids glued shut by pus. It was diagnosed as xerophthalmia. It was traced to malnutrition, like other afflictions of which the children were victims. When we went to Cornell at the end of our years in Karimpur, I registered for courses in nutrition to find some of the answers to their painful problems.

Our medicine cabinet was in constant demand. There were many ailments and a good deal of illness in the village. Their fear of outside contacts had kept them within the village and denied them the benefit of simple remedies like ours. Malaria was rampant and was responsible for many days of misery and fever and loss of work. Amoebic dysentery ranked next. Aches and a variety of pains brought others to our tent. After each special holiday, celebrated with rich homemade dishes, I could expect a line of men and women wanting "soda."

The unnecessary suffering of the women and children concerned me most. I tried taking a group of women to one of the doctors in town. His office was wide open to the noisy, dusty street. Patients sat around a large table at which the doctor presided. They were supposed to be examined by turn. I waited outside the door in our car. Relatives of patients squatted on a wide "shelf" at the front of the building and visited. Because the women were obviously villagers and found it difficult to explain their troubles to a strange man, they were given curt treatment. One final flourish made the visit worthwhile. As they went out of the door, a doctor's assistant met them with a syringe already used many times and gave each one an injection. This added to their prestige when they returned home.

After a number of such visits, I decided that the *hakim* in Karimpur who used roots and herbs could do more for them. Bill and I had met him often when we were called to visit a patient in his or her home. We had learned that a family felt free to call on several consultants at the same time. We were not competing, but cooperating with him. We had heard from several village leaders of his ability. He always carried a very large volume printed in Hindi. We never saw him open it and wondered if he ever read it. Then, several years later, we learned that he was better trained in Eastern medicine than the doctors in town were in Western medicine. His illiterate, humble oilpresser son told us proudly that his father had attended school in his home village, not Karimpur. And he had read the volume many times all the way through. It was on *ayurvedic* medicines. He had been called here to treat certain Brahmin families and had been invited to stay.

When Bill had similar experiences taking men to a doctor in town, he resented the air of superiority with which the doctors and their assistants treated villagers. This started him working on his first role. He went in search of a doctor who would treat villagers with the respect due them. He found one such man from Mainpuri willing to visit our camp once a fortnight. One of his outstanding cases was the daughter of Panditji, the village priest who had welcomed us. A growth had appeared on the side of her nose, and it was swelling. The disfigurement was serious for a girl approaching marriageable age. The doctor set Alfred's discarded playpen on its side under a mango tree and used it as an operating table. Villagers crowded around. To them it was awesome. They had never been in a hospital. With his few instruments dipped in alcohol, the doctor removed the growth and stitched up the wound. Her nose and her chances of a proper wedding were saved.

When the Mainpuri doctor could no longer visit the village, Bill went further afield. A doctor in a mission hospital in Kasganj, seventy miles away, agreed to come on alternate Sundays. Later, when there were more doctors in the hospital, they conducted regular village clinics. At that time he was alone and was prepared to hold a clinic at that distance, organized for him. Our office tent served his purpose. We had guessed the Karimpur needed professional help. And when it came, with a service motive added, it went far beyond our hopes. The village gradually came to life. It had been partially free from fever and dysentery, but there were other parasites and infections that remained. The doctor diagnosed and prescribed, and we were left to carry out instructions. This brought us into every compartment of the village.

The Kasganj doctor became interested in Ram Singh, an elder of the *Kachhi*, or farmer, caste. The *Kachhi*s lived apart from the rest of the village in their own exclusive community beside the district road. Ram Singh was one of the few *Kachhi*s who had accepted us. He had been blind since before we came and spent his days on his front stoop visiting with friends. Bill took the doctor to meet him. When Ram Singh heard that a doctor had come, he asked that his eyes be examined. The diagnosis was cataracts in both eyes. An operation could be performed and Ram Singh's sight restored. The word "operation" was frightening for any villager. Ram Singh talked it over at length with his sons and neighbors and finally agreed to go to Kasganj with Bill. The operation was successful and he returned, a hero. He no longer wanted sympathy. He was an important person.

We introduced the doctor to another case of blindness. The second case was a little old woman, grandmother of a carpenter, living near our grove. She was unhappy, feeling sure that she was not wanted by her grandson and his wife. I was with her often, trying to cheer her. When I explained the operation to her, she was terrified. But she trusted us and agreed to go to Kasganj if Bill and I went with her. The three of us went. The operation was as successful as Ram Singh's and she herself was a success. Instead of brooding in a corner of her small courtyard, she sat in the lane outside of her son's door, and to everyone's surprise, talked freely with visitors, not only with women but with men she would never have dared to face before. Soon she volunteered to teach me how to cook everything prepared in village homes. We set up a *chulha* at the foot of a mango tree, and there she sat giving me orders while I worked. She insisted that before each lesson I coat the *chulha* with the traditional plaster of fresh clay. The lessons helped me, not only to learn the details of village cookery, but provided me with a popular subject for conversation when I joined noonday circles with other women.

While Bill and I were absorbed with our individual roles, our sons were reveling in tree climbing. Without effort, they took on their own role. Arthur Dana was five years old and Alfred was a year and a half. Word of their tricycle and swings and little red wagon spread. Children of all castes, with several from the outcaste section, came to play. They were shy on the first day and watched from the edge of the grove. By the second day they joined our playground. They taught our two their games, like *kabaddi*, and our sons taught them games they themselves had known.

In the late afternoon when their friends left for home and evening meal, our two wandered into the village. We had made a rule that they were not to go into enclosures, where some infection might break out without warning. And our village neighbors easily understood. Their children were strictly limited to enclosures of their own relatives. Two spots were our sons' favorites. First, they went to the huts where the boys and girls, each with a small basket of grain--wheat or corn, barley or rice--went to have the grain roasted in blazing hot sand in a broken water jar. The inviting smell of roasting grain and the handful given them by a grain parcher, was tempting. Their second stop was the carpenter's outdoor workshop where there was always activity. Carpenters, old and young, were sawing logs or shaving boards, or making handles for trowels or plows. One or two men tossed the boys small pieces of discarded wood to use in camp as blocks. This was where we counted on finding them when it

was our supper time. As sons they were an asset in our
relations with the village. We were a family, and the family
in village life is very important.

We were still exploring our roles when two unfamiliar
words stirred our curiosity. One was *jajman* (pronounced
"judgemann"), and the other was *jajmani haqq--jajmani* rights.
When we asked what they meant, we were told that they were
part of an age-old *jajmani* system.

Everyone in the village was familiar with it. The
jajman was the person who paid others to work for him. And
the others, those who served him, were *kam karne wale*,
shortened to *kamin*. However, a *kamin* became a *jajman* as soon
as he hired someone else. In this way the head of each
family was *jajman* in certain relationships and *kamin* in
others. The one exception was the priest; he was given his
title of *pandit* instead of being classified as *kamin*.

Men of wisdom and experience must have pooled their
knowledge and made the *jajmani* system available to the small
communities exposed to inimical forces of nature and of men,
forces so strong that they could only be withstood by a
united front. The more we learned about its contribution to
the life of the village, the more certain we were that we
should better understand it. Bill's role was more strategic
than mine, but less time consuming. Mine had become almost
full time. The *jajmani* system seemed important enough for
him to make understanding it his chief concern.

Village leaders like Panditji and the council of five
encouraged Bill to study and record the system. In Allahabad we had found books on village life. They covered social
relationships as in caste and kinship, but we found nothing
on service interrelationships. Bill, with his interest in
research, welcomed the idea of delving into an untried field,
the *jajmani* system.

A Brahmin farmer, a friend of ours with plenty of land
but not enough cash, suggested that Bill use the services of
his son Prakash. Prakash was eighteen. He had spent his
life in Karimpur and was able to communicate with men and
women of all ages and levels. It was the beginning of a
close relationship between Prakash's family and ours. Many
years later, after Bill's death, Prakash's joint family moved
in with me in our enclosure. And two years ago when I
revisited Karimpur (Karimganj) with three grandchildren, they
found congenial friends in Prakash's grandsons, still in my
enclosure.

Bill discovered that long ago village leaders had laid down rules intended to strengthen the viability of individual families of the village and of the community as a whole. The rules provided for full scale interrelations in services among members of the village and of the community as a whole. The rules provided for full-scale interrelations in services among members of the village. In a given situation, a village family might be in the position of employer, or of *jajman* and at the same time could be in the position of employee or *kamin*. These were entirely different from the patron-serf relationship where one person or family is the established patron and others are their serfs.

Bill found that Topal, a Brahmin farmer was *jajman* to Balram, a carpenter. But Balram was not limited to the one *jajman*. He had twenty-four other *jajman*s whose implements he made and kept in repair. And from each of the twenty-five he claimed a specified amount of grain at the time of the spring and fall harvests, as well as other benefits. Following the rules of the *jajmani* system, Balram would not think of working for a farmer who already employed a different *kamin*. And each carpenter knew that he could count on his *jajman*s not to change to another *kamin*. While Balram was working for his *jajman*s, he himself was *jajman* to a particular *darzi* (rustic tailor) who made clothes for Balram's family. In this way, the whole village was involved and families were interdependent.

The carpenters were an example of the viability provided by the *jajmani* system. As apprentices they had been taught the rules and benefits of the system. By following the rules, their forefathers had retained their *jajmani* rights. The rights assured them of food for their families to last from harvest to harvest. This was important for people living near the edge of hunger. A few of them, like Devi, had as many as twenty-five *jajman*s. Others had fewer, some with only five or six. But no one interfered with the *jajman-kamin* (employer-employee) relationship of another. They worked together sharing tools, but did not compete. Tesu was an example of the system in action. He was a gentle, quiet-spoken man with a few *jajman*s. He had trouble with his eyes. This slowed him down and he came to us for help. Bill took him to a government eye hospital in Aligarh. His new glasses helped for a while, but again, he had trouble and his work deteriorated. If he had been located in a city, his patrons would have called on another carpenter. Here his *jajman*s continued to give him a little work until his son gave up a job in Mainpuri and came home to assist his father. He found his father's *jajman*s easier to work for than his city master who quibbled over every penny he paid. And once back in Karimpur, he found *jajman*s in neighboring villages where there were no carpenters. Everyone seemed to benefit.

Bill's research developed until it became a book, *The Hindu Jajmani System*, still used in conferences and round-table discussions on village life (1). It gave us personally a new appreciation of the stability of villages like Karimpur. While sustained by the traditional rules, they could still accept changes that assured them of better harvests and better living. At the same time the study has made us pause. Can the new ideas we might offer compare with the wisdom coming from centuries of experience?

Working with the woman doctor, I learned to hold a screaming child and treat inflamed eyes or an infected sore with equanimity. And I found ways to supplement a mother's dwindling breast milk for her two-year old child who looked like an old man. New ailments no longer worried me. I was viable. My role no longer claimed all of my thought, and I was free to watch what went on around me.

I discovered that the men did not question their roles, nor were they aware of their viability. Each one had been born into a family of farmers or tradesmen, grain parchers, potters, carpenters or one of the other occupations. He was free of any kind of discipline or training until he was seven or eight, and ready for his apprenticeship. He was sent to school if his work was not necessary for the benefit of his family. There is a familiar saying, "Treat your son as a prince until he is seven. Then treat him as a slave." This was the one period of adjustment for him. He started work under his father or older brother on the land or in the family workshop. When he reached the point where he no longer needed instruction, he was viable and took his place along with his elders.

For a girl, fitting into her role was more difficult. She started out like her brother, free as the wind. She could watch her mother working or play at cooking. Nothing was expected of her in her own home. Her mother and aunts did the same work as all village women, regardless of caste. They ground flour from any kind of grain available, husked rice, churned, cooked meals and scoured the brass. At that time very few girls attended school. Later, there were many more. They went until they reached the sixth class which was almost the marriageable age. Like most newcomers from the

---

[1] W. Wiser, *The Hindu Jajmani System* (Lucknow Publishing House, Lucknow, 1936).

West, we were shocked to learn that girls were still married at thirteen. For boys it might be fifteen or older. Laws were passed to make the thirteen illegal for girls. But the law was so worded that it could be bypassed.

When we objected to such unfairness to girls, two reasons for it were given. One was from the point of view of parents. When a girl reached puberty she was safer in her in-laws' courtyard where she would be closely chaperoned than free in her home village. We heard of only one case of a boy-girl affair and it ended with the murder of the boy. Both the boy and girl were of the same subcaste. And it was men of their caste who brutally killed the boy. It gave us an inkling of the village attitude toward extramarital romance. The parents felt that if any irregularities occurred, it would be "in the family." In the women's afternoon gatherings, I had heard of this happening. But I knew definitely of only one case. It resulted from the carelessness of the girl's father. He delayed going to her in-laws to bring her home at the end of the traditional three or four day visit where a bride was guarded by the mother- and sisters-in-law.

The second reason given was that a thirteen-year old girl adjusts more easily to the ways of the mother-in-law than a girl of 20. Every girl expected to be married. She knew that her "prince" would come riding in on an ox cart accompanied by as many cart loads of relatives as his parents chose. For three days of wedding ceremonies she was queen. But then came her first step in adjustment, a traumatic experience. She was carried to an empty cart and rode alone with the wedding party to the bridegroom's home. There she was led into a strange courtyard. She had not come to be with her husband, but with her mother-in-law. Three days were considered enough for her to be looked over by the women of her new family. From that time on, she belonged to her in-laws. Never again, in her husband's village, would she mention her own name or her husband's. She became daughter-in-law of her husband's father until she had a son. From then on she was mother of "Sundaro" or "Ramesh." She was awkward and frightened lest she make a punishable mistake. Painfully she became part of the household which may or may not be like her own. I have been impressed by young women I have known who left Karimpur as terrified brides and returned as poised matrons. And I have watched the reverse process when a bride came to Karimpur. I have never known a village spinster. When I meet a village woman or stranger without the two silver toe rings, symbol of marriage, I know that she has lost her husband. With the absence of two rings goes the absence of the familiar colored glass bangles broken after her husband's death.

After some time our place in the community was taken for granted. We were no longer under strain. We were free to try to understand village life. It was hard to believe that the men and women who had rejected us so coldly could be as friendly and ready to answer our endless questions as they now were. The contrast between our treatment as dangerous while we were outside, and the warmth and friendliness we met when we were inside, led us to associate threats to the viability of the village with outsiders. This impression was confirmed by the bards who came during our first year. They spent a fortnight. No one knew whence they came or where they went when they moved on. We took for granted that their visit was an annual event until we were told that only the oldest men could recall their last visit. Night after night we sat under the stars in a semi-circle of villagers and listened. Their tales were of the remote past, chanted or sung. With a tubla, an elongated village drum played at both ends, and a one-stringed instrument, they carried us into the past. We heard the beating of horses' hooves and the threatening shouts of brigands as they swept across the country. And the single string trembled with the dread of their approach or the desolation that followed in their wake. As I recall, there were six or seven bards. They were simply dressed and barefooted. Their songs and their chanting were in Hindi, simple enough for villagers (and foreigners) to understand. They expected no payment other than grain and vegetables or lentils which they cooked over open fires. They all wore the *chutia*, the long lock of hair on the crown of the head characteristic of conservative Hindu men.

Their tales brought to illiterate villagers a glimpse of their own history and added to the identity of the community as a whole. And for us, they did more than any books in English we might have read.

And they explained a number of features of life in Karimpur that had puzzled us. The walls of earth around family enclosures undoubtedly originated in the distant past when outsiders were cruel. And the walls had been retained when, to us, they seemed superfluous. Women were still confined to the family courtyard as the women were long ago when they were hiding from ruthless marauders. On brief visits to South India we passed villages with houses separated by small yards. And the women had more freedom. South Indians gave themselves credit for being more advanced than Indians of the North. But their early invasions had been by Portugese traders, looking for merchandise, and by men like St. Thomas.

Later we heard tales of the era following that of the invaders. These were brought to us by Madan, a young farmer, one of the few interested in the history of the village. He told us of a time when Karimpur was a large market town and Mainpuri was a village. Brahmins and *Kshatriya*s (warriors) were the two outstanding castes. Madan did not know the reason for a serious rift between the two. The *Kshatriyas*, without warning, killed all of the Brahmins except for two young men who were with their mother in her home village some distance away. When she heard the news, she set out to prepare her sons to revenge their father's murder. She had them trained in the arts of war. And when they had completed their training she sent them to join the service of a *raja* who lived in Karimpur. They are supposed to have been handsome and skillful. They won the admiration of the *raja*, and after serving him for a year or two, they told him of the fate of their people. He placed his army at their disposal. They marched into Karimpur and massacred the *Kshatriyas*. Thereupon they took over the town. Since then no *Kshatriyas* have been allowed to live in Karimpur. However, *Kshatriyas*, now known locally as *Thakur*s, occupied a hamlet on one side of Karimpur and a large, prosperous village on the other. There have been feuds between both of them and Karimpur ever since. Inadvertently we became involved.

Our housewarming was the occasion. At the end of our five years in Karimpur we knew that it would always be "home" to us. And we made a promise to the elders who came to the mango grove to bid us farewell. The promise was that when we would retire from our own service project, known as India Village Service, we would come back to Karimpur to live. Almost thirty years later we kept the promise and had an enclosure built on a corner of the village next door to Prakash who had helped Bill on his research project. We were welcomed with an all-village housewarming.

Village elders lent dignity to the occasion sitting with Bill on our front stoop. In the wide lane before them young men of the village conducted popular games, with voices like megaphones. All went smoothly until the final event which was a tug-of-war. The rope was heavy and long. It had been loaned by a farmer who had made it by hand. Young stalwarts of Karimpur took one end of the rope and young huskies of Nagla took the other. Nagla was the neighboring hamlet associated with the history of massacres of Brahmins by warriors and of warriors by Brahmins. And Nagla was occupied by *Thakur*s. Young men of Nagla had come to us the day before, asking to be invited to the housewarming. We saw no logical reason to refuse. In official records Nagla is a part of Karimpur. Also, an occasion as festive as a housewarming was rare, especially for farmers. We did not take into account the feud between the two. The Nagla team won the tug-of-war. And before anyone grasped what was happening, they picked up the rope, carried it across the lane and along the ridges of field after field. The crowd was scattering and talking at high pitch about the games. Only the elders were left. They were shocked when the Nagla team shouted defiance while they crossed the district road and headed for the hamlet.

Bahadur, Prakash's eldest son, was head of the village council at the time. He regarded this as an insult to Karimpur and to him. Because Bill was ill, we had retired to our dining room. Bahadur followed us storming. We were to blame. We had allowed the ruffians of Nagla to come to the housewarming. He would have refused. We must get the police to punish the men of Nagla.

No one in the villages of the North goes on the road at night. So we waited for morning. Bahadur came, prepared to go with me in our station wagon to get a police escort. Meanwhile I had decided that we were poor social workers if we called on police to settle the young men's prank, especially when the police had a record of cruelty. I explained this to Bahadur. His fury exploded. However, I turned the car toward Nagla instead of Mainpuri and police headquarters. Bahadur had always treated us with respect. Now he reverted to village *gali*, cursing. I turned into the long, straight lane that led between fields to Nagla. The station wagon seemed more conspicuous than ever as we bore down on the hamlet.

Bill and I had called several times on the head man, and now he was courteous as always. However, I noticed that he was surrounded by young men armed with heavy staves. Bahadur controlled his anger and responded with equal courtesy, although he was obviously seething. I excused myself and joined the women in the head man's courtyard. This has always been my practice in villages where I am a stranger. It would be inexcusable for any woman to sit in a public place talking with men. I stayed in the courtyard for about fifteen minutes. When I came out, the two men were discussing the coming harvest. As we walked to the car, I saw the rope neatly coiled in the back. Nothing was said, but apparently there had been quick action. The following day a telegram came calling Bill to a Punjab hospital for surgery. Concern for him overcame animosity. As far as we could discern, viability had been restored.

When we first came to live in Karimpur, land held by any family was in small, scattered plots. Every year the monsoon rains washed down the earth barriers between plots. Quarrels often resulted. When plots were adjoining those of members of another village, the quarrels became more serious. Anjini farmers and farmers of Karimpur made the most of this chance to quarrel and prove the other party wrong.

Anjini was a large, prosperous village of *Thakur*s next to Karimpur. It was on the road to Mainpuri and district headquarters. This gave it an advantage over Karimpur. Everyone going to town from Karimpur or villages beyond had to pass it. The *pradhan*'s house faced the road, and he spent his days sitting on his front stoop, checking every passerby. Most men looked straight ahead to avoid his glare or turned the other way. Women who passed were in ox carts with faces covered. After our initial call Bill and I did not stop again. On that one visit he treated us as village men had in the vicinity of Allahabad, making us feel unwelcome. We were not sure whether this was expressing his dislike of foreigners or his hatred of anyone associated with the Karimpur Brahmins. Anjini's location had a second advantage. It was between Karimpur and the small river that ran through the district. When rains were heavy and fields were flooded, the only outlet for excess water was a channel that ran through Anjini land. Several rainy seasons while we were living in our tent and digging trenches for our excess water, we heard that Anjini was blocking the channel between Karimpur fields and the river. The Anjini *pradhan*'s reason was that Anjini fields were being flooded from Karimpur fields. The Karimpur *pradhan*'s appeals were ignored. He finally interested the district canal officer, and after two more rainy seasons a new channel was dug leading to the river along the edge of Anjini.

Not satisfied with the constant bickering over field boundaries and floods, the two villages broke out into *lathi* (staff) fights. *Lathi*s are heavy, some bound with metal, top and bottom. Men of Karimpur, old enough for cool judgment, thought the battle not worth cracked skulls. Young men set out with clamor. The two "armies" met midway. We could hear loud shouts as *lathi*s came down on heads and arms. When both sides were confident that they had won, they withdrew. The Karimpur contingent came home with shouts of victory, bloody but unbowed. They had proved the superior strength of the Brahmins of Karimpur over the warriers of Anjini. And they were satisfied, until they found some new excuse to resume the feud.

In 1961 I returned to Karimpur and to our enclosure alone. It was two years after our housewarming and thirty years since Bill and I had left Karimpur for advanced studies and our own rural project, India Village Service. It was not long before Prakash who had helped Bill with his research on the *Jajmani* System, brought Jiya, his wife, and their large extended family to share my courtyard. Their high, thick walls had crashed down during the latest monsoon rains, the heaviest in anyone's memory. Prakash planned to rebuild, but a series of misadventures interfered. They both helped me in the study I had undertaken of four families of the village. When that was completed, I set it aside until this year, when it was published as *Four Families of Karimpur* (2). It then joined the book Bill and I had done together, <u>Behind Mud Walls, 1930-1960</u> (3).

I cannot describe each situation in which viability has figured. Instead, I have reviewed my impressions from two angles. One is as I found it coming from outside of the village, and the other is as I found it existing inside. Both outside and inside the village I have described the forces that endanger it and those which support it.

The compartmental character of the village, that is, occupational groups residing together, is an asset to viability. People are more at ease and can work with neighbors involved in the same kind of work. They may quarrel. But they understand each other and can more easily recover. The size of compartments varies. The largest is that of the *Pande* subcaste of Brahmins. Its influence is weakened by a sharp division. There are *Pande*s of the East and those of the West. And there is continual rivalry between them. The next largest is that of the *Kachki*s, farmers by birth. They remain aloof, living apart from the main village, along both sides of the district road. Other compartments are composed of members of other occupations.

The compartment occupied by carpenter families was the nearest to our enclosure. And on every return visit to the village I stop to watch them in their workshop under a large neem tree. Several are chopping or sawing, or using the lathe they have in common. One of them is usually at the forge, sharpening a plow tip or reshaping a *kurpi* (a flat trowel). Their implements have been passed on to them by their fathers and remade. Their work is unhurried but they meet the needs of their *jajman*s. There is always a *jajman* or two sitting on the ground waiting for a job to be finished and visiting with his carpenter *kamin* while he waits. An apprentice is sent across the lane to one of the small carpenter houses and brings back a *chilam*, a red clay pipe without a stem, made by the potter. The men stop work and sit together. They pass the pipe from hand to hand. Lips never touch it. Curved fingers serve as a stem.

They all work together, but each one has his own *jajman*s. A few have inherited as many as twenty *jajman*s, others only three or four. To us, this has seemed unfair. They quarrel over petty differences. But they refuse to compete. None of them will.

The old potter belongs in no traditional compartment. He composes a compartment of his own. He was working when we first came to Karimpur. And he was still working when I returned with my grandchildren two years ago. All through those years he gave faithful support to the viability of Karimpur. He squats on the ground beside his large homemade wheel and turns it with a stick. When it is whirling he sets a lump of clay at the center and begins to shape it. He may make fat clay water jars for village households. For every wedding or other celebration, he makes small plates and cups without handles. When the occasion is over, cups and plates are thrown away and revert to earth. He makes the *chilam*s, graceful pipes with wide bowls and without handles, which the men smoke each evening.

For *Diwali*, the Festival of Lights, he makes hundreds of the tiny saucers, the *diva*s, which give the festival its name. *Diwali* is the most loved of festivals in village families. Filled with mustard oil and with twists of cotton from the family fields serving as wicks, the *diva*s are lighted and placed on roofs and tops of walls until the whole village becomes a fairyland.

While we were living in Karimpur, three grain parcher brothers lived close together in what we called "Humble Lane." Their small enclosures were mud walled with a hut in front and with the furnace in which the parcher heated sand blazing hot, ready to roast grain. The parcher's son kept the fire going with fallen leaves he had gathered. Fallen leaves were the "right" of grain parchers. Once or twice a week the parchers started their fires and ladled the hot sand into old earthen water jars. Then they added grain to them. Children with small baskets of grain they had brought from their homes stood watching and waiting. The grain was quickly "parched." The parcher poured it into a handmade sieve over a container for the sand which would be reheated and used again. He poured the grain into the small baskets which the children held out, setting aside a share for his own family or to be sold in the small shop in front of his enclosure. This is where our sons joined the other children. They sniffed the aroma of roasting grain and waited for the handful the parcher gave them.

Soon after we left the village, one of the three brothers became a moneylender, and with the help of the secretary of the cooperative loan society, he became rich. He had a brick house built across the lane and established his family in it. The other two continued with their inherited task of grain parching. During the years the two parchers had been roasting wheat, popping corn and puffing rice, each in its season. The aroma spread over the village and into the open courtyards, adding to everyone's pleasure. Theirs has been an appreciated service to the village and a steady support of viability.

Four families of *darzi*s live close together in a row of small enclosures. They own no animals and have very little grain to store. Literally *darzi* means "tailor." But village *darzi*s are not like tailors who work in town. Tailors are expected to make garments that fit. *Darzi*s make garments to wear. I call them "rustic tailors." They have one thing in common; they are all poor. One family owns a treadle machine. The others sit on the ground and turn the wheel with one hand and stitch with the other. Each family has its *jajman*s. A *jajman* brings cloth from the town bazaar to his particular *darzi*. The *darzi* turns the cloth into garments and collects grain in payment at harvest time.

For some reason which no one has tried to explain, the *darzi*s and the oil pressers next door consider themselves as one compartment. Both are *Sudra*s, menials, but in entirely different trades. When we left the village in 1930, the oil pressers comprised one large extended family. Their courtyard was crowded with an indefinite number of adults and children. They had two oil presses, the crudest of any village contraption we had seen. A large tree stump gouged out served as mortar and a tall sapling held together by ropes was the pestle. A heavy beam provided pressure, with more pressure added by a woman and a child or two sitting on it along with a rock. The beam was pulled around in a circle by a small blindfolded bony ox. Everything in the courtyard reeked of oil. They lived near our grove beside the *darzi*s, and we stopped there often, fascinated by the pressers and the presses. The *charpai*s on which we sat were soaked with oil as were their clothes.

When I returned in 1961, the extended family had broken down. One branch had a courtyard and storerooms of its own, with its own *jajman*s. The other branch had moved to a new location behind a very large Brahmin enclosure. A long passageway led from the lane to their outer courtyard shared by three brothers. Each of the three had a separate small enclosure with two presses still functioning. All three were as poor as the *darzi*s. My impression had been that they were in a lower social bracket than the *darzi*s. However, I now noticed that there were ties between them and the *darzi*s. When an oil presser's son spoke of a *darzin* (wife of a *darzi*) as his aunt, I was puzzled. But when I asked how she could be his aunt, he laughed at my ignorance. Of course she was his aunt. I had to let it go as one more puzzle unresolved.

The oil pressers had always been poor. But they were sure of a regular income, even though small. After they pressed oil for a *jajman* who had turned his mustard seed over to them, the *jajman* got the oil and the oil presser could sell the oil cake left in the bottom of the mortar. Then, unknown to them, oil mills invaded Mainpuri. Farmers who had been loyal *jajman*s found that it was to their advantage to buy oil from a mill. They ignored the oil pressers and left them without the income on which they had depended and without a trade. The eldest brother got work in the government seed store. The next brother knew where their father had hidden his silver and gold and spent all of it for a cycle for himself. By carrying mustard seed to an oil mill in town and delivering the oil to farmers, he was able to make much more money than he had with his own press. Dinesh, the youngest brother, was the one who was lost. He had an additional handicap. Although he was not crippled from birth, when he was twelve years old, he was the victim of a scheme by a *Pande* Brahmin to undo a rival Brahmin by a fictitious robbery. Dinesh was taken by surprise, pounced on by the police as an accomplice in the robbery, and dragged six miles to Mainpuri. There he was beaten until he was unconscious and then his family was allowed to carry him home. He finally recovered but with a broken bone and a broken spirit. For years afterward, he avoided men of high caste. When I visited his mother in 1961, I noticed the limp and heard the story. It was so shocking that I had to check it with others involved. It proved to be even more unjust and more cruel than his mother's version. He was making a very small income as a vegetable peddlar. I wondered at his cheerfulness until I met his wife. She was beautiful, and she looked up to him as though he were a great success. When he came into their tiny courtyard, her eyes shone. If he brought home only a few wilted vegetables rejected by housewives, she was delighted. She had not been chosen for him by

his parents. He had found her when his first wife died. He
had paid her brothers for her with money earned on a building
project of the *pradhran*'s and had brought her to his courtyard. Without complaint she had endured his disagreeable
mother. He had given his mother the room where his press had
stood. And when she left to visit relatives, he closed the
opening between the room and his small courtyard and made a
new opening into the outer courtyard shared with his
brothers. This gave them a trifle more privacy. They had
lost three sons as infants. In spite of what seemed more
than their share of troubles, they loved each other and were
happy. They were viable.

Just over a high wall in front of their small enclosure
was one of the largest enclosures in the village and owned by
one of the richest Brahmins. He was isolated from the rest
of the village, partly from choice and partly because he
belonged to a *Dube* subcaste of Brahmins unrelated to other
Brahmins and even other *Dube*s. Also he was a newcomer. His
great grandfather had been granted a large piece of land for
services to the government and had moved here. The mango
grove in which we camped was part of it. While we lived in
the grove, there were two brothers. The eldest was Janak,
head of the family and a miser. He checked our every move,
especially when we had visitors. When I planned to sow
tomato seeds beside our tent, he objected. We had not been
able to buy tomatoes in the Mainpuri bazaar and they were not
grown in the fields of *Kachhi*s known as vegetable growers.
He was suspicious. If we planted anything in the grove, we
might lay claim to the ground. We knew that farmers were on
guard against this when they engaged sharecroppers.

In a rural village there was little demand for *Kahar*s as
personal servants. Only Brahmins employed them or their
wives to work in family courtyards. Others became field
workers. Prakash had two *Kahar*s who were like hired men on
American farms. A few emigrated, along with members of
scheduled castes (formerly outcastes). One family went as
far as Calcutta and became prosperous. During the 1960s the
wife, a *Kaharin*, returned to Karimpur with enough money for a
temple. Ironically, the village had its first temple after
Panditji's death. He had performed his duties as priest on
his large open stoop. Also, the temple was not presented by
a Brahmin but by a member of a menial caste. The *Kaharin* had
been living in a large city and was ready to deal with village leaders, all men. She stayed in the *Kahar* compartment,
but spent her days watching the building of the temple. When
it was ready, there was a full-scale opening with two visiting priests from Kanpur and a feast for the whole village.
After the ceremony, a procession was formed with the few

four-wheeled ox carts reserved for weddings. They not only had four wheels instead of the usual two, but decorated canopies. The *Kaharin* sat in the first cart, with Panditji's grandson then acting as priest. On the cart was a *lingam*, symbol of the god Shiva and behind him was Parbati, his consort, a doll that must have been purchased in Calcutta. They paraded up and down the village lanes and ended at the temple. There Shiva and Parbati were installed in the temple. And there they have remained with an iron grating fastened with chains protecting them. Once a year since then, the *Kaharin* returns and ceremonies and feasts are repeated. The annual occasion adds to the pride of the whole village as well as to the humble *Kaharin*, a novel source of viability in a Brahmin dominated community.

Only one occupation has been detrimental to the viability of the village, that of the shepherds. We might expect it to be most beneficial. The shepherd's compartment is on a corner of the village, where they have space for their sheepfolds. Several years ago, a number of them gave up their sheep and changed to goats. There are seasons every year when grass is brown and dry and sheep suffer. Goats thrive on the leaves of neem trees. Long ago the government forestry department planted the trees along main roads. By the time we moved to the village they were large and provided shade for travelers on foot or in ox carts. There were neem trees inside the village as well, shading the carpenter's workshop.

A shepherd walked ahead of his flock of goats carrying a long bamboo pole with a sickle tied to the tip. He cuts off branches of neem trees. And as fast as they fall to the ground, the goats devour them. The neem leaves are used by villagers for medicinal purposes. They are brewed as a drink for certain purposes, or are ground to make a plaster for sprains or breaks. The men make toothbrushes from the stems. When chewed for some time, they roughly resemble brushes. And when teeth are clean, the brushes are thrown away. Denuded neem trees along the roadside are the result of goat herding and many of the trees have died. No one has yet found a solution to the problem, and meanwhile viability suffers.

The village retains its independence by being self-sufficient. Their food comes from their own fields or from fields of neighbors.

Implements are made and repaired by village carpenters who also make door frames. It is customary to sit on the ground. But anyone is free to sit on a *charpai*. Visitors

Time Perspectives in Village India 151

expect to be seated on *charpais*. Village carpenters make them, a wooden frame like a cot, laced with twine which serves as springs.

Utensils for cooking and eating are of brass which is durable. Forks, knives and spoons are not needed, when fingers washed before a meal are just as satisfactory. Water jars, and plates and cups for feasts are made by the village potter who also makes pipes for men to smoke.

Tables are rare, usually in the homes of V.I.P.'s who can afford tables from town. Chairs are almost as rare, and not needed when the ground is more comfortable. Lamps would take too much oil. A few lanterns have appeared, but when the chimney is broken, the lantern is discarded.

Clothing is very simple. Shirts for men and blouses for women are made by the village *darzis*. Both men and women wear *dhotis* of cotton, usually white. A *dhoti* is simply a straight length of cloth. For men, it becomes a loin cloth. For the women, it is draped like a sari, with fewer pleats and without the drape over the shoulder. Brought up the back over the head, it makes it possible for a woman to keep her head covered. Prosperous families may have better material, but the garment is the same. *Dhotis* may be washed by the *dhobi*, the washerman. Or they can be washed at home. After the noon pour-over bath beside a pump or well, a woman can change to a fresh *dhoti* which also serves as a towel. Silk is not used. Men wear heavy leather, pointed slippers when going to town or to a wedding or temple fair. In the village or the fields their feet are bare. Women are barefooted. On special occasions away from home, they may wear sandals bought at the annual district fair.

They provide their own entertainment. The men treat themselves to an occasional singing party. The women and girls not only sing, but dance. They imitate the dancing girls who are engaged by prosperous villagers to entertain wedding guests. Weddings provide a variety of entertainment, and feasts, all enjoyed by everyone but the bride and her parents.

An annual event is the *Ram Lila* drama, still performed, although not every year. Ganesh, the leading singer, Panditji's grandnephew, chants the story verse by verse. And village boys follow with pantomine, scene by scene. They are in gorgeous costumes borrowed from special family chests. They need no rehearsals. They listen to Ganesh and know their part from watching older brothers in earlier performances. Between acts, two hired actors, one playing the part of a woman, insert slapstick entertainment greeted by roars of laughter. When I once asked why this is added to a classical religious performance, the answer was that farmers know the story by heart and would not come except for the comic addition. The drama continues for ten nights, with a large audience every night. No stage props or seats are necessary. The climax, on the tenth night, takes place in a large open space in a neighboring market town. A towering effigy of Ravan is ready, stuffed with straw. He was the king who kidnapped Sita and carried her off to Lanka (now Sri Lanka). The armies of Rama and Ravan clash and the effigy of Ravan is set ablaze while the extra large crowd cheers.

Changes have appeared during recent decades. Some are immediately helpful to viability. Others are still in the balance between positive and negative.

In the schools there were changes. More children were attending the three school sections, elementary, middle and the girls' school. The girls were not segregated because they were girls. It was simpler to put all of the girls into one section rather than try to divide all pupils equally among three sections.

More farmers were buying factory-made steel plows which were used for deep plowing when the ground had lain fallow and had been through the heat of May and June and had baked hard. After that first plowing, they use their old plows with a small metal tip, made by the village carpenters. One tractor was bought by a prosperous farmer and is always in evidence. The owner rents it to farmers able to pay the rent. The rest depend on their oxen.

At least twelve deep well pumps have been installed for irrigation. Farmers were not warned that there was not power enough for the increased demand. As a result all are limited to using their pumps one or two nights a week. The government deep well that had functioned since the early 1950's is still in use.

Chemical fertilizer has had a similar experience. Farmers could buy it from the government seed store. By adding it to the dung available they were getting much larger harvests. Then because of the reduction in the import of petroleum, the farmers had to resort to dung alone. They had found what abundant harvests they could have, which made the cutback more disappointing.

The consolidation of holdings led to more efficient farming for the privileged who discovered that a quiet payment to a member of the consolidation team would assure favors. Court cases followed. And the bitterness that ensued has been damaging.

Elections are among the later innovations. The voting for members of the village council has been disturbing. The men elected know who will expect favors and whom they can punish. But this happens everywhere. It has been the election of the *pradhan*, head of the council, that has disrupted relationships. It is done by secret ballot. At one of the elections I witnessed, there were eight or nine candidates. Each one chose a symbol to help illiterate voters: a plow, a cow and calf, a kite, etc. I wondered why the campaigning was so heated until I was informed that the post was highly lucrative.

The introduction of DDT was heralded as the end of malaria. The government sent teams to every city and village with DDT spray. And for several years we were free of malaria. Now to everyone's disappointment we have learned that there are dangers from the use of DDT. The only alternative thus far has been anti-malaria drugs. One new contribution to prevention which has not yet been questioned is aimed at cholera. Each year there are *mela*s (religious fairs) in different parts of the country. The larger ones attract vast numbers of worshippers. The spread of cholera across the country was traced to *mela*s, especially those where immersion in a river is part of the worship ceremony. Karimpur had its quota of victims. One year the carpenter compartment threatened to be wiped out. Fortunately for us, just before this, the School of Tropical Medicine in Calcutta had created a mixture that acted as preventive for treatment. It was miraculous. And it made it possible to treat cholera victims without risk. I recall vividly going into house after house of carpenters, armed with carbolic acid to spread on polluted *charpai*s and the earth floor underneath, and a bottle of the cholera mixture. Needless to say, we kept our sons segregated! We also attacked the wells. It made my role worthwhile. Now prevention has checked the spread of the cholera at its source. Doctors and their assistants armed with syringes are posted at every approach to a big *mela*. They check incoming trains and buses and cars and all travelers on foot. No one is allowed to pass without an innoculation. In our state, at least, we rarely find a case.

Men of Karimpur took the presence of castes for granted. They also took for granted that castes had always been in the rank familiar to them. Any change that occurred took place in an individual. A man who had been faithful in observing ritual in one incarnation would be promoted to a higher caste in the next. Brahmins could go no higher. They had reached the top. They were satisfied with what they had achieved. However, they must not neglect ritual, lest they be demoted in the next life. This affected relations between men of different castes. A man who was born a menial could not resent a man born a Brahmin. He could only blame himself. If he had been faithful in his ritual in the past, he too might be a Brahmin now.

Scholars might question this reasoning. But it has satisfied villagers. I have been bothered on discovering that a man's way of life, whether upright or corrupt, as we understand them, had no place in his rise or fall, caste-wise. Ritual was the determining factor. Again and again I have been shocked by Prakash and Jiya, Brahmins, in their unethical treatment of others. At the same time they have criticized me for helping others outside the family.

No one in the village was prepared for changes in whole castes. However, the changes did occur, led by caste leaders outside the village. First it came to the *Chamar*s, even below caste level. They removed the hides of dead animals and processed them, then sent them to leather factories in a city. Their name became *Yadav*, and on occasion, they softened the consonant to make *Jadar*, the name of a caste slightly lower than *Kshatriya*, warrior. They had always been more advanced than the other two scheduled castes, sweepers and *Dhanuk*s. They had taken advantage of offers by the government to scheduled castes for scholarships and government posts. They made use of government scholarships for their sons, some of whom found service in government offices. All of the carpenters accepted the opportunity to move up. They had held a respected place in the village. Now they jumped to the rank of Brahmins. Some became members of the *Maithil* subcaste and others chose the subcaste of *Ojha*. Both names were unfamiliar in Uttar Pradesh. They were South Indian. The carpenters donned the sacred thread with six strands, until then worn only by traditional Brahmins. And as *Ojha* and *Maithil* Brahmins, they rank higher than *Pande*s, which most Karimpur Brahmins are. This makes it impossible for the erstwhile carpenter to accept food from *Pande* Brahmins. The traditional Brahmins have always refused food from carpenters, so there is confusion. When I asked Prakash what he thought about Balram, his carpenter *kamin*, wearing the sacred thread, he laughed. All that concerned him was that Balram learn to keep it ceremonially clean. Only one son in the oil presser compartment changed his caste name and joined a caste slightly higher than that adopted by *Chamar*s. His father and uncles scorned the idea. They were proud of their heritage as oil pressers. However, his father was responsible for his change. His father had him trained by a city tailor to be better than the local *darzis*. His father also provided him with a treadle sewing machine. I expected the local *darzis* to resent this as unfair competition, but because of the strange tie between the two communities, there was no sign of competition.

Later, when I talked with Dr. Karve, an eminent anthropologist, about this upward movement of village castes, she exclaimed, "Good for them. Good for them!" She herself was a Brahmin of Brahmins, but understood.

An ordinary village like Karimpur is vulnerable even though surrounded by the invisible barriers described to us by the magistrate. The barriers succeeded in keeping us out until help came from inside. We were harmless. But there have been, and always will be, inimical forces just around the corner, ready to attack. To keep them at a distance, men and women of the village depend on two sources of strength. Their religion, Hinduism, offers them the support of gods and goddesses without number, enough to meet every need. Tradition offers stability provided by wise forefathers.

Hinduism is powerful enough to unite all of India. The diverse languages separate people of province or state from others. Members of each state are loyal to their inherited language. Madrasis think more highly of Tamil as reputed for its classical literature. People of Mysore use Kanada. People of Kerola are strong for Malayalam. There have been efforts to make Hindi the national language through the All-India radio. When for politics or business this is required, people accept it. But they easily revert to their own tongue. Meanwhile, Hinduism continues to draw them together in worship. The same is true of caste. Whatever their caste prejudices may be, they are all one in Hinduism. They may worship different gods, but all gods and goddesses are Hindu. The men and women of Karimpur are devotees of Shiva, the destroyer. In the South, there are more temples to Vishnu, the creator. But villagers, North and South, are prepared to worship both. And both are Hindu. In Karimpur, Shiva is more often worshipped as creator and destroyer. The *lingam*, his symbol, is found in the most personal worship centers just outside the door of high caste families. Villagers also invoke the help of Indra, god of rain, when fields are parched. And they invoke the help of others to meet some special need.

Congregational or group worship is rare. Only once during my years associated with Karimpur, from 1925 until the present, has there been an all-village gathering for worship. It was at the time of a confluence of eight or nine planets when in all parts of the world people were praying to be spared from the destruction prophesied by alarmists. The meeting, very rustic, continued for a whole day and night. It was held in an open space beside the district road. It had been set aside for such a purpose long ago, and still had a low mud wall to mark it. In the beginning someone had blessed it with a peepul tree, held sacred by village Hindus. Panditji presided. He and two younger priests, one seated on each side of him, provided the religious atmosphere. They sat on a slightly raised earth platform, each one with a large volume, the Ramayard, on the ground in front of him. They read aloud in turn all the way through. Men, farmers and tradesmen gathered directly in front of them, seated on the ground in rows. Their wives arrived later after their noonday chores. They were dressed for the occasion in white blouses and colored *dhotis*. They were the older women of their families with grown sons. Their heads were covered, but not their faces. They sat behind the men in small groups by compartments. They had not come to listen, but for the *darshan*, the aura of blessing of Panditji. For them it was an opportunity to visit with neighbors they seldom met. Only on such an occasion did they feel free to leave their courtyards. Children were everywhere, running, hiding, laughing. Young men with lusty voices sat on the low mud wall. They had volunteered to provide background for the reading with their singing. This they did with abandon. They chanted and sang, accompanied by any instruments they could find. They clapped their hands and cheered. Because their contribution was so strenuous, two groups performed, turn by turn. When night came, the women and then the older men left. Younger men came and departed, until only the three readers were left. Nights were chilly. The two young priests wrapped themselves in shawls and slept. Panditji sat straight in his white shirt and *dhoti*, whether reading or waiting his turn. The next morning a crowd of men and boys made the round of the village. They carried a bucket containing ghee and cow's milk and water. This they ladled out into cupped hands held out to them at each door. The ceremony included all the village, at least all of the caste members. It gave me the impression of a united community. In a village where every occasion is welcomed but usually limited to families, it might well be repeated without waiting to ward off danger from the heavens.

While I lived in Karimpur, first with Bill and the boys, and years later alone, I always counted on visiting a spring *mela*. It was held in a group of small temples on the near side of Mainpuri. The men of Karimpur stopped there when on trips to and from town or villages beyond. The women went only once a year for the spring *mela*. They all knew the names of the gods whose figures or lithographed pictures they had seen on other visits. And they remembered the correct procedure. Each one was careful to ring the right bell, to touch the feet of each god or goddess and to leave the prescribed coins or flowers purchased nearby. When they had finished every step, they were free to enjoy the holiday, away from the grind of daily work at home. They had brought a picnic lunch, an important part of a holiday. And they ate and relaxed beside an open well. They had gained merit in the temples and had feasted. Now they were ready for an exciting afternoon. They crossed the road to the district fairgrounds. Government officials in the department of agriculture found in this spring festival an opportunity to demonstrate improved equipment to farmers. And shopkeepers from surrounding towns found it an opportunity to make sales. Jiya made the round of stalls in a large circle at the center of the fairgrounds. Her several daughters-in-law and a few neighbors followed. They admired the jewelry, real and imitation. They looked at new gadgets for making festival sweets. Sandals were a big attraction. They handled every article that charmed them. They argued over prices with the stall keeper. But at the end of the round they had little to carry home, a nose ring or an imitation necklace, and a balloon for each child.

   Those who could afford the bus fare to Soron, about sixty miles from Karimpur, had an added privilege. Soron was on the Ganges and they could add the blessing of a ceremonial bath in her waters. I had just one trip to Soron with several families of Karimpur, including Panditji and Panditain. The women sang all the way. Their songs were chiefly about Sita, the ideal wife. The verses were without number. As we neared Soron, the crowds on foot, in ox carts, or in buses, increased. As we waited at a railroad crossing, a train passed on its way to Soron. It was loaded with pilgrims. Every coach was crowded, and men and women who were "overflow" clung to window and door frames. Passengers on the train shouted to those on the road and all cheered together.

   From the end of the bus line we walked over a mile to the first temple. On the way we passed stalls with effigies of gods and goddesses and large lithograph pictures for visitors to carry home. Monkeys were climbing and jumping from the peepul trees. They were on the alert to steal food or anything unguarded. One picked up the sandal of an unsuspecting young man, carried it to the branch of a tree and dangled it over the water while the owner watched. The monkey finally dropped it in the water and escaped. My duty was to watch over the bundles containing the leftovers of our lunch, while the others bathed. There were stone steps beside the temple leading down into the water. Panditji and Madan, a *Pande* Brahmin, were the first to go down the steps for the ceremonial bath. They took it seriously and performed the complete bathing ritual, ending with immersion. The younger men followed. I was amused when one of them asked to borrow my soap. They knew my habit of carrying soap and a towel on any trip. No one else thought it amusing, as long as it did not interfere with ritual. Last the women bathed, shivering and squirming in the chilly water. They went through an abbreviated ceremony and came out quickly. They changed their *dhotis* as they did at home, draping a clean *dhoti* around themselves, using it as a towel and exposing only their arms and shoulders.

When everyone had bathed and gained merit, we moved on to the larger, more pretentious temples. They were decorated to please village worshippers. There were colored tissue paper flags and streamers and hanging lamps with colored glass shades. Priests were seated on platforms beside the figures of gods. They were ready to bless worshippers and to direct steps in their worship and accept offerings. In each temple the members of our group followed, guided always by priests. On the return trip to the village, no one seemed tired. And the women sang all the way.

Natives of rural north India think of their villages not in terms of yesterday, today, and tomorrow but in terms of generations. They are benefiting from the experience and wisdom of forefathers who survived centuries of brutal attacks by invaders. Their safety depended on high walls of earth as uninviting as possible. Those solid walls are no longer needed and have been supplanted by the invisible walls described by the Magistrate. The new walls must serve as defense against attacks of prosperous neighboring villages or by tempting offers of mechanized farm implements that speed up production with less manual effort. I have known villages undermined by one or both of these. The resulting progress has been spectular, but it has been limited to the already affluent few, while sacrificing the sense of community. The attack long ago drew people within the wall closer together. The modern attacks have proven divisive. By retaining their self-sufficiency along with the best of their body of tradition and their sense of community, the villages of north India can hope to remain viable.

References

1. W. Wiser, <u>The Hindu Jajmani System</u> (Lucknow Publishing House, Lucknow, 1936).

2. C. Wiser, <u>Four Families of Karimpur</u> (Syracuse University, Syracuse, 1978).

3. W. Wiser and C. Wiser, <u>Behind Mud Walls 1930-1960</u>, rev. ed. (University of California Press, Berkeley, 1972).

Daniel G. Bates

6. The Middle Eastern Village in Regional Perspective

Kingsley Davis (1) writes that while we think of the Neolithic or food producing revolution as committing people to the soil and to a sedentary life, in fact, movement has continued to be an important part of human adaptation. In the Middle East, much of this involves people settling in new villages, resettling previously abandoned sites, or leaving villages in order to take up urban residence. Less commonly, but still an alternative to be considered under certain conditions, people may choose to adopt a pattern of regular movement or nomadism. This picture of regular population movement and shifting settlement systems does not accord with our more familiar stereotype of the ubiquitous Near Eastern village...timeless and as fixed in the landscape as the mud and stone from which it is formed. Nevertheless, virtually every village monograph known to this author describes a village population whose local or settled antecedents go back fewer than 150 years. Most Near Eastern villages described in the literature are of very recent settlement. Rural settlements are the products of people responding to particular problems and opportunities, and people change their economic strategies and residential or social groupings as these circumstances change. Settlement systems reflect this as the size and distribution of villages shift through time. This suggests that if we are to understand contemporary village life as well as to make practical recommendations affecting villages we should consider how and why such shifts occur.

Anthropologists have usually examined local level economic and social processes in the course of "case studies" of particular villages or communities in the Near East. Many problems facing the members of village communities originate, however, in the relationship of the local population to other comparable communities, to regional centers or cities, and to national political and economic institutions. The study of such relationships calls for a perspective which views each local community or village as functionally integrated in larger regional and supra-regional systems (2). In discussing the Near Eastern village in a regional perspective, I will review a number of studies in settlement history, and explore the implications of regional variability in settlement and land use in contemporary settings.

One striking aspect of the Near East is the extent to which humans have modified the natural landscape and the extent to which settlement systems responsible for this have changed through time. The 20th century has seen a proliferation of village settlements in conjunction with high rates of internal migration and population growth. In Turkey for example, the greater part of the country has been brought under cultivation through the establishment of a dense network of villages (3). According to Hütteroth, to whose work I will refer again, approximately two-thirds of today's villages in Central Turkey had been village sites in pre-Islamic and medieval periods, but resettled in the 19th or 20th centuries (4). Tunçdelik reports that 1575 villages were registered in official Turkish censuses between the years 1945 and 1965, and suggests that this results from the intrinsic growth of small clusters of households or hamlets which became villages as well as the settlement of new sites (5). The growth of villages, the formation of new village communities and the internal movement of large numbers of people is characteristic of the contemporary Near East, even when considered apart from rural migration to urban centers.

Most of the region is experiencing resettlement of areas where previously villages had been abandoned for a substantial period of time. Cases in point include inner Anatolia (6), eastern Mediterranean and the Aegean coastal plains (7), the Syrian Steppe (8), Palestine prior to the formation of the state of Israel (9), Mesopotamia (10), northcentral Iran (11), southcentral Iran (12), central Afghanistan (13), -- to name only examples selected because the processes and problems of settlement have been the object of direct study. Relatively high rates of rural population growth are obviously related to the expansion of rural settlement and land use intensification (14). The development of rural settlement systems is not consistent or uniform, however, and we cannot simply refer to population pressure as a primary causal factor. From the

16th to the end of the 19th century the central Middle East experienced a long period of rural population decline (15) now reversed by several generations of rapid increase. Still, some rural areas continue to decline (16), some urban centers decline or remain stationary in size in the face of rapid rural growth in their former 'catchment zone' (17), and some areas of rapid growth and settlement expansion in previous decades are today exporting population faster than they produce it (18). Clearly, some areas experience growth or decline simply because of exogenous factors -- for example, routes of communication shift, drought strikes or international agencies fund a local industrial complex. But it is also true for many areas that the development of regional variation as well as temporal changes in settlement and land use are understandable in terms of regular processes (19).

One study based on the assumption that regular processes underlie the development of settlement systems is English's classic study of Kirman basin in central Iran (20). This analysis focuses on patterns of interrelatedness among villages in the Kirman basin and most critically on the dominance of the city of Kirman (21). Urban dominance, English suggests, is the key to understanding settlement and economy in the Kirman basin and elsewhere in the Near East where one sees a widespread pattern of village-level functional differentiation and the primacy of urban-directed exchanges (22). In Kirman, English describes a hierarchical arrangement of diverse settlements: they range in size from a major city, a couple of market towns, large villages, through small villages and mountain hamlets. The organization of settlements is described as a series of concentric rings formed by villages of decreasing size and complexity as one leaves the city itself. English interprets the settlement history of the region in terms of Sassanian state-instigated establishment of a garrison center (ca. 240 A.D.) in Kirman, followed by the spread of village settlements as a result of the deployment of urban controlled capital. It was urban sources of capital which built the elaborate irrigation networks (qanat), dug wells and maintained access to water on which village agricultural life depends. His thesis, relevant to any consideration of village viability, is that urban centers both generate villages -- and keep villages relatively underdeveloped. Most of the villages around Kirman are heavily involved in craft production, especially carpet weaving, and agriculturalists are a majority in only the remotest hamlets and mountain villages. The capital which sustains this craft industry is centered in Kirman, and the urban elite dominate rural modes of production and exchange, preveinting the growth of rival centers.

Costello (23) using a larger sample focused on Kashan in central Iran essentially replicates English's study in describing a settlement hierarchy focused on one major urban center, one which likewise exerted primary political and economic influence over the villages with which it is functionally integrated. Villages in the Kashan region varied considerably in terms of size, crops grown, dependence on irrigation, and in a regular pattern with respect to effective distance from the urban center. Land reform, a factor which was not relevant to English's earlier study, is responsible, Costello maintains, for giving more economic and political power to rural communities, but not sufficient to upset the far-reaching dominance of Kashan city. In short, they conclude the Near Eastern village or the settlement system of which it is part, can be understood in terms of the same selective forces emanating from urban centers that have shaped European settlement history.

What emerges from these urban-focused studies of rural settlement that might help us understand the nature of contemporary village life in the Middle East? One contribution of the settlement hierarchy approach is to empirically describe the range of variation in land use, population size, and technology among settlements which are functionally integrated. Further, the studies become the basis for the comparative study of demographic processes. For example, Costello finds significantly higher rates of out-migration from the upland hamlets (24) reflecting the relative inability of inhabitants to intensify agriculture because of lack of capital or resource limitations. Also both studies establish the basis for the comparative study of the impact of schools, community health centers, developing wage labor markets, and other vehicles of social change. In both studies discontinuities in the distribution and effects of such services emerge according to the size and location of the community. Also the impact of capital is dramatically different in villages situated in different relationships to the regional urban centers. Finally, the studies demonstrate empirically the relatively underdeveloped pattern of trade and exchange among villages and towns, with the growth and dominance of urban centers achieved at the expense of the countryside.

Although these and other studies point to the pivotal roles cities and towns play in extant settlement systems, they do not indicate the historical processes which give rise to shifts in village settlement and in the distribution of rural populations. One recent analysis of late 16th-century settlement history in Palestine, Transjordan and southern Syria (25) focuses explicitly on the spread of village settlements and their changing relation with urban centers. Moreover, the events in greater Syria affecting settlement and land use seem to closely parallel developments elsewhere in the Ottoman Empire during the same time period (26). Hütteroth and Abdulfattah analyze Ottoman tax and census registers from 1595, together with supplemental archival and cartographic data. They document the rapid expansion of rural settlement during the 75 years preceeding the 1595 census as well as the reasons for a decline in village based rural population following the census and continuing until the 19th century. In the development and continuity of village settlements in this vast area -- located between two metropolitan centers of Cairo and Damascus -- security is seen as a primary determinant of village size, location, and indeed, in some instances, the ethnic composition of its inhabitants (27). One of the primary problems these rural dwellers have to contend with is competition from other local populations.

The Hütteroth-Abdulfattah study describes the geographic region of greater Syria in terms of three settlement components: nomads, village farmers and townspeople, with the first two numerically the most important. In fact, towns at the time of greatest rural prosperity in the late 16th century were relatively small. These towns increase in size only as the political and economic situation begins to deteriorate and the number of nomads increase. Here, what would appear to be urban dominance is really a product of village retreat and rural decline when seen from a historical perspective. In the period of strongest central administration, ca. 1595, villages were small with few over 500 inhabitants. These are found distributed in a network within the limitations imposed by rainfall and sources of ground water. There were three areas of particularly dense settlement, two in mountainous zones and one in the Gazza Plain. In general, villagers preferred hilly or mountainous land "except where wide, fertile and well drained plains allowed a concentration of villages to such a degree that the danger of nomadic raids is of relative unimportance -- for the 16th century at least" (28). By the 19th century the settlement frontier had retreated, towns increase in importance and the percentage of nomadic pastoralists increases relative to farmers. Formerly many tribes were taxed, both nomadic and sedentary, and according to the tax records the nomadic segments were probably dependent on markets for the grains on which they lived. By the 17th century the decline in central authority made it difficult to defend plains villages in most areas. The raids of Bedouin and the tribute they exacted defined the settlement frontier and set limits to the size of villages: it selected for larger concentrations of people although rural population in general declines. This is also a period during which local notables come to usurp many functions of the state, the system of taxation is shifted to a new basis, that of tax-farming, and the amount of "surplus production" exported out of the region drops sharply (29). Only in the mountainous zones does a comparison of the 16th century tax registers with 19th century maps and records indicate substantial continuity. Moreover, mountain marketing towns are found in a pattern which the authors describe as a "linear variant" of the Christaller system of rank-size distribution (30). Generally speaking, any such pattern is lacking in the lowlands as far fewer towns exist during the 16th century than would be expected on the basis of rural village population alone, since even relatively remote villages find their marketing needs served by the distant metropolitan centers.

There is other evidence for the integration of producers in an urban-focused system of exchange. The same tax records allow the authors to estimate that in 1595, 18-22% of rural food production was directed to the payment of taxes and land rents to urban based authorities or religious institutions located outside the region (31). Still more grain was marketed by villagers to meet their own needs, and much of this is presumed to have been purchased by nomadic tribesmen in market towns (not directly in barter with villagers). Taxes appear to have been paid in kind, with grain the primary produce. Cotton was raised in some plains villages and arboriculture of various sorts was important in others. In short, considerable functional diversity and regional integration is evident from the register and other sources.

How is all this relevant to an appreciation of contemporary village life and settlement systems? The picture that emerges is that populations in each sector of the economy and settlement system can be seen as committed in varying degrees to exchanges with other groups. As a result levels of agricultural productivity, local political stability, urban investment in agriculture, and the con-

tinued ability of the government to collect taxes and
maintain security are all closely interrelated.

In this system peasant and other rural based
producers vary in their dependence on external sources of
capital, protection, market-supplied consumer goods and foodstuffs. This dependency on external sources of goods,
markets, and political regulation is an important cause of
periodic shifts in economic strategy and in the level of
integration of entire regions. In general, the degree of
dependence might be estimated proportionate to the degree of
specialization of a particular mode of production. Economic
specialization at the village level is measurable in terms
of range and diversity of crops grown, commitment to crafts
or sources of wage labor, and degree of reliance on a
particular element of technology such as tractors, heavy
plows, deep wells or qanats. Functional specialization extends to the social and political areas as well. Tribal
villages, of which there are many in the Middle East, might
be thought of as politically less specialized than comparable non-tribal rural communities. This is because the
local tribal population of which the village is one segment
is more self-reliant in terms of defense, decision-making
and the adjucation of disputes. Remarkable continuity of
settlement sites and in the organization and continuity of
market towns is reflected in the mountains of southern Syria
and Palestine (32). We will return to this point shortly.

An earlier study by Hütteroth of settlement history
in central Anatolia suggests a similar pattern of rural
population increase, proliferation of villages in the plains
followed by a sharp and protracted period of settlement
decline (33). In Anatolia as well as in Palestine settlement remained more stable in the highlands. In the 19th and
20th century expansion of village sites proceeded outward
from the Taurus mountains which ring the southern and western
Anatolian plateau. Security is again a major consideration,
and with the strengthening of the government's control of
regional dynasties and nomadic tribes, resettlement of the
central plateau, and Mediterranean and Aegean coastal plains
followed fairly rapidly. Interestingly enough, resettlement closely paralleled pre-existing patterns of village
location with long abandoned sites reoccupied. Many of the
19th and 20th century settlers were Yoruk or Turkmen pastoralists whose traditional grazing areas became restricted or
whose migratory routes were disrupted. Other settlers (of
differing ethnic groups) were migrants from other regions or
countries to whom the government gave land and other support.
In short, the expansion of village agriculture reflects more

the government's ability to maintain control in the region than the intrusion of urban-based investment capital which did not become important until government control was firmly established. Even then most pre-W.W. II investment was concerned more with the acquisition of land than with increasing productivity (34).

This pattern of internal colonization, intensification of land use -- often accompanied by a shift to agriculture where formerly animal husbandry prevailed -- is not restricted to the Mediterranean littoral. Kortum, in a study of settlement history and land use in the now heavily irrigated Marvdasht plain in Fars, north of Shiraz, describes a long-term cyclical pattern of village expansion and subsequent decline (12). Today, the organization of villages and towns closely replicates the expanded settlement systems of earlier years. While Kortum notes that settlement expansion is associated with periods of strong central government, he supplies detailed information on the locally limiting factors. Certain environmental constraints and sources of hazard or risk for farmers have remained relatively constant over the centuries: irregularity in water supplies needed for irrigation, soil salinity, breakdown of critical elements in the system of water distribution, competition from nomadic pastoralists and political unrest all figure in the contraction of settlements at particular times -- with the most recent low point reached toward the end of the 19th century (35).

Colonization, nomadic settlement and investment in water works proceed in times of political security associated with strong state-level administration. Kortum's survey of 356 villages and three urban centers is remarkable for its use of archaeological and historical evidence in attempting to see the processes in settlement development which underlie the cyclical expansion of village life in the plains. His thesis is that historically the regulation and distribution of the waters of the Kor River through dams and feeder canals extended settlement into otherwise marginal areas. An inability to control the effects of salinization, together with a failure to effect appropriate repairs on the critical river dams, repeatedly led to the abandonment of previously intensively farmed zones -- and the reversion of these lands to pasturage (36).

Today, the Marvdasht Plain is one of the agriculturally most developed regions of Iran, and river supplied water is supplemented in many areas by mechanized deep wells which has significantly extended the settlement frontier and transformed village land use. Cotton is now a major cash crop. Industrialized sugar-beet production is another innovation which similarly increases rural cash income.

The effects of capital investment in irrigation are not limited to extending the frontiers of settled agriculture. It has substantially altered the internal organization of production within the rural community, and changed the relationship of local communities to each other and to the market places which develop to serve them. Kortum analyses the shift in land use and productivity following the completion of the Dariush Kabir Dam in 1972, using data from 10 villages whose lands are watered by the dam. Although sugar beet production was introduced as early as 1935, following construction of the new dam the acreage under beet cultivation increases three-fold and acreage in cotton increases twelve-fold. The proportion of land cultivated for food crops or animal production decreased by 42%, although the total amount of land put to food crops has increased.

In short, diversified subsistence farming has been replaced by an almost exclusively market-directed system of heavily mechanized agriculture. According to Kortum's estimate of agricultural labor, in the pre-irrigation system of land use human labor constitutes one of the principle inputs or "costs". In the new irrigation scheme labor inputs remain comparable to previous levels at 400,000 people/hours per 1000 hectares under cultivation while other costs (exclusive of water itself) rise 520%. All of this dramatic increase in overhead is accounted for by items which have to be purchased outside the farming communities themselves, particularly fertilizer and machine traction, not to mention the capital cost of canal construction. Labor then shrinks by comparison to become a relatively insignificant component of the agricultural economy. While this might be viewed as a measure of the efficiency of this newly commercialized system of land use, it is also indicative of increasing regional and national integration and the dependence of local farmers on distant markets and sources of capital. A commitment to the market place and a concentration on a limited range of intensively grown crops, such as cotton or sugar beets, seriously disadvantages the small producer, former sharecroppers and tenants. In Marvdasht, as elsewhere in the agriculturally developed Middle East, such shifts in land use have forced many to seek nonagricultural sources of employment even when this means migration to the already swollen metropolitan centers.

Quite apart from the not-so-hidden social costs, this high level of regional integration based on the marketing of cash crops may be inherently unstable for the same reasons suggested for earlier periods of settlement retreat. The environmental constraints Kortum identified remain as potential problems; in some cases they are exacerbated by modern technology. Not only does soil salinization persist as a long-term threat, but modern drilled wells have speeded up this process as wells have begun to alter water tables, disrupting the traditional small-scale qanat water supply system. Susan Lees in a study of irrigation in the valley of Oaxaca, Mexico, points out that irrigation sponsored by the government encouraged local farmers to intensify production and water usage beyond limits of environmental safety (37). Water, for example, is consumed in great amounts to grow profitable cash crops, threatening the water table and traditional water supply system (38). In Iran, as in many other countries, the government is interested in increasing food production and has done so through massive technological intervention as with the Dariush Kabir Dam. On a smaller but broader scale, it has made available credit and other supports for the individual farmer or investor. While impressive success has been achieved in productivity one must at least consider the possibility some of these innovations may be detrimental in the long-term, and that intensively worked lands may once again be given over to mixed farming on a drastically reduced scale.

This point is made as a more generalizable model by Robert Adams with respect to the settlement history of Mesopotamia which he describes as a shifting frontier represented by "...successive phases of unification and dissolution..." (39). He considers "agriculture and pastoralism on the alluvial plains of lowland Mesopotamia as interdependent forms of adaptation to the deep, prevailing uncertainties that largely originated with unpredictable water supplies for irrigation and a hot, arid climate" (40). The fact that villagers can and do regularly shift from farming to pastoralism makes such settlement systems inherently unstable. The most reliable adaptation to much of this region, he suggests, is not intensive agriculture but extensive diversified agriculture combined with a strong animal husbandry component (41). The unreliable flow of river water and precipitation together with water's critical role in determining crop yields, predispose villagers to over-irrigate. This increases the risk of salinization and concomitant long term degradation. Added to uncertainty arising from economic problems, political breakdowns also encourage people to pursue flexible subsistence strategies.

The cyclical patterns of settlement that Hutteroth, Kortum and others describe represent the outcome of individual strategies in making a living. If, as Adams suggests, an optimal strategy for the household is flexibility in managing its resources, it might be useful to see how rural people are coping in a rapidly changing economic environment. One region for which household-level economic data are available is the area of Turkmen settlement centering on the city of Gombad-i Kavus in northeastern Iran. Here, too, a regional perspective is helpful in understanding how households in different sectors of the economy and in different villages manage their resources in land and labor. The region resembles Marvdasht described by Kortum in high rates of capital investment in agriculture and in its dependence on national markets for the sale of a limited number of cash crops. It also is similar to Marvdasht in that rural wage labor is increasingly important.

In 1973 I carried out a survey of most of about 120 villages belonging to the Göklan Turkmen in northeastern Iran.(42). On the basis of this survey I selected as representative of the region about 40 villages occupying lands contiguous to one another, and served by the marketing and administrative center of Gombad-i Kavus. These villages in turn formed the basis for a sample of 16 communities selected for more intensive economic and demographic study. The villages were systematically selected on the basis of differences in environmental setting, village size and village wealth as measured by total holdings in land, livestock and major equipment such as tractors and combines. Within each community either all Turkmen households were interviewed, or a sample was drawn reflecting the distribution of wealth within the village. As the economic data from the 513 households interviewed are not completely analyzed I will restrict myself to general and preliminary observations.

The southern portion of the Gurgan Plain occupied by the Göklan Turkmen, and especially the area along and south of the Gurgan River, has been the locus of rapid mechanization, cashcropping, and urban-based agricultural investment. All of the Göklan villages find their primary marketing needs served by the administrative center of Gombad-i Kavus, a city of 25,000. Some marketing, provisioning and tractor repair is carried out in two smaller towns, but Gombad-i Kavus is clearly paramount in the local economy. Wealthy land owners frequently maintain urban residences here in addition to village dwellings. Major banks and national institutions have offices in Gombad-i Kavus, and here reside the businessmen, brokers and co-operatives which ultimately integrate the region with the national market.

The Göklan, formerly nomadic pastoralists, have been settled in the area for over 100 years although recently there has been an extension of village settlement into lowland areas. Villages range in size from 11 households, in one case, to over 150 with the median being 45 households. Although there is considerable variability in the size of households, the mean number of people who reside together and act as one economic unit is 6.3 per household for the entire sample. As might be expected, there is considerable variation in household wealth, and this is significantly reflected in the size of domestic units. Wealthier families have larger households. Throughout the region wealth is a close determinant of household size, with the only exception being one village which is virtually landless. The social structure of households similarly displays considerable variability. Without attempting to give more than an impression here, extended households comprised of parents and one or more married sons are almost exclusively found in the lowland villages, especially those where land values are high. Instances of more than one domestic family forming a unit of shared consumption and expense are entirely restricted to these communities and to relatively wealthy families within them. Polygynous households are relatively common (12%) in the areas of most intensive land use, the irrigated sectors of the lowlands, while averaging less than half this rate for the rest of the region.

With respect to population processes, the Turkmen might be termed a "natural fertility" population in that modern methods of contraception and deliberate techniques of family planning are not employed. The overall annual growth rate can be estimated provisionally at 2.5 per annum, with very high rates of general fertility as the number of births per year per 1000 women aged 15-44 is 214.62 (averaged over four years). Mortality is correspondingly high, particularly among children in their first year with 172.75 dying per 1000 live births (averaged over four years). Analysis to date indicates a consistent pattern regarding fertility throughout the region, with no apparent significant correlation with wealth or with particular land use

regimen. The one village which is dependent on wage labor
as its residents lack land has a substantially lower completed family size, 4.5 for women aged 40-44 as compared
with 7.3 for the other communities, but the small size of
this village sub-sample precludes concluding that this
difference is due to economic circumstances. What the
figures do indicate is that the Göklan Turkmen farmers while
experiencing rapid economic change have yet to respond
demographically to them. We might expect, however, that
such changes in fertility, mortality or migration as will
develop, will largely parallel the increasing economic
differentiation among villages, and more importantly, social
and economic differences among households.

Topographic characteristics and the availability of
water affect land use and agricultural potential...and hence
the structure of capital investment. Lowland villages where
flat terrain and either sufficient rainfall or a potential
for irrigation have attracted the highest rates of investment. This is evidenced by high land values, tractors,
water pumps, drilled wells, canalization, combines and motor
vehicles. Villages whose lands are irrigated, either by
water taken from the Gurgan River or by means of privately
owned drilled wells, display considerable internal economic
and social stratification. The first impression one gets is
of great contrasts in quality of dwellings, dress, and
general standard of living. These villages tend to be large,
and many are politically dominated by powerful families, the
heads of which are called "khan". The influence of the
khan, a traditional title for political leaders among the
Göklan, extends to most areas of social and economic significance. Their power is ultimately based in extensive
holdings in land, animals, and in the close relationship
these men maintain with such urban institutions as the office
for land registration, the district governor's office and
other national agencies. The khans farm their lands using
modern technology, and are often the first to adopt mechanized equipment.

Although land reform resulted in the distribution
of some land in every community, 28% of the population is
presently landless. Some households did not receive land
grants, some households were formed in the 11 years since
land was distributed and still others have sold the lands
they received. In the areas of most intensive agriculture,
particularly where cotton and grain are grown on irrigated
lands, rates of landlessness run much higher (about 45%)
among Turkmen households.

There appear to be two main reasons for this. The first is that small landowners are at a competitive disadvantage in an economy restricted to a limited number of cash crops. The cash required to plant a hectare of cotton is 15 times that required to plant grain in the less mechanized system of agriculture found in the uplands. Second, the demand for labor in cotton, combined with under employment in other sectors of the economy, attracts landless migrants. However poor conditions may be for those without land, it is preferable for them to live in communities where at least seasonal employment is available. Judging from patterns of indebtedness noted in interviews, and from the frequency with which small holders turn their land over to others to farm, it appears that alienation of land is an ongoing process.

A few communities have attracted migrants from Sistan and Baluchistan where drought conditions have led to the abandonment of villages in some areas. These non-Turkmen migrants are almost invariably without title to land, and compete with the landless or poor Turkmen in the rural labor market. While mechanization has, as Kortum suggests for Marvdasht, reduced the relative value of labor in farming, there is nevertheless a strong demand for workers in cotton. However, what distinguishes this labor demand is its seasonality and low level of remuneration. The seasonal nature of labor demand in heavily specialized agriculture means that employment opportunities are great enough during at least one part of the year to bring in workers from other poorer areas. In 1973 the region was attracting both seasonal and permanent migrants. These newcomers reside in separate sections of the Turkmen-dominated villages, do not intermarry with the Göklan, and by their presence contribute to a growing social differentiation which is in addition to that occuring within the Turkmen community itself.

This economic environment has produced at least one village comprised very heavily of the landless, both Turkmen and Baluch. Of about 45 households, half are Turkmen and the majority of both ethnic groups are without fields. Those who own land hold it in small amounts and the households are for the most part laborers on nearby estates. This functionally specialized settlement is representative of some of the changes associated with agricultural intensification. Villagers depend on variable opportunities for wage labor and almost entirely on purchased food items. It is quite uniformly poor, households are uniformly nuclear in social structure with pervasive evidence of economic deprivation. It is a rural slum in the social as well as the economic sense of that term.

Adjacent to areas suitable for deep-well and river irrigation are villages to the north whose crops depend on rainfall and where open rolling fields permit large-scale grain cultivation in conjunction with limited cotton production. These villages, too, display considerable economic differentiation among households in terms of land ownership, but are ethnically homogeneous as few non-Turkmen have settled in them. The demand for seasonal labor in grain production is less than in cotton. While most of the villages whose lands are substantially irrigated contain khan families, most of the lowland grain producing villages do not. The two or three men in this area who are considered "khan" have land distributed among several villages, some of it rented annually, some of it used on a share basis, and some purchased outright. These families are important in the organization of modern agriculture: they invest heavily in equipment, purchase crops for resale from others, and on occasion extend credit. Considerable effective power still rests with these rural-dwelling leaders among the Göklan.

In the villages of lowland grain production rates of landlessness (19%) are lower than in areas of cotton production. In areas of major cotton production small holders, owning under five hectares of irrigated land, usually work their fields themselves. In grain cultivation there is a stronger tendency for those owning less than ten hectares to rent their land out. It is not possible to isolate all of the factors involved in particular decisions, but over half the households with fewer than ten hectares of non-irrigated land rent their land to others. Most of these families then supplement this income by selling labor. Often this involves seasonal work in cotton. Families holding more than ten hectares almost always work their own fields, hiring labor as needed, and a number in each village systematically acquire access to other fields through rental or on a cropsharing basis. In these communities the system of "crop sharing" long considered the traditional means of access to land in the Middle East is partially reversed. Previously, landless families would gain access to land by working fields of others for a fixed share of the crop. Now it is the landed households who acquire land in this manner since they control both the capital and equipment needed, while labor inputs are less important. This is evident even where a small landowner works his own fields. Tractors are engaged to do the plowing and seeding, and combines are hired to harvest the grain.

In the upland areas to the east of Gombad-i Kavus where

the Gurgan River originates, there is a sharply different pattern of land use and labor deployment. Villages in the hilly uplands, along the course of the Gurgan River, and to the south in mountain villages, where semi-Alpine climatic conditions prevail, share a number of environmental features. Broken terrain usually prevents the organization of large open fields and the growing season is short. The mountain villages, and some of the villages along the upper Gurgan, are subject to prolonged snowfall, leaving them isolated for weeks - even months on occasion.

The principle grain crops are barley and wheat. Sunflowers and melons are occasionally raised as cash crops. Some fruit is grown for household consumption and in a few villages mulberrys are grown for a cottage industry of silk worm production. There has been little outside investment in these villages; no estates or large farms are owned by urban residents, and there is little local investment in machinery and no mechanized system of water utilization. Overt signs of economic and social stratification are comparatively muted, although there is clear differentiation by wealth in each community. The range of variation in wealth is quite limited; very few families have more than 20 hectares, most have between 5-10 hectares, with about 15% of the households of the six villages sampled being totally without land.

While spatially remote from Gombad-i Kavus, all households nevertheless depend on market-supplied goods to meet most consumption needs. Even grain is today ground in mills located in towns, and many who raise wheat simply sell it for flour. Barley, however, is rarely sold but consumed by the household. What distinguishes farming in this area is that small farmers are more likely to work their own lands, and unlike in much of the lowlands, those who rent lands from others are themselves more apt to be small rather than larger owners. Cash inputs are relatively low compared with other more mechanized forms of agriculture. Much plowing is done by tractors and most grain harvesting is done by combine. Combine equipment is usually owned by farmers in lowland villages and circulates through the high valleys after harvesting is completed in the lowlands. Modern self-propelled combines manage to follow almost any trail that can be handled by a tractor and thus appear unexpectedly in very remote villages. Tractors are not found in every village. A few are owned by residents of the highland villages while others are brought up from the lowlands. Some land is put to sunflowers and melons in cooperation with either lowland landowners or entrepreneurs who supply working capital.

The Middle Eastern Village   177

In general there is little entrepreneural activity involving capital investment in land development or intensification and there is little evidence of expansion of settlement, certainly nothing comparable to what has occurred in the plains.

If we look at the region as a whole we see growing differences among villages while they are integrated by patterns of investment and marketing. Agricultural equipment owned by families resident in one village frequently is used on a rental or share basis in other communities. A small number of combines serve the grain harvesting needs of many villages. This suggests that while every household is dependent on mechanized equipment, those owning it enjoy a substantial competitive advantage. They can employ it to secure additional sources of income, one that is less vulnerable to market fluctuations than are grains and cotton. Much of the marketing of cash crops, particularly cotton, is done through the medium of a "futures" market (<u>selef</u>) in which small producers usually sell their crop before it is harvested. Even the landless make use of this institution. Frequently households are engaged to plant, weed, and pick cotton for a fixed share of the crop. They most commonly sell this prior to harvest. A small number of buyers, both village and urban-based, act as middlemen in this procedure. This parallels networks of credit which are important in enabling households to secure purchased seeds, fertilizers, rent or to purchase and repair equipment. Most small landowners were found to be in debt. While there is some lending of money among families of nearly equal wealth, the common pattern is for debts to be incurred with merchants in town, or loans acquired from wealthier members of the villages (or outside it if related). These debts are usually secured by advance sales of cotton or other crops.

In this increasingly specialized and centralized system of production some individuals find their economic options restricted. Most families seem to attempt to stay as flexible as possible through the pursuit of mixed economic strategies. Their ability to do this varies with their circumstances. Landless families can sell labor or work a tract of cotton for a share of the crop. Rarely can they do both. They can also move, and we might see this option exercised by more in the future. Families with small holdings, the definition of which varies according to the productive value of the land, often rent their lands out on shares, while then working the lands of others for either cash wages or for shares. This, together with selling their produce as <u>selef</u>, or in advance of harvest, enables them to minimize some hazards. Some families owning more than median holdings in every village tend to be acquiring land and thus putting together sizable spreads on which they can raise a variety of crops. Often the same families own machinery which they can rent to others. The very wealthy invest in urban real estate, act as brokers, and purchase livestock -- the one agricultural commodity in Iran which has consistently risen in price.

While each household may be trying to cope through the maintenance of alternative sources of income and various means of "hedging bets", the net result contributes to increasing specialization and dependence on the national market. For example, owners of tractors and similar equipment seek to supplement their income by employing them in areas where local productivity would scarcely permit local farmers to purchase them. Farmers investing in deep wells find that they have to continually compete for water with owners of other wells, and often must pay fines or bribe officials to continue using the wells. All of which increases their dependence on high rates of cash flow, and encourages them to seek further investments. Some of the deep wells have adversely affected traditional means of irrigation. In one village private wells have replaced a communal system of water distribution in which all landowners could purchase water. This has resulted in considerable economic hardship for some. The spread of expensive equipment such as large tractors and combines is quite similar in effect. The use of such equipment where owned by a limited number of households, but utilized by many, tends to decrease household self-sufficiency. It raises the cash requirements of farming, while the relative value of household labor as an input declines.

Summary and Concluding Remarks

The preceding discussion has attempted to point out some of the obvious factors which have affected rural settlement and hence village life. The Middle East may be something of an extreme case in terms of the shifts which have occurred in settlement systems. However it is likely that, given global rates of population increase, widespread patterns of rural investment and changing methods of agriculture, most rural settlement systems are being transformed every bit as much as are the urban centers to which they are articulated. We have long focused on problems of urbanization in developing countries while assuming that rural sectors are relatively static.

In the Middle East it appears that some of the same processes which have in the past led to the expansion and decline of particular regional settlement systems are still operant. In brief, rural development based on agricultural intensification depends on high levels of security and results from urban demand for agricultural products. In meeting these, local producers find themselves increasingly dependent on far-reaching networks for marketing their produce, maintaining security, and ensuring access to externally produced items on which local specialization rests. In the Middle East it seems that agricultural intensification usually implies concentration on a few items, be they animals, tree crops, cotton or grains, with productivity increased through irrigation, field preparation and now, inputs requiring cash credits. Extreme specialization results in entire villages raising crops which they do not consume directly, or even in communities whose specialization is simply the supply of labor in agro-industry. While such specialization and attendant high levels of productivity may have great benefits for some households in the rural economy and for the nation as a whole, there are costs to be paid. One major cost is that any problem which affects one sector of the rural economy will have adverse effects elsewhere. For example, now even mountain villages in Gombad-i Kavus region rely heavily on mechanized plowing and harvesting. Should an oil shortage occur they will be affected. Moreover, the effects will not be limited to local shortages, but will produce disruption in the system by which goods are transported to and from markets. More immediate to most farmers in that region are changes in the price of cotton which, should it fall again, could result in drastic changes in the way in which land is used -- and who owns it. Another source of risk is environmental. Intensive agriculture pursued under the stimulae of market demand or organized by distant institutions may lead to the depletion of soil and water resources or making them more costly to get at. This has been a reoccurring problem in much of the world's arid and semi-arid zones. Other costs to be reckoned include the social costs of maintaining an increasingly under-employed rural labor force and the urban absorbtion of displaced rural peoples. In Turkey, for example, much rural-urban migration is from the developed rural regions rather than the traditionally poor eastern and mountainous zones.

These observations do not predict the demise of intensive agriculture in the Middle East, or even suggest that recent developments in the agricultural sector are, on balance, a bad thing. They simply suggest that probably village life today is no less precarious than in previous eras in the Middle East. And it is likely that areas where some of the most spectacular gains in productivity and land use intensification have been made will also be the areas hardest hit by any development which threatens the exchange which bind them to distant cities and markets.

What practical suggestion arises from this review of settlement and village life? One might be that planners concerned with rural development should view patterns of investment, deployment of machinery and labor within a regional perspective. Costs and benefits associated with agricultural development are borne differently by individuals in different sectors of the rural economy. Moreover, one cannot estimate potential costs and benefits in terms of individual villages. Adjacent to prospering villages one often finds communities whose residents have paid a price for the prosperity of their neighbors -- as where settlements of poorly paid workers serve the needs of agro-industry. As we have seen, villages are not uniform, and a regional perspective is needed in order to assess their variability, specialization and functional interdependence.

References and Notes

1. Kingsley Davis, "The Migrations of Human Populations," Scientific American, Vol. 231 No. 3 (1974), pp.92-105.
2. Paul English, City and Village in Iran: Settlement and Economy in the Kirman Basin, (University of Wisconsin Press, Madison, 1966), p. xviii. See also Daniel Bates and Susan Lees, "The Role of Exchange in Productive Specialization," American Anthropologist Vol. 79 No. 4 (1977), pp. 824-841.
3. Wolf-Dieter Hütteroth, "The Influence of Social Structure on Land Division and Settlement in Inner Anatolia," in Peter Benedict et al, Eds. Turkey: Geographic and Social Perspectives, (E. J. Brill, Leiden, 1974), pp. 19-47.
4. See Hutteroth (3), p. 21.
5. Necdet Tunçdilek, "Types of Rural Settlement and Their Characteristics," in Peter Benedict et al, Eds. (3), pp. 48-70.
6. See Hütteroth (3) and Wolf-Dieter Hütteroth, Landliche Siedlungen im südlichen Inneranatolien in den letzen vierhundert Jahren, (Göttingen Geographische Abhandlungen, Heft 46, Göttingen, 1968) for good discussion; see also H. Wenzel, Forschugen in Inner

anatolien II: Die Steppe als Lebensraum, (Geographisches Instituts Kiel, 1973).

7. See Mustafa Soysal, Die Siedlungs und Land haftsentwicklung der Çukurova, Erlanger Geographische Arbiten, Sonderbank 4, (Fränkischen Geographischen Gesellschaft, Erlangen, 1976); John Kolars, "Systems of Change in Turkish Village Agriculture," in Peter Benedict et al, Eds. (3); Mübeccel Kiray, "Social Change in Cukurova: A Comparison of Four Villages," in Peter Benedict et al, Eds. (3); Willi Johannes Eggeling, Beitrage zur Kulturgeographie des Küçük Menderes Gebietes, unpublished dissertation, Ruhr-Universität Bochum, (Bochum 1973.)

8. See Barbara Aswad, Property Control and Social Strategies: Settlers on a Middle Eastern Plain (University of Michigan, Museum of Anthropology, Anthropological Papers No. 44, 1971); Louise Sweet, Tell Toqaan: A Syrian Village (Ann Arbor: University of Michigan, Museum of Anthropology, Anthropological Papers No. 14, 1960); Daniel G. Bates, Nomads and Farmers: A Study of the Yörük of Southeastern Turkey (Ann Arbor: University of Michigan, Museum of Anthropology, Anthropological Papers No. 52, 1973).

9. See Wolf-Dieter Hütteroth and Kamal Abdulfattah, Historical Geography of Palestine, Transjordan and Southern Syria in the Late 16th Century, Erlanger Geographische Arbeiten, Sonderband 5, (Fränkischen Geographischen Gesellschaft, Erlangen, 1977).

10. See Robert McC. Adams, "The Mesopotamian Social Landscape: A View from the Frontier," in Charlotte B. Moore, ed., Reconstructing Complex Societies: An Archaeological Colloquium, supplement to the Bulletin of the American Schools of Oriental Research No. 20, (1972), pp. 1-22. See also Robert Fernea, "Gaps in the Ethnographic Literature on the Middle Eastern Village: A Classificatory Exploration," in Richard Antoun and Illiye Harik, Eds., Rural Politics and Social Change in the Middle East, (Indiana University Press, Bloomington, 1972) for a good ethnographic review.

11. See William Irons, The Yomut Turkmen: A Study of Social Organization Among a Central Asian Turkic-Speaking Population, (Ann Arbor: University of Michigan, Museum of Anthropology, Anthropological Papers No. 58, 1975).

12. See Gerhard Kortum, Die iranische Landwirtschaft zwischen Tradition und Neuerung, Fragenkreise, Nr. 23512, (Blutenburg Verlag, München, 1977); Gerhard Kortum, Die Marvdasht-Ebene in Fars: Grundlagen und Entwicklung einer alten iranischen Bewasserungsland-

schaft, (Selbsverlag des Geographischen Instituts der Universität Kiel, Kiel, 1976). Also see V.F. Costello, Kashan: A City and Region of Iran, (University of Durham Center for Middle Eastern and Islamic Studies Publications, Durham, 1976) and English (2).
13. See Louis Depree, Afghanistan, (Princeton University Press, Princeton, 1974). See also Robert Canfield, Faction and Conversion in a Plural Society: Religious Alignments in the Hindu Kush (Ann Arbor: University of Michigan, Museum of Anthropology, Anthropological Papers No. 50, 1973).
14. See Frederic Shorter and Tekce Belgin, "Demographic Determinants of Urbanization in Turkey," in Peter Benedict et al, Eds., (3) for Turkish example.
15. See Hütteroth and Abdulfattah (9) for a good case study.
16. See Peter Benedict, "The Changing Role of Provincial towns: A Case Study from Southwestern Turkey," in Peter Benedict et al, Eds., (3). Also see Brian Spooner, Ecological Research in Turan, American Institute of Iranian Studies Newsletter, Vol. 10, No. 2 (1978), pp. 3-5.
17. See Benedict (16) and Soysal (7) for examples.
18. See Kiray (7) for example.
19. For a good review of the behavioral implications of the regional analytic approach see Gregory Johnson, "Aspects of Regional Analysis in Archaeology," in Annual Review of Anthropology, (Annual Reviews Inc., Palo Alto, 1977); also see Carol Smith, ed., Regional Analysis Vols. I and II, (Academic Press, New York, 1976). To date most regional analyses of settlement in the Middle East have been descriptive and with little attempt at formal modeling. Costello (12) is a notable exception.
20. English (2), especially the introduction for good description of the utility of the regional approach.
21. English (2), 22-23; 86.
22. English (2), pp. 65-97.
23. See Costello (12), especially pp. 28 ff.
24. See Costello (12), p. 57.
25. See Hütteroth and Abdulfattah (9), pp. 1-16.
26. See Hütteroth (6), see Wenzel (6) and Soysal (7).
27. See Hütteroth and Abdulfattah (9), p. 47, p.53-4.
28. See Hütteroth and Abdulfattah (9), p. 86.
29. Hütteroth and Abdulfattah (9), pp. 56-59.
30. Hütteroth and Abdulfattah (9), pp. 86-87.
31. Hütteroth and Abdulfattah (9), pp. 107-110.
32. Fernea (10) and Xavier De Planhol, "Regional Diversification and Social Structure in North Africa and the Islamic Middle East: A Geographic Approach," in Richard Antoun and Illiye Harik, Eds., (10), pp. 103-115,

recognize this in their proposed typologies of different types of villages.
33. See Hütteroth (3) and Hütteroth (6) and Wenzel (6).
34. See Eggeling (7) and Soysal (7).
35. See Kortum (12), pp. 137-139.
36. See Kortum (12), p. 67 and p. 137.
37. Susan H. Lees, "Hydraulic Development as a Process of Response," Human Ecology, Vol. 2 No. 3 (1974), pp. 159-175.
38. See Lees (37), p. 160.
39. See Adams (10), p. 2.
40. See Adams (10).
41. See Adams (10), p. 8 and p. 15.
42. The work was supported by grants from the Ford-Rockefeller Program in Social Science, Law and Population Policy, and by an N.I.H. award, HD 08892. The fieldwork was coordinated with a project being carried out by Willian Irons among the Yomut Turkmen. His monograph (11) is an excellent source of information about the region, and about the contemporary Turkmen society.
43. I am grateful to Ülkü Bates, Francis Conant, Carol Hirsch, Gregory Johnson, Susan Lees and Priscilla Reining for their valuable assistance.

_____ *Molly G. Schuchat, James D. Jordan*

7. Continuities and Discontinuities in China: The Natural Village and the Production Brigade

Introduction

The Village we are discussing is a peasant village, that is, a community that is part of a system that includes cities. Redfield (1) says that the peasant lives where he has always lived and the city has grown up out of a kind of life that is his, too. Perhaps its influence came from nearby, and the peasant has been there to sell or contribute labor, or maybe the city is only far away and its influence reaches him after a delay. But in either event, the peasant is long used to the city and its ways are, in altered form, part of his ways.

Redfield further suggests that there are varying forms of political adjustment to the central power, which may be a city-state, a kingdom or an empire. The representative of this central power might be someone derived from the village itself, as when the literate Chinese villager who had passed an exam dealt on behalf of the village with the bureaucrats in the town and province.

It is worth noting here that Redfield, and Wolf (2) a decade later, relied primarily on the ethnographic work of native Chinese anthropologists for their baseline data. In many other parts of the world, the ethnographies of the nineteen thirties, forties and fifties were written by western anthropologists who moved into the area for their field work. But Fei Hsiao-t'ung was trained in China and in London and worked with Redfield in Chicago and Peking, and Martin Yang was trained both in China and at Columbia (3).

Villages are old and geographically fixed in China -- as is civilization. But Leeds suggests (4) that the persons who live in the villages, and their roles within and without them, may not be as fixed. Leeds also reminds us that when subsistence and market orientations coexist, the sources of each may be quite differentiated so that they may be capitalist and noncapitalist at the same time. The internal organization of peasant villages are of great complexity and into them are interwoven most of the important societal role structures and their institutions. In these, peasants are ceded the right to maintain internal organization by convention or contract with the state, until such time as peasantry is seen as stepping out of bounds. That is the point at which the right is abrogated and the peasants are crushed.

Leeds points out a role separation between peasancy, as he calls it, and the rural proletariat, who have no say in anything about the village. This is primarily because they have no jural rights to land at all, but are simply mechanical tools in the agricultural production whose capital, organization, administration, production and surplus value are controlled by incumbents of a mutually exclusive role category. Leeds' definition is quite similar to Mao Tse-Tung's 50-year-old description of a landless peasant (5).

Wolf, writing earlier than Leeds (6), had pointed out two characteristics of peasant social organization: a strong tendency toward autonomy on the part of households and an equally strong tendency to form coalitions on a more or less flexible basis for short-range ends. In entering a coalition the household cannot over-commit itself. Wolf says that this was clearly understood by those modern political figures who realize the potential power of peasants when aroused to common action, but are equally aware of their inability to remain organized both in action and afterwards. Chinese responses to this problem will be apparent through our discussion of the manner of turning indigenous villages into contemporary production brigades.

In summary, then, peasants in their village form a part-culture, the other part being in the city. The peasantry is aware of the city and of the idea of literacy. The city-state requires that the peasants live at more than a subsistence level so that they may pay taxes or tribute and/or supply labor for the usually distant state. For some of these purposes, the villagers may form short-lived groups, but the all encompassing needs of their own family organizations limits enduring extra-familial, extra-village ties in traditional peasant societies.

It is useful to keep in mind Wiser's discussion of Indian villages in this symposium. As she says, village walls keep strangers out. Chinese villages are like the

The Village in China   187

Indian ones, closely associated collections of family dwelling units. Farmers live inside their villages, not on their land, for security. For security, side walls adjoin those of neighbors. Villagers do not easily incorporate strangers, but deal with them through designated persons.

Also in this volume, Maccoby lists four psycho-social needs that should be met in village cultural development: (1) the need for security -- which is survival support; (2) equity, encompassing justice and freedom from exploitation; (3) participation; and (4) individuation. The following discussion should indicate to what extent the natural village responded to these social needs and to what extent the current socio-political organization in China allows villagers to retain or develop them.

No One Typical Village

China is a diverse continental nation with mountains, deserts, plateaus, highlands, oases, and river valleys. Extremes of heat and cold are encountered in several locations. As to the agriculture the peasants practice, it ranges from a complex of corn-sorghum-winter wheat to double crop rice, with rice-tea cultivation important in some areas. The most significant agricultural division, of course, separates the rice growing southern provinces from the dry-grain growing northern provinces where wheat and coarse grains dominate. Potatoes, grown in all regions, provide a not-inconsiderable part of the diet.

A "typical village" is difficult to pin down because of the just-stated variations in topography and geography, both of which affect the demographic realities of villages. Generally speaking, we are dealing with a collection of households containing somewhere between two hundred and two thousand individuals. In aggregates beyond that size it is hard to know everyone face to face, which is also essential to village life. We are talking, moreover, about more than one large extended family. In each village there are people who are not related to each other and wives come from other nearby villages to live in their husbands' households. In each village there are part-time specialists who perform needed functions for the continuation of local life. There are, as well, specialists who come to the village to supply seasonal needs and there are peasants with such small holdings that they serve part-time as hired laborers. And we are speaking of villages that are not only old but to the very recent time have exhibited a nature not only durable but largely static. Let us examine, therefore, a specific village, like thousands of other villages, but differing in minor ways.

188   Schuchat and Jordan

Evolution of the Natural Village

The example we present here is the village of Li Chia T'ai (The Li Family Place), in Yang Chou (Upper River) Prefecture, Ching Chiang (Clear River) County of Chiangsu (River Revival) Province (7).

Li Chia T'ai provides examples of most of the elements of a Chinese Village. Its name alone suggests the origin of many Chinese villages. Most villages in China, and elsewhere probably, develop around a dominant family. A couple of well known examples in China are Chang Chia K'ou (The Chang Family Depot), a commercial center on the Great Wall on the Inner-Mongolian-Chinese border; and Shih Chia Chuang (The Shih Family Store), now the capital of Hopei Province and an important railway center on the Chinghan (Peking-Hankow) railway line.

Li Chia T'ai has had a population ranging between 500 and 1000 during the Ch'ing dynasty (1644-1912), through the Republican period (1912-1949), and up to the present. It is situated a few miles north of the Yangtze River about 100 miles upstream from Shanghai, and is an agricultural village. There is one important family or clan in the village and that is the Li family. It has been this way for about 1000 years.

In the 1930s and 1940s, the Li family consisted of three households, each headed by a brother, and each encompassing three generations. The head of the Li clan, the second of four brothers, was the unofficial village head. He was called Lao Yeh, a term of great respect meaning "grandfather" or "old gentleman." Lao Yeh and his brothers met and dealt with each other occasionally in matters of village affairs, but otherwise were not close. The eldest brother was not much interested in administrative matters, and because of unfortunate business dealings was not an economic power in the village. Lao Yeh and his younger brother had had a falling out over a sliver of land years ago, and although their households were wall-to-wall, they hadn't spoken to each other for over twenty years. The fourth brother had been adopted into the family of a relative who lived in a village some twenty miles away. The Li family still met each spring during Ch'ing Ming, however, at the Li Tz'u Tang (the Li family ancestral hall) to clean and sweep and memorialize the Li ancestors. At this time they also tended the ancestral graves in the field. The Li family didn't own mountain land where elaborate tombs could be maintained. They buried their dead in the fields and built mounds over the graves. No stones marked the graves, but Lao

The Village in China

Yeh knew the identity of each grave. These grave mounds still exist in the fields, and the farmers cultivate around them. No one now knows who is buried under them.

In the family home of Lao Yeh, and Tzu Mu his wife, were three sons. There had been two daughters, but they had married and moved to the villages of their husbands. Lao Yeh's sons-in-law were of an equal social and economic status as the Li family. This fact had been carefully ascertained by both parties to the contract, and especially by the matchmaker who arranged the marriage. A matchmaker who arranged an unsuitable union would not only lose face, but might even find his "rice bowl broken." He could find himself out of business.

By the late 1930s and the 1940s, two of Lao Yeh's sons were married. The eldest had three sons and a daughter, and it is the eldest son of this eldest son of Lao Yeh to whom we owe this intimate glimpse into the Chinese peasant village. Lao Yeh's second son was married and had a daughter. Lao Yeh's third son was unmarried.

The Family Home

The farmstead of Lao Yeh was typical of a rich peasant of the region. He owned over 1000 _mou_ (160 acres) of land, a really grand holding considering the average farm for the area was 2.3 _mou_ (8), but only about 50 _mou_ were included in the home farmstead. The remainder was in plots of various sizes and scattered about the region and rented out. Lao Yeh, with his three sons and a permanent hired hand, himself farmed the 50 _mou_ of the farmstead. The entire village was situated between two parallel streams, and Lao Yeh's homestead extended from one stream to the other, where footbridges gave access to his fields.

The house itself consisted of a series of courtyards surrounded by living quarters and areas for animals and storage, comprising a general walled compound. The compound was set in a thick bamboo grove. From the front to the back, the layout was as follows: the first courtyard contained a few fruit trees, some potted flowers and a chicken yard; and the surrounding buildings housed the pigs (about 60 of them), a bullock, a waterbuffalo, a horse and a donkey. Horses were rare by the 1940s because every military levy invariably confiscated the horse. You can hardly go off to war riding a buffalo. In the corner of the barn was the privy, where animal manure could be dumped along with night soil. The cesspool was reachable from outside the walls. Pig manure was kept separate. According to Chinese traditional agricultural lore, the pig is the perfect fertilizer machine. Grass, leaves, sweet potato vines and garbage is put in the pig at one end, and immediately usable fertilizer produced at the other.

The transverse hall at the end of the first courtyard was the main reception room, and gave onto the second court which was surrounded by the kitchen, dining room and family and guest apartments. This tiled court also contained flowers and flowering trees, but no chickens or other farm animals. The final courtyard was primarily for storage of tools, farm implements and grains. It was here that the Communist troops, led by Marshall Ch'en Yi, quartered themselves (at Lao Yeh's invitation) during the anti-Japanese United Front in the late 1930s and early 1940s. It was here also that the Japanese quartered themselves, as did Nationalist troops in their periodic sweeps through the area. There were several semi-secret side doors which led into the bamboo forest, and a back door which opened on to a footbridge to the fields to the back of the house.

The Pao-Chia Control System (9)

The formal leaders (Chaing) of the village consisted of: the village head; the hsiang chang; several pao changs; and at the lowest level, the chia changs. A chia consisted of from five to ten families, a pao from five to ten chia, and the hsiang one or more pao. The whole system was designed for control downward, rather than representation upward, and dated from the period of Wang An-shih (1021-1086) in the Sung dynasty (ca. 1000). It was called the pao-chia system, and was designed to provide for control of elements below the lowest government level of the hsien or county. Although the system seems rather rigid and organized, in actuality, it was very flexible. When times were serene and placid, little attention was paid to it, but in times of military or political disorder, the pao-chia system was revitalized.

In Li Chia T'ai there were no chia changs, and the hsiang chang and pao changs were designated by the gentry families, of which Lao Yeh was doyen. Even higher level official appointees recognized the power of the gentry and made it a point to pay official and social calls on Lao Yeh and the gentry of the district.

The responsibility of the pao changs and the hsiang chang were all upward, in accordance with the central bureaucratic system. Each pao chang: (1) reported regularly to his superior on matters relating to births, deaths, marriages and criminal activities; (2) collected taxes and kept land records; and (3) kept population records to facilitate military conscription and civilian labor drafts.

A people's militia was theoretically a function of the pao. During the Republican period, pao changs received some military training at the hsien (county) level, but ammunition and weapons were left to the village to procure. In Li Chia T'ai, Lao Yeh provided an arsenal and organized the defense. He owned some 20 rifles and about 15 handguns, and an undetermined amount of ammunition, but probably no more than ten rounds per weapon. Some of these weapons dated from the T'ai P'ing Rebellion (1850-1864), and some were muzzle loaders. When danger threatened, weapons were assigned to individuals according to their known proficiency. Such dangers arose from various sources: T'ai P'ings from the period of the rebellion; wandering bands of looters following the Boxer Rebellion in 1900; disbanded soldiers during the early Republican period; deserters from the Northern Expeditionary Army of Chiang K'ai-shek; various warlord armies of Sun Chuan-fang, Wu P'ei-fu, Chang Chung-chang and others; army deserters in the wake of the Japanese advance, and renegade units of Communist, Nationalist or Wang Ching-wei Puppet Army troops. During the final period before the Communist victory, hurried and inadequate efforts were made by the Nationalist Government to organize grass-roots resistence. Each ti ch'ü (prefecture) organized a Pao An T'uan (Safety Corps). Each hsien (county) had its Kung-An Pu-Tui (Peace Corps), and each hsiang (village) had its Tze-Wei-Tui (Self Defense Corps). It was while commanding the Pao An T'uan Lao Yeh's eldest son was killed.

Thus, large clan families took the responsibility for organization for mobilization, tax collection and census. They also took the responsibility for public utilities and services.

Public Works and Utilities

Except for major military facilities, the building and maintaining of roads and bridges, dikes, canals and so forth rested mainly on the gentry, led by clan heads such as Lao Yeh. While each household of the village was responsible for its own bridges across the streams fronting their farmsteads, the larger bridge on the road to the market town was a community responsibility. A delegation of villagers came to Lao Yeh to seek his leadership in renovating the large bridge which had fallen into disrepair. Lao Yeh solicited (requisitioned is a more appropriate word) funds from the families according to their economic status. A bridge builder was engaged, and he and his professional crew were paid for their work in cash. Ordinary labor and draft animals were contributed by the villagers.

Provision for schooling was another activity of the gentry. The Li clan had always provided a school and school master. The school at Li Chia T'ai was held in Lao Yeh's house. Lao Yeh hired a hsiu ts'ai, holder of the third scholarly degree, to conduct the school. Families of the village who could afford it sent their children (boys) to the school, and made regular contributions for the hsiu ts'ai's salary and the maintenance of the school. The school master was housed and fed by Lao Yeh. There was no formal graduation classes. Students ranged in age from eight to eighteen, and read from the classics in the morning and practiced calligraphy in the afternoon, with some time each day devoted to the abacus. Some families sent their children to the modern school at the county seat at Ching Chiang, where science and social studies were included in the curriculum. After 1945, when the Communists had taken over, a school was established in the village and a modern curriculum with emphasis on political studies introduced.

Most activities generally thought of as public utilities were handled by individual families. There was no electricity. The rich had kerosene or coleman lamps, and the poor had oil lamps or tallow candles. Sewage was collected from the privy and, after curing in large vats, was used for fertilizer along with mud from the beds of the dredged streams and canals. Garbage was fed to the pigs. In Li Chia T'ai, water was dipped from the streams in wooden buckets and stored in large cisterns by each family. Chemicals were added to flocculate and precipitate the sediment; and water carefully decanted from the top in order not to roil the cistern. Other villages had wells which averaged one per every two or three families.

The Market Town and Village Industry

The market town which served Li Chia T'ai lay about two miles away, past two other villages. It was called Ch'ang An Shih (Perpetual Peace). The population of Ch'ang An Shih was not much greater than that of each of the villages it served, but on market days the population increased ten fold. It boasted a rice brokerage, a teashop for the latest news, a pawn shop, canned food store, butcher shop, pharmacy, tobacconist, and other such facilities. There were no government offices in Ch'ang An Shih. These, the county magistrate's yamen, police station and health clinic were at the county seat of Ching Chiang.

After 1945, when the Communists had firm control of the village, the oldest male in the Li family still living in Li Chia T'ai was twelve years old. Each day he made the trip into the market town to buy daily necessities. These always included meat or fish; often herbal medicines prescribed by the village herb doctor; sometimes needles, thread or other notions; or to get a pot mended that couldn't wait for the itinerant tinker. Each morning, his grandmother would measure out a few catties (1 cattie = 1-1/3 lb.) of rice which he would sell to the rice broker. With the money from the sale, he would make the purchases which he would carry home in the wicker baskets slung on the ends of the carrying pole.

In general, the village provided for most of its own needs. The major home industry was weaving of cloth, which was sold at the market town on market days. Home-loomed cloth was eventually supplanted by factory cloth from Chinese and western cotton mills. Other village industries included an oil presser, a winemaker, a beancurd maker, the noodle shop, and a candy butcher. Itinerant tradesmen and artisans visited the village several times a year. Dyers came twice a year at times they calculated there would be enough cloth woven to make it worthwhile. A blacksmith-tinker came twice a year and set up his forge in the village square, where he mended pots and tools, and fashioned knives. Village children surrounded him from morning to night for the entire week he was in the village, clamoring to be allowed to pump the double-action piston bellows, marvelling at the cherry-red iron as it came from the forge, and wide-eyed with awe at the shower of sparks that followed each ring of the hammer. A dentist came about once each year, and set up his stool and pulled teeth; and the barber visited the village about once per month where he shaved heads, trimmed eyebrows, and cleaned ears.

Some local enterprises were part time, and served several villages. Li Chia T'ai boasted a cormorant fisherman with his flock of birds perched on the edge of his sampan. Rings around their necks prevented them from swallowing any of the larger fish they caught, and cords tethered them to the boat. One man made a living catching frogs, toads and snakes, which he sold to the pharmacist in the market town. Another netted rice birds when they were in season and trapped quail, pheasant and wild ducks.

The Village and the State

Only on rare occasions were members of the village required to come in direct contact with the government, whose official representation ended at the hsien (county) level. Hsien officials might make a yearly call on Lao Yeh and other gentry of the area, or police might come to Lao Yeh to seek his help in the investigation or apprehension of a villager. Government directives, such as those regarding turning in gold for bank notes, military conscription levies, smallpox vaccinations or cholera shots were passed from the hsien level to the hsiang chang and pao changs. Posters announcing these regulations were pasted on the walls, along with advertisements for Ruby Queen, Pirate or Rat Cigarettes.

As a general practice, the village avoided and tried to ignore the state government. The villagers quietly submitted to government exploitation. They expected nothing in return from the government. They paid their taxes and kept up with responsibilities regarding military recruiting and labor corvees.

Regardless which government was in charge, taxes continued to be collected, often by several contending factions, and often in advance for several years. It mattered not whether the collectors were the imperial agents, the Nationalist Government, warlords, provincial governors or Communists. Conscription was also a daily fact of life. Only the Communists were careful not to conscript -- until they gained control. After years in which the pao-chia had all but vanished, it was revitalized in the 1930s. Its primary function was to function as a mobilization center for government indoctrination and military training, first against the Communists, then against the Japanese, and then against the Communists again.

Through the entire period of the twentieth century of revolution, war, and national chaos, the village persisted in the traditional way, with the sources of political power stemming from the traditional gentry, clans and large families. Few individuals in the village had the desire or interest to concern themselves with affairs of state. For example, the concept of suppressing Communism as a state objective had no meaning for the ordinary villager. He had not participated in the decisionmaking on government matters beyond the village in the past, and saw no reason to do so now. The important things in life revolved around the family and its welfare.

Both the National Government and the Japanese were content to use the existing sources of political power. The Nationalist Government sought to instill an allegiance to itself, and the Japanese attempted to build a loyalty to the puppet government of Wang Ching-wei. Only the Communists seemed to know that the traditional system had to be destroyed if national loyalty were to supplant one based on family and clan.

Communes and the Production Brigade

Communist control came to various parts of China at different times. By 1944, Li Chia T'ai was under the control of the Communists, and in places of traditional sources of political power were Communist "cadres." (10) Lao Yeh's brothers were dead, and Lao Yeh himself had been smuggled to a distant village where he supported himself as a school master until his death. His sons had been conscripted into the Nationalist Army. Other adult male clan members had left the village, and some had been imprisoned. Two of Lao Yeh's nephews had been tried by "people's courts" and executed. Only women and children in the Li family remained in Li Chia T'ai. Destruction of the village political system came rapidly.

First came the abolition of the pao-chia system which supplied the only link between the people and the Nationalist Government. Next came the imprisonment or dislodgement of the traditional gentry, and the confiscation of their property. Gentry, such as Lao Yeh were no longer referred to by their honorific titles. Instead, they were called ti-chu (landlord), with the pejorative connotation that attaches to slumlord, exploiter and criminal. Confiscation of property eliminated the economic power and influence of the gentry, and the seizing of the weapons rendered the village militarily helpless. Finally, a "peasant's organization" was formed of the villagers, and led by an "active element" of local Communist cadres who had been trained by "party organizers." A militia was established to guard against destruction of the new political system from within or without.

The two main features of government relations with the village continued: exploitation and control. Taxes (or quotas) continued to be collected, and conscription and corvees levied. The pao-chia system leaders were replaced by various "responsible persons," local Communist cadres (leaders). Two important additions were made to the village-government relationship. One was the introduction of government assistance and control at all levels by means of the cadre system, and the other was the incorporation of the people into the decisionmaking process. It was not that the people were allowed to take part in the political process; they were forced to do so under the slogan of "from the people, to the people." Furthermore, the new government intruded and interested itself in the most intimate details of the life of each individual peasant: his marriage, his children; his sex life; his possessions; his crops; and, most important, his thoughts. It also provided for organization of work, a function formerly exercised by the gentry and large families.

Mutual Aid Teams and Agricultural Producers Cooperatives

The first step to bring the peasant out of the family farm as a working unit, was the establishment of Mutual Aid Teams. These were later amalgamated into Agricultural Producers Cooperatives (APC's) on the basis roughly of one village-one cooperative. As collectivization proceeded, the APC's became Production Brigades and elements of a commune.

Mutual Aid Teams were not alien to the natural village. For centuries, Chinese farmers had pooled their labor resources and exchanged or rented labor. The Communist Mutual Aid Teams, later called Production Teams, consisted of up to twenty peasant families, whose labor, tools and draft animals were combined to perform specific tasks (tilling, terracing, combining fields, extension of irrigation projects, etc.)

The cooperative farming of communal land did raise the productive capacity of individual peasants, but mostly because private family plots which were allotted, contributed significantly to the supply of supplemental food: i.e., vegetables, meats, fruit and edible oils. The success of the Production Brigade (former APC's) brought on a euphoria for organization which resulted in the consolidation of Production Brigades into huge supercommunes, administering over 10,000 adult workers and farming over 6,000 mou (1,000 acres). By 1958, private plots, the last surviving element of family unity and cooperation, were taken from the villagers and incorporated into commune land. The family lost its identity as a unit of production. This created a catastrophic loss in production as well as in morale.

Eventual recognition (1960-1961) that communes so constituted were counterproductive prompted the Chinese government to make revisions. The natural village was returned to its original function as a traditional work group. The villager worked the land he had always worked, in many cases with the same tools he used before. As a Production Brigade, the village became the basic unit for planning and organization. The Production Team, consisting of from five to twenty families of the same village, became the basic element of production, the de facto unit of ownership, and the basic level of accounting in the commune. (11)

After some unsuccessful attempts to bypass the family and enter into an era of familyless Communism, the present regime in China has recognized that the family is an important basic element of production. And a village is more than a collection of people, it is an organization of families. Larger kinship groups, such as the clan, no longer exist in China as sources of village political power. Gentry and clan chiefs have been eliminated as village leaders, but leadership has returned to the villages themselves. Communes are administrative organizations, but Production Brigades, that is, villages, are the units of ownership. (12) The natural village, notwithstanding the changes in political power, has resumed its traditional function. The power of the Li clan is gone, but ninety percent of the former village inhabitants, including some Li's, still live in Li Chia T'ai.

Under the emperors, the scholar officials related to the village through exploitation and control. The Nationalist Government during the Republican period, convinced that the basic traditions of village society could not be changed, similarly relied on exploitation and control. The Communist plan includes a structured political and economic system. Even with changes in leadership and incorporation of the villagers into the decisionmaking system, the village as an organized collection of families is a working social, political and economic component of the present national structure. Given its present recognition its viability is newly affirmed.

Present-Day Observations

Population Movements

This, then, is the outline of change within the village-production brigade. But there have also been movements of people throughout China that have affected populations.

The central government sets quotas for local units in production and also moves people throughout the enormous land to develop new production and to thin overpopulated areas. After the cultural revolution (1966), educated youth from the cities were sent to perform productive labor in the countryside either on the land itself or in new factories developed out there. The purpose of this dispersion was twofold: first, to improve production and second, to get the youth to settle, marry and successfully root their future away from the cities.

Basic supplies of rice, cooking oil and cotton are

rationed. In the cities, at least, individuals carry identity papers noting pertinent characteristics. Without these documents individuals are cut off from both necessities and legal travel. At the beginning of the youths' move to the country, the local units to which they were assigned provided extra supplies to cover their needs. After this initial period, the new residents received their fair share of local rations, depending on their work.

The program was widely unpopular. Some youth ran away from their country stations back to their families in the cities. Once returned they had no access to food rations, housing or jobs because they were not legally present.

In the Fall of 1976, at least in Canton, there was word of some criminal activity -- theft and prostitution, time honored ways of acquiring food and money. After Mao Tse Tung's death, relaxations in programming began. In January, 1977, youth from the countryside crowded the streets of cities like Shanghai, home to visit for the upcoming spring holiday. The public transportation systems, including recently opened railway lines, were jammed then and on through the year, with Chinese newly permitted to travel. By the Fall of 1977, it was reported that workers who were unhappy in one location, might be able to move elsewhere, if they could find workers to switch jobs with them. That fall, entrance requirements for post-middle school education were revised and it was announced that some youth would be exempt from the countryside period to go directly into scientific programs and other would only have to serve six months. The process of re-evaluating who should be technically educated continues. What does all of this auger for the urban-rural wage and education differentials that have been one of the major past concerns?

In the production brigades visited in 1977 and 1978, the local leaders with whom we met were all home grown men and women. Their husbands and wives were also born in the local counties. Those cadres speak to the continuing local nature of local leadership. On the other hand, several of the men of the families whose homes we visited in these production brigades worked "in the city" and returned only on their weekly day off and for holidays. They are not counted as members of the production brigade. While these absent workers provided labor without crowding their families into urban residential slums, still it suggests a dreary life for the men in town. They live in factory dormitories and foreigners can see them eating their non-family supper in badly lit cafes on side streets in all the cities.

It also leaves the bulk of village work -- agricultural work -- to women. Riding in our buses or trains, we observed platoons of workers in the fields, predominantly women, turning the earth with long-handled hoes. There was little evidence of the tractors that the revolutionary committee members list in their statistical presentations of the extent of current agricultural mechanization. In the production brigade and commune level enterprises visited, many more men than women are working -- and earning more money than the field laborers. It is obvious, then, that even though men and women are now said to be equal, i.e., "women hold up half the sky" -- their sky is certainly more agricultural and rural than is men's.

Although we saw a few women in army uniform in town, in the countryside it was the sons who were off in the army, and it was young men whom we saw wearing huge paper flowers and being given a gala send-off as they left their production brigades for the army. And the army is a major pathway to a more powerful voice in group control as it is, to date, the major route to preferment and Party jobs.

Communication - Ties Between City and Countryside

The hold of the Chinese tradition, with its great historical depth and its homogenizing effect throughout that time, is no new story. Redfield discussed it and much more recently Barbara Ward has examined it in her study of the River Boat People in Hong Kong (13). Dramatic performances have entertained villagers for many generations, the performers consisting either of local amateurs or professional troupes that travel from community to community. Although the content of the drama has changed since liberation, the format and the symbols (traditional dances and songs) have continued. They are the same as that taught the children in the schools, both as participants and as spectators. This schooling is now available to all. In addition, teachers from the cities are sent to the communes and production brigades to share their knowledge. We were told by members of the International Language Institute in Peking that English teachers were working at the Taching Oil Fields, preparing the children there to serve as auxiliary guides to explain the commune to its stream of foreign visitors.

Radio, tv and movies spread the national culture as well as ideology. In January, 1977, the first anniversary of the death of Chou en Lai was "celebrated", and that term is used advisedly, since it was really an extension of the "victory over the gang of four". At the time of the Premier's death, the year before, the Chinese people were not allowed to mourn as fully as they wished to. An interpreter explained, "We were told not to wear mourning bands, but we dared to, at great peril". Now, on the anniversary, mourning bands were distributed throughout the schools, factories and offices of Canton, and there were memorial services at all locations. In addition, a movie, made after the Premier's death but shown only once throughout the country, was available for several days.

The film documented the variety of delegations of famous and ordinary people who traveled to Peking to pay their respects at Chou en Lai's bier, the funeral itself, and memorial services held in the natural villages on the communes in far-flung areas of China. Scenes of mourners in minority costumes alternated with other scenes showing mourners in plain blue peasant garb. Following these moving, moving scenes of unity in emotion with some slight diversity of expression, the second half of the 2-1/2 hour film recalled the life of Chou en Lai -- greeting villagers at the many factories and production brigades which he visited, dancing the local dances, addressing a fantastic variety of audiences.

Perhaps the railroad network is weak, but airplanes make this kind of communication possible as well as making it easy for far-flung delegations to attend national events and conferences. Professor Fei-Hsiao-t'ung talked with us about the Earthquake that the Province of Lioning suffered in 1975, the Earthquake that had been successfully predicted in time to evacuate more than one-million people from the area subsequently devastated. Professor Fei said that to help the evacuees celebrate the New Year in their make-shift locations, the government sent in planeloads of the dumplings that signify good luck for the year to come.

Effect of Self-Reliance

Notwithstanding the directives on change that have appeared, been revised, redirected and reappeared at the production brigades, villagers have managed to keep certain basic traditions. And today, in 1978, the plots where chickens, ducks, vegetables, herbs and tobacco are raised for the household are still <u>family</u> activity, although the plot size is determined by the number of <u>individuals</u> in the household.

The pig requires separate treatment because of its paramount position in rural China, always at the heart of peasant life whether in villages or production brigades. Even in America we have the child's piggy bank as a symbol of savings. But in Chinese culture, the very ideograph for home is a pig under the roof.

Early on, Chairman Mao instructed the peasants to raise a pig apiece. For the pig is the basic rural enterprise, the primary fertilizer factory. Pig manure is also used to light the lamps of rural China, through the production of methane gas for lights.

The pigs are produced on pig farms by production brigades. One such we visited had brick pigstyes with solidly constructed arches. But once weaned, the pigs are raised by households and the manure collected from the animal's way of life as well as the products resulting from harvesting the animal are paid to the household in cash by the commune and the meat markets.

Under the infamous "Gang of Four", it seems that the honorable family custom of raising pigs was attacked as capitalistic, but now it is again praiseworthy to breed pigs for the Revolution and to have fat pigs for sale to the state. Production points for collective work are, then, not the only way to achieve bank accounts. The cash generated from the sale of pigs and produce from family plots has undoubtedly made possible most of the sewing machines and bicycles and electric clocks seen in the homes we visited.

These individual plots are miniscule (.06 _mou_ per individual) by our standards, but they produce bountifully under the tender loving care of the Chinese peasants, who in most of their agricultural activity, whether individual or collective, garden rather than farm. A Texas rancher with whom we traveled through China reminded us that this is a characteristic of Chinese as they continue their lives outside of the Peoples Republic of China as well as within it. She had been shown around the New Territories of Hong Kong and was startled by the concept of farm applied to a half acre of private cultivation from which a refugee family lived well. "Postage stamps", she said, "and they called them farms! We could play hop scotch between them."

The agricultural Mecca for the Chinese and their guests is a commune named Tachai, from which all rural agriculture communes are expected to "learn". Tachai exemplifies the collective spirit in raising production, extending production and developing alternatives to back-breaking labor expended in reaching this condition. It is, therefore, a comparatively wealthy commune, at least the pay is the highest in Hsiyang County, with every family having both bank savings and a store of surplus grain. As a mecca, however, it enjoys the additional economic advantages accruing to any showplace tourist attraction. Although it is located in a ravine in the foothills of the mountains of northern Shansi province, there is a special bus route to make it accessible to tourists and it accomodates tourist-workers as well. We have not been there ourselves, but have been to communes accessible to visitors from cities and assume they are also on the tourist route. For example, at Ren Ho in Kwangtung Province, adjacent to the Hall in which we were briefed and later lunched, there were signs in English designating the way to the bathrooms (well-built large quarters with cement floors). Leaping to generalizations from both the signs and the bountiful meal provided us, we assume that such production brigades have enterprise opportunities not available to most of China's villages.

For example, in the literature churned out by travelers to China, the same production brigades and factories keep reoccurring. These are by no means Potempkin villages, but they have both the advantages and disadvantages to continued organic development and autonomy that accrue from their distinction. How does their "favored" status affect village life in other production brigades on other communes, since word does get around? In the last analysis, how does that affect the self-reliance it is celebrating?

Future of the Village in China

"Inside a People's Commune" is an English language book published in 1974 "to help foreign readers understand the character, make-up and functions and advantages of these new-type socialist collectives." (14) Certainly its illustrative example, the commune of Chiliyang, must be typical. Before 1958, Chiliyang was made up of 38 villages. Today it has 38 production brigades, still acting as a network radiating from what used to be the market town.

As to other things, they are more complex. Clans provided, according to Martin Yang (15), "a transitional grouping between the family and the village as well as a sense of social orientation." By now their role has been replaced by the Communist Party. However, everyone belonged to a clan, of which there were usually more than one in a village. But the party is the one national party which runs the Peoples Republic of China. Its local membership is probably never more than 5% of the adult brigade members.

While every effort seems to be made to include the local party personnel in the administrative apparatus, it would seem likely that the whole group still is more locally oriented and would act as one unit to stand its ground against the monolithic party structure bearing down from outside. The National Party Congress held in February, 1978, heard a new Constitution which encouraged workers to report inefficient superiors and to freely criticize production methods. This was an about-face, presaged by other announcements throughout the last year, from the previous focus on "correct" political statements   being more important than production. It should increase the ability of the local production brigade to say "no, that's too much to ask from us" or "this is the way we should do it here", both to achieve production quotas and to share them out, internally and externally.

From our reading and observations, the concept of the village is still a viable one in China. The structure and cohesion of the production brigade are a direct legacy of the natural village. Agriculture is the mode of production unifying the group, basic relationships are in a family household, and interaction is face to face. There still is a continuity of population. More than that, it seems to us that the psycho-social needs delineated by Maccoby are nourished no less in the production brigade than in the natural village. In fact, equity is far greater, there is more participation according to sex and age, and at least as much security. Individuation is far less for some and far more for others.

References and Notes

1. R. Redfield, The Primitive World and its Transformation (Chicago, U. of Chicago Press, 1953), p. 35.
2. E.R. Wolf, Peasants (Prentice-Hall, Englewood Cliffs, N.J., 1966).
3. Fei Hsiao-t'ung & C. Chang, Earthbound China (Chicago, U. of Chicago Press, 1945); Fei, Peasant Life in China (London: Kegan Paul, 1939); M. Yang, A Chinese Village: Taitou, Shantung Province (New York: Columbia University Press, 1945). For an interesting documentation of Chinese-America cross-fertilization, see W. Fairbank, America's Cultural Experiment in China, 1942-49 (Department of State Publication 8839, June, 1976).
4. A. Leeds, "Mythos and Pathos: Some Unpleasantries on Peasantries" in R. Halperin & J. Dow, eds., Peasant Livelihood: Studies in Economic Anthropology and Cultural Ecology (New York, St. Martin's Press, 1977).
5. Mao Tse Tung, "Analysis of the Classes in Chinese Society (1926)", in Selected Works of Mao Tse-Tung (Vol. 1) (Foreign Language Press, Peking, 1967).
6. Wolf, 91.

7. Li Chia Tai is an actual village, but the name has been changed, as has the name of the family. The earlier status and recent changes in the organization and among the villagers have been closely followed through an informant who is a member of the Li family, and presently living in the United States.
8. R.H. Tawney, Land and Labor in China (Boston: Beacon Press, 1966 (originally published, London: George Allen & Unwin, 1932)), p. 30.
9. For a detailed description of the pao-chia system, see Franz Schurmann, Ideology and Organization in Communist China (Berkeley: University of California Press), p. 408ff.
10. _____, 162ff, for a discussion of the "cadre concept".
11. _____, p. 492.
12. _____, p. 494.
13. B. Ward, "Readers and Audiences: An Exploration of the Spread of Tradition" in B. Kapferer (ed.) Transaction and Meaning: Directions in the Anthropology of Exchange and Symbolic Behavior.
14. Chu Li and C. Tien, Inside a Peoples Commune (Peking: Foreign Language Press, 1974).
15. Yang, 134.

Part 3

Development and the Village

Clive Bell

8. The Future of Rice Monocultures in Malaysia

> "There is no certain knowledge about the future [...]. The New York State Legislature has deliberated these difficulties, and enacted in Section 899 of the Code of Criminal Procedure that persons 'Pretending to forecast the future shall be considered disorderly under subdivision 3, Section 901 of the Code and liable to a fine or $250 and/or six months in prison.'"(1)

Speculations about the future economic and social organisation of rice production in any country are likely to be rather idle unless they are informed by a well-founded view of what the future holds for certain features of the economy and society at large. Similarly, it is difficult to address the theme of this Symposium, <u>Village Viability in Contemporary Society</u>, in the chosen context of this paper without first establishing what form the future economic and social arrangements for producing rice are likely to take. For by their very nature, the economies of the villages of Malaysia's "rice bowl" areas are presently very specialised, and it so happens that there are few opportunities for diversification into other agricultural activities. Hence, it is important to distinguish between their viability as primarily rice-producing villages and as settlements whose inhabitants earn much of their incomes from non-farm jobs, the production

---

I am indebted to Barbara Lenkerd and Priscilla Reining for extensive comments on an earlier draft. Bela Balassa, Randolph Harris, Peter Hazell, Kevin Young and two anonymous colleagues also provided useful suggestions. None of them is to be held responsible for the errors which survive or the opinions to which I have obdurately clung. It must also be said that the views expressed in this paper do not necessarily reflect those of the World Bank.

of rice being relegated to a (comparatively) minor role. As Malaysia is already a middle income country, with good prospects of rapid economic growth over the next decade and more, this distinction is central to the argument of this paper.

Thus the paper begins with a brief sketch of the probable growth of, and structural changes in, the Malaysian economy over the next one or two decades. In section II, there follows a more detailed account of the present economic and social organisation of paddy (2) production, which lays the basis for speculations about the future. Section III deals with more aggregative issues at the sectoral level: output, demand and government policy towards the sector, the future course of which have a strong bearing on the incomes of the paddy farming community. In the light of these considerations, section IV lays out the most plausible outcomes for the future economic and social organisation of paddy production in Malaysia. Finally, in section V, an attempt is made to see to what extent the findings from the Malaysian case carry over to other countries in Southeast Asia.

I. Malaysia's Paddy Sector in Its National Setting

Malaysia is hardly a "typical" Southeast Asian economy. Partly for that reason, the position and role of her rice-producing peasantry are somewhat atypical also. To start with, the level of GNP per head is far higher than in Thailand, Indonesia, the Philippines, Burma and the countries of Indochina. Moreover, Malaysia's paddy sector is a relatively small branch of the national economy, accounting for about 2 percent of GNP and providing the principal means of livelihood for about 8 percent of the population. As these statistics suggest, Malaysia's paddy farmers are also poor by the standards of society as a whole. Indeed, one careful estimate for 1970 puts two out of every three paddy farming households below a poverty line of M$25 per person per month (3). Yet, as a group, they are of considerable political and social importance. Almost all of them are ethnically Malay, in a society in which just over 50 percent of the population are Malays and the ruling party is an ethnic coalition dominated by Malay interests. Moreover, the government has recently espoused a strategy of both wiping out poverty among all racial groups and giving Malays special access to expanding economic opportunities outside agriculture (4). Thus, today's paddy farming families ought to enjoy a growth in incomes which is above the national average over the next decade and more, whatever their future occupations.

That Malaysia's rice sector is comparatively small simplifies matters a great deal. What happens in the sector has little bearing on growth and structural change in the national economy. Rather, the causal chain runs in the other direction: to form a view of how the rice sector will look in 10 or 15 years time, one must begin establishing an outline, however rough, of the future development of the whole economy.

First, there is the pace of economic growth in aggregate. Output has been expanding rapidly for the past decade or so, the average rate for the period 1970-75 being 7.4 percent per annum (5). The Third Malaysian Plan projects an annual rate of 8.5 percent for 1975-80, and the perspective for the 'eighties is scarcely lower at 8.1 percent (6). Failing a war, or a collapse of the international trading system (on which Malaysia is heavily dependent), or prolonged civil strife at home, a long term growth rate of 7 percent should be attainable. In the nature of things, there must be some uncertainty surrounding this estimate; but while the actual outcome could easily be somewhat higher or lower, a rate of about 7 percent seems to be the most probable one.

Secondly, the population has been growing at a fairly rapid rate too. The annual rate averaged 2.6 percent per annum during 1970-75. It is expected to accelerate very slightly to 2.7 percent for the period 1975-80, before dropping back to 2.6 percent throughout the 'eighties. By 1990, the total fertility rate for Peninsular Malaysia should have fallen to 3.3 (from 4.9 in 1970), at which point the demographic transition will be largely complete (7).

Compound growth rates of this magnitude produce important changes, even over a decade or so. In 1975, the population was just over 12 million and GNP per head about US$750 (at 1975 market prices and nominal exchange rates). From this base, if the above projections are to be believed, we should expect the population to reach 18.5 million in 1990, with a GNP per head of US$1500 (in the above units of account). Even if the growth of output slackens somewhat thereafter, by the turn of the century Malaysia's average output per person will be on a par with that of Italy today.

Profound structural changes will accompany this aggregate expansion. The primary sector will continue to contract relative to the secondary and tertiary sectors, and by 1990 or thereabouts the workforce engaged in agriculture will have ceased to grow altogether. At the same time, there will be a large shift in population towards the towns, although urban dwellers are unlikely to attain a majority until the 'nineties (8).

It seems safe to conclude that the present economic and social organisation of rice production will not survive this combined onslaught of material affluence and urbanisation. Indeed, within one generation the "agrarian problem" will no longer be characterised by the position of a numerous and growing small peasantry in a middle income, "dualistic" economy. Rather, it will have much in common with that confronting France and Italy over the past decade and more: how to give decent incomes to a declining peasantry through a system of subsidies paid for by taxing other, presumably richer, social groups. This is the salient proposition of the paper, which the remaining sections are intended to support and amplify.

II. The Economic and Social Organisation of Paddy Production

Malaysia's paddy producers are peasants. There are no estates, nor are there capitalist enterprises cultivating hundreds of acres. There are a few Chinese households whose entrepreneurial energies are devoted, in part, to 50 or at most 100 acres — and most of this land is rented from Malays. The peasantry shows a measure of social and economic differentiation (9), but compared with South Asia, say, such differentiation is not especially marked. A high proportion of the land cultivated is rented from others — as much as 50 percent in the main paddy areas — but a high proportion of rental contracts appear to involve kin. In such cases, rents seem to be influenced by the needs of landlord and tenant as well as market forces: a newly-married couple may pay a nominal rent to a well-off parent or uncle, whereas a farmer in his prime is likely to pay the going market rate on land rented from his widowed mother. Absentee landlordism is significant in some areas; but although it is a source of inequality, it does not bear down upon the peasantry with the force of its counterpart in Eastern India, for example. Thus, while tenancy is extensive, it is not oppressive in the large, much of it being a reflection of kinship relations linked by the domestic life cycle (9, 10, 11, 12).

The typical head of a paddy farming household, as he emerges from the studies cited in Table 1, is a Malay in his late thirties or forties who has some formal schooling and a claim to being functionally literate. The household has 5 or 6 members, and its structure is generally nuclear (9). As we have seen, tenancy and kinship are usually closely intertwined, as are tenancy and the domestic life-cycle. The pure tenant is often a young man who has just started a family, while the mixed owner-tenant, whose holding is usually larger than the average in his locality, is usually a successful cultivator in his prime, who has also scaled to the peak of the domestic cycle. The Chayanovian parallel in all this should not be overdrawn because paddy land is very scarce, rather than being there for the taking at the extensive margin. Nevertheless, in other respects the parallel is close enough to have some suggestive value in the Malaysian context.

By no means all of the 940,000 acres under paddy in Peninsular Malaysia are cultivated by households which depend mainly on this crop for their livelihood. According to the 1960 Census, 296,000 farms grew paddy; 58 percent reported paddy farming as their main source of livelihood, and just under a half allocated more than three-quarters of their holdings to paddy (12). If we call the latter category "specialist" paddy farmers, they accounted for 74 percent of all paddy farms in the states of Perlis, Province Wellesley and Selangor, 57 percent in Kedah and 51 percent in Perak. Outdated though they are, these data suggest that a fair proportion of the paddy acreage still falls under diversified holdings, in which paddy is a subsidiary crop and the peasant pays most of his attention to treecrops such as rubber. However, these holdings do not concern us here. Instead, we shall focus on farmers in the main irrigated areas, which are virtually rice monocultures: Muda, covering 250,000 acres in the states of Kedah and Perlis; Kemubu, 50,000 acres in Kelantan; 35,000 acres in North-Central Province Wellesley; Krian, 62,000 acres in Perak and South Province Wellesley; and Tanjong Karang, 50,000 acres in Selangor.

Thanks to the painstaking survey work of Selvadurai and others, it is possible to piece together a summary picture of farm holdings, the allocation of land and the sources of household incomes in these areas — albeit at different times over the past decade. At the times surveyed, the areas were also at different stages of "agricultural intensification", a catch-all phrase to cover irrigation, double-cropping, the adoption of high yielding varieties and new cultural practices. Thus, if their statistics are put together in a comparative way, they can yield a "development story" of sorts, although one must keep the following caveats in mind. First, the terms of trade drifted against paddy farmers from 1967 to 1972. However, the farm gate price of paddy varied little over the surveys' dates, with the exception of 1974/75, when its level was almost double that of two years before. Secondly, the data for Muda are almost certainly more reliable than those for the other areas: households in both Muda surveys were interviewed weekly, whereas those in the other samples were interviewed once. Thirdly, the surveys do not employ a uniform concept of income: those for Kemubu, Krian and Province Wellesley (1967/68) omit the value of the house-

Table 1. The salient characteristics of paddy farm households.

Area Characteristic	Muda 1972/73	Muda 1974/75	Province Wellesley 1967/68	Province Wellesley 1971	Krian 1971	Kemubu 1967/68
Average farm size (acres)	4.6	n.a.	4.1	n.a.	3.8	3.0
Average paddy area (acres)	4.0	4.0	3.3	3.1	3.1	2.2
Proportion rented	0.45	n.a.	0.51	0.56	0.48	0.37
Average household size	5.6	5.6	5.8	5.2	5.8	5.2
Average household income*	2,405	4,001	1,314	1,578	1,111	647
Proportion from paddy	0.78	0.78	0.68	0.72	0.62	0.42
Proportion from off-farm sources	0.10	0.09	0.23	0.16	0.27	0.44
Average per capita household income**	557	714	312	406	257	171

*Current M$.
**1975 M$, using the consumer price index as deflator.
Sources: Muda (10, 13); Province Wellesley (14, 12); Krian (15); Kemubu (16).

hold's consumption of own-farm produce other than paddy, which might amount to 10 percent of total net income; and none of the estimates includes the value of housing services — an important omission, as most farmers own their dwellings.

In 1967/68, the Kemubu scheme was a single-cropping area in which most of the land was sown to traditional varieties, with very low doses of fertiliser and land preparation by animal draught power. Krian was in transition in 1971: high yielding varieties and double-cropping were almost universal, along with (relatively) heavy fertiliser inputs; but owing to deep water logging, most land preparation was done by hand using a tajak. By 1967/68, most of the paddy land in Province Wellesley was under irrigation. However, the next four years saw important changes in the form of the widespread adoption of high yielding varieties and mechanised ploughing. Muda in 1972/73 was in transition in a different sense again. Although high yielding varieties, fairly heavy fertiliser use and mechanised ploughing formed the dominant technique of cultivation, 30 percent of the command area was still unirrigated (and single-cropped). In 1974/75, Muda reached project maturity, just as paddy farmers benefitted from a very favourable shift in the terms of trade.

The "development story" which Table 2 represents is clear enough. Rises in real incomes are associated with an increasing dependence on paddy cultivation as a source of livelihood. And the proportions cited there understate such dependence inasmuch as the definition of "off-farm income" includes wages and rents earned through hiring out labour and land to other farmers. This is not to say that the strategy for raising the incomes of paddy farm households over the past decade has been wrong-headed. After all, the impoverished paddy farmers in the Kemubu area of 10 years back, who were cramped on small, unirrigated holdings and made do with low-yielding cultivation practices, had no choice but to seek out income earning opportunities beyond paddy cultivation on their own farms. Better by far to enjoy the comparative affluence afforded by specialisation in the Muda of 1974/75 than the privations of (rational) diversification in the Kemubu of 1967/68.

Moreover, that diversification is more apparent than real, for *per capita* off-farm incomes vary little across the samples. One reason for this is that farmers in monoculture areas cannot easily diversify into other crops and animal husbandry; for the paddy fields in these areas are best suited to paddy — indeed, in many cases, they will grow virtually nothing else. That leaves the kampong land of the farmers' houselots, which is higher and better drained than the rice paddies. These tiny parcels of a quarter-acre or so already support poultry-raising, vegetables and fruit crops. One-third to a half of this produce is consumed at home, and it provides about 10 percent of net farm income (10, 12). Farmers also raise buffalo and cattle; but livestock numbers, especially of buffalo, have fallen sharply as double-cropping reduced the supply of grazing land and tractors began to provide draught power at lower costs.

* * * * *

We turn now to some aspects of the social organisation of paddy production, paying particular attention to the significance of the "village", or kampong, as a unit of aggregation for analysis. Husin Ali (9), in particular, is one Malaysian scholar who has argued strongly that the kampong is well-defined in the peasants' eyes and that it serves as a focus for their most important social, economic and political dealings. He bases his argument on a set of characteristics which give the village its identity: territory, kinship, local economy, religion and politico-administrative base. Let us consider each of these in turn, taking special note of the fact that much has changed in the paddy monocultures since he carried out his fieldwork intermittently between 1961 and 1968.

In these paddy monocultures, the settlement pattern usually takes the form of linear strips along roads, canals and drains, as can be seen from a glance at the land-use maps. The natural boundaries which confer identity on the South Asian clustered settlement are palpably missing, for each village "runs into" the next. It does not follow, of course, that this layout precludes the "villagers" from having a sense of their "village" as a well-defined socio-economic community — though it can hardly reinforce such feelings of community, especially if it is easy to travel along the whole of the strip in question. Husin Ali recognises the point that extended linear settlements lack natural divisions along their axes. Indeed, two of the villages he studied in the Muda area were adjacent to one another. In these cases — whatever the confusion of outsiders — the villagers seemingly had no difficulty in identifying themselves with one village as opposed to the other. All well and good; but it must also be established that such identification has a functional basis, and here some doubts begin to intrude.

Marriages are not endogamous, but there is a kin-based bilateral system of settlement. Immediately after marriage, residence can be either virilocal or uxorilocal. Thereafter, it tends to be neolocal, not least because <u>kampong</u> land is in short supply. Subdivision of the parents' houselot spares the children an outlay of cash and keeps them in close proximity. It accounts also for the prevalence of kin homestead clusters, even in linear <u>kampongs</u>, and is undoubtedly connected with the intertwining of kinship with tenancy (9). However, as each <u>kampong</u> is composed of many such clusters, the identity conferred on the <u>kampong</u> by kinship is not entirely clear-cut.

It is when we turn to socio-economic relations in the context of good communications, rising incomes and new crop production technology that the <u>kampong's</u> significance as a unit of aggregation must come under close scrutiny. In the traditional system, communications with the outside world -- or even adjacent <u>kampongs</u> on the same strip -- were often poor and the cultivation of a single crop with labour, animal draught power and a little seed put by from last year took place within the framework of the so-called "natural economy" of the family farm. It is small wonder, then, that the village was relatively closed both socially and economically. Hence, widespread endogamy in the past was simply a reflection of the law of large numbers. Conversely, exogamy is gaining ground today, because girls go to coeducational schools serving several villages and later make chaperoned trips to town. There are, of course, many successful village systems in the world which are exogamous — South Asian villages are classic examples. Thus, this structural shift, while important, does not necessarily imply the demise of the kampong as such. However, it implies some dilution of the kinship basis of the kampong's identity inasmuch as exogamy entails a strengthening of kinship links across village boundaries.

To pursue other examples involving structural changes, two systems of labour mobilisation symbolised and supported the self-sufficient character of traditional cultivation: the derau, a group of women who undertook the crucial transplanting operation on the basis of completely reciprocal trades in labour among households; and gotong royong, a term covering collective work in production, such as the digging and cleaning of canals and drains that affect output on all farms. Nowadays, however, the farmer employs a technology which forces him to trade mainly with a larger economic system. What is more, he must deal with many kinds of agents: the irrigation authorities, who control his water supply; the dealers in farm chemicals; the specialist contractors, who plough his land (and increasingly combine harvest it, too); and the agricultural bank, which must supply him with the working capital to finance such trades. Where final expenditures are concerned, less than a quarter of all outlays go on the household's own produce; virtually all of the rest are spent on goods and services from the non-farm economy outside the "village" (17).

In Muda, at least, even the labour market is now to all intents and purposes fully commercialised. The derau continues to function, but the strict reciprocity of old has been replaced by money contract rates payable to the group as a whole. And as the road network has grown along with the canals and drains, so labour has become more mobile. Moreover, seasonal workers are drawn in across the border from Thailand and Kelantan, and even from rubber smallholdings and estates in Baling and Sik in Southern Kedah — all in search of the high wages that rule at harvest time.

Under these conditions of production and exchange, it is hard to argue that there is a strong nexus of economic transactions which confer identity on the kampong, especially as tenancy is based on kinship. Thus, while they may have been valid in the light of the conditions ruling 10 or 15 years ago, Husin Ali's arguments that the kampong derives its identity in part from an extensive network of economic dealings now appear to be untenable.

Improvements in personal mobility and communications also pose a threat to the religious and politico-administrative bases of the Malaysian kampong. The village prayerhouse, which encourages a sense of community and identity qua village, stands to lose its Friday congregation to the nearest Mosque. Where administration is concerned, the old hereditary system, in which the village headman came under the authority of the pengulu of the mukim, who, in turn, was responsible to the Sultan, has given way to something more "modern". Sultans are now titular figureheads, and headmen and pengulus are elected, enjoying no patronage of their own. The pengulu must approach the District Officer, who is an administrator, not a politician. Thus, "traditional leaders" in the village have been reduced to little more than civil servants at the lowest rungs of the administration (9).

In politics, as in their economic dealings, the villagers must look outwards to the larger society — in this case, to political parties. At the branch level, the new leaders include labourers, peasants, ex-officials and teachers. However, the people holding the most important offices — chairmen, secretaries and treasurers — are people of high status within their own communities (9), who are also more likely to be aware of, and responsive to, political issues at the national level. In any event, the "modern" system involves a more thorough-going incorporation of the village into the political mainstream of the nation's life, and the village's identity is diminished accordingly.

It is plain from the foregoing that the kampong is no longer a very convincing unit of aggregation where the peasant's economic dealings are concerned, at least in the agriculturally "advanced" areas such as Muda. The social and political elements in the kampong's identity also seem to be rather weaker than they were even a decade ago. Moreover, the prospect is that this steady erosion of the traditional basis of the kampong's identity will continue. It does not follow, of course, that the kampong will lose all significance as the society at large undergoes structural change. But while the kampong will keep its population for a long time to come, its future role in shaping their lives will surely be more limited than it was in the past. Just what that role will be is a question which will be taken up in section IV.

III. <u>The Sectoral Picture: Supply, Demand and Prices</u>

We turn now to the prospects for output and prices in the paddy sector over the next 10-15 years; for these two variables have a large say in determining the incomes of paddy farmers.

There are about 940,000 acres under paddy cultivation in Peninsular Malaysia. All but 20,000 acres or so are "wet paddy" lands, and about 530,000 acres are irrigated, producing two crops a year (18). There is little scope for extending the physical area under cultivation except at very high cost, all the river valleys and their plains having been settled and brought under cultivation some time ago. Instead, cultivation has been steadily intensified through public investment in irrigation, the diffusion of new varieties and increasing inputs of chemical fertilisers. As recently as 1960, only 21,000 acres were double-cropped; but a number of schemes began to mature in the late 'sixties, bringing the double-cropped area up to 325,000 acres in 1970. This expansion of double-cropping was also facilitated by the introduction of photo-insensitive varieties of paddy, which have shorter growing periods than the traditional (photo-sensitive) varieties they replaced. Not surprisingly, paddy output also grew apace in this period, as Table 2 reveals.

Turning to the growth of supply over the longer run, it is envisaged that the area under irrigation will reach 700,000 acres by 1990 (21); but the extra 170,000 acres will add only 12 percent to the gross area sown in 1975. Table 2 suggests that the growth of output began to slow during the seventies as the area brought under irrigation expanded less rapidly than in the 'sixties. Hence, the main impetus to raising output in the 'eighties must come from higher crop

Table 2. Growth rates of paddy production and net sown area in Peninsular Malaysia (%p.a.).

	1960-65	1965-70	1970-75	1975-80*
Area	0.4	0.9	-1.0	n.a.
Production	5.9	6.1	4.7	3.6

*Projected.
Sources: (19, 20).

yields, which can be achieved in three main ways. First, irrigation systems can be remodelled to improve water control and so raise the returns to other productive inputs. These are public investment decisions, and some are under close consideration. (In particular, work is already underway on the construction of a fine network of tertiary and quaternary canals in sections of the Muda and Krian project areas, which are the two largest irrigation schemes in the country.) Secondly, plant breeding programmes may lead to varieties which are more resistant to pests and diseases, more responsive to nutrients, and of shorter maturity (which may permit five crops in two years if there is enough water). In Malaysia, such programmes will also be funded from the public purse. Thirdly, fertiliser inputs can be increased and standards of husbandry improved, not least in response to agricultural extension. In the first case, the farmer gets water control whether he likes it or not. If a new variety is released, he can at least decide against adopting it — though in the past, Malaysia's paddy farmers have been quick to try out new releases, and to persevere with those varieties which turn out to be profitable (10, 12). Only in the third case does he have much room to vary the bundle of farm inputs in response to changes in the structure of economic incentives, especially prices, in textbook fashion.

If investments in irrigation and the development of new crop varieties are under the control of public authorities and there is little scope for extending the area under a particular crop, either by land reclamation or by switching land from other crops, the long run price elasticity of supply of the crop in question may not differ much from its short run value. So long as the level of such public investments is unresponsive to the market price of that particular crop and the rewards to farming are such as to keep all land under cultivation, the long run and short run price elasticities of supply will differ little. In the present case, another government agency intervenes in the market for paddy with the aim of keeping its price at a level which will give paddy farmers "reasonable" incomes, whatever the world price of rice. Until 1974/75, the domestic price of paddy was maintained at a level well above the equivalent c.i.f. price of imported rice; but since then, the difference between them has been slight, and this is expected to continue. However, the connection between the price of paddy and public investment in irrigation and agricultural research directed towards paddy is rendered somewhat tenuous by the fact that the government has declared itself for a target of complete self-sufficiency in rice by the mid 'eighties — presumably irrespective of the world price of rice. Thus, it is plausible

to argue that these investments — and hence the stream of
output they generate — will be independent of paddy prices
for at least a decade.

Now the short run price elasticity of paddy supply is
likely to be rather low, primarily because all the farmer can
do is change his inputs of farm chemicals and the diligence
and time he devotes to husbandry and management, the draught
power and variable labour requirements of cultivating the
crop being virtually fixed. Production responds to these inputs, but it does so in a rather feeble way. Some research
on Muda suggests that even if farmers' input decisions adjust fully over a season to changes in paddy prices, the
short run supply elasticity for paddy is less than 0.1 (22).
It follows that the growth of paddy output over the long run
will depend largely on public investments and rather little
on changes in prices — although the latter do have a large
say in determining farmers' incomes.

In making guesses about the growth of paddy yields in
the future, it is wise to start by looking at what happened
in the past. Between 1962 and 1974, total output grew at
5.6 percent per annum, largely through the growth of double-
cropping; yields in the main- and off-seasons rose at only
1.3 and 2.2 percent per annum, respectively. In this period, a number of successful new varieties were released (12).
As for the barter terms of trade, these reached a modest peak
in 1967 before moving gently against paddy producers until
1972/73, when they staged a strong recovery. On this evidence, then, together with the prospects for extending and
improving irrigation, the annual rate of growth of paddy
output will not exceed 3 to 3.5 percent during the 'eighties
— unless there is a remarkable breakthrough in the characteristics of plant varieties.

Some may regard this estimate as unduly pessimistic,
reasoning as follows: Wet paddy yields in Malaysia are
about 3 tonnes per hectare, which are far lower than those
achieved by farmers in Korea, Japan or Taiwan, or even on experiment stations in Malaysia. Therefore, the scope for increasing farm yields is large enough for one to take a bul-
lish view of the potential for expanding output. Over the
very long run, the argument clearly carries some force,
though the logical connection between observation and conclusion is by no means unassailable, not least because Northeast Asia enjoys the agronomic advantage of longer daylight
hours in the growing season. However, over an historically
short period, such as a decade or two, the argument becomes
no more than a piece of wishful arithmetic. For it is difficult to entertain seriously the notion that the entire set of

attitudes to work, standards of husbandry, social and economic institutions, and history of plant breeding and cultivation that underpin the yields attained in Korea, Japan and Taiwan can be transferred to Malaysia over such a period. Even if such a transfer were possible, it is by no means clear that superimposing such a package upon the Malaysian peasantry would be desirable. While the past is rarely an infallible guide to the future, it seems preferable to stay with 3.5 percent per annum as the outer limit on how fast Malaysia's output of paddy can expand over the next 15 years.

Turning to the demand side of the story, we shall make use of a simple relationship between the rate of growth of demand for a consumer good (c), the rate of growth of population (g) and the rate of growth of real income per head (y):

$$c = g + \eta y \qquad (1)$$

where η is the income elasticity of demand for the good in question. This relationship holds good for any set of prices provided relative prices stay constant and the distribution of incomes and consumers' tastes do not change. Now the own-price elasticity of demand for rice is low, so that even in the fact of large shifts in the price of rice, equation (1) will remain a good approximation. The income elasticity of demand for rice is also very low, in aggregate, for a middle income country such as Malaysia, and its value declines as incomes increase. By international standards, the distribution of incomes in Malaysia is fairly unequal (23), so that, <u>ceteris paribus</u>, the government's strategy of redistributing income to the poor should arrest somewhat the tendency for η to fall as real incomes grow. However, under the circumstances considered here, the income elasticity of demand for rice would be 0.1 at the very outside; some would even put it at zero (24). As we noted earlier, the population is expected to grow at just over 2.6 percent per annum over the next 15 years. Also, per capita private consumption will probably grow at just over 4 percent per annum. Thus, from equation (1), the annual rate of growth of domestic demand during our time perspective will not exceed 3.0 percent, and may be as low as 2.7 percent. Moreover, this long term growth rate of domestic demand is only slightly sensitive to the long term growth rate of GNP.

If we match this demand projection with that for supply, it is clear that there will be some downward pressure on domestic paddy prices over the longer term, unless international trade possibilities are admitted into the picture. Historically, Malaysia has been, and remains, a net importer of rice. The proportion of rice consumption accounted for by imports fell from 21 percent in 1970 to 13 percent in 1975 (25). Hence, abstracting from year-to-year variations, the remaining scope for import substitution will probably absorb the difference between the growth rates of domestic supply and demand until about 1985, or perhaps a little later. Thereafter, the downward pressure on the domestic price can be relieved only by exporting the surplus over domestic consumption. Except for a brief period in 1974/75, the domestic price of rice has exceeded the c.i.f. price of Thai rice, although the difference has been small in recent years. As the Malaysian dollar does not appear to be overvalued — if her consistently strong balance of payments position is any guide — it is fair to conclude that Malaysia is a rather high cost producer of rice relative to one of her principal sources of imports. Hence, exporting rice surpluses will ultimately entail export subsidies, which may be large if the gap between domestic and world prices is wide.

This, then, is the supply-demand framework within which the paddy sector must evolve. At best, Malaysia's paddy producers can expect to raise their aggregate real output by 3.5 percent annually over the long haul, irrespective of how many of them are thus engaged and what form of production organisation prevails.

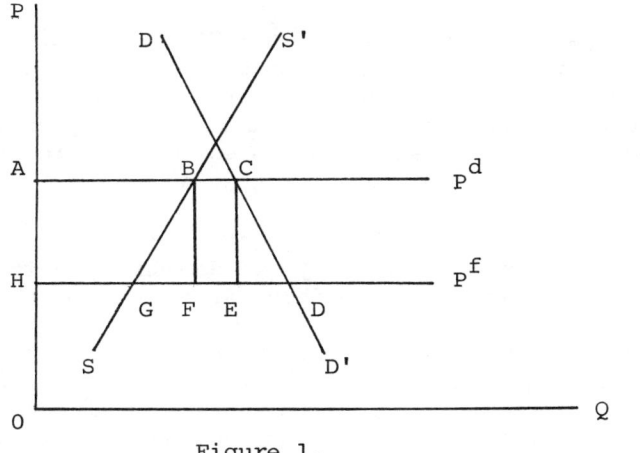

Figure 1.

As the growth of real output in the economy as a whole will probably be twice as rapid as that in the paddy sector, it is natural to look at the consequences for allocation and income distribution of subsidising paddy producers by keeping the domestic price of rice above the world level. This can be accomplished, in some measure, using the standard price-quantity diagrams of elementary supply-demand analysis of the partial equilibrium kind. Figure 1 depicts the situation ruling before 1974. The domestic price, P^d (= OA) is well above the c.i.f. price of imports, P^f (= OH), the tariff on each unit of imports being $P^d - P^f$ (= HA). Domestic production is AB, imports are BC and domestic consumption is AC. In the absence of the tariff, production, imports and consumption would have been HG, GD and HD, respectively. Thus, the imposition of the tariff leads to a gain in producers' surplus of HABG, a loss in consumers' surplus of ACDH, a tariff revenue of BCEF and a "deadweight loss" of BFG plus CDE. In the present case, while the producers are relatively poor, their output is also consumed intensively by all the poor. Thus, it is far from clear that income distribution as a whole has been improved as a result. The "deadweight loss" is a measure of the allocative inefficiency introduced by the tariff: it is the fall in the sum of producers' and consumers' surpluses resulting from the intervention. It should be noted that this measure takes no heed of income distribution considerations; for it is based on the assumption that the marginal utility of income is independent of the level of income. In any event, as both the supply (SS') and demand (DD') schedules are inelastic, the modest levels of the tariff and imports during the period up to 1974 meant modest "deadweight losses" and government tariff revenues.

Figure 2 depicts the post-1974 situation, in which the c.i.f. price of rice imports has risen to domestic levels without the intervention of a tariff. Production, imports and consumption are AB, BC and AC, respectively. (These are not the same quantities as those in figure 1, since SS' and DD' are shifting over time; P^d had also risen sharply.)

In figure 3, the supply and demand schedules shift over time, as described in the above discussion of the growth of supply and demand. In period 1, there is no difference between the domestic price and the c.i.f. price of imports, a situation just examined in figure 2. Between period 1 and period 2, domestic output grows faster than domestic demand. If the domestic price is maintained at its old level, there will be a surplus of output over domestic demand of magnitude B_2C_2, which must be exported. As there is usually a significant difference between the c.i.f. price of imports and the f.o.b. price of exports ($P_1^f - P_2^f$ in figure 3), the government must subsidize exports by that amount and so incurs a revenue loss of $C_2B_2E_2F_2$. Without this official intervention to keep the domestic price at its former level, the market price would have settled at the intersection of S_2S_2' and D_2D_2', to the advantage of consumers and the detriment of producers.

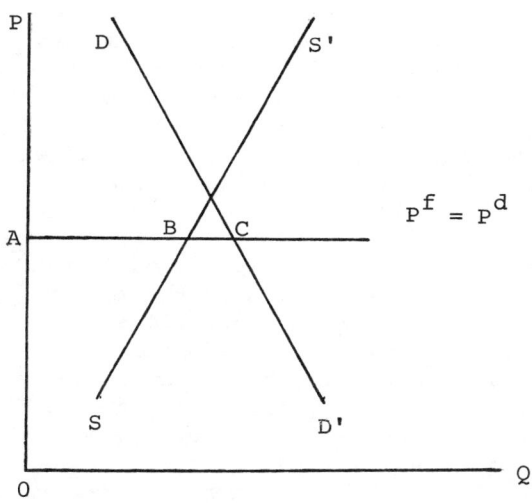

Figure 2.

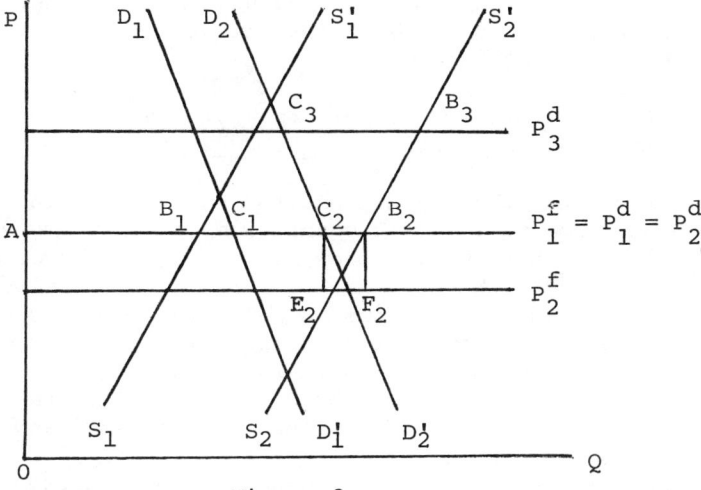

Figure 3.

This last case is a suggestive illustration of the situation which is likely to arise in the late 'eighties after import substitution is complete. If the supply schedule continues to shift faster than the demand schedule, the size of the exportable surplus — and hence the subsidy needed to sell it on world markets — will increase steadily. And if producer incomes are deemed to be inadequate at a constant domestic price, intervention to raise the domestic price, to P_3^d say, will entail a still larger unit subsidy, $P_3^d - P_2^f$, on a now bigger exportable surplus, B_3C_3. The need to increase paddy producers' incomes may, of course, prompt intervention to raise paddy prices above world levels well before the late 'eighties. That being so, the story is contained in figure 1.

To complete this simple exposition of the most likely form of government intervention in the market for rice, it is worth noting that so long as the world and domestic prices of rice differ little, the effective protection granted to the domestic production of paddy is likely to be small also. For intermediate inputs make up only a modest fraction of total cost, at market prices, of all inputs going into paddy production — about 15 percent in Muda (26). Hence, the ratio of value added in paddy production measured at domestic prices to that measured at world prices will not depart much from unity unless the ratio of the domestic to the world price of rice does so (27). While the rate of effective protection is not without drawbacks as an indicator of the efficiency of resource allocation, it seems plausible that, for the next few years at least, the continued expansion of paddy output through public investment involves no serious misallocation of resources.

IV. The Economic and Social Organisation of Paddy Production in the Future

In laying the foundations for the discussion of this section, some of its main conclusions are already apparent. It is clear that the strategy of raising the incomes of paddy producers through the provision of irrigation, new varieties, agricultural extension and price supports has been successful. Yet now that this intensive strategy of increasing paddy output has run most of its course, and the lives of most paddy farming households have changed for the better, the macroeconomic considerations in sections I and III must be confronted once again. Comparatively well-off as they are — taken as a group — Muda's paddy farming households are still much poorer than the national average: in 1975, the levels of income per head defined on a comparable basis, were US$330 and US$600, respectively. Moreover, 80 percent of the farmers' income was derived from paddy cultivation. Thus, if paddy output will grow no faster than 3.5 percent annually, while the rest of the economy grows at twice that rate or more, paddy farmers must diversify their sources of income in the future if their living standards are to lag no further behind the national average, a difference we will call the "income gap". The only question is: what form will diversification take?

It is also clear that the traditional basis for the socio-economic significance of the kampong as a unit of aggregation is weakening and that the future role of the village is intimately bound up with how paddy farming households seek to diversify their economic activities. Nevertheless, there remain powerful kinship bonds, which are intimately connected with tenancy arrangements and the domestic life cycle. In peering into the future to see what forms diversification might take, we ignore the kinship-tenancy-life cycle nexus at our peril.

As the population is a very young one and the "momentum" effect is powerful, the decline in fertility will not make itself felt in lower natural rates of growth for at least 15 or 20 years. Within that perspective, therefore, the starting point is the growth of the farm population on a fixed land base. Moreover, the natural rate of increase of the paddy farming population is no lower than that of the population at large. But even if paddy holdings stayed at their present size, so that outmigration would have to run at 2.6 percent annually for at least another 15 years, the "income gap" would tend to grow, and so speed outmigration further. This rate of outmigration is not without precedent in Malaysia. In Muda, the population of a sample of paddy mukims grew at a mere 0.8 percent annually between 1957 and 1970 (26), a period during which the incomes of paddy farming households lagged far behind the levels ruling elsewhere in the economy. Even with heavy investments in water control and the diffusion of ever-improving varieties, outmigration from Muda's paddy farms will continue apace.

It seems likely, then, that paddy holdings will not shrink much, and they will grow larger if the creation of jobs outside the paddy sector encourages a stream of migrants which outpaces the natural growth of the paddy farming population — although this is not a tangible prospect until the late 'eighties. But even if holdings and households stay roughly at their present size and paddy producers' terms of trade remain constant, the already large relative "income gap" is likely to grow at 1 to 1.5 percent annually — unless incomes from other sources increase rapidly — since per capita GNP will probably grow at 4 to 4.5 percent per annum.

The first possibility to be considered is that farmers will diversify into other crops and animal husbandry. These products have a high income elasticity of demand, and given the growth of incomes in the towns and a good transportation network, there will be no difficulty in finding markets to absorb them at remunerative prices. Rather, as we have already seen in section II, the problem is on the supply side, there being an acute shortage of suitable land. Perhaps the stall-feeding of selected stock has some promise, as do systematic poultry- and vegetable-raising. But the income thus arising would have to grow at 12 to 15 percent per annum initially just to keep the relative "income gap" where it is, even with the assistance of a 3 to 3.5 percent annual growth rate in paddy output (28). Hence, the prospects for profitable on-farm diversification are not sufficient to relieve unaided the pressures making for outmigration over and above that keeping operational paddy holdings at their present size. Sadly, Malaysia's paddy farmers do not have the option of switching heavily into higher value crops on their present holdings — unlike, for example, Israel's moshavim, which send daily supplies of fresh carnations in winter to Northern Europe.

Thus far, the terms of trade have been kept constant for the sake of tidiness in exposition. But the government could reduce the "income gap" below what it would otherwise have been by propping up the farm gate price of paddy above world levels and subsidising farm inputs, such as fertiliser. (Indeed, if the world price of rice grows more slowly than the prices of commodities the farmer purchases, keeping the paddy producer's terms of trade constant entails a subsidy anyway.) As we have seen in section III, the long period price elasticities of demand for, and supply of, paddy are rather low in Malaysia, and the sector accounts for only 2 percent of GNP. Hence, the long run fiscal burden of raising the price of paddy relative to other commodities at a rate of 1 or 2 percent annually, which would keep the "relative income gap" constant, should not be intolerable. For domestic supply and consumption will alter little, so that the loss of tariff revenue on imports, or the outlay on subsidising exports to be "dumped" on world markets, would be modest, too. After some time, the domestic price of rice might get out of line from world levels. But such happenings are not unheard of in Northeast Asia, where small rice farms survive in the midst of relative or absolute affluence. Of course, the drawback of this form of intervention is that it bears heavily on all poorer households, since rice is a wage good. However, there is no real prospect of subsidising paddy farming households through lump-sum transfers, so the adverse effects of price support policies will have to be borne as necessary evils.

The remaining possibility is that part-time paddy farming will become the rule, as in contemporary Japan. With a good road network and the growth of off-farm jobs in provincial towns such as Alor Setar in Kedah, farmers might commute to work. Islamic rules and ethos make it less plausible that farmers' wives will commute to off-farm jobs in any numbers, although some of their unmarried daughters do so already. Moreover, recent changes in techniques of paddy cultivation make part-time farming a distinct possibility, with women managing cultivation. The arduous task of land preparation is now fully mechanised, and combine harvesters are already dealing with 20 percent of the land area in Muda, a figure which may ultimately approach 50 percent. Women do the transplanting anyway, and could probably cope with the heavier operations given occasional help from their husbands, adolescent sons and hired hands. Indeed, there appears to be no reason why they should not develop and exercise the management and husbandry skills possessed by their husbands. After all, many widows do well enough as cultivators, and there is some recent, but fragmentary evidence from the Muda area that important farm decisions are usually made jointly by the married couple. Thus, if part-time paddy farming were to develop, it seems plausible that an important change in the economic role of women would be involved. However, this does not necessarily pose any threat to the present system of patriarchy, even though some vestiges of the matriarchal pre-Islamic order have survived to the present day.

If these forms of diversification and/or government subsidy failed to keep the "income gap" within bounds, outmigration would accelerate to the point where farm holdings began to increase in size, and so provide higher incomes. Two "models" offer themselves for consideration. First, Malays finding jobs elsewhere in the economy may rent out their holdings to entrepreneurial Chinese households. (They cannot sell out to non-Malays owing to the Land Alienation Act.) These entrepreneurs seem to have no difficulty in managing 70 to 100 acres with great efficiency — when they can muster such a holding through leases. But social and political factors weigh against these arrangements on a large scale, except perhaps in the implausible event of a mass exodus of the paddy farming population. In particular, the social pressures to lease to one's kin — if one leases at all — are very strong. As one farmer put it to me: "If land is rented to outsiders when kinsmen are in need, then heads will get broken." Only when a large sum of money is needed in a hurry can the claims of kin be ignored with safety. The land is then leased for 3, 5 or 7 years in exchange for a lump sum in advance: only entrepreneurial Chinese households can raise that sort of cash.

This leads to the second "model", which might be called the kulak variant in the development of agrarian capitalism. Changes in cultivation techniques have pushed back the management diseconomies usually associated with paddy production, as the success of the Chinese entrepreneur farmers testifies. Also, those families with marginal holdings may be more tempted to sell up when there are fair prospects of permanent jobs in the government's land settlement schemes (which involve rubber or oil palm), or in the non-farm economy. They can certainly sell to other Malay farmers, and those who are already relatively well-off will be in the strongest position to buy. This is a familiar enough story, and there is no need to dwell on it (29).

One question still remains unanswered, whether holdings stay at their present size or increase with the advance of the kulak farmer: what will happen to the ownership rights of those members who leave the household on attaining maturity, for they will make up the main part of the stream of migrants from paddy farms? As matters now stand, inheritance practices lie somewhere between the Islamic Law (two-thirds shares for all males and one-third for females) and the older "animist" tradition (equal shares for all offspring). In the strict sense, therefore, the outmigrants become rentiers. In this connection, the terms of the above discussion of the "income gap" assumed implicitly that they claim no rent. The traditional ethos of paying rents to kin according to one's ability is in tune with that assumption provided the outmigrants are doing well enough economically, which seems plausible if their decisions are fairly rational and well-informed.

Over a generation or so, as the migrants' contacts with their native villages grow more tenuous, the hereditary claims of the second generation may begin to lose their de facto force. Thus, in the much longer term, the rapid growth of the Malaysian economy may well lead to a uni-geniture system in practice, and because of the influence of Islam, it will almost certainly be a patrilineal one. Such a development would be consistent with the domestic cycle and a part-time farming system if the favoured son held down a nearby non-farm job until middle-age, when he would assume the responsibilities of farming from his aging father. If he were to retain his non-farm job, his wife could take over the day-to-day tasks of paddy cultivation, as was suggested earlier.

Over the next two decades the exodus from paddy farms will probably not be heavy enough to allow holdings to grow much in size in the face of the rapid natural growth of population. Thereafter, the demographic transition should be well beyond the half-way point, so that continuing and strong outmigration will far outweigh natural increase and farms will start to become significantly larger. Under these circumstances, those who stay behind will be under less pressure to seek local off-farm jobs, and having few children, farmers will find it easier to pass on the farm to one son or a son-in-law. However, a system of this kind lies far off in the future, if it should ever get established.

And what of the outmigrants themselves? If the economy grows as rapidly as it has done in the past decade they will be absorbed fairly easily and the population in paddy farming households will grow very slowly over the next 15 years. Moreover, their material well-being will improve over the long run — though whether they will be happier in their new occupations is perhaps less certain. Some of them will acquire small holdings in settlement schemes specialising in tree crops; most will become production and clerical workers; and the well-educated few will enter business, the professions or government. But their new status — whether commercial farmer producing export crops, proletarian or bourgeois — points to a steady decline of the rice producing peasantry.

In the light of all this, the doubts expressed earlier about the identity of the Malaysian paddy village become more compelling as one looks at the likely future changes in paddy technology, personal mobility, communications, the opportunities of accessible off-farm jobs and expenditure patterns — to say nothing of incorporation into the nation's political structure. But there is also a clue from the past which must not be ignored: the historical weakness of secondary and tertiary economic activities based in the villages (17). Unlike South Asia, there are no traditional village artisans — weavers, potters, blacksmiths and the like — to provide the skills for growing, labour-intensive activities in manufacturing. Moreover, even the physical topography of the __kampongs__ discourages the establishment of factories and workshops there because expensive land-filling of the poorly drained soils is essential if these buildings are to have adequate foundations. Good communications and mobility have pre-empted that sort of development anyway, as the towns — large and small alike — flourish. The village shop has a secure, if limited, future; the local small scale rice mill can still grow through illegal commercial sales; and farmers will continue to build, extend and maintain their lovely stilted houses with new materials and some help from the local carpenter. Thus, the kampong will retain its significance as a settlement in which people live and conduct the ordinary business of daily life — and a very pleasant one it is by the standards of most villages in the Third World. But there is no prospect that it will remain the focus of economic, social and political life which apparently constituted its significance in the past.

V. Some General Conclusions

The special features of Malaysia's paddy sector need no further emphasis; but it should not be concluded that this case is so atypical that it holds no lessons for the future of paddy farming in the rest of Southeast Asia. First, there are the characteristics of the demand and supply sides of the market to be considered. When incomes are very low, the aggregate income elasticity of demand for rice will be relatively high, albeit still less than unity. Thus, an expansion in supply will not put domestic prices under pressure to the same extent as it would in Malaysia. Of course, low cost producers can always resort to exports, as Thailand has done. However, the world market for rice is rather "thin" and may not provide a reliable buffer, let alone stable prices. Hence, if paddy farmers are to grow more affluent along with the rest of the society, the forces demanding diversification will make themselves increasingly felt. In those countries which now have low and slowly growing incomes, as well as relatively large paddy sectors, appreciable gains in paddy producers' incomes may not be realised for many decades. If the physical area under cultivation cannot be extended, farms will become smaller and cultivation more intensive; but with living standards altering little, the structures of output and consumption in paddy villages will tend to stay as they are.

Secondly, there is the existence, or otherwise, of a strong tradition of secondary and tertiary activity in rural areas. As we have noted, this tradition is weak in Malaysia, so that the establishment of a good communications network has caused the rapid growth in manufacturing and services to be centred in towns. However, that is by no means an inevitable path. At a similar stage of development, a large part of Japan's industrial employment and output was based on rural enterprises, which made heavy use of part-time workers from farms. Likewise, the emphasis on rural industry in the People's Republic of China stems not only from the country's rather inadequate transportation system, but also from the view that village industry promotes strong linkages in the economy (30).

These examples suggest that the poorer countries of Southeast Asia can adopt a strategy of bringing non-farm jobs to the peasants, in line with rising incomes from a sustained growth in farm output. In such cases, the village economy will be diversified and strengthened. Villagers will have a wider choice of occupations and income-earning opportunities without being forced to uproot themselves in search of jobs in the larger towns and cities. Moreover, a diversified economic base will provide a range of profitable uses for local savings within the local economy itself, thus giving an impetus to new growth based, in part, on local resources. Naturally, some of the basic infrastructure needed to support a diversified village economy will have to be provided by the central government. In the past, with a few notable exceptions, villages have not fared well in competing with the cities for government funds. This is not to say that the pattern of past allocations has been socially efficient, although it has undoubtedly served some interests in a handsome way. But whether the social groups which dominate the regimes in these countries will perceive — and act upon — any advantage in pursuing a development strategy based on a diversified rural economy remains to be seen.

References and Notes

1. B.J. Loasby, Imperfections and Adjustments (University of Stirling Discussion Papers, No. 50, 1977).
2. The crop is paddy, which becomes the consumer good rice after milling. The term "rice" is sometimes used where "paddy" would be correct, but the context should dispel any ambiguity.
3. S. Anand, Inequality and Poverty in Malaysia: Measurement and Decomposition (London, Oxford University Press, forthcoming).
4. This strategy is spelt out in Malaysia, Second Malaysia Plan: 1971-75 (Government Press, Kuala Lumpur, 1971) and reiterated in Malaysia, Third Malaysia Plan: 1976-1980 (Government Press, Kuala Lumpur, 1976).
5. Malaysia, ibid., p. 11.
6. Malaysia, ibid., p. 53.
7. Malaysia, ibid., p. 66.
8. Malaysia, ibid., p. 331.
9. S. Husin Ali, Malay Peasant Society and Leadership (Kuala Lumpur, Oxford University Press, 1975).
10. F.A.O., The Muda Study (Rome, 1975).
11. S. Jegatheesan, Land Tenure in the Muda Irrigation Scheme (Alor Setar, Muda Agricultural Development Authority, 1976).
12. U.N. Bhati, Some Social and Economic Aspects of the Introduction of New Varieties of Paddy in Malaysia (United

Nations Research Institute for Social Development, Geneva, 1976).
13. M. Yamashita, S. Jegatheesan and Wong Chee Yoong, "Agro-Economic Studies in the Muda Region: Farm Management Report" (Alor Setar, Muda Agricultural Development Authority, unpublished, 1976).
14. S. Selvadurai and A.B. Arope, <u>Socio-Economic Study of Padi Farms in Province Wellesley, 1968</u> (Kuala Lumpur, Ministry of Agriculture and Cooperatives, 1969).
15. S. Selvadurai, <u>Krian Padi Survey</u> (Kuala Lumpur, Ministry of Agriculture and Cooperatives, 1972).
16. S. Selvadurai, A.B. Arope and N.H.B. Mohammad, <u>Socio-Economic Study of Padi Farms in the Kemubu Area of Kelantan, 1968</u> (Kuala Lumpur, Ministry of Agriculture and Cooperatives, 1969).
17. C. Bell, S. Devarajan, P. Hazell and R. Slade, "A Social Accounts Analysis of the Structure of the Muda Regional Economy" (Washington, D.C., World Bank, unpublished, 1976).
18. Malaysia, op.cit., p. 295.
19. The Treasury, Malaysia, <u>Economic Report: 1975-76</u> (Kuala Lumpur, 1975).
20. Malaysia, op.cit., p. 286.
21. <u>Ibid.</u>, p. 74.
22. C. Bell and P. Hazell, "A Formal Analysis of Muda's Paddy Farm Sector" (Washington, D.C., unpublished, 1977).
23. M.S. Ahluwalia, "The Dimensions of the Problem", in H.B. Chenery, <u>et al.</u>, <u>Redistribution With Growth</u> (Oxford, The Clarendon Press, 1974).
24. M.S. Ahluwalia and S.D. Tendulkar, "An Input-Output Analysis of Growth in the Malaysian Economy: 1970-1980" (Washington, D.C., World Bank, unpublished, 1976).
25. Malaysia, op.cit., p. 294.
26. C. Bell and P. Hazell, "Measuring the Indirect Effects of an Agricultural Investment Project on Its Surrounding Region" (Washington, D.C., World Bank, unpublished, 1978).
27. Let the cost of intermediate inputs needed to produce a unit of paddy be c^d and c^f, evaluated at domestic and world prices, respectively. Then the value added associated with a unit of paddy output is $p^d - c^d$ at domestic prices, and $p^f - c^f$ at world prices. The rate of effective protection is defined as:

$$\frac{p^d - c^d}{p^f - c^f} - 1 \ .$$

28. If per capita incomes elsewhere in the economy are growing, on average, at 4.5 percent annually, then the <u>ratio</u> of their level to that of members of paddy farm house-

holds will stay constant provided the non-farm incomes of the latter grow at a rate y_o given by $4.5 = 3.0 \times 0.8 + y_o \times 0.2$, 0.8 being the weight attached to incomes from paddy cultivation (see Table 1), and the growth of paddy output being 3 percent annually.

29. For an account of the forces making for inequality in the traditional paddy system, see M.G. Swift, "Economic Concentration and Malay Peasant Society", in M. Freedman (ed.), <u>Social Organisation: Essays Presented to Raymond Firth</u> (Chicago, Aldine, 1967).

30. J. Gray, "The Chinese Model: Some Characteristics of Maoist Policies for Social Change and Economic Growth", <u>L'Est</u> (Milan, 1971, No. 2).

David Shear

9. The Role of the Village in Sahelian Development

I. Introduction and Overview

Background of the Drought

The economic consequences of the drought between 1968 and 1973 in West Africa were profound. Extreme rainfall deficits which occurred in 1971, 72 and 73 caused 40 percent losses of livestock in Mali, over 30 percent in Upper Volta, Niger and Senegal, and possibly more than 60 percent in Mauritania. Cash crops also suffered severely. Ground nut harvests in Niger and Senegal plummetted. Mali and Chad harvested between one and two-thirds of their normal cotton crop (1). It is much more difficult to measure the impact of the drought upon food production, because food is grown almost solely for local consumption. There is, however, no question that cereals production also declined substantially. During the period when suffering was at its greatest and international aid at its highest, from 1972 to 1974, over one million tons of cereals were delivered to the Sahelian states by the external donor community (2).

While the economic consequences of the drought were great, the cost in human terms was even greater. As many as 100,000 persons may have died. Literally millions of people were forced to change their place of habitation and between eight and ten million persons were directly affected. This substantial temporary displacement resulted in creating considerable pressures on other populations, especially in areas to the south of the Sahel.

On the positive side, local response to the impact of the drought showed the resilience of the Sahelian population. Acreage allocated to cereal production increased significantly while that allotted to cash crops declined (3). Cattle herders, rather than retain their herds and see them die, rapidly responded by selling off a large proportion of their animals while retaining those only required for subsistence. The relationship between pastoralist and sedentarized farmer was also reinforced and, in many instances, pastoral nomads became semi-sedentary and turned to farming (4).

The political consequences of the drought were also profound. The Governments of Niger and Chad were overthrown, primarily because they could not respond effectively to the needs of their hungry populations. Perhaps more importantly in the long run, an awareness of the importance of the rural populations to the ruling groups in each country was made manifest. Correspondingly, the Sahelian Ministers of Rural Development have become increasingly important. So much so that when the Interstate Commission to Combat the Effects of the Drought was established in 1973 in Ouagadougou, it was comprised of the Ministers of Rural Development from each of the Sahelian states. This Interstate Commission, known as the CILSS, became the political forum through which the Sahelian countries made their plight known to the world at large. That their appeal was effective was seen in the magnitude of the donor response (5).

The donors, despite a somewhat unsteady beginning in 1972, rapidly mobilized resources in both food and financing and coordinated their efforts through the Office of Sahelian Relief in FAO. A million tons of cereals and thousands of tons of other emergency supplies were moved through most difficult circumstances into the Sahelian states themselves and were distributed where needed most; amongst the rural populations. In addition to food aid, some donors such as the European Economic Community, provided special grants to the Sahelian states in order to permit a moratorium on livestock taxes normally collected from the pastoral herders. Emergency road and bridge repairs and other logistics requirements for the movement of cereals were actively undertaken by donors such as Canada and the U.S. and a special Sahel office was created in the Secretary General's Office of the United Nations. In all, some $900 million was expended during the period 1972 and 1974 by the donor community for both cash and food aid in order to help prevent a calamity of major proportions from occurring in the Sahelian zone.

The Long-Term Response to the Sahelian Drought

As a result of the Sahelian drought, certain fundamental development problems were laid bare. One analysis indicated that the process of desertification was clearly accelerating as a result of increases of people and cattle (6). Perennial grasses were being replaced by annual grasses, and, in many places, deforestation was occurring at an alarming rate. Increased population pressure meant decreasing periods of fallow and a decline in soil fertility. Analyses by development planners also indicated declining per capita food production over the 15 years prior to 1974 at a rate slightly in excess of one percent annually. It became evident that if the long-term environmental decline of the Sahel was to be reversed and if the Sahel was ever to become resistant to future droughts, a sustained, concerted development effort of a considerable magnitude had to be launched.

This was done within the context of the Organization for Economic Cooperation and Development (OECD), primarily through the initiative of France and the U.S. The result of this effort is the Club du Sahel which now comprises twelve principal bilateral donors and all of the principal international development agencies (7). The Club is, in effect, an alliance between the industrialized world and the Sahelian states. The African states are represented through their Interstate Commission to Combat the Drought (the CILSS).

The first meeting of the Club took place in Dakar in late March 1975. This launched the planning process which is now well under way. Technical working groups have been established for the key production sectors of Agriculture, Livestock and Fisheries. Integrating technical groups have also been launched for Ecology, Human Resources Development and Health, Infrastructure and Transportation. Special technical commissions have also been formed to deal with such important questions as agricultural price policy, marketing and storage, local and recurrent project costs and criteria for the selection of programs. The originators of the Club planning methodology also saw that conventional sectoral planning would not be adequate to deal with the large number of interrelationships which had to be examined if a Sahel-wide integrated program was to be achieved. Therefore, a special unit for program integration has also been established.

The consultative and planning process has in one measure been extremely successful. The core problems of the region have been identified and the analysis for their technical solution is under way. An intense interchange among donor and recipient planners is well advanced and a clearer understanding of the priorities of the Sahelian states has emerged. Finally, a very significant mobilization of resources has already been accomplished. Over three billion dollars was pledged in the second meeting of the Club du Sahel in Ottawa in May 1977. As a result, the external resources have in large measure been made available for the first phase of what must be a 15-20 year development effort (<u>8</u>).

Village Emphasis

While the resources, both financial and technical, have been mobilized, there are some significant constraints to bringing about the realization of these programs. The problem of the absorptive capacity of the Sahelian governments to receive and properly utilize the external assistance being made available poses significant problems. It also presents a unique opportunity. If we assess where the absorptive capacity in the Sahel is greatest, it is at the local level. That is, at the level of the village. The long-term development program for the Sahel, therefore, is focusing on the village as a principal channel for delivery of development assistance. It is this method for administering assistance almost directly to the local level which also makes the Sahel Development Program a unique enterprise.

We must look, therefore, at the village as the delivery vehicle in greater detail. Using the village as the principal channel for development programs will give us a safeguard against some of the dangers of the macro-planning which has taken place at the national level and sometimes even outside of the Sahel itself. Planning from the top down, while useful in identifying macro constraints to development, clearly has severe limitations. Local societies can be changed and even destroyed by the development process. The impact which technological change brings about at the village is rarely well understood. And indeed the lack of local feedback and evaluation often brings about significant dislocations at the local level and can presage the doom of any large-scale development effort from the outset.

The proposed approach through the village has three primary advantages. First, it utilizes the existing, responsive, administrative structure at the local level. Secondly, it avoids the creation of large government bureaucracy, with the resulting high continuing costs for its maintenance. Third, it assures sensitivity to local conditions which would be impossible if the program were primarily administered from the capital city. This is critical to the creation of an evaluation system so essential for the success of any long-term program which includes the need for relative ease of obtaining information feedback.

II. Village and Underdevelopment in Historical Perspective

One has to be extremely careful in discussing "the village" in any universal sense since the societies of the Sahel are so varied. The history of the area from empire and dissolution to recent national reconstitution from the colonial period is extremely complex. The grouping of villages, their internal composition, the way in which they use land and indeed the way in which they are ruled and guided varies considerably from one area to the other (9). Nevertheless, the village, despite its diversity, has certain elements of permanence. Part of this permanence is based on the ability of the village system to be flexible and to adapt to external pressures and hence to survive.

Unlike their colonial rule in Asia, the French and the English in West Africa chose to govern through existing institutional structures. They did so not because of any feeling of reverence towards the local cultures but rather because of the difficulties of Europeans living in West Africa on any permanent basis (10).

Lord Lugards' policy of indirect rule in Nigeria, while perhaps the most extreme and clearest example, was in some ways a model for much of colonial administration throughout West Africa. Therefore, the basic composition of the village, the role of the headman and the chief remained reasonably intact despite a whole series of external pressures brought about by the nature of colonial rule. During the colonial period, there were many changes in responsibilities laid upon the village and, therefore, to some degree some changes in the village unit survived extremely well as the tool for local administration.

Examples of Permanence and Change

Permanence and change should be seen in several examples in order to fully appreciate the special capacity of the village in this portion of West Africa.

Djoliba is a Maninke village in Mali at the edge of the Niger River's annual flood plain, originally settled about the time of the arrival of the first Englishman in North America. Djoliba has remained a functioning organization of local government ever since (11). The present chief traces his descendants back fourteen generations even though the location from whence they first came is not known. Established after the period of Empire, the village maintained its independence during the local political turmoil which existed intermittently from Empire up to the military victory of the

French in 1883 and the firm establishment of its colonial rule in 1888. The impact of French rule in Djoliba which lasted 72 years up to 1960 was fairly typical. Colonial control brought peace, greater personal freedom to travel and trade plus taxes. While the revenue from villages like Djoliba was never very great, its collection did force important changes in agricultural practices. Cash crops were introduced and peanuts became the means of revenue for Djoliba farmers. As production increased and local incomes rose, the village also became an important consumer of French manufactures.

Following the end of World War II, the French began a substantial investment program in Mali. Included in this effort was the rice scheme for Djoliba. The project, which was physically completed just before independence, failed. It failed under French colonial administration and under an independent Mali as well. It did so because both the French and Malian planners failed to understand the dynamics of the village institutions and the relationship of those institutions to labor and agricultural production. Jones points out (12) these key relationships between clans, the internal family structure and the failure of the Malian political system as well as the French to read properly these interactions. Strongly resisted was the imposition of labor practices which did not honor the work relationship of elders to the rest of the village force.

The failure of an AID housing project at Djoliba during the same period was also related to a lack of understanding about the village structure, especially the central position of the residential lineage. Even though they refused to inhabit the AID-financed housing that did not conform to their own family patterns, the residents of Djoliba were not opposed to change per se. They enthusiastically supported those Malian political programs which tied them to the Mali which was also a nation state when those programs did not run counter to traditional institutions.

The introduction of the plow to Djoliba in the mid 1960s is a powerful indication of the flexibility of these Maninke when it is in their own interest. Plows mean draft animals and a wholly new relationship of sedentary farmers to cattle. Manuring of fields was possible thereby increasing productivity. The area farmed was theoretically tripled but in more real terms it was doubled. The use of carts for hauling became common and with the introduction of pit silos, it is now possible to begin to plow when the rains first come instead of waiting for grass to grow high for the oxen to regain their strength after the dry season.

The Village in Sahelian Development   241

The introduction of the plow and oxen to Djoliba may also, in time, bring about another and even more profound change. The need for very large families will diminish somewhat as the labor output by farmers increases with the use of animal traction. This factor, when combined with rural health programs currently being planned which include maternal and child care, gives some hope that child spacing is a reasonable prospect in the future.

Djoliba has changed and will continue to change. It has, however, remained largely intact and gives every prospect of retaining its basic characteristics into the foreseeable future.

In addition to seeing both the resistance as well as the adaptability of the people of Djoliba, it might be useful to examine briefly two other groups in Mali in order to see how they have adapted to external change.

In late June 1975 a colloquium was held at the Institut de Recherche en Science Humaine at the University of Niamey in Niger. The colloquium dealt with the effects of drought on the productive strategies of Sudano-Sahelian herdsmen and farmers. One of the reports presented at the colloquium was prepared by an American researcher who had been resident in Doukolomba, Mali, where AID was undertaking a livestock production activity. Grayzel reports in some detail how the Peul, while adhering to the basic herding systems with which they had been so long associated, were flexible enough to turn to the production of sorghum and millet in times of extreme adversity (13). It should be pointed out that one 8-year old steer is worth approximately 175 dollars on the market or the equivalent of some 3.5 metric tons of millet at local prices. The possession of cattle, however, also carries with it significant benefits for agricultural undertakings. There is the availability of large quantities of manure and hence, while neighboring Bambara agriculturalists have to rotate their fields every 7 or 9 years many Peul have been able to use the same field for over 18 years. In addition, all the Peul use plows which are pulled by their oxen. This system actually sustained the Peul through the worst periods of the drought. Rather than changing their basic practices, the Peul in the Doukolomba area had their agricultural system reinforced. Using animal traction it was also possible for the Peul to increase the acreage under millet production in contrast to that normally undertaken. Grayzel points out in his paper that while neighboring Bambara gave up cultivating cotton and peanuts for increased millet planting, the Peul merely had to expand the acreage they already had under production. He also reports that

Bozo and Somono fishermen in the area who had not before cultivated millet have over the past five years begun to participate in the production of this cereal.

The Peul of the Doukolomba area work a mixed farming and herding system. These activities do not take place at the same time and frequently overlap. They show, however, that such a mixed farming and herding system while dependent upon a limited, seasonal transhumance of cattle into richer grasslands is clearly a viable option under certain circumstances.

One has to be careful about generalizing, however, for I have seen south of Lake Chad a similar system that is leading to the rapid deterioration of range land. This is primarily because sufficient amounts of rich rainy season grasses are not available and, therefore, rather than trekking 200 miles, as the Peul of Doukolomba do in search of new grass, the Peul in Chad are forced to work a system approximately 50 miles in extent. This system cannot sustain the numbers of cattle being held by the Peul and some basic change in their production systems will have to be brought about if they are to even survive in their current environment.

While the Maninke and the Peul in Mali indicate two different ways of reacting to external forces, the Dogon of the Songa Plateau in Mali show how even within a highly structured system, one with a very elaborate cosmology, external technical innovations can be absorbed within the societal construct. During a visit to Songa in 1974 at the height of the drought, I asked the paramount chief how much emergency grain had been made available to his village. He informed me that no grain had been needed. He pointed out to a number of crypts carved in the sandstone side of a cliff in which the victims of the drought of 1916 to 1918 had been enterred. The chief said that during the current drought no one had died. None had died because during the prior thirty years the Dogon had established an agronomic technique which gave them a millet crop even in times of extreme adversity. This labor-intensive method has also permitted a mixed cropping of millet and onions; the onions find their way as far as the coastal cities and bring to the Dogon a very substantial return on their investment of labor and time. The intensive agriculture of the Dogon is based on the use of heavy composting and, therefore, the high degree of moisture retention. This technique, introduced by a French extension agent in the early 1920s, was clearly a practice which the Dogons seized upon following their unfortunate experience during the 1916-18 drought.

We see in Dogon agriculture today a technique which has considerable applicability elsewhere in the Sahel and indeed AID and the Malian government are currently undertaking research to see what aspects of these agronomic practices can be adopted by others in the Sahel. Implicit with this analysis and research is an understanding of the Dogon social structure so we can better understand how the basic agricultural system was factored into their basic cultural system.

Forced Migration and New Lands Settlement

In striking contrast to the Maninke of Djoliba and the Dogon at Sanga is the history of the Office du Niger irrigation project in which thousands of Bambara and Mossi were forcibly settled by the French beginning in 1932. This project, established by the colonial regime as a public enterprise and continued by an independent Mali in the same vein, sought to make the area around Ségou one of the world's principal cotton-producing regions. It was also intended to produce enough irrigated rice to supply Mali's rice-short neighbors in Senegal and the Ivory Coast (14).

By 1945 the development of much of the infrastructure for the project had been completed. More than 20,000 persons had been forcibly "colonized" and some 50,000 acres of land was under production. This is in contrast to the original objective of 570,000 acres to be established. In that year, there was produced only 22,000 tons of rice paddy on 85 per cent of the irrigated land. Cotton seed production which was to have been the other major agricultural crop was only 1500 tons. A pause in the expansion was then called for in an attempt to increase individual yields since per capita production was extremely low, indeed even lower than traditional rice production at the village level. The pause was only a brief one, however, and by 1962 the Office du Niger, comprising 80,000 acres of irrigated land, had a population of 37,000 persons. These farmers produced 41,000 tons of rice paddy annually and 7,000 tons of cotton seed. Both types of production represented substantial increases over the 1945 figures, even though the 1962 level of production was much lower than the original goals. In that year, the administration of the Office du Niger was handed over by the French to the Malians. The Malian government, under Modibo Kéita, saw the Office du Niger as an example of how it could forward his socialist policies with respect to agricultural production on the collectivization of land. The imposition of an ideological overburden on an already shaky project further inhibited its growth and efficiency.

In addition to the many technical and managerial problems which the Office du Niger faced, perhaps the most overwhelming burden was that of the forced colonization of the farmers themselves. In the 1940s, Mossi and Samogho from Upper Volta were settled on the project. Bambara and Maninke from Mali were also forcibly established at the project. Since independence, however, forced in-migration has been halted. Despite attempts by the Government of Mali to improve the management of the project, the number of settlers has actually declined, owing to voluntary departures and the eviction of farmers who failed to pay their debts or to cultivate the land properly. In 1964, almost 3,000 persons left the Office and, in that year, the total settled population of 33,000 persons was smaller than the number reached in 1961. Some improvement in price incentives to the farmers has increased the production of cotton so that now two tons per hectare are produced as compared with the previous average .8 tons. Nevertheless, the primary constraint to production remains labor output and the incentive to farmers. Despite the staggering investment of $175 million since its inception, the project still produces only a small portion of what its potential might well be (15).

In fairness to the Malian government, it should be noted that the government is currently undertaking an extensive analysis of the project in order to see how it can be restructured to be made more productive. Fortunately, within that analysis is a clear understanding, albeit belatedly, of the importance of the attitude of the local farmers to the overall scheme. Inherent within this is, of course, the need for the Government of Mali to look at the whole construct of cereals price policy in order to assure that the farmer is given the proper incentive to produce -- a fair price.

Other Historical Constraints

Historically, the farmers of most of West Africa have supported the urban centers by their own labors. These centers, historically the seats for colonial administration and governance, have since independence continued to grow at approximately twice the rate of rural population. In addition, the city has continued to be the center for commerce, industry and general administration of the entire country. The city, therefore, has a population which tends to be reasonably educated and is certainly at the seat of power. Governments believe, therefore, that the Civil Service has to be fed at all costs. And the cost is usually at the expense of the farmer.

Grain marketing systems in the Sahel vary from country to country but they can be seen as having certain common elements. Private marketing systems are generally held suspect and individual commerçants are discouraged to the extent possible. National price marketing systems have been established which tend to provide cereals to urban consumers at a subsidized price. At the other end of the spectrum, the price to the farmer tends to be extremely low and not reflective of true demand. There was also historically considerable suspicion that the farmer "did not know enough" to respond to price incentives or to know when to sell or how to store his grain (16).

Events since the great drought have indicated the fallacies of at least some of these policies. The focus after the drought on food production has forced attention into the whole area of rural development and the need of the individual farmer. Price policy is now considered an important element in production incentives. And while there is still a very significant mistrust of the private sector's role with respect to marketing of food grains, there is at least a grudging acceptance of the fact that the Government itself cannot be the sole arbiter of national production, policy and distribution.

Official grain prices are currently rarely respected by either producer or consumer. Prices fluctuate according to production and distribution and, hence, prices sometimes find their level through supply and demand despite substantial attempts by the Government to intervene. The thrust of current policy emphasis is only now and grudgingly to look to the farmer as one of the principal arbiters of price since he has the ultimate responsibility for production.

Measured against this understanding, however, must also be seen the need for some means of national storage systems to assure against periods of drought such as the western Sahel experienced again in 1977 and to assure a reasonable price to the urban consumer.

III. Promoting Village Development through the Sahel Development Program

Alternate management structures to the village cannot be created in the time available to Sahelian planners. For while the long-term development program in the Sahel aims at the year 2000 as its horizon, some fundamental changes will be undertaken in the agricultural production systems of the area within the next decade. This means that large cadres of conventional civil servants cannot be trained and indeed, as noted earlier, the creation of such institutional infrastructure in the capitals is probably not even desirable. We must look at different ways for bringing about development in the rural areas. Such systems are currently being developed in the context of the Club du Sahel although they are not yet placed "on the ground" in large numbers. The implementation of the first phase of the program over the next five years will, however, begin to place extreme strains on local village systems and in that context we should look at how development programs in the Sahel can promote village development and how it can bring about change in the most constructive way possible.

In order to do this, however, we must first look at the basic strategies recommended for the Sahel Development Program (17). The overall objectives are: (1) to reduce the consequences of emergency drought situations in the future; (2) to assure regionwide self-sufficiency in staple foods (cereals and meat) while rehabilitating the basic environment of the Sahel, and finally (3) economic and social development particularly in the rural areas.

Given this set of objectives for the development of the Sahel, the following sub-strategies have been agreed to. These are: (1) development of traditional non-irrigated crops; (2) development of irrigated crops; and (3) development of animal husbandry and the achievement of a new agriculture/livestock balance.

The first phase of this program places very heavy emphasis upon developing traditional non-irrigated crops. For centuries past the Sahelians have coped with the difficult climate in their region by practicing "dryland farming". This, of course, is in reality seasonal farming making maximum use of the short rainy season. This traditional form of agriculture occupies most of the population and furnishes the bulk of its food supply which is approximately five million tons of cereals produced in an average year in the Sahel from non-irrigated crops. Ninety-nine percent of those five million tons are produced by small farmers. All of the technical studies undertaken on the Sahel in this sector emphasize the necessity of developing these dryland crops using to the maximum extent possible the technology developed by the farmers over the prior centuries. We are certain, nevertheless, that significant increases in production can be brought about by improved seeds and some changes in agronomic practices. Finally, at least a 25 percent increase in production can be achieved merely through the reduction of losses due to pests and birds.

The means of obtaining higher yields are well known, and most of the experts referring to them indicate the following:

- better soil preparation;

- use of improved varieties which are selected for high yields and if possible shorter maturation periods;

- some use of fertilizers and pesticides;

- protection from locusts and other predators;

- improved facilities for grain storage and transport.

All of these improvements can be undertaken at the local level with the single exception of the need to improve transport throughout the Sahel. Another factor, already mentioned, of extreme importance to increasing yields is to assure the farmer a reasonable return for the investment of his labor and meager capital.

Despite these improvements, almost all reports on the Sahel note that yield increase brought about by dry-land farming will remain highly sensitive to the vagaries of weather and, therefore, the development of non-irrigated crops cannot alone provide a solution to the future problems of drought.

The long-term alternative to the reliance on existing dry-land farming is the cultivation of new lands. Some of these lands are currently being held in escrow because of the presence of the tse-tse fly along the southern Sahel. There are also lands currently under-utilized which lie in the great river basin systems which traverse the Sahelian region. The Sahel is unique in the sense that five major water systems exist in its arid zone; Lake Chad, the Volta River system, the Senegal River Basin, the Gambia River system and the mighty Niger system; all have been virtually untapped to date. The development of these systems, however, is a very long-term undertaking requiring (1) massive inputs of capital, (2) long-term assessments of the environment impact of the damming of the rivers, and (3) the education of farm populations in utilizing new irrigation systems. Perhaps most importantly, however, is the need to bring about in-migration into these new lands in a way which does not disrupt basic social patterns. This is currently being done in Upper Volta in the Onchocerciasis Control Program which is leading to the resettlement of the White, Red, and

Black Volta Rivers. In this system basic village structures are being respected and ethnically cohesive groups are being introduced into the cleared land. With the development of these new lands, it is estimated that the Sahel could produce 18 million tons of cereal using present techniques and yields per hectare. Twenty-five million tons with current yields can be envisaged by 1985 and 29 million tons are possible by the year 2000.

The extension of cropland can be achieved in two ways: (a) by extending the land cultivated around existing villages and (b) by creating new farm land and establishing new villages. This, however, can only be achieved through migration, otherwise the extension of currently cultivated areas would be detrimental to soil fertility because of reduced fallow periods. We have already seen, however, how difficult migration can be if not handled with great care.

Along with the development of new lands will also be the introduction of new technologies. It is a basic premise of AID, however, that certain conditions must be fulfilled by any new technology for its adaptation by the farmer.

It must:

- be suited to local conditions;
- be economically profitable for the farmer;
- involve no more than acceptable risk levels;
- and, finally, fit in with the general sociocultural pattern.

Despite the macro planning being undertaken for the Sahel at this time, it is fortunate that no one has suggested the large scale introduction of very modern energy-dependent technology might be a solution compatible with the Sahel's sociocultural tradition (18).

While a major development effort is now going forward, the fact remains that farmers' incomes in the Sahel have actually been declining over the past decade. Annual cash incomes in Niger amongst the Hausa cereal-producing farmers average only $17. In Upper Volta and Senegal farmer cash incomes are somewhat higher but only due to the remittance from immigrant workers to members of their families remaining in Upper Volta and from ground nut cultivation in Senegal. Cash income by no means represents the farmer's real income since a large proportion is in the form of produce grown and

The Village in Sahelian Development 249

consumed on the farm; on the other hand taxes paid have to be deducted from money income. The FAO has attempted to estimate the trend of agricultural income between 1960 and 1970 and it has drawn two conclusions: One, in all the Sahel states agricultural income is lower than the urban worker's agricultural income and urban income deteriorated over the ten-year period. From 1960 to 1970, overall agricultural production increased slowly and prices remained static on the whole. At the same time, by the end of the decade the cost of essential inputs purchased by the farmer was increasing faster than the selling prices for crops, therefore, the value added on the farm actually decreased. Inequality between rural and urban dwellers which was already considerable in 1960 worsened during the subsequent 10-year period.

This trend has continued beyond 1970. The Center for Research in Economic Development (CRED) at the University of Michigan has examined trends in agricultural cash incomes between 1970 and 1974. In nominal values these incomes declined during the period except in Mali and in Upper Volta. Further, the uncertainty about price trends was such that in these two countries it was impossible to decide whether the trend of real income was upward or downward. The general conclusion reached by CRED was that the cash incomes of African producers have dropped between 1970 and 1974.

Using Basic Human Needs as an Approach to Integrated Rural Development

The obvious means to effect this declining situation, particularly in light of the prospects for substantial aid which now is very real, is the development of a major rural support effort. The development and large-scale adoption of new cultivation techniques demands more than a technical research effort for the rural communities of the Sahel, i.e., the villages. Past experience such as that at Djoliba has amply demonstrated this fact by the failure of many operations and it was not possible to break the bottlenecks of financial constraints by merely strengthening general rural support services. On the other hand, if the various technical and financial constraints were the subject of coherent measures insuring that the farmer was not thwarted by other bottlenecks, we would probably see more optimistic behavior on his part in favor of adopting new techniques. One way of assuring this is by introducing these techniques through systems which are his own.

One way of assuring local participation, particularly within the village context in an investment program as massive as that proposed for the Club du Sahel, is to view it within the context of a basic human needs policy. A basic human needs development policy is a fairly recent innovation and as a development tool it still is being refined and needs considerable further definition (21). There is hope, however, based on the recent conference at the Development Assistance Committee of the OECD that the principal donors of the world are now assessing basic human needs in much more analytical terms.

The DAC Chairman's Report for 1977 (22) places very heavy emphasis upon the need for further refinement of this development philosophy. The concept, however, is a relatively simple one. First, it includes certain minimum requirements of a family for private consumption. Adequate food, shelter and clothing are obviously needed as are certain household equipment and furniture. Second, the concept includes essential services provided by and for the community at large, such as safe drinking water, sanitation, transport, health and educational facilities.

The basic needs-oriented policy implies a very high degree of participation of the people in making the decisions which affect them. Their participation interacts with two main elements of the basic needs strategy. For example, education and good health will facilitate participation and participation, in turn, will strengthen the claim for basic needs. The satisfaction of an absolute level of basic needs as so defined should be placed within a broader framework, that is, the fulfillment of basic human rights which are not only ends in themselves but contribute to the attainment of other goals. Inherent within this concept of rights is the respect for basic value systems.

In all countries employment enters into a basic needs strategy both as a means and as an end. Employment yields output. It provides income to the employed. Further, it gives a person the recognition of being engaged in something worth his while. While the concept of basic needs has a universality of application it seems particularly relevant to development in the Sahel. If we look at the basic factors of human needs as already outlined, we can see that many of them already exist within the village construct. This is especially so with the participation which is at the core of a basic human needs approach. Only in this way can development objectives be made responsive to local will and locally perceived requirements.

In the Sahel the basic needs objectives can be found in increasing food production and storage, improving health and nutrition, bringing about the creation of dependable potable water and assuring the worker an adequate return for his or her labor.

Health

An excellent example of this approach can be seen through the basic rural health strategy developed by the Club du Sahel and now in the process of being accepted by all the Sahelian states themselves (19). The underlying premise of the village-based health delivery system is that it is organized by and for local residents. It is supported by a back-up health infrastructure which provides those services which are not possible at the local level. However, by basing the principal systems at the local level it offers the most effective and efficient way to promote and to protect community health for the majority of the people dispersed in rural areas.

Indigenous systems of health care exist in almost every Sahelian community; these systems could well be integrated into low-cost technologies and simple primary care methods. Local healers and practitioners, including traditional midwives, are effective to the extent they are because these local providers enjoy the confidence of the community.

It is possible to train village practitioners and selected village residents to enhance their skills in prevention and to provide simple diagnoses and treatment of common health problems and, thus to facilitate their effective intervention in the health status of the community. At the local level, the common disease patterns of infants and young children -- respiratory infections, diarrhea, malaria, and malnutrition -- are the major killers and can be effectively managed at the village level, along with a wide variety of prevalent infectious and parasitic diseases. Village health workers, as they continue to serve their communities, can expand the scope of their knowledge and problem-solving skills.

The implementation of the village-based system can take place in a phased incremental way allowing resources to be allocated as they become available.

The closeness of such a community health system to local residents creates an incentive and an opportunity for the citizens to contribute to the successful development of the system.

The use of village health workers in the development and collection of health and vital statistics offers an effective mechanism by which to develop a health information system.

Birth-spacing services are most appropriate when provided within the context of maternal and child health services that effectively reach the village level, and where the community itself has made an informed choice regarding these services. The estimated 80-90 percent of the population that do not have access to the existing health systems in the Sahel countries can be reached.

The expected operating expense of this system is justified on the basis of the benefits anticipated from the equitable distribution of resources for basic health services to rural populations. The <u>capital</u> investment outlay is minimal relative to existing expenditure patterns.

The existing health infrastructure in the Sahelian countries can provide the basis of technical and logistical support for a village-based strategy. Successful pilot efforts have already been undertaken ([20]).

   a. The Maradi ten-year village-based regional experience in Niger has strongly influenced a fundamental health service reform in Niger -- reflected in the current three-year plan.

   b. Villaged-based projects, using existing health infrastructures, are being implemented in Mali and Senegal and perhaps in other Sahelian countries.

   c. The successful experience of other countries which have undertaken health service reforms with scarce resources strongly favor this approach (China, Tanzania, Sri Lanka, the Kerala state of India).

   d. The health services technologies appropriate and applicable to any particular Sahel village would require country- and possibly area-specific definitions and adaptations to fit localized customs, patterns, and resources.

Demographic and Health Planning

Planning of health and social services, as well as other sectoral planning, requires reliable data concerning population growth and distribution combined with an accurate assessment of health and disease patterns. Unless national censuses, surveys, and epidemiologic studies in the Sahel take special account of the following three factors, considerable uncertainty will remain concerning purported future demographic patterns:

   a. Migration: nomadism, rural settlement, and also rural-to-urban population shifts.

   b. Isolated rural populations.

   c. Changing fertility and age-specific mortality rates.

Further, an understanding of small-area variations in local demographic and disease patterns is essential to the planning, implementation, and evaluation of health and other projects.

It is important that these data be used in all development programs. This can only be done by enhancing the understanding of relationships between population and Sahelian development objectives and by expanding the capability of planning institutions to incorporate these population dimensions into their development programs.

The health risks to Sahelian mothers and children can be significantly reduced by the spacing of births. This has long been recognized in the Sahel and accomplished by tradition methods of abstinence, contraception, and prolonged breast-feeding. There is evidence that urbanization and other modernizing forces are eroding these traditions. The lengthening of birth intervals by modern child-spacing measures (combined with improved child and maternal nutrition) markedly increases the survival chances of infants and young children, and also improves maternal health.

Components of an Integrated Village-Based System

To make most effective use of a village-based organizational structure for improving health, the preventive/community health orientation of services delivered should include components focusing on nutrition, clean water, environmental sanitation, and communicable disease control.

In general, the successful implementation of such components within the delivery mechanism of a village-based system depends on the effectiveness of a health education effort emphasizing the importance of each of the above components. Unless villagers are convinced of the importance of the component programs, successful implementation will be most difficult.

For each particular component, the strategy postulates a number of program premises, which are outlined below. (Of course, these components are in addition to, and complementary of, other primary health care activities.)

Nutrition

Improvement in the nutritional status of the Sahelian population, particularly mothers and infants, is dependent upon:

a. "Self-sufficiency" in a nutritional sense, i.e., having available adequate supplies of a nutritionally sound diet, preferably produced locally.

b. Future planning and implementation of nutritional self-sufficiency through new crops, livestock, or other foods being derived from the definition of specific localized (village or regional) nutritional requirements.

c. Ultimate achievement of a <u>constant</u> local availability of a nutritionally sound diet.

Significant improvement in the nutritional status of the Sahel population can be effected by a well-developed village-based health structure.

a. Changes in feeding practices of infants and children can substantially contribute to nutritional improvement and can most effectively be accomplished within a village-based system.

b. In addition to nutritional emphasis on infants and young children, emphasis must be placed on the nutritional needs of pregnant women and lactating mothers.

After initial training and deployment of village health personnel, continuing education/skill upgrading workshops should be provided periodically at the intermediate level (i.e., at peripheral health centers and dispensaries serving in support of village health workers), and should include nutrition training. Also, at the intermediate level of the health infrastructure resources for the nutritional rehabilitation of severely malnourished children need to be available. Stress should be placed on the health and nutrition education of the mothers of these children and the use of locally available weaning and supplementary foods.

Sex Roles

By looking both at the village and at a basic needs approach, we also can perceive a great gap in development planning in the Sahel today. This weakness is not unique to this portion of Africa. It is implicit within development planning on a worldwide basis. It is simply that the role of women has been virtually ignored. Only by pushing development planning down to the village level and by forcing planners and sociologists within the planning process to assess the interrelationships of village clan and family will the role of women be properly perceived. The focus on sedentary farmers living in small extended family villages has recently been examined by Kathleen Cloud in her paper prepared for AID (23). In it she describes the sex roles in food production among sedentary farmers as follows:

Grain Production. The grain is usually millet or sorghum. These are most often seen as men's crops, and the husband or a group of brothers will control the field and its product. The division of labor is often:

a. Clearing the land - done by boys and young men during the dry season. Trees and large plants are cut down and the area is burned to prepare for planting.

b. In planting - men make holes, women plant seed. Often women are responsible for selection of seed from previous harvests to be used. Because of erratic rainfall they will sometimes plant four or five types of seed in the same plot.

c. Weeding - This is the most labor-demanding part of the grain farming, and in most instances every available hand will be used in hoeing weeds. Young men come home from the city to help during this period. Wives will take turns staying home to cook and care for the children while the others go to the fields for the day. A man with several wives and many children has a distinct advantage in agriculture because of the labor he can call upon during the weeding and the harvest. The crops may be weeded one, two or three times. The amount of weeding has an effect on the amount of grain harvested. There is some indication that when grain reserves are high, less weeding is done -- there is not the urgent need for grain.

d. Harvesting - Again, every available person will be used.

e. Storage - Generally men are responsible for building the family storage sheds and supervising the grain stored in them. Women are responsible for the household storage of the grain.

f. Threshing - This is the women's job, and it will be done just before pounding the grain into flour each day. This threshing and milling may take a woman two to three hours, and is one of the most arduous, time-consuming tasks she has to perform.

There are some exceptions to the pattern of male dominance of grain production. In addition to assisting in their husband's millet field, women from some groups will have their own grain fields where they and their children do all the work. Notable among these are some of the Hausa women. In Mali, women grow corn in fairly large quantities and in some areas swamp rice is grown by women.

Vegetable Gardens. Women in most sedentary farm groups have hut gardens where they grow vegetables for the sauces eaten with the millet as well as for trade. They may grow carrots, red peppers, onions, garlic, tomatoes, eggplant, gumbo and various kinds of beans. It is these sauces that provide the necessary additional amino acids to the millet to make a complete protein chain. In addition, they provide many necessary vitamins, minerals and fats to the diet while also providing variety in flavor and appearance.

Extraordinary as it may sound, any number of food production projects have been designed with a very imperfect understanding of the basic divisions of labor as indicated in the Cloud paper. While it is not germane to this paper, the sex roles in food production among pastoralists is also poorly understood, and even worse what is known is infrequently utilized in the planning of livestock development activities. By promoting the village development through an understanding of the village dynamics the role of women can, should be, and must be factored into future Sahelian development programs.

Conclusion

Increasingly, donors are coming to understand that rural change can only be brought about through integrated rural development programs focusing on the village. AID, the World Bank, the Canadians and most other donors now agree that Integrated Rural Development is a system of related economic, cultural and social changes which are designed to improve the material welfare of rural people in terms of minimum levels of food, clothing, shelter and vital services such as health and education. An integrated approach to rural development, therefore, is nothing more than a systematic means of attempting to achieve the basic human needs of the rural population.

Implementation: Timing and Decentralization

A recent assessment of an AID rural development activity in Upper Volta by Michigan State University (24) confirms that rural development cannot occur in the short time periods in which most donor agencies conceive and execute projects. The MSU assessment team recommended (and AID has now agreed) that projects for Rural Development be framed within a ten-year period. The report states that: "Only within such a period of time can social, economic, agronomic study, experimentation and application take place to begin to perceive substantial progress toward integrated development. For example, building a road may take six months while setting up a viable animal traction system may take seven or eight years. But both should be seen as integral parts of the same long-term process."

Rural development in Upper Volta can be seen as an interesting harbinger of the future. Beginning in 1965, Upper Volta has pursued a general approach to rural economic development which is essentially decentralized. This decentralization sought to bring about social development through regional development organizations called ORDs, which in effect are local development institutions. These institutions are directly responsive and responsible for a fully integrated approach to development in the rural areas of Upper Volta. The decentralization permits greater flexibility and adaptation to local conditions which vary widely across Upper Volta depending on the ethnic composition of the populations being serviced. Decentralization is also a process which permits greater local participation in determining the very scope of the ORD activities and who will be the beneficiaries of these new programs.

Reinforcing the Village-Based Approach

The ORD approach in Upper Volta also reveals a very important element in supporting the village-based development system. That is, the village itself, despite the very considerable strength we have already identified, has certain very real limitations. One is that the principal families in any given village will tend to accumulate the greatest benefit from any development effort. And while most village systems are essentially egalitarian, there are, however, hierarchic structures, including lineages, which take a percentage "off the top" of most programs. It is, therefore, important that some external and more independent body have a role in the administration of the development process. Clearly, however, when that administration has historically been lodged in capital cities the gulf has been much too great. By placing development administration in the rural areas the Government of Upper Volta has achieved, I believe, a very important balance between the village system and a management process which is sufficiently removed from the traditional village hierarchial structure in order to permit a somewhat greater degree of objectivity in the allocation of resources. Also important, a secondary administrative system external to the village permits a more independent judgment in terms of actual progress.

There are certain technical elements of development which are also outside the capacity of the village to undertake. For example, field trials for the local adaptation of new strains of millet and sorghum must be undertaken in a reasonably controlled circumstance; one in which scientific observations can be made and fed back into an overall nationwide agricultural research system. While the demonstration plot should take place at the village level, it is important that the actual management of the plots be related to some more objective external system of assessment.

Similarly in the health area, as we have already noted, the village itself can form the absolute core for any rural health delivery system. It must, however, be backed up by institutions and structures which permit a greater degree of scientific review as well as have the capacity for terminal analysis which the village itself cannot contain.

Much of the infrastructure which is needed to tie the village to the outside world must be administered by bodies external to the village. This is clearly accepted as a reality on the part of the villagers and is seen as one of the important functions for the central government or as in the case of Upper Volta, the ORD. What is critical here is the participation of the village in selecting the optimal placement of a rural farm network system in relation to production units. Inputs of fertilizer and seed on a regular basis as well as the supply of credit and technical assistance cannot take place without a rural road system. Similarly, crops cannot be marketed in a timely manner and central storage assured unless a basic farm to market system is in place and being maintained.

A decentralized approach to rural development focusing on the village also has distinct advantages for participation by donors. For example, in the Eastern ORD of Upper Volta, AID and the FAO are the principal donors. Here, where AID will be involved for at least a decade, it is possible to develop an in-depth knowledge of the Gurmanchi society with which the AID technical personnel are dealing. Ethno-specific data can be verified. Similarly, other donors such as the French working in the Sahel ORD in northern Upper Volta have an ability to focus their attention on the Peul and to understand in detail the nature of both the pastoral nomads of the area as well as those Peul who are becoming semi-sedentarized. The correlation, then, of this information by a national social research center is, therefore, also of extreme importance. Here, then, support for national and regional social research institutions becomes an important element of any assistance strategy.

In this regard, the Institute of the Sahel, established in Bamako this past year will become an increasingly important institution. The primary functions of the Institute are three-fold. It will serve as the basic coordinator and dissemination center for research information concerning the social sciences as well as the hard sciences. Secondly, it will train Sahelian researchers in research techniques and in the management of research systems. Thirdly, it will become the locus of a great deal of information currently scattered throughout the Sahel and indeed throughout the developed world. Much of the information which currently resides outside of Africa will find a home at the Institute. In the longer term it is hoped that the Institute will build a sensitivity on the part of national planners to the social systems which are functioning in their respective countries. And that by training researchers and social scientists the Institute can increase the degree of sensitivity on the part of national leaders in the Sahel concerning the importance of their local institutions.

The Donor Community's Ability to Respond to Village-Based Activities

There is a very real limitation on the part of the donor community to support and sustain large numbers of activities such as those we have looked at in the eastern ORD of Upper Volta. Problems in recruiting adequate numbers of technical personnel are striking. Of over 100 technical positions in the Sahel established by AID over the course of the last year, more than 40 percent remain unfilled. Problems of finding American technicians with both French capacity and a desire to live in difficult rural circumstances is a major constraint. While the Peace Corps has a major role in the implementation of many of these AID programs, there is frequently needed a degree of technical expertise greater than that possessed by volunteers.

While social scientists in AID field posts are now readily accepted, the problem is in finding properly trained sociologists and anthropologists who are prepared to work in the area on a full time basis. For them this usually means taking up residency in the Sahel for a minimum of two years. This is not necessarily a life-style which is amenable to most American academics. This is especially so since many of them feel that two or four years outside of their academic system will work to the detriment of their future career opportunities. One way of countering this problem is a recent attempt by AID to bring into its foreign development service a number of young social scientists who are prepared to consider AID on a career basis so that they will apply their training to development problems of the Third World on a long-term basis.

The social science community on the whole has a much larger and substantive role to play in the development of assistance strategies than has been the case heretofore. The social scientist has historically been an examiner of local systems in a static sense. This has permitted the creation of a very valuable critical analysis of local institutions. The time has come, however, for the addition of certain further responsibilities. These responsibilities relate first of all to the people being assessed. It is no longer adequate for social scientists to study local cultures in isolation. These cultures should be analyzed in such a way as to permit the findings to be made available to a much larger audience; particularly that audience which is charged in helping to bring about economic development in rural areas.

Social scientists also have a responsibility to the countries in which they work. It is a responsibility to pursue, with perhaps greater diligence than has heretofore been the case, the analysis of policy constraints which impinge upon local change; which either inhibit it or bring about change in such a way as to be destructive to the basic fabric of the indigenous society. Key in this process is a better understanding on the part of the social scientists of the decision factors of any local system being examined. Here then, social scientists must become increasingly attuned to how economic as well as cultural decisions are arrived at. Only in this way can those persons charged with macro planning be made sensitive to such fundamental decisions as to how and when a farmer will sell the product of his labors or under what circumstances cattle will be moved into a marketing system.

The social scientists must also be prepared to do battle if need be on a much more continuing basis with the hard scientists. Glenn Johnson, in a paper presented at the annual meeting of the Canadian Agricultural Economic Society in August 1977 (25), came forward with the following conclusions:

1. Social scientists and particularly agricultural economists have not contributed successfully to food and nutritional appraisals.

2. Social scientists and particularly agricultural economists have not successfully made the case for needed social science research on food and nutrition.

3. The failure of social scientists has not been due to their being excluded from food and nutrition appraisals and research priority setting exercises. Instead, it appears to be due to a deep-seated philosophical orientation of natural and social scientists.

4. Some of the constraining philosophical orientations are shared by natural scientists and by some social scientists. Shared constraining philosophies include positivism and conditional normativism (a la Myrdal). Among the social scientists who often share positivistic orientations for the natural scientists are some production economists, econometricians and some policy analysts.

There is much truth in what Johnson is saying -- the need for social scientists to be prepared to expose their ideas to a much more critical assessment by those who are natural scientists, planners and even politicians.

The social scientist, therefore, has an increasing responsibility to the world in which he is operating. That responsibility encompasses the need to assess existing data in a problem context: a context that is somewhat alien to much of the analysis which has been conducted; especially with respect to sociology and ethnography. Along with this increased responsibility, however, has evolved an enormous opportunity for an understanding in a much larger arena by politicians and planners who had heretofore been insensitive to the subtleties of social science disciplines.

There is also a responsibility with respect to the ultimate recipients of the vast amount of development aid currently being mobilized in areas such as the Sahel. It is, hence, a responsibility to the very individuals who benefit from that aid. Based on the analysis, the findings and the data developed by social scientists -- planners and politicians - local administrators and headmen and the families in thousands of villages, all will be impacted upon in a way which was thought impossible only a decade ago. Social scientists, therefore, have a unique opportunity as well as a profound duty if the village is to continue as the primary arena for human existence and growth in the Sahel.

References and Notes

1. Agency for International Development, Development Assistance Program 1976-1980 - Central West Africa Region, Volume I (Department of State, Washington, D.C., November 1975).

2. Agency for International Development, Special Report to the Congress (June 1977).

3. E. Skinner, Social Institutions in the Sahel (United Nations Secretariat, Special Sahelian Office, March 1974).

4. M. Horowitz, D. W. Brokensha, T. Scudder, The Anthropology of Rural Development in the Sahel (Institute for Development Anthropology, Inc., Binghamton, N.Y., July 1977).

5. Agency for International Development, Special Report to the Congress (April 1976).

6. E. Eckholm, Losing Ground (Norton Publishers, 1976).

7. Development Assistance Committee Chairman's Report for 1977 (Organization for Economic Cooperation and Development, Paris, September 9, 1977).

8. Record of the Second Conference of the Club du Sahel, held in Ottawa, Canada, from 30th May to 1st June, 1977 (Permanent Interstate Committee for Drought Control in the Sahel - CILSS, Organization for Economic Cooperation and Development, OECD, Paris, August 10, 1977).

9. E. Skinner, Social Institutions in the Sahel (United Nations Secretariat, Special Sahelian Office, March 1974).

10. M. Perham, Lugard (Collins, London 1960).

11. W. Jones, "The Food Economy of Ba Dugu, Djoliba, Mali" in African Food Production Systems, P. F. McLoughlin, ed. (Johns Hopkins Press, 1970).

12. Ibid.

13. J. A. Grayzel, The Drought and Fulfulde Speaking Herder/Farmer in Doukolomba, from proceedings of symposium held

in Niamey on Response of the Sahelian Drought (M. M. Horowitz, ed., June 1975).

14. W. Jones, "The Food Economy of Ba Dugu, Djoliba, Mali" in African Food Production Systems, P. F. McLoughlin, ed. (Johns Hopkins Press, 1970).

15. J. DeWilde, Experiences with Agricultural Development in Tropical Africa (Johns Hopkins Press, 1967), vol. 2.

16. CILSS - Club du Sahel Working Group on Price Policy and Storage, Marketing, Price Policy and Storage of Food Grains in the Sahel (Center for Research in Economic Development, August, 1977).

17. Organization for Economic Cooperation and Development, Development Strategies for the Sahel (Paris, November 1976).

18. J. W. Howe and the staff of the Overseas Development Council, Energy for the Villages of Africa. Recommendations for African Governments and Outside Donors (February 25, 1977).

19. S. Joseph and S. Scheyer, A Strategy for Health as a Component of the Sahel Development Program (Family Health Care, Inc., May 1977).

20. Ibid.

21. International Labour Office, Employment, Growth and Basic Needs: A One-World Problem; The International "Basic Needs Strategy" Against Chronic Poverty (Praeger Publishers, 1977).

22. Development Assistance Committee Chairman's Report for 1977 (Organization for Economic Cooperation and Development, Paris, September 9, 1977).

23. K. Cloud, paper prepared for AID, Sex Roles in Food Production and Distribution Systems in the Sahel (January 1978).

24. Michigan State University, An Analysis of the Eastern ORD Rural Development Project in Upper Volta: Report of the MSU Mission (Michigan State University, January 1976).

25. G. L. Johnson, Recent United States Priority Assessments for Food and Nutrition: The Neglect of the Social Sciences, presented at the proceedings of the Annual

Meeting, Canadian Agricultural Economics Society, Guelph, Ontario, August 1977.

Bibliography

Agency for International Development, Development Assistance Program 1976-1980, Central West Africa Region, Vol. I, November 1975.

_____, Opportunity for Self-Reliance: An Overview of the Sahel Development Program, 1977.

_____, Report to the United States Congress: Proposal for a Long-Term Comprehensive Development Program for the Sahel, April 1976.

_____, Submission to the Congress Fiscal Year 1978, Africa Programs, February 1977.

_____, United States Response to the Sahel Drought, Third Special Report to Congress on the Sahel Drought, August 1977.

Charlick, Robert, Power and Participation in the Modernization of Rural Hausa Communities, a Ph.D. Dissertation, University of California, 1974.

CILSS/Club du Sahel Working Group on Price Policy and Storage, Marketing, Price Policy and Storage of Food Grains in the Sahel, Center for Research in Economic Development, August 1977.

Cloud, Kathleen, Sex Roles in Food Production and Distribution Systems in the Sahel, January 1978.

Club des Amis du Sahel, Development Strategies for the Sahel, Organization for Economic Cooperation and Development, November 1976.

_____, Record of the Second Conference of the Club du Sahel held in Ottawa, Canada from 30th May to 1st June 1977, CILSS, OECD, Paris, August 10, 1977.

_____, Synthesis Report - Proposal for Drought Control and Strategy for the Sahel, May 1977.

Development Assistance Committee, DAC Chairman's Report for 1977, OECD, Paris, September 1977.

deWilde, John C., Experiences with Agricultural Development in Tropical Africa, vol. 2, IBRD, 1967.

Eckholm, Eric, Losing Ground, Norton Publishers, 1976.

Glantz, Michael H., ed., Desertification: Environmental Degradation in and around Arid Lands, Westview Press, Boulder, Colorado, 1977.

Grant, James P., Basic Human Needs, Food and the World's Poorest Billions - What Future Prospects? Overseas Development Council, October 1977.

Grayzel, John A., The Drought and Fulfulde Speaking Herder/Farmer in Doukolomba, from proceedings of symposium held in Niamey, Niger, on Response of the Sahelian Drought, M. M. Horowitz, ed., June 1975.

Hopkins, Nicholas S., Popular Government in an African Town, Kita, Mali, University of Chicago Press, 1972.

Horowitz, Michael M., Brokensha, D. W., Scudder, T., The Anthropology of Rural Development in the Sahel, Institute for Development Anthropology, Inc., Binghamton, N.Y., July 1977.

Howe, James W., Energy for the Village of Africa - Recommendations for African Governments and Outside Donors, Overseas Development Council, February 1977.

International Labour Office, Employment, Growth and Basic Needs: A One-World Problem: "Basic Needs Strategy" Against Chronic Poverty, Praeger Publishers, 1977.

Johnson, Glenn L., Recent United States Research Priority Assessments for Food and Nutrition: The Neglect of the Social Sciences, presented at the proceedings of the Annual Meeting, Canadian Agricultural Economic Society, Guelph, Ontario, August 1977.

Jones, W. I., The Food Economy of Ba Dugu, Djoliba, Mali from African Food Production Systems, Thesis and Theory, Peter F. M. McLoughlin, ed., Johns Hopkins Press, 1970.

Khan, Akhter Hameed, Comila Revisited, Michigan State University, Department of Social Economics, June 1977.

Lele, Uma, Designing Rural Development Programs: Lessons from

Past Experience in Africa, Economic Development and Cultural Change, Vol. 24, no. 2, University of Chicago Press, 1976.

Michigan State University, An Analysis of the Eastern ORD Development Project in Upper Volta: Report of the MSU Mission, Michigan State University, Department of Agricultural Economics, January 1976.

OECD, Development Strategies for the Sahel, Paris; November 1976.

Quimby, Lucy G., The Local-Level Dynamics of Development in the Sahelian States, prepared for AID, August 1977.

Scheyer, Stanley C., Joseph, Stephen C., A Strategy for Health as a Component of the Sahel Development Program, Family Health Care, Inc., May 1977.

Skinner, Elliott, Social Institutions in the Sahel, United Nations' Secretariat, Special Sahelian Office, March 1974.

Smith, James, Economy and Demography in a Mossi Village, Ph.D. thesis, University of Michigan, 1977.

Thompson, James T., Trouble Case Investigation of a Problem in Nigerien Rural Modernization: Forest Conservation, Indiana University, Department of Political Science, Bloomington, Indiana.

United Nations Economic and Social Council, The Sahel: Ecological Approaches to Land Use, UNESCO Press, Paris, 1975.

United Nations Research Institute for Social Development, Famine Risk and Famine Prevention in the Modern World. Studies in the Food Systems under Conditions of Recurrent Scarcity, Geneva, June 1976.

_____, Agriculture and the New Technology in Tropical Africa, Brigit Dommen, ed., Geneva, March 1977.

Ware, Helen, The Sahelian Drought: Some Thoughts on the Future, Australian National University, Demographic Department, 1975.

James W. Howe

10. New Village Uses of Renewable Energy Sources

I. Current Energy Use in Developing Countries

There are three characteristics of the energy regimes in the Third World: (1) not much modern energy is used, (2) very little of that amount is used in rural villages and farms, but (3) a great deal of traditional energy is used -- especially in rural areas.

A. Not Much Modern Energy is Used

There are about 2.4 billion people in the developing countries excluding China. About 2 billion of these people live in areas without electricity. This includes virtually all of the rural people and a number of people in urban slums as well.

Moreover, the bulk of the people living in rural areas at some distance from cities are not likely to be reached by the electrical grids for the foreseeable future.

The following table summarizes how much less energy is used in selected developing countries than in the United States:

Table 1. Ratio of energy used in the United States compared to selected countries.

Nepal	957 to one	Bangladesh	380 to one
Burundi	883 to one	India	57 to one
Upper Volta	820 to one	South Korea	12 to one
Mali	478 to one		

Source: U.N. Statistical Series J for 1976. (Per Capita 1974)

Table 2. Energy use per hectare in rice production in various countries.[a,b] From Energy and Agriculture in the Third World, Copyright 1975, The Ford Foundation. Reprinted with permission from Ballinger Publishing Company.

Country	Installed horsepower hp per ha[c] farm machines and draft animals[d] only	Energy for farm operations million Btu per ha[e]	Energy for irrigation and nitrogen fertilizers manufacture million Btu per ha	Total energy input per ha million Btu	Rice yield kg/ha	Energy intensity million Btu per ton of Rice
India	0.7	20	6.5	26.5	1,400	19
China	0.7	20	12	32	3,000	10.7
Taiwan	0.5	10	22	32	4,000	8
Japan	1.6	10	25	35	5,600	6.2
U.S.A.	1.5	7	25	32	5,100	6.3

Sources: See Chapter One, Table 1-2, and Appendix A; notes 1, 2, 3, 4, 5.

[a]We have chosen to compare a single grain (rice) since total grain production not only depends on seed variety, soil quality, etc., but also on the mix of grains grown. Comparing a single grain, therefore, gives a better comparison of the energy intensity of various farming methods.

[b]Installed horsepower and energy use are based on national average energy use in agriculture. *The numbers in this table are very approximate.*

[c]For India and China about 20 percent of the installed horsepower is in tractors; for Taiwan 50 percent; for Japan 90 percent; for the U.S. 100 percent.

[d]We assume that one draft animal (ox, horse, mule) is approximately equal to ½ horsepower. This implies a draft animal of about 250 kg^3. For lack of data, it is assumed that draft animal weight is about the same in all poor countries. *Since a bullock or horse weighing 250 kg. is a rather small animal, this assumption may give rise to an underestimate of installed horsepower for some countries (e.g., Taiwan).* It is assumed that 75 percent of the energy output of the draft animals is used on farms, the other 25 percent being used for transportation, pumping domestic water, and similar nonfarm activities (which are excluded from the calculations). *Installed horsepower numbers include tractors, but exclude irrigation equipment, trucks, and autos on farms.*

Annual energy input per draft animal is assumed to be 25 million Btu. Tractor fuel input 7 million Btu/ha/yr for fully mechanized farms (U.S. data).

[e]The energy for irrigation varies according to the irrigation method, terrain, rainfall, water table depth, etc. For the purposes of comparison we have used 15 million Btu of energy input (3 million Btu of useful work) per irrigated hectare per crop. Thus in India, about 40 percent of the rice-producing land is irrigated, so that the irrigation energy input per hectare of rice-producing land is taken as 0.4 × 15 × 10^6 Btu or 6 million Btu. The energy input for chemical nitrogen fertilizer manufacture is about 75 million Btu per metric ton of nitrogen. No energy cost is assigned to the preparation of organic fertilizer. The energy requirements for potassium and phosphorous are small compared to those for nitrogen fertilizers.

B. Most Modern Energy Use is Concentrated in Urban Areas

As noted above, almost all electricity is used in urban areas. Other common "modern" forms of energy consist of petroleum driven engines, and industrial heat supplied by electricity, coal or petroleum. The latter (industrial heat) is confined almost exclusively to urban use. Trains, trucks and buses travel to rural areas but most vehicular travel is in urban areas. In many rural villages the only contact with modern energy may be a diesel driven pump or generator which lights a few commercial or public buildings and the trucks and buses that pass through. Although we have no comprehensive data on the share of modern energy consumed in urban areas, Brookhaven estimates from its work in Mexico that a resident migrating from the countryside into the city becomes ten times as energy intensive. (1) A.K.N. Reddy estimates that in India the ratio between the rich urban and the poorest 60% of the people (mostly rural) is from 4.3 to 8.6 to one (2).

C. Much Traditional Energy is Used in Rural Areas

Farmers and villagers use a great deal of crop residue, charcoal and cattle dung as fuel for cooking, crop or meat drying and space heating. In addition they use much animal traction in tilling the land and harvesting crops. In fact, one source estimates that farmers in developing countries use more energy per unit of crop produced than a U.S. farmer. See Table 2 and reference 3.

But the story changes dramatically if one considers only fossil fuel energy in farming. The U.S. farmer uses from four to ten times as much fossil energy per unit of protein output as a farmer in the Third World, as is shown in Table 3.

Table 3. Comparison of fossil energy inputs for corn, rice and wheat (4).

(K Cal of fossil energy input per K Cal of protein input)		
	United States	Developing Countries
Rice	10.1	1.31 (Philippines)
Corn	3.63	.08 (Mexico)
Wheat	3.44	.65 (India)

II. The Connection Between Energy and Development

The effort to improve human material wellbeing over the past many millenia has consisted in major part of finding and applying substitutes for human energy. Some of these substitutes have been sources of energy completely separate from the human body such as fire, wind, sun, draft animals, and flowing water. Others have been tools to enhance the power of human muscles such as wheels, hoes, levers, and gears. One respected authority, Professor Marion J. Levy, has defined the whole of modernization in terms of using "inanimate sources of power and (...) tools to multiply the effect of effort." (5) That definition goes farther than this paper, which limits its inquiry to economic development. Moreover, we recognize that scientific knowledge has contributed to economic development through better seeds, fertilizers, and a host of other inputs which are not substitutes for nor extensions of human energy. Nevertheless the pervasive transformations that have occurred as humans evolved from primative hunters and gatherers to twentieth century urbanites are largely the result of finding substitutes for and supplements to human muscular energy, or, since the computer age, human mental energy.

Most of the energy used in rural areas is for cooking. A recent workshop directed by David Pimentel (6) concluded that from 60 to 90% of the energy in rural areas of developing countries is used in the food system, of which cooking accounts for 60%. The energy for such cooking comes almost entirely from organic sources such as wood, crop residues and dung.

Most village tasks are done with human or animal muscles. This is true of soil preparation, planting, tilling, harvesting, threshing, grinding, pumping, hauling crops or water and gathering wood, dung or crop residues for cooking. Aside from the sheer arduousness of these physical burdens this condition inhibits development in five ways. First,-- recognizing the great variations among ethnic groups -- for a substantial number of people there is an important labor shortage at critical times of the crop cycle. "Labor bottlenecks at one or more stages of the annual cycle of cultivation are a very obvious feature of peasant agriculture..." (7) This reduces the extent of acreage cultivated or the putput harvested per acre or both. Second, goods are transported by foot or by animal power which puts a low ceiling on the extent of trade. Without much trade, villagers are limited to the rather low level of material wellbeing that is typically provided by a subsistence economy.

Third, most villagers are condemned to darkness after the sun has gone down which inhibits formal education. Fourth, villagers are confined to water hauled from a nearby stream or open well which is inadequate for irrigation and may perpetuate diseases. Finally, they cook with wood, dung or crop residues with the result that the land is progressively being devegetated, drained of nutrients and eroded. Hence, whenever a village must rely chiefly on traditional energy it is likely that the residents of that village have a low income and a low physical quality of life. Unfortunately, this is true of most rural people in the developing countries. Since rural people make up nearly half of the people in Latin America, 78 percent in Asia and 81 percent in Africa, this is not an unimportant problem. Of course some of these same factors apply to the urban poor people as well. In fact, many well established villagers are better off than people in urban slums.

III. Conventional Sources of Modern Energy

What are the chief conventional sources of the energy for development?

A. Petroleum

First and most important in the short run is petroleum. Although relatively little petroleum is used in Third World villages, almost all modern energy in the villages now is petroleum based and everywhere one looks in rural Third World, plans are being laid to start down a petroleum based energy path. Kerosene is being used for lighting, diesel engines for electricity generation, pumping and grinding, and gasoline motors for transportation or farm tasks. The problem with petroleum is clear and inescapable: these countries are already having trouble paying for oil for their modern sector and many will not be able to pay for extending it to rural areas; but even if they had some way of financing such oil costs they would be establishing an obsolescing economic infrastructure--one they will be compelled to begin dismantling before the end of the century as physical limits to the availability of oil begin to be felt.

B. Nuclear

The smallest nuclear generators now commercially available are 600 megawatts and, for economic reasons, industry strongly favors increasing the size. Even the 600 mw generator is too large to be reliable for the power grids of all but a handful of developing countries. For this reason

alone, quite apart from the many economic, environmental and
security problems that have been raised, nuclear energy does
not now appear to be a promising source for most developing
countries.

C. Other Site Specific Sources

Coal, major hydroelectric, and geothermal energy all
have important potential for selected countries, but all
share the common feature of being poorly distributed. Thus,
the energy potential of each is restricted to certain specific sites. Although the exact location and extent of coal
reserves is not known it appears that the distribution of
ultimately recoverable coal reserves is about as follows:(8)

	Coal (% of World Total)
United States	25.3
Soviet Union (including Eastern Europe)	49.6
China	14.2
Western Europe	4.1
Australia	2.6
Africa	1.7
India	0.05
Other America	1.4
Other Asia	0.05

Thus, apart from China the developing countries do not
appear to be well endowed with coal.

Major hydroelectric sites are fairly widely distributed
and their exploitation promises to make a significant contribution to energy supplies for urban industrial centers. However, the energy they produce can only be economically transported a limited distance. Moreover, the large initial costs
of generation and transmission together with potentially
serious health and environmental problems associated with
damming large streams will inhibit exploitation of some
sites. Geothermal energy sites offer another significant
source of energy for selected developing countries once
certain technical and environmental problems are resolved.
It is unlikely to be a major source.

In summary, the sources of energy mentioned above, all
of which tend to be centralized (except oil which can also
be used as the basis for decentralized energy) will be useful in greater or lesser degree depending upon local circumstances. I do not believe they will be adequate to meet the

Village Uses of Renewable Energy Sources   275

needs of the developing countries especially the needs of the poor majority living in rural areas. If that is true, what are the prospects for meeting village energy needs for such tasks as pumping, lighting, grinding and (above all) cooking through harnessing locally available renewable sources? To answer this question we turn now to a consideration of solar energy technology.

IV. Solar Energy Technology

The current energy of the sun comes to earth in one of four major systems. First, the power of falling water is made renewable through the action of the sun in raising the water from sea level back up to the hills and mountains. Second, the wind is caused by the differing intensities of soalr energy falling on different parts of the earth. Third, the photosynthetic character of green plants enables them to store solar energy in their edible tissues which is the basis of all life on earth. Finally, the direct energy of the sun's rays may be converted to heat or directly into electricity.

There is now an array of proven technologies, some of which are commercially available to convert solar energy into useable energy. We will identify five of them here.

A. Mini-Hydroelectric Generators

China today is reported to have about 60,000 such units averaging between 35 and 50 Kw in capacity and ranging to less than 3 Kw. Even the U.S., which at one time depended primarily on small mechanical and electric hydropower especially for New England industries, is reconsidering the potential of tapping its own small rivers and streams for electric power. A recent study by the U.S. Army Corps of Engineers estimated that new generating equipment at existing abandoned dam sites alone could contribute 54,000 mw to U.S. generating capacity. (9) The U.S. Federal Power Commission maintains that partially developing only 10% of the U.S.' 50,000 small dams would contribute power equivalent to using 180 billion barrels of oil per year (or the same as reducing our daily oil imports of 7.5 - 8.5 mbd by 1/2 mbd). (10)

B. Wind

Wind has served as a source of power for over two millenia, ranging from the earliest windmachines used for pumping and grinding in the Persian empires to the windpumpers and aerogenerators which helped make the Great Plains of the U.S. habitable and productive for stock raising and farming well into the 1930s. In the U.S. alone over 6 million windmachines have been used within the past 100 years. (11) There are still reported to be 100,000 - 150,000 windmachines (mostly windpumpers) in use in the U.S. today. (12) Perhaps as many as a quarter of a million standing but broken windmachines in the U.S. are in suitable condition to be easily repaired and operational again. (13) In addition, the U.S. is experiencing a rebirth of interest in windmachines, especially aerogenerators, with sales up at least five-fold since 1974. (14) Both government and private groups in the U.S. and other industrialized countries have begun more seriously to explore the potentials of wider scale use of aerogenerators, ranging in size from less than 1 Kw capacity to some well over 1 mw.

At a less complex level, the use of locally assembled sail wing windpumpers among the Geleb people of the Lake Rudolf/Omo River area of Ethiopia over the past few years demonstrates that there may well be good prospects for much wider use of the wind for mechanical uses in the rural areas of the developing world. (15)

C. Generating Methane Gas from Organic Wastes

The third proven technology is the generation of methane gas from organic wastes. Biogasification involves the fermentation of animal dung, human night soil, and organic farm and household debris and wastes in relatively air tight tanks, to produce methane gas. The gas may be used for farm, household, and cottage craft purposes. The process leaves a residue which is a liquid fertilizer in partially sterilized form. The technology is known and reliable, particularly where livestock are abundant, and has been used by thousands of farmers in Korea, Taiwan, China, and India and has been experimented with in Tanzania, Mali, and Ecuador, among other countries. There are problems with consistency of output during the cold session in high latitude or high altitude areas, and with costs of construction materials like steel, cement, tubing, gas appliance fixtures and adapted equipment.

The degree to which biogasification can be accepted and used will depend heavily on both the number of sedentary cattle or other animals from which dung can be collected and the willingness of villagers to collect and handle dung. For example, for most family size biogas units, dung from a minimum of five head of cattle is usually necessary. For village scale use, of course, there would have to be a substantial degree of cooperation involved both in collection of dung and in distribution of gas and fertilizer by-products. Biogasification has promise for those cultures with domesticated sedentary cattle, particularly if animals are penned or corralled (a practice which facilitates collection), and provided the people are accustomed to using dung (to build mud walls for homes, for example) or are otherwise willing to handle dung. It would require some careful investigation of cultural habits for each village or community to ascertain this potential.

D. Photovoltaic (pv), or Solar Cells

The fourth proven technology is photovoltaic (pv), or solar cells such as are used in space craft. They are usually made of wafer thin slices of silicon attached to wires and covered with or imbedded in glass. The action of the sun on these cells creates a continuous electric charge which is collected and carried off by the wires. Although the technology to make these cells is high, it takes virtually no technology to maintain them because there are no moving parts and the use of electricity requires only a moderately skilled operator.

The costs of the technology are currently too high for it to compete with diesel but rapidly declining pv costs plus expected rises in the costs of diesel fuel make it likely that pv will be competitive in the next five or ten years. This new technology may already be the best choice for certain uses in remote areas (e.g., water pumping or communications systems in villages where delivery of fuel and servicing a diesel engine present problems).

E. Simple Flat Plate Solar Collector

The fifth technology is the simple flat plate solar collector, an insulated box painted black on the inside, and covered with glass. The glass lets the sun's rays through where they convert to heat on contact with the black paint and the glass traps the heat from escaping. That heat can be used to dry fish, grain or tobacco, distill water, heat water and run a pump among other things. The technology for most uses does not require great skill either to construct from local materials or to maintain and operate.

V. Solar Energy Costs

Despite the numerous experiences with solar energy hardware, there are no systemmatic data on actual cost

Table 4. Solar energy applicability matrix. Animals are included as a solar technology (based on photosynthesis). For many villages the use of animals would represent a modernizing step. It includes the use of dung for burning or fertilizing. Source: adapted from a presentation by J.R. Williams at the Tanzanian workshop. Symbols: ++, applicable; +, potentially applicable; -, not applicable. Reprinted with permission from ENERGY II: Conservation and Supply, ed. by Philip H. Abelson and Allen L. Hammond (American Association for the Advancement of Science, 1978), p. 36.

Solar technology	Energy use							Heating					
	Water pumping	Lighting	Cooling	Communications	Water desalting	Spinning	Sawing	Cooking	Space	Domestic water	Grinding	Drying	Transport	Fertilizer
Solar cells (flat plate)	+	+	+	++	-	+	-	-	-	-	+	-	-	-
Flat-plate collectors	+	-	+	-	++	-	-	+	++	++	-	++	-	-
Concentrating collectors	+	+	+	-	+	-	-	+	-	-	-	-	-	-
Solar, Stirling	+	+	+	-	-	+	+	-	-	-	+	-	-	-
Solar, Rankine	+	+	+	-	-	+	+	-	-	-	+	-	-	-
Wind (mechanical)	++	-	-	-	-	+	+	-	-	-	++	-	-	-
Wind generator	++	++	+	++	-	++	++	-	-	-	++	-	-	-
Water (mechanical)	++	-	-	-	-	++	++	-	-	-	++	-	-	-
Hydroelectric	++	++	++	++	-	-	-	++	++	++	-	++	-	-
Bioconversion wood/pyrolysis	-	+	-	-	-	-	-	++	-	+	-	+	+	+
Biogas	+	++	+	-	-	-	-	++	-	+	-	+	+	++
Draft animals	++	-	-	-	-	-	-	+	-	-	++	-	++	++

performance of solar hardware compared with (say) diesel or an extension of the electric grid. In August of 1977, however, the U.S. National Academy of Sciences sent a team of experts to Tanzania to sit down with the Tanzanian National Scientific Research Council and experts from the Government and the University to consider the matter of solar energy for the villages of Tanzania. These experts spent a week pouring over calculations of the costs of performing certain village tasks (a) with diesel engines, (b) with electricity from Tanzanian electric grid, and (c) with the five small scale solar technologies identified above. What they learned was encouraging for solar energy. Each of the five technologies is either now able to compete with diesel or will be able to do so within the next few years. Whereas the costs of diesel are about 2.3 shillings per Kilowatt hour of electricity, the cost of mini hydro ranges from .26 to .97 shillings, of wind is 1.5 shillings, and of flat plate cooling is .98. Photovoltaic costs are now 11.6 shillings but if the U.S. Department of Energy target for price drops are achieved, the pv cell will cost .83 shillings in 1985. Currently the cost of energy from the electric grid in a village would be .88 shillings if it were available. (16)

Moreover, there is a wide range of applications of such technologies to the performance of common village tasks as is shown in Table 4.

VI. Testing Solar Energy Potential

A. The Need for Village Level Tests

The Overseas Development Council was asked by AID to evaluate the prospects for solar energy for the villages of Africa. After completing our research we reported to AID that we could not answer the question whether solar technology holds great potential for village use for the reason that there exists no systemmatically recorded body of the experience of such technology at the village level. We recommend a period of actual village level testing and described the testing process needed. AID asked ODC and others to help set up some tests with the result that projects to test solar hardware in a sample of villages have now been identified in seven African countries and a project identification effort will be undertaken in two or three more countries. If these projects are then well designed and skillfully executed, some answers to the questions of solar energy potential for Third World villages should be emerging within a few years. Without reliable evidence on this subject, Third World policy makers will be understandably reluctant to make a major commitment of resources to solar technology. Hence by default this technology will be by-passed and choices will be made among the proven conventional technologies--largely petroleum based.

B. The Nature of the Tests

These village tests should be designed to answer six questions:

1) How well does a given device perform technically within the physical conditons--including the all-important variable of settlement pattern--of the village?

2) How do its costs compare with alternative energy technologies?

3) How does it fit the local culture?

4) How does it match existing or prospective village institutions that could own, operate and maintain it?

5) What can be learned about the best techniques for introducing the technology into the villages?

6) What is the effect of the increase in available energy upon such indicators of community well-being as literacy, infant mortality, income, migration and birth rates?

Each of these tests deserves further comment.

1. Physical Conditions. The selection of technology must match the physical circumstances of the village. A windmill requires a certain velocity of wind for a reliable period of time to function. Sandstorms may damage the glass on a photovoltaic cell, hydroelectric generators will not work if the stream is dry for several months during the year, humidity or salt spray may corrode metal parts, bio-digesters are less effective at low temperatures and require the right mix of organic wastes and water, and a pyrolitic converter requires a ready supply of woody material to make charcoal, gas, and oil. Such a test should match various kinds of hardware with a range of physical conditions and measure and record technical performance, maintenance problems, safety record, breakdowns and the like.

2. Costs. Initial capital costs are easiest to measure. Other costs include maintenance, repair, and the

costs of operating personnel. Solar equipment tends to have relatively high costs for purchase and installation but in many instances it costs very little for maintenance and operation over the remainder of its life. It is therefore important to know as soon as possible the approximate life of the project in order to compare it with diesel which costs less to install but a great deal more to operate.

3. <u>Local Cultural Factors</u>. Some devices may be less than acceptable to local residents than others because they offend local beliefs. For example, the design of a device may be reminiscent of an evil omen. Some devices may stir up family problems. For example, men may resent it if the first device introduced is one that only helps women. Since the men may be dominant in the locality this may kill the prospect of a successful experience with the device. The device may require the handling of cow dung which in some societies may be unacceptable.

4. <u>How Does it Fit Village Institutions?</u> Some technologies can be operated by an individual family. This might be true, for example, of a bio-digester in a culture where families own several cattle each, pen them up at night, and are willing to handle dung. A solar cooker that cooks by concentrating the sun's rays on a cooking pot could also be operated by an individual family in those cases where cooking is done in a pot, where there is no objection to cooking out of doors when the sun is high overhead. Other technologies are not amenable to management by single families. Thus a technology that produces electricity calls for some kind of village public utility. In some villages there is a tradition of carrying on activities on a village-wide basis. In others there may be no such tradition and hence it may be necessary either to avoid such a technology, or have it operated by a unit established from outside the village, or experiment with forming untried forms of village organization. Some technological applications might lend themselves readily to private enterprise. Thus, for example, a photovoltaic cell-driven grinder might be operated by a village entrepreneur who would sell the service of grinding corn or millet to people in the village. Similarly a pyrolitic converter to make charcoal out of fibrous waste, (e.g., wood, sawdust, coconut husks or peanut shells) might in some cultures be best managed by a small industrialist.

The range of applications is great and the cultural-institutional variations within and among villages are almost limitless. In order to give the technology the best chance of performing well, at low cost, and being well maintained, a great deal of thought needs to be given to the best institutional arrangement within the village for "owning" and operating the device. A great deal of field research has been done in many cultures and individual villages by sociologists and anthropologists. Techniques need to be found to draw upon this knowledge during the period when the project is being designed. The village test should make provision for observing and recording the performance of various kinds of village institutions in utilizing various kinds of hardware.

5. <u>Introducing the Technology</u>. Although there is much evidence that several technologies work, there is also a disquieting record of failures at the village level in many developing countries. Anyone who has travelled in developing countries extensively has come across the skeletons of windmills or the remains of abandoned bio-digesters. Although the reasons for these failures are not well documented, they probably include the normal quota of bad design and bad management by the project directors. One may also generalize that a leading cause of failure had to do with the technique for transfering the technology from the lab to the village. Outside experts came to the village with a preselected piece of hardware to do a preselected task (e.g., a windmill to pump). They erected the device, operated it for a time, tried to enlist the interest of certain villagers and then left. Shortly after their departure the device fell into disuse. Perhaps its parts were canabalized for other purposes. The failure may not have been technical or even economic. Rather it may have been a failure of the technique of transfer to enlist the enthusiasm of local persons or institutions so that they would incorporate the new device into the economy and the cultural practices of the village. The device was brought in by aliens and it remained alien. It never became part of the village.

No doubt the technique for introducing a project into a village will affect importantly the success of the project. My hypothesis is that involving innovative villagers in the very early stages of a project will increase the enthusiasm and involvement they have over the life of the project. It will increase the likelihood that the project will be incorporated into the life of the village, and the villagers maintain and operate the new device well and get the most out of it. Moreover, involving villagers will improve the design of the project because villagers may have the most reliable opinions on (1) what task to select for energizing (e.g., pumping, grinding or cooking), (2) what primary energy to use (e.g., sunshine, organic waste, animal power or wind), (3) what device to use (e.g., wind pumper, wind generator, solar pumps, or solar cell), and (4) what village institutional arrangements to make for the operation of the device.

On the other hand, involving villagers in project planning has some drawbacks. It may be time consuming and hence unattractive to impatient Americans (or other foreign) aid officials or to host country operators. It calls for skills not always possessed by energy technologists. In many countries the normal method of dealing with villagers is to impose change from above. This normal technique, of course, requires the governmental office that imposes the change to supply a corps of people to operate and maintain the new technology. It is a much greater budgetary burden than if villagers could be motivated to take over maintenance, operation and simple repairs.

It is for each government to consider these advantages and disadvantages and decide whether to impose technology from above or to attempt to involve villagers in designing and implementing the changes. The fifth purpose of a well-designed test would be to furnish such governments objective data on the advantages and disadvantages of each technology transfer technique. Hence, the test should attempt to determine whether involving villagers in the early stages of the project enhances the prospects for success.

6. _Impact on Community Well-being_. Finally, the tests should be able to tell policy makers of developing nations something about the impact of new energy sources of the life of the villagers (or urban slum dwellers) and therefore ultimately upon the nation.

What is the impact of energy on agricultural production? Is a substantial portion of the labor released from other tasks devoted to raising additional crops or livestock? Does employment occur as a result? Are small industry or handicrafts stimulated by the coming of energy to the village? Does the provision of lights for reading improve the pace or quality of education? What effect is there with respect to health services or the incidence of disease (for example, from clean drinking water)? What effect is there on the role of women? Is there an increase, a decrease, or no change in the number of babies born each year? The AID-financed Evaluation Study of the MISAMIS Oriental Rural Electric Service Cooperative in the Philippines, concluded that, "The sharp decline in the crude birth rates (in the wake of electrification) is one of the most interesting phenomena uncovered by the study." Is there a change in infant mortality? What changes, if any, take place in the pattern of migration? Does energy set up a demand for imported items that drain limited foreign exchange? These and other evidences of the impact of energy on village life should be measured and analyzed in order to better understand the importance of village energy, to anticipate problems and opportunities it may create and to differentiate among the effects of different uses of energy (lighting, clean water, cooking fuel, for example, contrasted with irrigation) and different forms (electricity versus gas, charcoal or mechanical energy).

VII. Summary

The goal of improving the physical quality of life is dependent upon finding substitutes for human energy at the village level. We see no prospects of meeting such a large energy requirement from conventional sources such as petroleum, nuclear, coal or major hydro. In some instances (e.g., Zaire or India) there may be enough hydroelectricity or coal but the problems of distributing the power to the distant countryside have proven to be overwhelming. Three factors make solar energy appear to be promising enough to give it a thorough test. First, solar energy is plentiful. There will be no shortage of primary energy in the combined potential of direct sunshine, photosynthesis, running water and wind. Second , it is already well distributed to the villages. There is no problem of transmission and distribution lines. Third, the technology to make use of this primary energy, although very imperfect and high priced, is progressing rapidly both in performance and costs. We do not know that solar energy will prove to be practical for village use, but it is sufficiently promising to warrant a careful test. If the widespread use of modern machinery becomes possible as a result of making energy available, the residential attractiveness of villages will improve and the quality of life for this majority of the world's people will be enriched. Thus, a great deal is dependent upon the outcome of the next few years' tests of solar energy in the villages of the developing nations.

Notes

1. Orally obtained from Brookhaven staff. To be included in a forthcoming study.
2. Reddy, A.K.N. and Prasad, K.K., "Technological Alternatives and the Indian Energy Crisis" in The Economic and

Political Weekly, Special Number, August, 1977, pp. 1465 to 1502.
3. Makhijani, Arjun, Energy Policy for the Rural Third World, International Institute for Environment and Development, London, September, 1976, p. 21.
4. Adapted from Pimentel et al. "Energy and Land Constraints in Food Protein Production," Science, November 21, 1975, p. 755.
5. Levy, Marion J., Jr. "Modernization and the Structures of Societies -- A Setting for International Affairs." Vol. 1. Princeton, New Jersey, Princeton University Press, 1966. Pages 10,11,12,35. We disagree with Professor Levy's exclusion of draft animals from the definition of modernization. While an economy based on animal power can scarcely be regarded as modern, it is certainly more developed than an economy that relies on human muscle, as many still do.

   For a more recent statement on the subject, see MacPherson, George and Jackson, Dudley, "Village Technology for Rural Development", in International Labour Review, Vol. III, No. 2, February 1975, I.L.O., Geneva, p. 99. These authorities "define 'technology' to mean a method of operating on the environment for man's benefit -- usually seen in terms of sources of energy."
6. "Energy Needs, Uses and Resources in the Food Systems of Developing Countries", December 23, 1977. Prepared by David Pimentel with the assistance of workshop participants, College of Agriculture and Life Sciences, Cornell University, draft.
7. MacPherson, George and Jackson, Dudley, "Village Technology for Rural Development", in International Labour Review, Vol. III, No. 2, February 1975, I.L.O., Geneva, p. 99.
8. W. Peters and H.D. Schilling, "An Appraisal of World Coal Resources and Their Future Availability" in World Energy Conference, Conservation Commission, World Energy Resources, 1985-2020, (New York: IPC Science and Technology Press, 1978), pp. 64-71. Percentages are based on "geological resources" estimates submitted most recently to the World Energy Conference. "Geological resources" are defined by the authors as "within an order of magnitude that can be regarded as realistic for those resources that may some day be of economic interest (sic) for the population of the world." The authors suggest that this may be a better frame of reference than current technology and economics since these are both going through a period of rapid change and are in part a reflection of a lack of exploration and development particularly in the Third World.

9. Lilienthal, David E. "Lost Megawatts Flow Over Nation's Myriad Spillways", in *Smithsonian Magazine*, September 1977, p. 83.
10. *Ibid.*
11. Metz, William D., "Wind Energy: Large and Small Systems Competing". *Science*, September 2, 1977, pp. 971.
12. Hayes, Denis, *Rays of Hope*, 1977.
13. "Spreading Windpower Gospel", *Washington Post*, July 30, 1977 (estimate of Professor M. I. Rashussen of New Mexico State University).
14. *Ibid.*
15. Fraenkel, Peter, "Food from Windmills", ITDG, London, 1975.
16. Brown, Norman L. and Howe, James W., "Solar Energy for Village Development" in *Science*, February 3, 1978.

John Simmons

11. The Political Economy of Education for Village Development

Education can promote development, but how it does so depends on how development is defined. If it is seen as mainly economic growth, which tends to benefit upper-income groups, then schooling has contributed to it by widening the skills and raising the productivity of future workers. If development is defined as mainly improving the standard of living of the poorest 40 percent of the population, most of whom are either illiterates or primary school dropouts, then formal schooling has not done much for them. In fact, the data show that investment in education widens the gap between rich and poor in most countries. This results from mechanisms like regressive tax systems, expensive secondary schooling, and free higher education all of which mainly benefit upper-income families. (1) For this article I will define development as movement toward a more humane society than now exists in both developing and developed nations. This requires political systems more responsive to the interests of the poor. It also requires rising real income as well as a more equal distribution of wealth and more participatory management of institutions.

I would define a more humane society as one based on four principles: security, equity, democracy and individuation. Briefly, security refers to job security, health and safety. Equity means fair practices in the community and on the job like fair pay differentials, the sharing of productivity increases between labor and capital, and the overcoming of discrimination based on race, sex or age. Democracy includes giving each worker and citizen the opportunity to have a say in the decisions that affect his life, both at work and outside. Individuation is the development of the individual's talents, compassion and capacity for reasoning. (2) The patient application of these principles to the problems that face villagers will result in a more humane society.

I. Types of Education

Before looking at some of the issues, a description of the terms might be useful. Formal education or schooling describes the learning that takes place in schools, and trains students mainly for urban, modern-sector jobs. Learning, however, also takes place outside school, at home, on the street, and on the job. This is learning by living or learning by doing, and can be called informal education. One of the few countries which recognizes the importance of informal education during the first ten years of school is China; it has captured some of its benefits by getting the students into informal learning situations on the farms and in the factories. All over the world professional training in some disciplines like medicine has long recognized the importance of informal on-the-job training.

Nonformal education is organized learning outside the normal school university curriculum - examples include the training of agricultural extension agents in short courses and teaching adults literacy. Thus nonformal education coexists with formal education, but it receives little funding and less prestige than formal education. Upsetting the existing balance between the two it is a major source of conflict among educational interest groups.

Finally, there is adult education for self-reliance and participation, which has its roots both in community development and worker participation in management. Although Paulo Freire, Julius Nyerere, Saul Alinsky, and Adam Curle have developed the concept recently, Mahatma Gandhi and others preceded them. Mao Tse-tung, however, gave the approach its most comprehensive elaboration and application. It helps groups of people learn how to study together and become aware of the political and economic determinants of their poverty. They then learn to organize and mobilize to improve their circumstances. This differs from the often paternalistic community development approach of the past which relied on outside experts. These adult groups learn that with cooperation and organization they can build roads, manage water distribution, reduce neighborhood crime, and grow more food. They learn that they can select their own people to be sent for training as paramedics and teachers. Through cooperative saving they reduce their dependence on money lenders. And when these things happen to them, they develop a self-confidence which in turn generates further initiatives.

Julius Nyerere has emphasized that "People can only develop themselves; they cannot be developed. Adult education is the key because it will help men and women to think for themselves, make their own decisions, and execute those decisions for themselves." (3) The rural poor have to transform themselves from being acted upon to being actors. If they do not, they will continue to be dependent on the rural and urban elites to plan and manage future investments in towns and villages to the detriment of the poor.

II. Failure of Present System

During the last ten years many observers saw that formal education in developing countries was not meeting the needs of most of the poor. Formal education provided training for urban, white-collar jobs while most jobs tended to be manual and in rural areas. The students from most poor families, moreover, were generally unable to continue formal education to the university level. In fact, what the poor do learn from formal education is that they are failures. They fail to be promoted from one grade to the next in primary school, or they fail the entrance exam to secondary school. Educators, the gatekeepers to job security and high incomes, reject them as unfit. In most countries, the poor are resigned to letting the educational establishment decide their fate and legitimize their poverty. Gunnar Myrdal, the Nobel Laureate in economics, has explained that "The poor are not educated to see their interests and they are not organized to fight for their interests." They lack education for critical awareness and organization.

We can illustrate the nature of the problems with a few facts from Pakistan. (4) Other countries in Asia, Africa, and Latin America share many of Pakistan's problems, or will soon encounter them.

- About 6 percent of the labor force is estimated to be unemployed and twice as many are seriously underemployed.

- One third of those who are unemployed, about one million adults, have completed primary education or more.

- Illiterate workers find jobs more quickly than the unemployed with education, even though there are three times as many illiterates who are unemployed.

- 40 percent of the vocational school graduates have been unemployed for two to four years after graduation.

- 27 percent of the population tell the census-taker that they can read. However, when literacy is measured as the ability to read and understand a newspaper, only 14 percent of the population is literate (19 percent of males and 6 percent of females).

- Although universal primary education has been a government objective for almost 30 years and total enrollments have been steadily increasing, the percentage of children completing primary school is falling. Only 30 percent of the present 15-19 age cohort have completed primary school, as opposed to 35 percent of the 20-24 age cohort. See Figure 1, below.

- Because of dropouts and low reading achievement, we can say that less than 8 percent of those who turn 12 years old each year can read and understand a newspaper.

Given these conditions, the 36 percent of the nation's education budget allocated to primary education goes <u>either</u> to producing generally illiterate primary school leavers, or to financing a most expensive, and inefficient, means of selecting students for secondary education.

- At the nation's eight universities we find the classic diploma factories. In one hour teachers grade 30 exams, each covering two years of a student's work. While observers agree that student and teacher performance has fallen, the number graduating with highest honors has quadrupled. Four years ago only 10 percent graduated with "first divisions," and now more than 40 percent do. Some university libraries have added no books in the past several years. Instead, funds have gone to more buildings.

- Nine out of ten graduates in the university courses in pharmacy have taken jobs abroad in the past few years. One reason is that there are not even posts for pharmacists in hospitals or clinics. Those who have gone abroad do not expect to return.

- There is only one doctor for 24,000 rural people, one of the lowest ratios in the world. The doctor-nurse ratio is about three doctors for one nurse instead of one to three, a more normal standard (even with these conditions, the government allows most new MDs to emigrate).

- Free education in Pakistan, in theory, gives equal opportunity to the poor to reach high-paying jobs. The data, however, show that children of upper-income families are overrepresented by 2,700 percent at the university level in comparison to the percentage of upper-income families in the population. No one could possibly argue that the rich are 2,700 percent more able to benefit from a university education.

Is Pakistan the extreme sole example of these educational problems? Unfortunately not. Similar problems are visible in countries as economically and educationally different from Pakistan as Brazil, Tunisia, and Liberia.

These problems can be grouped into three categories:

(1) inefficiences within the schools and the education system which are measured by high dropout rates, illiterate graduates, and the lack of paper, pencils, textbooks, and even teachers in the classrooms;

(2) mismatch between what the schools are producing and what employers, citizens, young people, and parents need - these problems are seen in educated unemployed, and parents and citizens from low-income groups who lack information about sanitation and child care; and

(3) inequities in distributing both educational opportunities and educational results to the rural and urban poor.

These problems have been around for so long, and appear so intractable, that analysts have reluctantly reached four main conclusions.

First, neither the lack of knowledge nor the limitations of educational planning have been a major reason why education systems have been so slow to change. A recent international meeting of educational planners concluded that even when better information is available, it is not used; even carefully prepared plans are shelved or partially implemented.

Second, both formal and informal education are shaped by the political and economic institutions of a country. Reforming education, therefore, means that successful political and economic reform comes first. Even seemingly minor changes, like replacing the "irrelevant" academic curricula, with vocational training, will be resisted by the present leadership in most countries since the academic curricula tends to reinforce the existing power structure. The authors of the Vth Plan in Pakistan, which called for reducing expenditure on higher education, argue that "the interest groups affected ... are likely to protest vigorously."

Third, as Torsten Husen, the Swedish educator and reformer has acknowledged, within the past ten years around the world "the mood has swung from the almost euphoric conception of education as the Great Equalizer to that of education as the Great Sieve that sorts and certifies people for their (predetermined) slot in society." (5)

Fourth, the evidence suggests that further investment in most aspects of the existing education systems of non-socialist developing countries would work against the interests of the poor, not for them.

III. Solutions

What can a government such as Pakistan's, which has made some commitments toward increased equity and participation, do for the one million educated who are now unemployed, plus the next million who will soon suffer the same fate? If it reduced the number of new graduates from the high schools and universities, the middle and upper class, which put the government in power, would withdraw their support. These groups want more school places for their children, not less. If the government required employers to hire the one million educated unemployed, thus increasing by 5 percent the number of their employees, the employers would complain of higher costs and lower profits. They could threaten to withdraw their political support. Finally, if the educated unemployed were hired, then the two million who are unemployed, but uneducated, might take to the streets to demand equal treatment with the educated.

Can the mismatch between the labor market and education be reduced in the future? There is some hope for the discussions of the reform of technical training. Training institutions in Brazil and Singapore are managed by employers, craftsmen and educators. This cooperative management approach permits the close supervision of both quality and quantity. Pakistan officials are studying this approach.

Lack of funds and lack of local responsibility for primary schools and secondary schools are two major problems. Although successive governments have promised universal primary education, no one can predict when it will happen. While the solutions are at hand, they all upset the status quo.

For example, in Pakistan, 40 percent of the educational capital budget at the Federal level goes for university training, but some of it contributes to the brain drain and to the numbers of educated unemployed. Because primary school costs per student are less than 1 percent of the costs of a university student, the Pakistan Government could educate 100 students through primary school for each student not admitted to the university. As the authors of the Vth Plan argued, this would be politically unacceptable: children of upper-income parents would be denied university places.

Similarly, providing control over schools to neighborhoods and villages would upset the socio-political balance and the central administration in some of its power. Villagers with new confidence might then challenge the rural elite - the landlords.

What can the government do to eliminate a dual education system which trains some for mental labor, and others for manual labor? Quite simply, with a possible exception, they can do very little now. If my analysis is correct, and the government aim is to avoid widened confrontation, then the government first has to continue to decrease slowly the economic power of both the present landowning elite and the bureaucracy and continue to decentralize political power in order to reduce the support for a dual educational system. The exception is for the government to expand its support for the existing pilot projects in education for self-reliance and participation.

Successful pilot projects provide an opportunity to develop programs of education for self-reliance, and not threaten the priority concerns of powerful interest groups. While from one perspective this may be coopting the energies of the reformers, which could be used instead on changing the power structure, it is also a form of anticipatory action which provides the experience needed before a reform can expand at a later date, similar to the educational work of Mao Tsetung in Yennan in the 1930s.

These examples reveal the interest groups of the society which prevent educational reforms from taking place. The landlords require a low-cost and docile labor force. Thus they neither want peasants to become independent nor unemployment to shrink. The educators do not want to "lower academic standards" by adopting more nonformal methods, nor to lose their own jobs. Similarly the middle and upper-class parents fear that opening more primary schools for the rural poor may mean losing places for their children at secondary school and the university. Governments are inevitably sensitive to these conflicts and, even in an ostensible period of transition to socialism, hesitate to alienate the support of any of these groups. The Pakistani government of Prime Minister Bhutto shared these problems.

IV. "Expert Solutions"

Many educational experts have recently agreed that nonformal education is a useful approach for poor countries. They urge the expansion of nonformal education to reduce the mismatch between educational supply and employment demand. And most of them agree that the expansion of formal education at the secondary and higher levels should be stabilized at present rates of enrollment growth, or slowly reduced.

The greatest economic need, the experts perceive, is in training specialists in all aspects of rural development or self-employment. World Bank authors wrote in 1974 that formal "educational systems have been irrelevant to the needs of developing countries for the past two decades." (6) The Bank then urged a program of nonformal and basic vocational education. But other observers have not been so enthusiastic about replacing formal education with a substitute that has been little tried. Ministers of education have been noticeably cool to such suggestions.

Why? The short answer is that the expansion of nonformal education will cut into the funds allocated for formal education which is more prestigious and in greater demand. But there is another, equally serious problem. The expansion of technical and nonformal education will reinforce a dual system of education, with one side of the system training students for manual labor jobs, and the other for mental labor; one side for mainly rural employment, the other for urban. The dual system reinforces the social and political status quo; unchanged, it adversely affects the poor and their interests. Thus, unwittingly, the nonformal strategy works against the poor, except in countries like China and Cuba where the reduction of poverty is the highest priority of the leadership. In nonsocialist countries, it appears, nonformal education streams poorer children into manual jobs and reinforces the class structure.

The extent of the opposition among educators and middle-class parents to nonformal education is impressive. They feel that formal education *is* relevant to their needs. Lower-income parents would also object to a dual education system that would stream *their* children into manual jobs while still in primary school. Can theory provide some insight?

V. Conflicting Theories

Formal education is often viewed as central to economic growth. Years of schooling, where rote learning is the basic method, and literacy rates become essential measures of human development for some observers. Other observers argue that the few years of primary schooling or the ability to write one's name, which is all that the majority of the poor receive and will continue to receive for the next twenty years, are neither a basic need nor an effective means of getting more food, shelter, or health care. (7) They prefer a form of learning that teaches the poor to define their own problems, and how to organize themselves to overcome them. Dialogue is the basic method. Thus there are two quite different approaches to learning for the poor. They actually reflect different theories of economic and human development, one stressing the control of the poor by national elites, the other stressing self determination.

The different approaches are exemplified by the experience in the Northeast of Brazil in the early 1960s and in China in the early 1950s. In Brazil the government closed down three major adult education programs which reached more than 5 million peasants and landless laborers. The programs had been successfully teaching the poor to identify and analyze their own problems. The graduates organized cooperatives, threatened the rural elite, and were suppressed by the army. As a substitute the government expanded adult literacy training and formal education for children. (8) In China, the government expanded its efforts to organize people in both the cities and countryside into study groups of 10 to 15 people. Their purpose was to analyze their work performance and their problems, and then develop solutions which they could implement without outside assistance. (9) It is important to note, however, that problem-posing education for adults is not limited to socialist countries like China, Mozambique, and Jamaica but has spread to other countries like Pakistan, Swaziland, and Colombia.

There are important assumptions about human development shared by the advocates of both formal and problem-posing education, although they might differ in emphasis. They would agree with Julius Nyerere that "people can only develop themselves; they cannot be developed." They would agree that the people who are successful in most cultures have faith in their abilities to master their own destinies in order to become better human beings. Carl Rogers, the psychologist and educator, has shown that the fully functioning person relies on his own feelings and judgments, rather than on what his friends and relatives expect. People who have a high degree of trust in themselves are able to look at all kinds of information. Psychologist Abraham Maslow found that men and women who were highly effective in their daily lives have a positive self-concept; they tend to view themselves as being acceptable and able, living in a world where they can make a contribution. They perceive the world as it really is, and people as they really are. This means that these people are operating with valid information; they tend to get more done than others. They can solve problems more efficiently because they make their decisions on the basis of how things really are rather than on how they wish they were. Maslow and others have found that feeling good about oneself generates a trust in oneself, and an appreciation and respect for others. (10)

Contrast these descriptions of effective and successful people with descriptions of the poor by Paulo Freire, a Brazilian educator. "So often do the poor hear that they are good for nothing, know nothing and are incapable of learning anything that in the end, they become convinced of their own unfitness... They distrust themselves." (11)

The central theoretical issue is, how can the poor learn to analyze and solve their own problems. Traditional educators have maintained that literacy training and schooling are the way to develop human resources for both the rich and poor. In the past forty years, however, a small but growing number of educators who have worked with the poor for most of their lives have observed that "school is a war against the poor." (12) And even UNESCO acknowledges that literacy training for adults has failed to achieve its objectives in most of the non-socialist countries. (13)

This group of educators argue that most of the poor either have no chance to attend primary school, or fail to complete it. Failure in school erodes self-confidence, that essential trait for self-development and success. These educators describe formal education as it is practiced in most countries as a form of banking. They see schooling as an act of depositing. The teacher makes deposits which students patiently receive, memorize, and repeat. Banking education resists dialogue, the essential process in problem-posing education. These educators argue that men can be truly human only through inquiry, thought, and action. Education for self-reliance and liberation from poverty is active learning, not the transferral of information. These educators include such successful and diverse leaders as Julius Nyerere, Mahatma Gandhi, Mao Tsetung, Paulo Freire, and Saul Alinsky.

This brief description of the difference between the proponents of formal schooling and of learning for critical awareness and self-reliance does not do justice to the arguments of either side. For example, some educators maintain that it is possible to have both effective adult education and formal schooling. While a number of countries are struggling to initiate effective adult education without substantially altering the formal system, a dual education system is likely to develop: one mainly for the rich, the other for the poor. The exceptions are those societies where the poor have played a major role in shaping the formal system. In China, for example, the formal system has radically changed to reflect the needs of the poor.

VI. Outlook

Hope may lie with new programs of education for self-reliance and participation, which Pakistan and other countries hope developed. The Pakistani Government is putting more and more faith in the people in the villages and neighborhoods to study and solve their own problems. A project in one province has 80 villages selecting their own teachers, managing their school affairs, and maintaining the buildings. When faced with the lack of space, several village school councils decided to use the mosque which was empty most of the day. The council has employed students to clean the school and maintain the grounds. Teacher attendance has improved as villagers, not distant supervisors, are responsible for the selection of teachers and their attendance.

The Bhutto government, which was in power when the author was in Pakistan, avoided conflict with possible opposition forces by keeping the project small and experimental. Significantly, the project created a climate to encourage self-help efforts by stressing its motto, "Power to the people."

Another project for 400 villages across the country is encouraging village planning and management of community development efforts, including both health and education. Initiated with the Ministry of Education and the cooperation of the U.S. Agency for International Development, the Government is supplying partial finance of the improvements.

It is too early to say whether these projects will succeed after the initial enthusiasm and government attention. However, the objective of the decentralization of educational planning and administration is consistent with World Bank policy to increase the participation of target groups in planning and managing Bank projects.

Although the Chinese acknowledge problems with their education system, their programs in education, health, and rural development come closest to the World Bank's description of the ideal programs for a developing country. In education they have a curriculum relevant to the needs of the mass of the population, ten years of schooling almost universally available, and a university selection process that minimizes discrimination against the poor - all achieved at low cost within twenty years. Even countries with five times the per capita annual income in China, $250, and the same objectives in their developing plans, have not achieved these results. A major reason, however, for the Chinese success is that effective political and economic reform provided a supportive context.

In other countries, education programs are emerging that benefit the poor and some have Bank support. Tanzania has made remarkable progress but, as President Nyerere has recently emphasized, the implementation appears to have slowed down. Other countries like Angola, Botswana, Ecuador, Ethiopia, Guinea Bissau, Somalia, Zambia, Guyana and Jamaica are reshaping the old education system to the new development needs, but have neither developed a comprehensive strategy nor sufficient implementation based on the participation of target groups. The failure in the 1960s to support and expand the efforts of peasants to organize and pursue their needs in northeast Brazil should remind us that the approach may not work in some countries. The desirable transformation of education cannot take place without the effort and struggle of the mass of the population and the support of the government leadership.

VII. **Strategy**

> The poor are not educated to see their interests, and they are not organized to fight for them.
> – Gunnar Myrdal

The educational objective is to promote types of learning which will help the poor to satisfy their needs in housing, food, and health and to become more self-reliant in their development efforts. It would be a program forged with, and not for, the poor to assure that they receive what they need. The major issue that faces most national officials and staffs of international agencies is whether they will trust the poor to participate in planning and managing such programs.

The two groups for which learning may be most cost-effective in moving toward more humane and productive development are adults, and children under five years old. Adults are a priority since they can make decisions daily to affect their basic human needs. Younger children are a priority because of the crucial impact of the first years of life on developing full adult potential. The evidence suggests that 50% of IQ which is measured at age 16 has already developed by age four.

Three components would comprise cost-effective training for poor adults: developing a critical awareness of the causes and consequences of their poverty through small group discussions, learning the skills of organization and leadership, and extending their production skills. The evidence indicates that when this process is implemented, peasants become active in face of their problems instead of passive. As their fatalism is replaced by hope, positive achievements result. As a Brazilian peasant said at the end of his training, "The peasant begins to get courage to overcome his dependence when he realizes that he is dependent. Until then, he says, 'What can I do, I am only a peasant?'" An awakened consciousness leads people to comprehend their situation as an historical reality susceptible to inquiry and transformation, a process over which people can feel themselves to be in control.

The second priority group is children from infancy to school age. Early environmental factors, both physical and psychological, are critical for the child's continued capacity to develop. It appears that the single most important input in the school performance of students is not budget size, class size, teacher experience or training, or physical facilities, but rather the characteristics of children at the time they enter school. (14) Thus one way to optimize learning is to invest in meeting the nutritional and cognitive needs of young children. Equally important to school performance are affective behaviors learned before age five which positively affect job performance and responsible citizenship.

While heredity determines an important fraction of intellectual abilities, it is not known how important this is compared to environmental factors. The best guess is that heredity accounts for less than 50% of IQ at age five. Important environmental factors include prenatal and early malnutrition, which affects brain growth and mental alertness, frequency of infectious diseases, and parental attention. Jerome Kagan, Harvard University psychologist, states that "...A child's experiences with his adult caretaker during the first 24 months of life are major determinants of the quality of his motivation, expectancy of success, and cognitive abilities during the school years." (15)

Improvement of early environment might well prove to be the most effective means of improving learning. This theory supports a new urgency in meeting basic needs of children. Because children can be reached only through their parents, this requires the same needs-oriented strategy for parents, with attention to productivity as a means of increasing income "and to access to basic resources." Improving early environment requires training parents about child-rearing practices like breast feeding and providing better health and nutrition. Thus these two strategic priorities of reaching adults and very young children overlap, since adult education should be used to teach parents about the importance of the early years for children's development.

VIII. Illustrations of Education for Self-Reliance

Education for self-reliance and participation takes many forms, although the problem-posing process is shared across them. The possibilities are best described through examples. They each have their strengths and weaknesses. Even this learning process which appears best adapted to the needs of the poor, will not achieve its potential if the technological conditions and political support for change are not also present. We include examples from Brazil, Columbia, Bangladesh, People's Republic of China, Senegal, and Sri Lanka.

The Problem-Posing Method: Brazil

Paulo Freire, as coordinator of the national literacy program in Brazil, would go to a village and enter into conversation with people. (16) He would ask them to help him to observe the village life. He would have them help him take pictures of scenes of village activities which were familiar and common to most of the villagers. The villagers would then come together to see the pictures. Freire would ask them to describe what they saw in detail, writing words under the pictures as they reflected on what they were seeing and feeling.

Then Freire would question the villagers about the contradictions in the explanations which they were giving about why things were the way they were. For example, in one village, the people described the harvest as being very poor. Freire asked them "Why?" Some of the villagers said: "Because the land is tired." Freire then asked them why some of the land seemed to be very productive and other parts of the land seemed tired. They explained that the rich farmers had fertilizer and they didn't. Freire then asked them how that was the case. The questions and answers continued. The topics discussed ranged from those which were primarily theological, political, or economic in nature to those which were basically philosophical in nature.

Frequently, villagers gave fatalistic answers. Freire would always come back to the contradictions which the people themselves had exposed. The people then began, as a result of this process, to think for themselves and to become aware of alternative ways of viewing and coping with problems that had seemed to be insurmountable for themselves and their communities.

In the process, people learned to read, to care, and to have a sense of worth. Freire called what happened to them conscientizacao (awareness). As soon as they could read and write, they could register to vote. They began to form cooperatives and to join unions. Literacy, as taught by the problem-posing method, became a means to questioning the status quo, and organizing to improve their conditions.

Reaching the Poor by Radio: Columbia

Mass media campaigns are an example of how low-level modern technology can be adapted to the needs of the rural poor, and can be used to affect the attitudes and behavior of larger numbers of people. Like all approaches, it must be carefully used: Are the media used understood by the

poor? Is the language, accent, and vocabulary appropriate?
Is the message suited to the needs of the rural poor? Do the
poor have access to the media, and are they attracted to the
message?

The most cost-effective approaches are often based on
radio, and use other media in order to reach target groups.
(17) One major campaign which did this with some success is
Accion Cultural Popular (ACPO) in Columbia. (18) It runs the
largest radio network in Columbia and provides an education
program to an audience in the hundreds of thousands. The
"Radio Schools" alone have enrollments of up to 240,000 students and a write-in survey attracted 97,000 responses. ACPO
uses not only the radio, but also a weekly newspaper, textbooks, book series, and local classes and parish organizations, all of which are coordinated to reinforce the same
content. ACPO also coordinates its activities with several
national agencies involved in rural development.

Despite a large and growing budget ($4 million in 1972),
the earnings of the radio network, which carries advertising,
and the publishing house, which does commercial work, allows
ACPO to be 75% self-supporting. The remainder comes from government, contributions, and loans. It has a full-time staff
of over 300, about 200 field workers who receive small stipends, and more than 20,000 unpaid volunteers. The radio
network broadcasts 19 hours a day, including six hours a day
of structured courses and various programs of informal education, such as practical advice on agriculture and the home
and news. Programs are oriented to an audience with little
or no formal schooling; the language is simple and the general content is relevant to all rural inhabitants.

ACPO demonstrates the possibilities of the multimedia
approach for raising standards of living. Evaluative studies
have indicated significant positive effects on literacy, general knowledge, participation in community affairs and behavioral changes, for example improved child vaccination and
nutrition as a result of the ACPO. The experience of ACPO
indicates the need for multimedia coordination: radio plus
printed matter plus personal contact. It also demonstrates
the possibility and need for mobilizing large-scale local
voluntary efforts to support a mass educational program.
The emphasis on motivation and attitude formation more than
specific information is believed to have contributed to the
broad impact of the program. Specific information provided
was based on real-life needs, rather than duplicating formal
school curriculum. Maintaining a large degree of flexibility allowed ACPO to respond to feedback through research and

criticism and to gear programming to the needs of the target group of small landholders.

Radio and multimedia campaigns have been used in many other countries, including the US, Canada, Ghana, Tanzania, India, and China, with a large degree of success. The Colombia example of ACPO demonstrates both the potential for such campaigns and the specific elements which contribute to their success. Such campaigns are well-suited for the education objectives of reaching large numbers of people with relevant materials at low cost and with maximum flexibility.

Education through Rural Cooperatives: Bangladesh

The Comilla project in what was at the time East Pakistan included an educational program based on a 'bottom up,' rather than 'top down,' effort. (19) Village cooperatives were the prime agencies for agricultural improvement and rural education. Rather than using an outside extension worker, an internally-selected "organizer" and a similarly chosen "model farmer" were the key teachers and served as educational liaison with outside sources of information relevant to self-perceived village needs. Central cooperative associations were formed to serve the common needs of the many small local cooperatives, providing skill training in response to specific requirements, such as for accounting and equipment operation and repair. The central organizations become a natural focus of the cooperatives and began providing services going beyond agriculture per se, including a women's program, family planning programs, expansion of primary education by utilizing mosques, and improving school facilities by involving students, teachers, and the community in planning and construction.

At the time of its disruption in the war of independence of 1971, the Comilla project showed impressive results in giving local people a larger voice and practical role in rural development. It showed that the two-way system of educational communication can be more effective than the familiar one-way, top-down extension model. The success was not unqualified, however. In most villages, less than half the farmers joined the cooperatives and often the greatest beneficiaries were the better-off farmers. Educational efforts other than those focused on agricultural production remained peripheral and poorly coordinated. Also the level of investment - about 25 million rupees over eight years to reach about 230,000 people - could not be widely replicated.

Barefoot Doctors: China

A well-known example of the adaptation of learning to meet basic health needs is the training of over one million "barefoot doctors" in China since the Cultural Revolution in 1966. (19) Mao Tsetung's guidelines for health care stretched back to pre-Revolutionary days: it should serve the needs of the people, stress prevention, combine western and traditional medicine, and be coordinated into mass medical education campaigns. The barefoot doctors are ordinary peasants, chosen in their communities to receive paramedical training. They provide basic health and medical care at the local level in a country where an estimated 20,000 western-trained doctors are hardly adequate to cope with the health needs of 850 million people. An alternative system of medical and health training was designed to meet these needs.

Barefoot doctors are chosen by their peers on the basis of their interest in helping others, as well as in medicine or science. They are initially trained in the commune medical facilities, or in short (one to three month) courses in the hospitals and medical schools of nearby cities and towns. But the emphasis of their training is to maintain ties to their own people - rather than becoming part of a special elite, as in so many other countries. This first stage of medical education gives enough basic training to become a part-time health worker, including first aid, diagnosing and treating common ailments, giving injections and some common drugs, and acupuncture. They handle up to 85% of the requests for care. The barefoot doctors also begin assisting and observing trained physicians, in order to graduate to practicing under supervision. Further responsibilities, such as vaccinations leading to public sanitation movements, and family planning, are then added. They are taught primary medical care and post-illness follow-up, plus more about diagnosis and referral. After two years, they have a broad spectrum of medical and public health training - and are on their way to additional training and practice, some of them gradually becoming qualified as fully professional physicians.

Thus, in a relatively short period of time, China has been able to significantly upgrade its health care system by instituting a non-traditional system of health education based on wide-scale non-professional training based on community needs, rather than on highly selective, high quality professional medical training which would produce relatively small numbers of doctors without close ties to the needs of the communities. Not only has the ability of the medical system to respond to the needs of hundreds of millions of rural people been greatly increased, but a solid foundation for the development of more extensive medical services and better trained personnel has been formed. Furthermore, this has been achieved not only in a small pilot project, where a concentration of attention and resources may yield results not broadly replicable, but has actually trained over one million new health workers spread across the largest country in the world.

China's unique political system, which allowed the desire to provide better health care to generate a commitment capable of implementing this desire without being defeated by self-interested groups or professional associations, was clearly a major factor in the success of the program. Countries without a strong commitment to meeting the needs of the poor have often tried to implement positive programs, only to find them sabotaged by elite interests. Animation rurale in Senegal provides such an example.

Building Local Initiative: Senegal

Animation rurale was a program aimed at "mobilizing the rural masses" for a sweeping reorientation of attitudes and agricultural improvement, begun in Senegal in 1959. (19) Villagers chose people among themselves to be trained as animateurs. The animateurs took intensive courses in general civic duties, national planning, cooperative management methods, and agricultural and animal husbandry techniques. They often returned to their villages, where they organized their fellow villagers and put into practice the techniques they had been taught. The animateurs also returned periodically to the training centers for four to five day consultation and training sessions. They served both as local guides to grass-roots development and as liaisons to outside sources of technical and material assistance.

Animation rurale achieved considerable success. It stimulated rural development projects and created a greater awareness among people of their capacities for self-help. However, the program itself was phased out after 1967 when government reorganization and resistance, especially from traditional local leaders, to movements challenging the status quo led to withdrawal of official support. Although in this institutional respect animation rurale failed – and in doing so demonstrates the sorts of problems faced by programs which actually address the real needs of the village poor and try to build local initiative – it did have both immediate and lasting effects on the villages which took part in the program. The lesson of animation rurale in Senegal is that the process of transforming rural life and institutions requires a serious commitment of resources, strong regional planning and coordination, and concerted effort by civil administrators. Most importantly sufficient political will is necessary to overcome the political factions eager to preserve the status quo for their own advantage, even where this status quo manifestly fails to meet the basic needs of the majority of the people.

Self-Reliance for Community Needs: Sri Lanka

The <u>Sarvodaya Shramadana</u> Movement, founded in 1958, is now the largest non-governmental organization in Sri Lanka. (20) It combines traditional Buddhist social values with local economic development and the provision of basic services for women, children, and youth. There is heavy emphasis on full community participation at all levels and on a self-reliant approach to development. <u>Shramadana</u> (the mutual sharing of labor) is used as a way of educating people about their potential to improve their own standards of living, as well as an effective way to actually develop physical infrastructure. The Sarvodaya organization teaches villagers the skills needed to utilize the resources available, trains community workers who are drawn from the villages, helps communities form into functional groups, aids in relief from debt burden, promotes cooperative marketing, launches cottage industries, creates agricultural farms for unemployed youth, and supports a range of educational activities.

Sarvodaya has special programs to meet the basic nutritional needs of children up to six years old and pregnant and lactating mothers, such as the community kitchen program started in 1973. In 1976, 450 kitchens were providing over one million meals a year. Most of the food itself was provided by the participants. Malnutrition was not treated so much as a lack of availability of food, as a lack of knowledge about nutrition, improper cooking habits, improper diet of infants, children, and mothers, illnesses, and unequal distribution of food. Nutrition needs could therefore be approached through self-reliant community activities.

In 1972, when the national school entry age was raised from five to seven, Sarvodaya began a pre-school education program, with special attention to child development needs, such as nutrition, health, love and protection. The schools are run by mothers' groups, with one woman selected by the group to be trained at a Sarvodaya Training Center. The program has been approved by government education authorities. In 1976, there were 150 preschools in operation.

Other programs for children include day-care centers, an extremely popular library service, and an extensive health program. As in the preschool and community kitchen programs, the mothers in the community nominate a health worker trainee who is given a six-month training course before returning to the community to organize health activities.

Activities of all Sarvodaya projects were financed within the communities wherever possible. In less able villages, financial assistance is provided. The Sarvodaya Movement itself was totally self-financed for its first ten years. Through the establishment of money-making activities, Sarvodaya expects to become financially self-reliant again by 1985.

In summary, programs using problem-posing education differ widely in specific objectives, structure, management, staffing, methods, content, and means of support. But they share a basic conception of rural development. They also share the underlying premise that rural transformation must and should be brought about primarily through transformation of the attitudes and behavior of rural people themselves. For this to happen, rural people must be given a large piece of the action; they should not simply be "programmed" to comply with plans and instruction devised by outsiders. They need to select their own members to receive outside training, if it is necessary. They should have a large voice in diagnosing their own needs, in making decisions that affect their lives, and in managing their own destiny.

Effective adult learning places heavy emphasis on the creation and strengthening of local institutions, such as cooperatives, local councils, and voluntary discussion and action groups through which rural people can participate in collective decision-making and concerted local actions.

IX. Policy Issues

> A real humanist can be identified more by his trust in the people, than by a thousand actions in their favor without that trust.
> — Paulo Freire (11)

What are the implications of these problems and illustrations for policy makers in developing countries and international agencies? The implications and policy questions can be briefly summarized:

- The planning and management of effective learning requires a deep understanding and political commitment among the national leadership. Existing educational and economic interest groups have a vested interest in the status quo. How can this commitment to change the status quo be developed and maintained?

- Effective education for the poor requires a trust by the national leadership and foreign experts in the ability of the poor to know their needs and in their willingness to work to meet them. This means local control of the programs, including the selection of trainees. How can this trust be developed where it does not exist?

- Appropriate technology like improved husbandry practices or crop varieties should often complement adult education. How can these efforts be usefully integrated at lowest cost?

- Primary education requires reform to assure that what children learn corresponds to their needs. How can villagers improve local primary schools?

The obstacles to mounting genuinely effective programs are large, as many past observers have learned. While there is support in the countries like China and Sri Lanka which have undertaken broad programs to meet the basic needs of the poor, there is often resistance in countries without the same commitment. The experience suggested by our illustrations, however, indicates that it is possible to design and implement projects which have a chance of overcoming basic obstacles. Even if they do not have the full expected support, they can still improve people's lives and provide hope for the future.

In conclusion, it is easy for technicians to come up with what appear to be theoretically sound solutions like non-formal education that in practice may even work against the very groups the technicians are trying to help. Small, but important, steps like those taken by Pakistan to place more confidence in local decision-makers are significant. New education programs will probably remain small and experimental until the political and economic power shifts to a more responsive and representative leadership. If international agencies are committed to the goals of more equitable distribution of wealth and education, and in building a more humane society, then they should support country efforts in education for self-reliance and participation.

Annex I

The Widening Gap: Literacy and Formal Education

Between 1950 and 1970, estimated total enrollments in the developing countries grew dramatically. Primary level enrollment grew over 200%, secondary level by 450%, and higher level by 500%. Estimated adult illiteracy in the developing countries fell from 63% in 1950 to 59% in 1960, and to 50% (40% male and 60% female, and ranging from 11% to 95%) in 1970. The percentage of school age children (5-14 years) out of school has fallen from 56% in 1970 to a projected 53% in 1975. (1)

These successes, however, have not been costless. Developing countries are spending an average of 4% of GNP and 18% of total public expenditures on public education, compared to about 6% of GNP and about 16% of public expenditures for developed countries. The poorest countries are spending twice the proportion of their budgets on education in 1970 as in 1950. Investment priorities from other sectors of the economy, moreover, are bringing an end to the era in which educational expenditures per capita have doubled by growing at double, and in some cases, triple, the rate of GNP. For example there is recent evidence of declining primary enrollments in Egypt, Nigeria and Pakistan.

The basic quantitative problem with relying on the expansion of formal education can be demonstrated by several projections. These show that the number of people who will be illiterate will continue to increase throughout the century, even at the highest possible rates of school expansion. Table 1 takes the growth rate of school enrollments in the developing countries in the 1960s, which created an additional 150 million literates in ten years, and projects this trend into the future. This is a highly optimistic assumption,

---

(1) Data sources for this section are the Education Sector Working Paper (Washington, D.C.: World Bank, 1974); Shahid Javed Burki and Joris Voorhoeve, "Global Estimates for Meeting Basic Needs: Background Paper" (World Bank, mimeo, 1977); John Simmons and Philip Brock, "Educational Issues in Pakistan: A Sector Memorandum" (World Bank, mimeo, 1977); and UNESCO, Statistical Yearbook (Paris: UNESCO, 1972 and 1974).

Table 1. Optimistic Literacy Projections

YEAR	ADULT POPULATION (millions)	LITERATE POPULATION (millions)	ILLITERATE POPULATION (millions)	PERCENTAGE ILLITERACY	DECADE INCREASE IN LITERATES (millions)
1950	1045	382	663	63	–
1960	1183	482	701	59	100
1970	1502	746	756	50	264
1980	2000	1150	850	42	404
1990	2650	1700	950	36	550
2000	3400	2400	1000	30	700

Table 2. Realistic Literacy Projections

YEAR	ADULT POPULATION (millions)	LITERATE POPULATION (millions)	ILLITERATE POPULATION (millions)	PERCENTAGE ILLITERACY	DECADE INCREASE IN LITERATES (millions)
1950	1045	382	663	63	–
1960	1183	482	701	59	100
1970	1502	746	756	50	264
1980	2000	1150	900	45	350
1990	2650	1700	110	41	450
2000	3400	2100	1300	38	550

Table 3. Functional Literacy Projections

YEAR	ADULT POPULATION (millions)	LITERATE POPULATION (millions)	ILLITERATE POPULATION (millions)	PERCENTAGE ILLITERACY	DECADE INCREASE IN LITERATES (millions)
1950	1045	191	854	82	–
1960	1183	241	942	80	50
1970	1502	373	1129	75	132
1980	2000	575	1425	71	202
1990	2650	850	1800	68	275
2000	3400	1200	2200	65	350

Source: Data for 1950-75 from Education Sector Working Paper (World Bank, 1974), and Statistical Yearbook (Paris: UNESCO, 1968, 1972, 1974). Projections by the authors.

given the high costs of expansion, but nonetheless the educational gap, defined by the absolute number of illiterates, continues to widen. (After 2000, the illiterate population would stabilize at one billion, since the projected rates of population growth and enrollment growth would be equal.)

Table 2 is based on what we feel to be a more realistic expansion rate of six million new school places per annum, or 100 million additional literates per decade, and shows an increasingly growing gap.

These tables show that given moderate population projections and steadily growing school systems, the number of illiterates in the developing countries will increase for the next 25 years. With the most optimistic projections, the gap

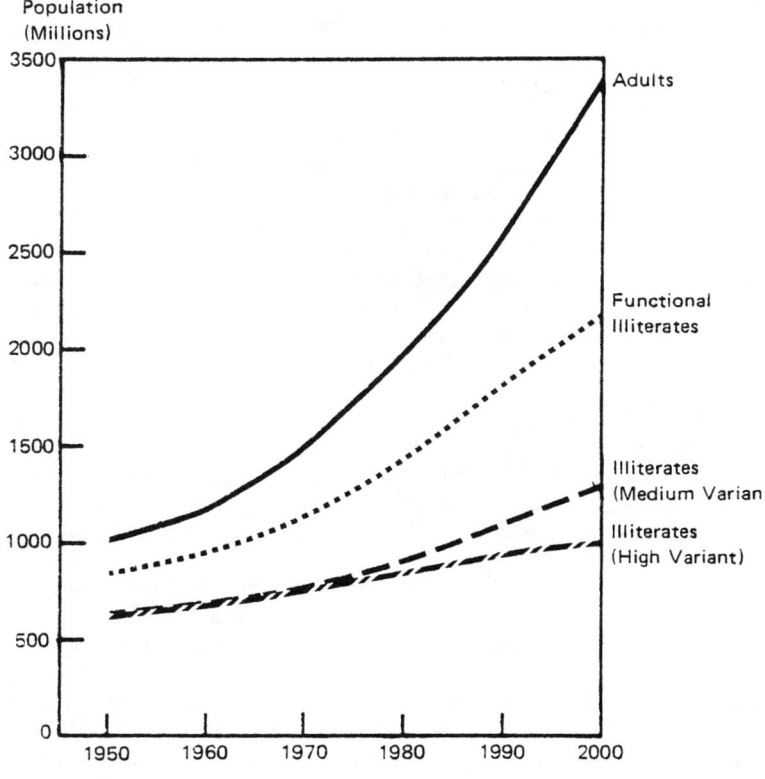

Figure 1. Illiteracy Projections

Source: J. Simmons and T. Phillips, "Education for Basic Human Needs" (Washington, D.C.: The World Bank mimeo, 1977; World Bank - 18410).

will cease to grow around the year 2000; with the more realistic projections, the gap will continue to widen for the indefinite future. In fact, the gap at any point in time will be wider than shown in these tables, because it will also include those under age 15 who are not in school. This additional number is projected to grow from 269 million in 1970 to 290 million in 1975, 375 million in 1985, and 500 million in 2000, based on the optimistic set of figures.

These projections also optimistically assume that all primary school graduates will be literate, when in fact less than half of primary school graduates are functionally illiterate.

The usual measure used to describe educational achievement is literacy. This can be, however, a troublesome concept. Much data is for census literacy, which is the percentage of people who answer yes to some survey questions as "can you read and write?" or "can you write your name?" The wide variation in census methodology restricts the comparability of census data, and leaves a great deal to be desired in the interpretation of the results. Another measure is simple literacy, the percentage of people who have graduated from primary school. It is presumed that a four or six year cycle of primary education yields literate graduates. But many primary graduates are not competent readers. In Pakistan, an estimated 70% of primary graduates are unable to read and understand a newspaper and thus are functionally illiterate. Although functional literacy is probably the most relevant definition for policy purposes and for evaluating the success of educational systems, almost all analysis is based on census or simple literacy figures, which are overly optimistic. Simple literacy data overstates the achievements of formal education by making its effectiveness tautological. In terms of functional literacy, the educational gap may well be double the size described in the text as shown by Table 3.

If we assume that one half of primary school graduates are literate, and use the optimistic expansion rate we find that the number of functional illiterates will grow to 2 billion in 2000 as shown in Table 3. This more realistic treatment of the effectiveness of schools makes the gap much wider (Figure 1). If there is to be any hope of meeting the literacy needs of the poor people in the gap, alternative approaches to education must be used.

References

(1) Asim Dasgupta, "Education, Wealth and Income Distribution" (Washington, D.C.: mimeo, World Bank, 1974).

(2) Michael Maccoby, "The Bolivar Project of Joint Management-Union Determination of Change According to Principles of Security, Equity, Individuation and Democracy" (Washington, D.C.: Institute for Policy Studies, 1976). See also Maccoby in this volume.

(3) "Adult Education and Development," Literacy Discussion, Winter 1976-77.

(4) Pakistani information is based on data from the census and other government publications.

(5) Torsten Husen, "Problems of Securing Equal Access to Higher Education: The Dilemma between Equality and Excellence," Higher Education (Vol. 5, 1976, p. 411).

(6) World Bank, Education Sector Working Paper (Washington, D.C., World Bank, 1974).

(7) While some studies show a correlation between literacy and farmer productivity, other studies do not. And for the studies that do, their poor design does not permit an analysis that indicates whether it was the literacy they learned, other affects of being at school, or the nature of the entering student compared to the one who does not enter which affects productivity.

(8) Thomas J. LaBelle, Nonformal Education and Social Change in Latin America (Los Angeles: UCLA Latin American Center Publications, 1976) pp. 113-114.

(9) Gerald Tannenbaum and John Simmons, Reform in China (Washington D.C. World Bank, 1977).

(10) James O. Lugo and Gerald L. Hershey, Human Development: A Multidisciplinary Approach to the Psychology of Individual Growth (New York: MacMillan, 1974), pp. 181-188.

(11) Paulo Freire, Pedagogy of the Oppressed (New York: Seabury Press, 1968) pp. 49-50, 47.

(12) The School Boys of Barbiana, Letter to a Teacher (New York: Random House, 1971).

(13) The Experimental World Literacy Programme: A Critical Assessment (Paris: UNESCO Press/UNDP, 1976).

(14) John Simmons, The Education Dilemma: Policy Issues for Developing Countries (Baltimore: Johns Hopkins University Press, forthcoming).

(15) M. Selowsky, "Preschool Age Investment in Human Capital," in Simmons, The Education Dilemma (Baltimore: Johns Hopkins University Press, forthcoming).

(16) J.A. Farmer, "Adult Education for Transiting," in S.M. Grabowski, ed., Paulo Freire: A Revolutionary Dilemma for the Adult Educator (Syracuse, N.Y.: Syracuse University Press, 1972), p. 1.

(17) Dean Jamison, Peter Spain and Emile McAnamy, Radio for Education and Development: Case Studies (Washington, D. C., World Bank, 1977).

(18) Steven Brumberg, "Colombia: A Multimedia Rural Education Program," in Manzoor Ahmed and Philip Coombs, eds., Education for Rural Development, pp. 1-60 (New York: Praeger, 1975).

(19) Philip Coombs and Manzoor Ahmed, Attacking Rural Poverty (Baltimore: Johns Hopkins Univ. Press, 1974), pp. 85-87.

(20) A.T. Ariyaratne, "A People's Movement for Self-Reliance in Sri Lanka," Carnets de l'enfance, Vol. 39, 1977.

_____*Michael Maccoby*

12. Human Development in Traditional and Modernizing Villages

The purpose of this paper is to stimulate those involved in village development to question and rethink policy, by focusing attention on human development.

What is the goal of village development policy? Is it merely economic, to raise income, or is it to make life better for people? If we agree that enough has been learned to reject a crude equation of material growth with well-being, then what is the alternative? What can we do to help make life better for villagers?

An argument can be made that the greatest service we the rich industrialized countries can provide to villagers would be to leave them alone. While compelling in its simplicity, this argument is naive. There is no way we can avoid influencing village life throughout the world, including the rural towns in America. As Redfield[1] and Foster[2] have taught us, practically all villages are part-societies, responsive to the great socio-economic and cultural movements created within cities. Most folk traditions are vestiges of more complex cultural creations, and for centuries, peasants have obeyed commands given in palaces, statehouses, and bureaucracies. The village has long danced to the city's tunes, but in our time the beat has become faster and more frenzied.

The changes Erich Fromm and I[3] observed in a Mexican village are occuring throughout the world. The populations grow and there is no longer enough land to go around. Instead of being freeholders, a majority of the young have become day laborers. Some have left the village, attracted by the glamor and glitter of the city. Over a period of ten to fifteen years in the Mexican village, the new electronic entertainment from the city drove out its rural competition; movies, radio and TV replace traditional popular culture. Local plays were the first to go, then the band, and finally even the Christmas posadas. A new school was built and inaugurated with hopes that it would boost village children into a better life, but the minority of village children who reached the sixth grade were practically all the sons and daughters of the richest peasants.

Changes benefitted some economically and not others. A generation before, after the Revolution, everyone had been more or less equal. Now, some villagers were becoming rich and others teetered on the edge of starvation. More than one third of the men had become alcoholics or heavy drinkers, while the women had become angry and disillusioned by irresponsible machismo.

The accelerated process of development could be seen as a process of <u>social selection</u>, favoring an entrepreneurial social character. In contrast to the respectful and independent productive hoarding type adapted to small farming or the passive and dependent receptive type adapted to peonage, the villagers who adapted best to the new conditions were exploitative, ambitious and least tied to traditions of the past. These entrepreneurs took advantage of new capitalistic opportunities, new technology, new sources of credit and schooling. The new styles of success shown in movies and TV best fit them and reinforced their authority; they became models. Government policy-makers decided that they were the hope of the future, creators of agribusiness, surplusses. When they took over <u>ejido</u> lands, which were supposed to be unalienable plots held only by the individual who farmed them, officials in charge of enforcing land tenure regulations ignored this subversion of the law. Rather than stimulating human development, this process of economic development and social selection left a few people rich and many perhaps poorer than before the Revolution. Nor were these entrepreneurs happy. They distrusted the people they controlled and feared revenge from those whose land they had taken. They did not like the fiestas, and were contemptuous of the poor, condemning the landless day laborers as lazy and stupid. Their relationships with wives and children were full of conflict.

In the new village society, when the exploitative entrepreneurs take over, the traditional productive hoarding peasants manage to adapt, but their best instincts for equity and respect are frustrated, while their cynical and egoistic tendencies are strengthened. In contrast, the receptive peasants become more passive, less capable, more despairing in a society which provides neither the slavish security of the old hacienda system nor the artistic and cultural stimulation of the traditional village.

The evidence from other villages in Mexico and elsewhere (e.g. Kenya) tell a similar story[4]. To intervene responsibly in the process of development, we must take account of social and human as well as economic and technological factors. This requires understanding social character and the social-cultural values and institutions which stimulate human development.

In the Mexican part of the AAAS study on the ethnology of reproduction [4], two villages were studied by an anthropologist and a psychoanalyst [5]. One, Santa Maria, is much like the village Fromm and I described. Many in Santa Maria have the unproductive character common to descendants of peons. Given land by the government, they lack the self-confidence and activeness to make good use of it. Nor do their values stress self-sufficiency, dignity, or mutual aid. Their solutions to problems is to hope that someone (e.g. the government) will provide. Their relationships are full of rivalry, envy and animosity. Within families, men dominate their wives and both parents treat children as exploitable property. Village leadership is authoritarian and arbitrary. Cultural stimulation is limited to the mass media and for some to the Church, another place they go to beg for help from the powerful.

The other village, Tierra Alta, is no richer than Santa Maria, probably poorer in land, but there is a long tradition of independent landholding. The women supplement their income by raising animals and through cottage industry, and their economic independence has allowed them to challenge the traditional patriarchy. But their economic activity cannot be separated from character and values. In Santa Maria, the war between the sexes remains underground. The women appear to accept male domination, but are in fact resentful, and both men and women undermine each other. In Tierra Alta, the struggle between the sexes is open and acknowledged, but it is tempered by values of human respect. By affirming values of equality, bringing women into the new economy and strengthening their ability to limit their families, the village's capacity to adapt to change is strengthened. This process is supported by local leadership, both religious and secular, which is responsive and democratic.

If the integrated culture of Tierra Alta supports adaptation, the fragmented culture of Santa Maria can lead to cancerous growth. Women in Tierra Alta told Dr. Millan that they wanted to practice birth control either in order to be free to enjoy life more or to have enough resources to provide well for their children. In contrast, mothers in Santa Maria were not interested in birth control. Because they lived in a violent untrusting society, they wanted more children: someone to provide for them in the future, replacements if a son were to be murdered, children to take their side against the father.

Development policy must deal with villages like Santa Maria and those like Tierra Alta, and their needs are different. To gain confidence and competence, receptive submissive descendants of peons on haciendas or plantations need a type of education which confronts their hopelessness and stimulates hope in the context of new economic possibilities. In the early 1960's, I worked with a group of adolescent boys, some from the poorest class, in a cooperative experimental farming project[3]. An essential element in its success was the group's analysis of resistance to development, the unconscious fear of authorities rooted in childhood and hopelessness about one's own ability to change a pattern of submission and dependency. A year ago, I visited the village again and spoke with a man in his early thirties who had been one of those boys. Now, he owned two stores and had a prosperous chicken and egg business. His sons worked at the counter. I asked him if our project had helped him to succeed at business. "Yes, of course," he answered. "Was it that you learned how to raise chickens and market them?" "Not so much that," he answered "You taught us that we were just as good as anyone else, that we knew as much as the authorities and could do more than they could." He and the others recognized, however, that they were not able to teach these lessons to other boys. Given the social character and the pressures of modern development which favored the exploitative entrepreneurs, these boys were likely to use their new found confidence to adapt by joining the winners and separating themselves from the losers. A different result would have required a program that not only supported the cooperative development, but also stimulated cultural development.

If submissive defeated villagers need special programs to develop, productive free peasants such as those in Tierra Alta need protection from exploitation, from big projects that destroy cultural integrity and human dignity. Ideally a development policy will recognize that human development requires not only material goods, but institutions which satisfy psycho-social needs for a sense of security, equity, participation, and individuation. Communities which best satisfy these needs are best able to establish shared goals and ideals which support human development.

The need for security refers of course to needs for nutrition, water, shelter and care in times of sickness, and protection from invasion and crime[6]. Cultures fill these needs in different ways, depending on climate, productive possibilities and tradition. However, in all societies, children must depend on the family to meet these needs. As Erikson[7] writes, the sense of trust first depends on the child's relationship to mothering persons. For the adult, as Fromm points out, one's emotional attitude becomes more important. The more productive and adaptive is one's character to economic and social conditions, the greater the sense of security. People feel secure, because they produce - through farming, craftmanship, etc. - and because they can work cooperatively with others. But even the most productive person will be insecure and frightened, if there is no one he can trust. Traditionally, the family is the main source of this security, and when one can count on help from neighbors, there is an even greater sense of security. In contrast, where there is little trust even among family members, individuals tend either to maintain infantile, symbiotic relationships and/or become hostile and predatory with each other. Life becomes a jungle. Here we see that the various social needs are interrelated. By satisfying needs for equity and participation, a society also increases the sense of security, since there is less to fear from others and a more cooperative spirit. In contrast, where there are extreme inequities and some people are excluded from participation, exploitation and resentment increases hostility and insecurity.

Equity refers to the sense of justice and fairness based on freedom from exploitation. The sense of justice is the basis of dignity and respect. Where individuals experience injustice and indignity, they are outraged. Although exploitation may appear to crush the sense of equity so that it no longer seems part of the social character, where people do not express anger about inequities, unconscious resentment poisons the social atmosphere. In contrast, as Foster[8] points out, by developing limits to wealth and inequality many cultures protect their members from envy and resentment. The AAAS study[4] suggests that in the modern world, greater equality between the sexes may be a precondition for a united and adaptive family.

Participation refers to the need to have a say in decisions that affect the individual, the need to have a valued role and experience oneself as a contributing member of society. The society's structure of authority and decision-making may limit this role in childhood and expand it as the individual grows up. In some societies, it is true, children are made fearful and submissive, but in the more humanly developing societies, even small children starting about the age of five or six have clear-cut responsibilities and experience a sense of dignity and respect as they participate in society according to their abilities.

Individuation refers to the process of individual development of active capacities for creative work and love. The degree to which society supports and stimulates this development -- through education, arts, traditions of craftmanship, and valued roles for musicians and artists -- measures its affirmation of life. Individuation in this sense is not the same as individualism which sanctions jungle-like competition. We must be cautious about generalizing from our own concepts and values. In North American society, particularly in the middle and upper classes, we encourage individuation and put a high value on originality. We are ambivalent about conformity. In village society, people are more cautious about being different and its risks to the maintenance of security and equity. There are many examples of gifted individuals who have suffered in villages because they were different. Once when I was visiting Tzintzuntzan with George Foster, I gave Rorschach tests to a number of villagers[9]. One was an exceptionally original potter who in responding to the ink blots kept asking anxiously whether other villagers saw the same things. Professor Foster later told me the man had suffered rejection and internal conflict because of his individuality.

Although these four social needs for security, equity, participation and individuation can be met in different ways and are experienced differently according to social character, they are best satisfied when the shared values and religious system support the view that the meaning of life includes human as well as material development. The result is the stimulation of reason, mutuality and creative expression in work, play, arts and sciences. Where they are least well-satisfied, the result is a society where individuals suffer from a sense of distrust, resentment, powerlessness, and hopelessness.

While these needs suggest universal principles of human development, as valid for modern communitites as for traditional villages, their application is by no means obvious or simple[10]. In contrast to current thinking by development experts, these needs do not imply a hierarchy, in the sense that people would be concerned about equity only after needs for security had been satisfied, and so on.

As the case of Santa Maria shows, satisfaction of material needs without consideration of cultural values leads to social conflict and the perpetuation of inequity between classes and sexes that threaten the viability of the village. When basic material needs are considered as separate from psychosocial development, the result is likely to be a policy of aid that increases dependency and decreases the chances for the self-sufficiency which is essential for human development. The sense of security is strengthened not only by food, shelter and health care, but also by institutions that guarantee equity and participation; support for individuation requires security and a sense of equity, and these are needs for the poor as well as the rich.

When I discussed this paper with my colleagues, Dr. Douglass Carmichael, who has been a consultant to the World Bank, thought it would be all too easy for a mechanistically minded economist who is unaware and uncritical of his own social character to take these four social needs to construct a new checklist. It is significant that policymakers at the World Bank and AID have begun to redefine goals of development in terms of security, equity and participation as well as economic indices, and they point out that social and economic goals need not be inconsistent. This is progress from a simplistic view of economic development, in terms of material growth, but unless he takes account of culture and social character, the economist will likely assume that his own social character is "human nature" and that social needs can be met in the same way everywhere. He will tend to seek ways of increasing security and equity by better distributing land, access to market, roads, and technology. Participation will be a matter of calling meetings of villagers to articulate their needs. These "needs" are likely to be interpreted by the developers in ways which can only be met by spending money and by employing sophisticated and costly experts. Needs for individual development will be met by schools, needs for health by doctors, needs for production by technology we want to sell. In attempting to meet needs, in fact new needs will be stimulated in a way that furthers the social selection process, favoring village leaders who know what we want them to ask for. Ignored or undermined will be the culturally rooted forms of satisfying social needs which might or might not be strengthened by outside help.

In the final analysis, a policy of village development requires constant testing in terms of individual lives. It cannot be measured by cash income for three reasons. One, some villagers will meet their needs through food they grow, gather or raise. Second, those with a higher income may lack the social integration and values necessary for long-term viability, including self-sufficiency, population control, and ability to adapt to change. And third, economic measures do not correlate in any single way with fulfilling the psychosocial needs for human development.

What this analysis suggests for policy is that evaluation should be made only by individuals who understand macro issues but who also have learned how to experience the world from the villagers' point of view, who can understand their categories and ways of making sense of life, who understand their social character and the limits it sets on change. Most important is the ability to recognize cultural forms that stimulate human development which can be destroyed by well-meaning economic development. This does not mean trying to stop change, but rather to influence it so that it strengthens positive cultural trends. Until now, those who make policy have either ignored the reports of participant observers or attempted to refine them into macrotheories that can be used for mechanistic across-the-board policies. But just as the policy-makers cannot integrate the micro-studies, so the anthropologists or Peace Corps volunteers usually do not focus either critically or creatively on policy issues. Policy that seems correct from the viewpoint of human development may not fit the national goals of less developed countries whose priorities may be measured in terms of balance of payments. Although representatives of either the U.S. or international development agencies are limited in pursuing policies which conflict with the goals of these governments, it does not follow that these priorities and goals should be supported when they do not meet criteria for human development.

A pragmatic development policy must continually test humanistic principle against practical experience, by transforming intervention into participative study and experimentation. It is unlikely that such a policy can be formed and carried out either by people who are unable to experience the village world or those who do not understand broader socio-economic and political factors. This suggests that, as a precondition for becoming policy-makers, development workers be trained to become resources to communities attempting to adapt to change.

PSYCHOSOCIAL NEEDS

Security

> food - nutrition
> water
> housing
> health
> protection

Equity

> freedom from exploitation
> sexual equality
> limits to wealth

Participation

> political structure for community decisions
> productive role at each age

Individuation

> cultural stimulation
> free expression
> education

References and Notes

1. Robert Redfield, Peasant Society and Culture: An Anthropological Approach to Civilization (University of Chicago Press, Chicago, 1956).

2. George M. Foster, Tzin Tzun Tzan: Mexican Peasants in a Changing World (Little Brown, Boston, 1967).

3. E. Fromm and M. Maccoby, Social Character in a Mexican Village (Prentice Hall, Englewood Cliffs, N.J., 1970).

4. P. Reining, et. al, Village Women: Their Changing Lives and Fertility (AAAS, Washington, D.C., 1977).

5. I supervised the work of the psychoanalyst, Dr. Sonia Gojman de Millan, who interviewed mothers in both villages.

6. Charlotte Wiser, in this volume, points out that the greatest external threat to security in an Indian Village is no longer the invader but the media which seduce villagers and destroy social patterns which protect village integrity.

7. E.H. Erikson, Childhood and Society (W.W. Norton & Co., New York, 1950).

8. George M. Foster, "The Anatomy of Envy: A Study in Symbolic Behavior" Current Anthropolgy, Vol. 13 No.2 (1972).

9. M. Maccoby and G. Foster, Anthropological Quarterly, Vol. 43 No.4 (1970).

10. The joint management-union (Harman International-UAW) project to improve work in Bolivar, Tennessee is based on principles of security, equity, individuation and democracy. Participants have learned to evaluate change in terms of these principles. See Maccoby, Working Papers, Summer 1975.

_____*Shahid Javed Burki*

Comment

I will divide my comments on Professor Maccoby's paper into three parts: First, why is there at present such a great deal of emphasis on meeting basic needs? Second, what is meant by "meeting basic needs"? Third, in what way do I understand Professor Maccoby's emphasis on human development and why is it relevant for the concept of basic needs as it is understood by myself and my colleagues at the World Bank.

So, first, why basic needs? I would like to suggest that the present preoccupation with basic needs as an important objective of development is largely because of the industrial countries' disappointment with the performance of the developing countries over the past two and a half decades. This disappointment is not with the rates of growth in the national product of developing countries but with their inability to solve the problem of poverty. I do not have the time to go into various indices but it would be useful to recall at this time that in the last 25 years the combined wealth of the developing countries has grown at a rate of over 3.4% per annum. This is not a mean performance but despite this very rapid increase - rapid in a historical perspective - these countries continue to face a massive problem of poverty. It is this problem that is now receiving a great deal of attention and which has led to the emphasis on basic needs as a central concern in development. There are now some 920 million people who can be considered as seriously poor in the developing countries out of a total population of slightly over two billion which means, defined one way or another, something like 40 to 50% of the population of the developing countries is living in abject poverty. In laying this emphasis on basic needs, the developed countries are borrowing, I would also suggest, from their own recent experience, that of the Great Society Programs of the mid-sixties. In the 'fifties, there was a great deal of emphasis on growth, an emphasis that we can trace back to the developed countries' own experience with the Marshall Plan. The Marshall Plan's success with rebuilding the war-torn Europe was reflected in the growth-oriented strategies followed relentlessly by the "donor countries" in assisting the developing world in the 'fifties and the early part of the 'sixties. The Marshall Plan was concerned with the transfer of large amounts of capital from the U.S.A. to Europe. Likewise, the strategies pursued in the Third World were based on the premise that if the shortage of investment capital could be overcome by transfers from abroad, the problem of economic backwardness would be solved. The Johnson Administration's Great Society Programs grew out of the disappointment with the inability of the capitalist process to help the less privileged segments of the society. These programs, therefore, undertook to provide state support directly to the poor rather than through the market. The "basic needs approach" is based on a similar direct intervention by the Third World governments in meeting the minimum requirements for food, water and social services of <u>all</u> people. I can use a quote from Professor Maccoby to describe the way the West's own preoccupation with different facets of human development has influenced its thinking about the problems being faced by the developing countries. The earlier growth-oriented strategies and the present basic needs based strategies are the outcome of, as he put it while presenting his paper, "making your own personality and your own views reflect on the problem of other people."

Let me now describe the way the people of the Third World perceive this concern with meeting basic needs. The developing countries - or, more accurately, the elites that govern them - are worried about poverty but they are even more worried about being left behind. Despite the very impressive performance of the developing countries during the past quarter century, the fact remains that the per capita income gap between them and the developed countries has widened considerably. In 1950, incomes in the developed world were fifteen times as much as those of the developing nations; twenty-five years later, they were sixteen times as much. The gap has widened much more quickly for the poor nations. In 1950, the incomes of the developed countries were twenty-eight times those of the poor countries; in 1975, they were forty times as much. Accordingly, when the political and intellectual leaders of the Third World talk about solutions to the problems posed by their economic backwardness, they don't talk so much about the problem of meeting basic needs but about the equality of opportunity for their people in an equitable international economic order. They believe that such equality of opportunity does not exist in the present international order. Hence, their demand for restructuring the order, for restructuring it in such a way that the people of the developing countries, the goods they produce and the commodities they grow would no longer be discriminated against.

A situation of conflict is inherent in these two perceptions about the causes of the economic backwardness of the Third World and the action needed to improve its wellbeing. According to the developed countries, mass poverty in the Third World owes a great deal to the neglect of the problem of poverty by the Third World governments. This neglect cannot be allowed to go on and the developed countries must pull all the levers at their command to make these countries focus on poverty. The developing countries view the situation from the opposite side: they regard poverty as a consequence of an international economic order which does not allow fair play to their people and the goods and commodities they produce. Accordingly, their solution is to restructure the international economic order.

What do we mean by "basic needs"? While a satisfactory definition remains to be provided explicitly, it is possible to find three different interpretations in the literature on the subject. The first comes from the International Labor Organization, the institution that made the term "basic needs" popular. The ILO does not draw any distinction between ends and means. For them, "basic needs" means attainment of a number of objectives that range from adequate nutrition to participation in the development process. The U.S. Administration and Congress define basic needs in three different ways. First, "basic needs" is defined as "right to life" and absence from torture. The term "basic needs" is also defined at times to mean civil and political rights. The first two definitions combined, encompass the so-called "human rights." Finally, "basic needs" are also defined in terms of minimum requirement of several items of consumption: food, water, clothing, education, shelter, etc. As in the case of ILO, no distinction is made between ends and means. For, one may well ask the question: Can societies with certain political systems meet the basic consumption needs of all their people without tampering with the human rights of those in power? In some situations, there can indeed be a conflict between allowing human rights and meeting basic needs.

The third definition of basic needs can be attributed to myself and some of my World Bank colleagues who have been working on the development of basic needs as an operational concept. We define basic needs as those needs for consumption which are essential for maintaining productive life. In other words, we feel that people, in order to become a resource for the societies in which they live, must develop their potential. This potential can be developed only when they have access to all "basic needs" defined as food and nutrition, water and sanitation, basic education, basic health and basic shelter. From my point of view, it is interesting that Professor Maccoby, in presenting his paper, should have ascribed a certain crudity to the economists when they habitually translate meeting basic needs into the erection of fancy structures such as schools, hospitals and waterworks for which the world's poor have little need. The fact that this sort of translation occurs all too often cannot be disputed. What can be disputed is that economists are responsible for this translation. I would suggest that politicians must take a major share of the responsibility for this kind of vulgarization of the concept of basic needs. I would also like to point out that it is to escape from this vulgarization that we have defined three of our basic needs as "basic education," "basic health" and "basic shelter." No fancy buildings and structures here. Our emphasis is on providing education that prepares the individual for participating fully and productively in developing the economic, political and social environment in which he is placed. Basic health and basic shelter are meant to serve the same purpose.

Let me now get to the third part of my presentation: comments on the paper delivered by Professor Maccoby. You will find that the first two parts of my presentation are useful in understanding the main analytical thrust of Professor Maccoby's paper. I find the following five themes running through the paper.

First, the villages in the developing countries cannot be treated as autonomous units. Second, rapid change is occurring in the villages of the developing countries for essentially two important reasons, demographic pressure and the pressure of urban-biased modernization. Third, this change has introduced a considerable amount of tension in the village societies, tension which has led to some further changes in which the traditional groups have suffered and what Professor Maccoby calls "new entrepreneurs" have gained. Fourth, these imbalances can be exacerbated if basic needs-types of strategies are followed in the crude way in which they have been enunciated by the economists. This is so because economists tend to interpret basic needs in entirely material terms disregarding four important non-material needs: security, equity, participation and individuation. If the economists take account of these non-material needs they recognize them in only a vulgar way. Fifth, in incorporating these needs in strategies of development, the economists (and also those who work to bring about change) must be sensitive to the peculiar demands of the societies with which they are dealing.

If my rendition of Professor Maccoby's argument is correct, there is little that I find I could disagree with. But our agreement would be only on the surface for there are a number of things implicit in these hypotheses with which I do not feel entirely comfortable. Let me restrict myself to the following four:

- I find that the analysis presented in the paper has a Latin American bias. We have to get away from this bias if we want to generalize about all developing countries. Let me go back to the numbers that I gave earlier: out of the 920 million people that live in abject poverty, only 55 million are in Latin America. Conclusions that are based entirely on the Latin American situations would serve only 6% of the world's rural poor. To serve the rest, we should look at the rural situations in other parts of the globe. These situations are considerably different from that of Latin America.

- While accusing economists of being insensitive to micro considerations, Professor Maccoby's approach is equally insensitive to the demands of the less developed countries. As I pointed out earlier, the emphasis on basic needs is an emphasis placed by the developed countries. By and large, the less developed countries do not endorse this emphasis. They don't like this emphasis for the following three reasons:

    first, this emphasis is considered as a cheap option being picked up by the developed countries to help the developing countries. It is cheaper than the other options that the developing countries would like to have adopted;

    second, it is a way of deflecting the attention of the developing countries from their demand for a new international order; and _third_, the developing countries perceive the emphasis on basic needs as a way of keeping them from being modernized. I would suggest that Professor Maccoby's approach on human development adds one further constraint which will result in slowing down the process of change in LDCs or at least that is the way they will perceive it. The less developed countries want change, and they want change very rapidly. They will not be very sympathetic to any attempts to slow it down.

- The tension that Professor Maccoby notices in the villages between traditionalists and non-traditionalists is also present at the national level. Invariably and understandably it is the non-traditionalists - or to use his term "the new entrepreneurs" - that occupy positions of decisionmaking in these countries. They want change and modernization. Attempts to introduce different objectives of development would be seen with considerable suspicion by these people.

- For societies as poor as that of Asia and Africa, our primary emphasis has to be on meeting shortfalls in the consumption of basic needs as I have defined them. In many societies, security, equity, participation and individuation would be important and necessary means for delivering these needs. In many others, there may be a trade-off between material needs and non-material needs or non-material means for delivering these needs. In those cases where such a trade-off exists, I would suggest we must choose in favor of material needs.

In sum, therefore, there are several reasons why the type of emphasis that Professor Maccoby places on human development would not be acceptable to the countries in the Third World. They may be wrong in rejecting this - I don't think they are - but those who propose it must be aware of the pitfalls they are likely to encounter.

_____*Michael Maccoby*

Reply

Mr. Burki is on the side of elites who want change "and they want it very rapidly." They ask for a new international order which gives them a "fair deal on their products, particularly commodities." Yet, they resent America's concern with human rights and a fair deal for the rural poor in their countries. I do not believe the elites should have it both ways: a fair deal for them but not the poor. Why should the United States be concerned with a new international order which fattens the rich and ignores the poor? Why should we be interested in "modernizing" the Third World, when the means of modernization undermines values and institutions that support human development.

From a practical as well as a moral point of view such a policy appears unwise. Stability in the Third World will not be achieved unless there is greater security, equity, participation and individual development in these countries. Otherwise elites will find themselves sitting on the top of dynamite kegs.

The principles sketched in my paper appear as valid for The Philippines and parts of Africa as for Latin America (Reining et al., 1977). They have also proved applicable in rural America. The reason I concentrated on Mexico is because having lived and worked in that country for over eight years, I was able to draw on personal experience as well as the work of others.

Mr. Burki has confused ends and means. The goal of responsible policy should be to promote human development which can be defined in terms of security, equity, participation and individual development. Material goods, health services, food may all be essential means toward this end, but as means they must be continually evaluated in terms of the goal: human development. In speaking of a "trade-off between material needs and non-material needs," Mr. Burki is conceptually confused. It is not a matter of feeding people first and then worrying about other needs. The question he should ask is how we can help meet material needs in such a way that people in need become stronger and more self-sufficient. Such a policy requires individuals who understand how cultural values and institutions satisfy human needs and strengthen the members of a society.

Part 4

Discussion

Francis P. Conant

13. A Concluding Comment

<u>Village Viability in Contemporary Society</u> is an exploratory volume, made up of papers written from several points of view and representing research on most of Earth's continents and subcontinents. Given such a spread, the most a discussant can do is to attempt a kind of running commentary based on the individual papers, some of which show a concern for the universal aspects of village life and the village setting, while others are geographically based field studies analyzed from the perspectives of several different disciplines and questions. These categories provide an organizing framework for the discussion which follows, and I conclude with some comments on the notion of "viability."

Universal Aspects of Villages

The contributions of Mead, Maccoby, Howe, Simmons and Shear share a concern for highly generalized features of village life: features that contribute to the definition and identification of a village (Mead), its psychosocial attributes (Maccoby), the importance of energy sources (Howe), the role of education (Simmons), and the possibility of the village as the principal channel for development programs (Shear).

Mead's comments stress not only the characteristics of the village as a kind of settlement, but also the qualities of being a villager. These last I find of great importance because the village defined without reference to its inhabitants and the behavioral patterns seems an empty exercise. Mead's remarks stress what other papers in this volume also show--the changing patterns of village life, and the capacity of villagers to adapt to new conditions generated both within the village setting and outside of it. In this respect I find Mead's discussion of the <u>elective</u> village of great importance. The elective village is one in which the individual chooses to live, and is by no means a small world into which one is born. While villages have perhaps always served as a refuge for those in flight--a kind of forced election--I believe what Mead means is the open choice of the village as a setting in order to realize the positive qualities of that setting. Furthermore, commitment to the elective village need not be for the lifetime of the individual. In my own experience in West and East Africa, being a villager seldom means being confined to a one-village scene; long absences are common, and even expected. But, as Mead points out, there is a reservoir of local knowledge such that, on return, the individual can rightfully claim a place in the village setting.

Maccoby's paper, primarily concerned with the goals of development policies as directed at villages, stresses the psychosocial needs which best serve human growth and development. Maccoby contrasts the quality of social relations in two Mexican villages, one of which is deficient in providing positive psychosocial support, and the other of which is far more supportive. Maccoby identifies four human needs in order to maximize growth and development: security, equity, participation, and individuation. Maccoby warns that too often the process of development selects in favor of an entrepreneurial syndrome or social character which then becomes a model for others and all too frequently leads to a deterioration of interpersonal relations and cultural values.

Maccoby suggests that a development program, as a matter of policy, should require constant testing in terms of individual lives and the quality of interpersonal relations. Such evaluations could be made by participant observers, anthropologically trained, and sensitive to local values and expectations. The purpose of these evaluations would be to assess the impact of development on the cultural forms enhancing human growth and sociability. The problem remains, which Maccoby recognizes, of integrating these local evaluations into development planning and to keep the latter flexible enough so that changes can be made before too much damage is done. Anthropologists, Maccoby notes, do not often focus on policy-making, and those who make policy either tend to ignore or seek to mechanize the findings of anthropologists or others acting as participant observers.

In Burki's commentary on Maccoby's paper as well as in Maccoby's rejoinder, an important disagreement is clearly set forth. As I see it, the essence of their disagreement involves an inherent divergence between those, like Maccoby, who stress improvement in humanistic qualities of life as the goal of development policy, and others, like Burki, who emphasize the delivery of basic material needs so as to enhance economic productivity. Their divergent points of view involve basic moral, philosophical, and political issues, a discussion of which would take one far from the central topic of this volume.

Achieving the kind of feedback Maccoby feels is necessary, and which certainly seems essential, will require a variety of solutions, according to the nature of the planning agencies as well as the nature of the recipients. I feel that not all villages and villagers are quite so much at the mercy of changes being fostered by development programs or emanating from urban centers as Maccoby's paper suggests and illustrates from his Mexican examples. Perhaps there are profound differences in villages and villagers such that some are less responsive to commands issuing from palaces, statehouses, and bureaucracies--again, I would point to the African setting in which the village and the quality of village life seems much more independent of urban and national developments. By independence I think I mean the ability to sift and sort and select those kinds of change which the villagers prize, and to contain or reject those which they do not. In Africa the feedback mechanisms which are so necessary to the success of development programs might well be different than in Mexico or Latin America. Perhaps the distinction between "peasant" and "tribal" villages is operative here, but I myself tend to think in terms of differences in subsistence strategies--where villagers enjoy a mixed economy by means of which they can sustain themselves as well as participate in cash cropping, perhaps then they are in a better position to safeguard their own interests, and select positively for those interests, among all the changes impinging on them from exogenous sources.

Like Maccoby, Howe argues effectively for maximum local participation in deciding on local needs and how they may best be met in his discussion of the implications of renewable energy sources in the village setting. In a wide-ranging set of examples, we see the village environment as the appropriate setting for effective use of potentially revolutionary sources of energy. Technological innovation can improve the quality of life by providing a substitute for human energy expended in arduous physical labor. But local decisions are essential in the application of the new energy sources if the new technology is to be productively integrated. In this respect, I wish in Howe's paper there were a greater emphasis on the role of women in the early stages of consultation and decision-making as well as in the later periods of actual application of the new energy sources. Much of the human labor to be saved by the new renewable energy sources is the labor of women who, as I perceive it, have generally lost out and lost out badly in the context of rural development as it has taken place in the past and is still taking place. If the general quality of life is to be improved (whether by education for reliance and participation or by the application of new energy sources), there is another very real policy issue to be addressed; specifically, how to develop confidence in the existing leadership (national and local) in the abilities and capabilities of women to participate in directed change.

Like Maccoby and Howe, Simmons injects a strong humanistic note into the goals of development policy: development should be movement toward a more humane society than now exists in both the developing and the developed nations. Specifically concerned with the role of educational programs in development schemes, Simmons suggests a focus on young children and adults. Edcuational policy for the former should concentrate on improving the learning environment, and for the latter on enhancing self-reliance and participation. Since young children can be reached largely if not only through their parents, the two priority groups overlap and should be interlocked in planning. Simmons offers a wide-ranging set of examples of educational programs which have achieved a variety of results: good, bad, and mixed. The importance of his paper I find is in the policy requirements and strategies necessary to achieve the goal of development toward a more humane society. One policy requirement is a profound political commitment by national leadership to undertake a change in the status quo. Where this commitment is lacking, how can it be developed and maintained? Similarly, how can the national leadership and the foreign experts be convinced of the ability of the poor to identify their needs, as well as their capability to manage development programs at the local or village level?

From the extensive set of examples which Simmons provides, it seems apparent that programs emphasizing formal education have tended to bypass the rural poor and to increase the gap between them and urban dwellers. Informal and non-formal educational programs centered on the village, including those aimed at developing self-reliance and participation, have a greater chance of success, especially when there is local control at the village level.

There may be an additional point to be made here, perhaps ancillary to the main concerns of the paper by Simmons. The evidence he presents very strongly suggests that the village is a viable setting for the initiation and development of programs. If these are successful, they will have profound effects on urban and national centers. This makes of villages and villagers something other than passive respondents to urban-directed change. It means that the village setting and the village actors may be the <u>source</u> of widespread change as well as its recipients.

Shear's paper makes clear that the village is emerging as a principal channel for delivery of development programs. He explores this question in the context of the African Sahel, so that his paper is also geographically based and could appear in either section. The editors have grouped it with the several other papers that specifically address questions of development policy. In the recent, tragic droughts which have afflicted the region, assistance delivered at the national level too often failed to penetrate into areas where it was most needed--the remote and widely scattered villages of the semi-arid areas. Shear points to the deadening effect of the large bureaucracies which are created when massive assistance becomes available at a distance from its designated destination. Sometimes very little assistance trickles through. A way to ensure more effective delivery of short-term assistance, as well as to develop the entire Sahelian area, is to utilize local village authority structures.

Shear himself injects a note of caution by emphasizing the fact that throughout the Sahel there is a great variety of settlement types, each perhaps requiring a different approach in encouraging local control over development programs. In my own experience in the Sahel not all villages, for example, are nucleated; some are "village areas" with individual households surrounded by fields brought under cultivation by household members. Authority patterns may be less clear in the dispersed settlements than in the nucleated, and this may require a different approach in encouraging local control over development programs. Some Sahelian populations tend more or less strongly to transhumant or nomadic patterns of exploitation, and for these a still different approach may be necessary. Perhaps in these cases the seasonal aggregations of herders at traditional points of assembly might serve as the starting place for developing or reinforcing local controls over development programs. In both West and East Africa I have found that administrators tend to ignore the very delicate relationships nomadic pastoralists must maintain with sedentary populations if the herders are to survive. Development and administrative policies tend to treat the nomadic and sedentary populations as though they are separate entities, sometimes to the detriment of either or both. One approach might be to consider the nexus of the connection between pastoral and sedentary peoples as providing a potential structure for the administration of development programs.

Field Studies

Although less global in approach than the papers considered thus far, some of the same emphases are apparent in the contributions to this volume which are field-based studies, often in a regional context. With the possible exception of Bell's paper on Malaysia and Reining's on Hungary, the village setting in the Middle East, in India, in China and in Europe seems to be viewed as an active, even dynamic stage for the working out of larger problems. Perhaps I am over-reading what these diverse authors have to say, but my impression is that they view the village and villager not so much as a problem in the context of development and change, but as a solution.

In the paper by Schuchat and Jordan on what has happened to the "natural" (traditional?) village in China under successive regimes there may be both a moral and a predictive model for those concerned with development policy and the use of the village setting as a platform for change. The moral might be that the more things change, the more they remain the same, with the village persisting as the basic unit of production and ownership. But if this is so, there are nonetheless pervasive changes in the qualities of life identified as necessary for human development by Maccoby. Schuchat and Jordan note that in terms of these psychosocial needs, in the village-as-production-brigade, equity is far greater, there is more participation according to sex and age, and while individuation is less for some and more for others, security is at least as assured as in the context of the traditional Chinese village.

Schuchat and Jordan recognize the difficulty in generalizing from a single case or a single type of village in so large and complex an area as China, and their conclusions are carefully drawn. I would summarize these as saying, in effect, the village remains, as it has for centuries, the appropriate setting for the working out of adaptive strategies by local residents. Insofar as national centers in the past and in the present attempt to interfere with these strategies, the new equity and the greater degree of participation now found in at least some villages will reinforce villagers' capacities to say "no" to unacceptable proposals emanating from outside the village. Perhaps the 1978 National Party Congress cited by Schuchat and Jordan as encouraging criticism of production methods was itself in part stimulated by increasing self-reliance and self-confidence of village delegates to the Congress to speak up and be heard.

A similar kind of confidence in villagers is expressed by Wiser in her paper on North India. From a perspective of 50 years involvement, Wiser sees Indian villages as continuing to provide a necessary degree of security and an appropriate setting for the learning and expression of traditional roles. Throughout Wiser's paper there is a series of wry comments, gently made, on the subject of viability. During her half-century involvement in India the question hardly arose as to the viability of the roles she observed or the appropriateness of the village setting for their enactment.

Both Bell and C. Reining, respectively concerned with villages in Malaysia and Hungary, are faced with the kind of pervasive change absent from Wiser's experience of villages in North India. Bell predicts the demise of the paddy subsistence base of the Malaysian kampong village, and with it will go much if not all of the kampong's present social characteristics. I am myself not quite so certain that these characteristics are as ephemeral as Bell suggests. There is evidence presented elsewhere in this volume (see Bates and Weatherford, for example) to the effect that there may well be profound change and even complete substitution of subsistence strategies but that the village persists as an appropriate setting for continued social relationships.

In his paper on Hungarian villages, Conrad Reining points out that the traditional preoccupation of villagers with the acquisition and management of land seems certain to be replaced with other preoccupations—such as the choice of a village strategically placed so that the younger generation of residents have access to jobs in nearby centers. In many respects Reining's analysis of the trends affecting Hungarian villages point to their survival as elective settlements—one of the possibilities outlined by Mead and mentioned at the outset of this discussion. Because of striking changes in subsistence strategies, economic organization, dramatic shifts in the age structure of village populations, new goals and different techniques for attaining them, Reining is exceedingly cautious in his predictions for the future. Villages or rural settlements may well survive but for different economic, social, and psychosocial reasons than have existed in the past.

What may well be part of the future of the village in Hungary and elsewhere seems to have been part of the past in the Middle East—at least this is how I interpret the evidence offered by Bates in his paper on that region. Drawing on both historical and contemporary sources of data, including his own fieldwork, Bates delivers several messages of some importance to those concerned with the viability of the village

in contemporary society. The first message I infer is that
viability is assured to the extent variability of the village
format is maintained within a region, so that if a profound
change occurs not all forms of village settlement are affected equally. This seems to have been true of past history in
the Middle East as well as the contemporary period. The
second message I get from Bates is that in addition to the
different kinds of villages found within a given region, each
village settlement is likely to have a far greater capacity
for change and tolerance of change than is usually associated with settlements in rural areas. Villages are far more
than repositories of traditional or "folk" traditions. They
are also appropriate settings for the working out of individual, familial, and household strategies. As such, Bates
documents shifts in subsistence strategies--farming to wage
laboring, for example, or from livestock management to irrigation agriculture--for which the same village may remain a
viable setting.

Surprisingly (to me, and perhaps to others), the residents of many Middle Eastern villages have relatively shallow
genealogical depth in situ--in many cases less than 150 years,
according to Bates. And as a corollary, many villages are
new settlements. So there are at least two possibilities
here: one is a village settlement reoccupied and reused by a
series of populations, for each of whom different subsistence
strategies may be appropriate; and the second possibility is
the demise of an existing village and its replacement elsewhere by a new settlement. There is no reason of course why
both processes should not be going on at the same time, leading to the proliferation of villages in the 20th century.

Finally, Bates demonstrates for his area the importance
of perceiving villages within a regional context. The variability found in the Sahel of Africa, and with respect to
responses to change or planned development, no one village
type is likely to serve as a model for all existing village
formats. Although it goes beyond his mandate, I wish Bates's
paper had included more of the defining characteristics of
the regions with which he is concerned. Perhaps some of the
variability within regions might then become interpretable in
terms of common regional characteristics--or, perhaps not.
Bates's materials are based on recent research, still in
the process of being analyzed.

The two site-specific studies included in this volume
offer striking examples, in considerable historical depth,
of some of the observations made elsewhere by authors concerned with the universal characteristics of village life or
with the village setting as perceived regionally. Weatherford's

study of Kahl am Main in what is now West Germany shows above all the ability of the village format to survive throughout a thousand years of change. The changes are no less than sequential shifts from an original base as a tribal settlement engaged in agriculture and hunting, to milling in feudal times, industrialization in the 19th century, and to a pioneer site for the development of atomic energy in the 20th century. Yet another change is still in process for the residents of Kahl am Main insofar as productive industries are giving way to those providing services. Despite this long history of change, Kahl am Main still preserves a political and cultural identity as a village, a kind of moral community within which there also survives a concern for individual household subsistence locally supplemented even if mostly obtained from non-local resources.

From the turnover of populations Weatherford describes I would infer that at least several times in its past Kahl am Main has been elected by newcomers as their favored setting, a possibility which we have seen Mead believes must be allowed for, and which C. Reining also reports as a possibility in contemporary Hungary. From Weatherford's account, Kahl am Main may at times have been more supportive of the kinds of psychosocial needs identified by Maccoby than it was at other times, especially in the context of depopulation and flight of residents to the surrounding areas. A kind of opposite population movement now seems to be taking place, with residents of nearby centers moving into Kahl am Main either as settlers or as visitors utilizing the recreational facilities the village has developed. Although Weatherford does not develop the point, one wonders if in this new context--as well perhaps at different times in the past--Kahl am Main is both affecting as well as being affected by its surrounding environment. The villager as an active agent of change as well as its recipient is an important theme developed by Simmons, Shear, and others in this volume.

Of comparable antiquity to Kahl am Main, the alpine village of Törbel in Switzerland presents a quite different profile through time--a persistence of population, boundaries, and exploitation of multiple resource zones. In the paper by Netting and Elias, Törbel presents a rare opportunity to study a relatively complete demographic record, including the gradual population growth which commenced in the eighteenth century. Netting and Elias relate this phenomenon to an improved nutritional base, as supplemented by cultivation of the potato. The hypothesis is that improved nutrition positively affects fecundity, decreasing intervals between births, and leading to an increase in children ever born.

Netting and Elias rightly state that the biochemical and physiological pathways by which nutrition and fecundity are related are beyond the scope of their present paper. Perhaps what could be discussed further in their paper, however, is the statistical reliability of regulatory mechanisms hypothesized to be at work in populations as small as those of Törbel's. The regulatory mechanisms relating to non-human species and their social behavior, which the authors cite at the outset of their paper, are derived from studies of quite large populations. This is true also of the Frisch-Revelle hypothesis linking nutrition and body composition to fecundity. While it is true there is some confirmation of the nutrition--fecundity linkage as detectably operable in small groups of gatherers and hunters, I also believe that in these cases there is a drastic change in both nutrition and activity levels which would seem considerably more dramatic than those described for Törbel. In view of this, it would be of extreme interest to know more and in greater detail the nutritional status and activity patterns of Torbel women before and after the introduction of the potato.

Viability

This discussion ends with a few comments on viability. To me, the word more properly applies to the villager than the village itself. The reification of the term village is an error to be avoided if at all possible. It is not villages that survive so much as it is the strategies which people undertake and for which the village setting--in scale and other attributes--is particularly suitable.

The setting itself, composed of mortar, thatch, stone--whatever--can disappear, but this has little to say about its viability. As we have seen, the setting can be rediscovered and rebuilt from old materials or new. Finally, and in my opinion, an over-riding requirement of rural development policy is to protect the option of people to live at the scale and in the setting which for millenia have been the hallmarks of village life. In this regard, the notable humanist concerns expressed by several authors in this volume is both reassuring and most welcome.

Index

Abdulfattah, Kamal, 165-166
abortion, 91
absentee landlords, 210
absorptive capacity, 238
academic curricula. *See* education
Accion Cultural Popular (ACPO), 302-303
adaptive strategies, 340
adolescents (Mexico), 318
Africa, 331
Africa, West, 235. *See also* Sahel
age distribution (Hungary), 115
Agency for International Development (AID), 240, 247, 257, 259, 298
agrarian capitalism, 228
Agricultural Producers Cooperatives (China), 196
agriculture, 6, 37, 39-40, 53-54, 179, 241, 246, 261
  in China, 201; employment and, 163, 306; in Hungary, 115; income trend, 249; intensification, 211, 212, 217; in Malaysia, 207, 209, 213, 226. *See also* farming, food
alcoholism (Mexico), 316

Ali, Husin, 213, 214, 216
Alinsky, Saul, 288, 297
amenorrhea, postpartum, 100
Anatolia, 167
Angola, 298
anthropological theory, 21
anthropologists,
  policy-makers and, 322; village and, 21
appropriate technology, 282-283, 308
Arensberg, Conrad M., 7, 8, 11
atomic power. *See* nuclear energy

Bambara tribe (Mali; Upper Volta), 241
Bangladesh, 303
barefoot doctors, 304-305
basic needs, 11, 249-251, 325, 327, 330
  of children, 300; in China, 308; conflict with human rights, 327; consumption shortfalls and, 330; definitions of, 327-328, 329; economics and, 328; education and, 299, 308; government intervention and, 326; Great Society Programs and, 325-326; nonmaterial, 328-329, 330; political factions and, 306
Bavaria, 35-67

Bedouin, 166
birth interval, 95, 100, 101
Botswana, 298
Bozo tribe (Mali), 242
Brahmins, 149
Brazil, 292, 295, 298, 301
Budapest, 111, 118
bureaucratization, 6
bus/rail network (Hungary), 116

cadre system, 195
calories, 100, 106. See also food
Canadian Agricultural Economic Society, 261
carrying capacity, 69
caste (India)
 changes in, 154, 155; division of labor by, 145; interrelationships, 137-138; in Karimpur, 142
celibacy, 70, 90, 102
census, 190-191, 251-252
 Swiss, 73
Center for Research in Economic Development, 249
central settlement policy (Hungary), 119
change, 152, 324
 educational systems and, 291; in rural systems, 178
chastity, premarital (Törbel), 87
children
 cognitive needs of, 300; in Santa Maria, 317. See also nutrition
China, People's Republic of, 185-204
 barefoot doctors, 304-305; communal land, 196; communes, 193, 195, 197, 201-202; communication, 199; education in, 192, 295, 296, 297, 308; local leadership in, 198; market-town in, 192; mini-hydroelectric generators in, 275;
pigs, 200-201; population movements, 197; private plots, 196; production brigade, 185-205; property confiscation, 195; public utilities, 191-192; radio and multimedia campaigns, 303; rationing, 197-198; rural industry, 230; study groups, 295-296; village/central government relationship, 193
Chinese Nationalists, 191, 194-195
Chinese villages
 changes, 191; education in, 192; evolution of, 188; typical, 187
Ch'ing Ming celebration, 188
cholera control, 153
Chou en Lai, 199, 200
Christianity, 38-39, 41-43, 317
CILSS (Interstate Commission to Combat the Effects of the Drought), 236
city
 attraction of, 28; dominance of, 163. See also urban life
Club du Sahel, 236, 246, 248, 259-260
 financial support, 237
coal, 274
collective memory, 7, 20, 24-25
Colombia, 296, 301, 302
colonial period (Mali), 239-240
Colyton, 83, 91
Comilla Project (East Pakistan), 303
commerce, 37, 40, 44-45, 53
commercialization, 4
communication
 face-to-face, 36; hearing/seeing, 23. See also education; Hungary; multimedia
community
 development (China), 298;

health system (Sahel), 251-253; moral, 54-56; needs (Sri Lanka), 306-307, 308; participation (Sri Lanka), 306; services in, 52-54
commuters (Hungary), 114
composting, 242
conception
 premarital, 90; seasonality of, 100, 101
conscientizacao, 301
consumption needs, 328. See *also* basic needs
contraception. See family limitation
cooking. See energy
Cook Islanders, 27
cooperatives, 112, 113, 128, 295, 318
 in Senegal, 305; in Sri Lanka, 306
cottage industry, 77, 86, 102, 306
cotton (West Africa), 235
critical awareness. See education
Crulai, 86, 91
Cuba, 295
cultural values. See values
culture, in Mexican villages, 317
"culture shock," 26

DAC (Development Assistance Committee), 250
decentralization, 13, 257-259, 339
decision-making, by married couples, 227
democracy, development and, 287
demographic and health planning, 252
demographic methods, 78, 79, 81, 82
demographic pressure, 328
demographic transition, 11
 in Malaysia, 229
demography, historical, 76

desertification, 150, 168, 170, 179, 236
detoxification. See migration
developing countries, national product of, 325
development
 advantages of village, 238; definitions, 287; in diversified rural economy, 231; integrated rural programs, 256; media campaigns for, 301; objectives, 246, 325, 330; policy for, 315, 318, 322, 331; problems, 236; Sahel, 236; social needs and, 321; village role, 258; village viability and, 1, 4-5, 12
diet. See food
diversification, economic, 230, 231
Djoliba (Mali), 239-241
Dogon tribe, 242, 243
domestic animals, 113, 150, 241
domestic cycle, paddy farming households, 211, 228
dominant family. See family
Doukolomba (Mali), 241
drought. See Sahel

East Pakistan, 303
economic activities, 229, 230
economic autonomy, 21
economic backwardness, causes of, 327
economic development, policy issues, 336
economic specialization. See labor, division of
education, 48, 57, 287, 290, 291, 293, 299, 302, 308, 318
 in Angola, 298; appropriate technology and, 282-283, 308; in Bangladesh, 303; in Botswana, 298; in Brazil, 292, 295, 301; in China, 295, 296, 297, 308;

in Colombia, 296, 301, 302; for critical awareness, 289, 297, 298, 299; in Cuba, 295; curriculum decisions, 292; dialogue method, 295; dual system, 293, 297; economic growth and, 287, 295; in Ecuador, 298; employment and, 289-290, 292; equal opportunity and, 291; in Ethiopia, 298; "expert solutions," 294; formal, 288, 296, 297; in Ghana, 303; in Guinea Bissau, 298; in Guyana, 298; health, 304; human development and, 295, 296; informal, 338; in Jamaica, 296, 298; in Mozambique, 296; multimedia and, 303; nonformal, 288, 294, 295, 308; in Pakistan, 289-292, 297; policy issues, 307-308, 338; the poor and, 287, 289, 295, 299, 308, 338; problem-posing, 296, 297, 307; production skills and, 299; radio schools, 302; reforms, 294; for self-reliance, 288, 293, 299, 300-307, 308; in Singapore, 292; in Somalia, 298; in Swaziland, 296; in Tanzania, 298; technical, 292; types of, 288-289; wealth and, 287, 308; in Zambia, 298. *See also* literacy
ejido lands, 316
electrification (Hungary), 116-117
elites, 289, 293, 295, 326, 331
employment, agricultural/nonagricultural, 163. *See also* labor
endogamy, 7, 111, 215
energy, 272, 273
for cooking, 117, 272; division of labor and, 283; needs, 275; photovoltaics, 276, 277; renewable, 21, 337; in rural areas, 271; in Third World, 269; traditional, 269, 270; in urban areas, 270; use per hectare, 271; in villages, 270, 272; wind, 275, 276. *See also* hydroelectricity; nuclear energy; solar energy
entrepreneurs, 228, 318, 330
epidemic disease, 83
equity, 11, 287, 321, 329
as psychosocial need, 318-319, 323; as Third World stability need, 331
Ethiopia, 276, 298
exogamy, 7, 140, 187, 215

FAO (Food and Agricultural Organization), Office of Sahelian Relief, 236, 249, 259
family
in China, 197; completed, 91; dominant, 188; enclosure (India), 141; in Santa Maria, 317; security in, 319. *See also* household
family limitation, 91, 95, 101, 105
in Bangladesh, 303; in Mexico, 318
family plots (China), 200-201
family reconstitution, 71
farmers, 12, 139, 339
farming
dryland, 246; real income from, 248; part-time, 227, 228. *See also* agriculture, Sahel
farms
in China, 189; cooperative, 112, 113, 318; private, 111, 113, 196; size of, and labor, 175-176; state, 112
fecundity, 91
Fei Hsiao-t'ung, 185, 200

fertility, 86, 91, 95, 100, 101, 102
  indigenous methods of control, 253; Industrial Revolution influence on, 77; malnutrition and, 100; rates, 91, 92, 172, 253
feudalism, 40-46
food, 99, 100, 107, 117, 235, 246-248, 255
food production, 236
Foster, George, 315, 319, 320
Freire, Paulo, 288, 296, 297, 301, 307
Fromm, Erich, 315-316, 319

Gandhi, Mahatma, 288, 297
"Gang of Four," 201
gardens, 36, 40, 54, 112-113
Gazza Plain settlement, 165
gentry, Chinese, 195
Germanic tribes, 38-40
Germans, ethnic, 60, 109-110
Ghana, 303
Göklan Turkmen, 171
Gombad-i Kavus (Iran), 171
grain
  bread, 107; market, 245; parcher, 136, 147; production, 246-248, 255
Great Society Programs, 325, 326
growth-oriented strategies, 326
guest workers, 55, 61-63. *See also* migration
Guinea Bissau, 298
Gürgan Plain (Iran), 171
  migration from Sistan, 174
Gürgan River (Iran), 173
Guyana, 298

Harman International, 324
Hausa tribe (Niger), 247 248
health delivery (village), 251-253
health education, nontraditional, 304
herders/farmers, 12, 242, 339
Hindi, 125
Hinduism, 126, 155, 156, 157
hoarding, 316
household, 22, 69, 87, 113, 210, 212, 215, 224, 342
  peasant, 70, 90. *See also* family
human development, 320
  in Africa, 331; basic needs and, 325; change and, 330; development and, 322; in Latin America, 331; modernization and, 331; national goals and, 322; in Philippines, 331; as policy goal, 331; psychosocial needs and, 318-319; religious systems and, 320; self-sufficiency and, 321;
humane society, 287, 308
humanist, 307
human rights, development and, 331
Hungary, 109-121
  communication in, 116, 118; commuters in, 114; cooperative farms in, 112, 113; gardens in, 112-113; transportation networks, 116
hunters/gatherers, 69
Hutterites, 95
Hütteroth, Wolf-Dieter, 162, 165-166, 167
hydroelectricity, 274, 275

illegitmacy, 70, 90
ILO (International Labor Organization), 327

income
  alternative, 178;
  diversified, 224; gap,
  225; household, 224; of
  paddy farmers, 218; per
  capita, 326; of rice
  farmers, 210
India, 123-159
  cooperatives in, 127, 128;
  health problems, 134-135;
  invisible village walls,
  132; *jajmani* system, 13,
  137-139; radio and multimedia campaigns in, 303;
  roles in village, 133;
  walls, 141. See also
  caste
individuation
  as nonmaterial need, 329,
  331; in North America, 320;
  as principle of development, 287; as psychosocial
  need, 318, 320, 323; requirements for, 321; in
  village, 320
industrialization, 36, 45-
  49, 56-57
industry
  in Germany, 37; in Hungary
  110-111, 118; occupations
  in, 86; rural, 230; in
  villages (China), 192-193
inequality, rural, 210, 228
inheritance, 87, 228
Institute de Recherche en
  Science Humaine, 24
Institute of the Sahel, 259
intercourse, premarital, 70
Interstate Commission to
  Combat the Effects of
  the Drought (CILSS),
  236
irrigation, 168, 169, 247

jajmani system, 13, 137-139
Jamaica, 296, 298
Japan, 227
justice, as freedom form
  exploitation, 319

Kahl (West Germany), 35-67
kampong, 12, 213-217, 225
  230. See also Malaysia
Kanpur (India), 127
Karimpur (India), 129
Keita, Modibo, 243
Kenya, 317
kinship and tenancy
  (Malaysia), 210
Kirman basin (Iran), 163
Kor River (Iran), 168
kulak, 228

labor
  division of, 167, 255;
  markets, 215; mobility of,
  215; nonfarm, 139, 145, 146,
  147-148, 227, 229
land, Hungarian attitudes
  toward, 112-113
Land Alienation Act (Malaysia), 227
landlessness, 175-176
land reform, 164, 173
land tenure (China), 196
leadership, 175, 239, 299,
  308, 317
  in China, 190-191, 198;
  in Senegal, 305; tradi-
  tional, 216, 305; in West
  Africa, 239
learning. See education
Leeds, A., 185-186
life expectancy, 83, 86
life tables, 83, 85
lineages, village organization and, 258
literacy, 301, 309
  in Brazil, 301; projections,
  310, 311, 313. See also
  education

machismo, 316
Main River (West Germany),
  35-36, 63-64
Mainz (West Germany), 42-45
Malaysia, 207-231
  agricultural diversification
  in, 207; economic growth

rates, 208-210; GNP per capita, 226; Land Alienation Act, 227; population growth rates, 209
Mali, 239-241
Malthusian checks, 69
Mao Tse-tung, 288, 294, 297, 304. *See also* China, People's Republic of
marriage, 70, 86, 91, 101, 102, 111
Marshall Plan, 326
Marvdasht plain (Iran), 168
mass-media campaigns, 301, 303
material needs, 321. *See also* basic needs
material well-being, 273
matrilocal residence, 29-30
McLuhan, Marshall, 20, 22
media (Hungary), 118
medical services (Hungary), 118
medicine
  Eastern, 134; modern, 79, 83, 134
memory, continuity of, 24-25
methane, 201, 276
methods, demographic, 103, 107
Mexico, 316
  cooperative farms in, 318; human development and, 331; villages in, 317
migrants, 127, 174
migration, 20, 44, 46, 56-63, 70, 77, 78, 102, 164, 174, 243, 244, 247, 253
  detoxification through, 27, 28; internal, 162; temporary, 27
Millan, Sonia, 317-318
milling, 35-47
mining, 37, 47-49
mobility, personal, 216, 229
modernization
  definition, 272; human development and, 331; in Hungary, 341; urban-biased, 328
moral order, 3, 6, 320
mortality, 70, 79, 102, 172
  adult, 83; crop failure and, 83, 100; Industrial Revolution influence, 77; infant, 83, 84, 85; rate, 79, 83, 253
Moslems, in Germany, 28-29
Mozambique, 296
multimedia campaigns, 303
mutual aid teams (China), 196
Myrdal, Gunnar, 289, 299

Napoleonic Wars, 43-44
National Party Congress (China), 203
National Socialism (Nazis), 48-49, 58-59
needs. *See* basic needs, consumption needs, nutrition
Neolithic era, 3, 161
New International Economic Order, 326-327, 329, 331
nuclear energy, 35, 50-51, 273-274
nuptiality, 88, 89, 90
nursing, 100, 101
nutrition, 99, 101, 102, 254
  of children, 300, 306; of lactating mothers, 306
Nyerere, Julius, 288, 289, 296, 297, 298

Oaxaca (Mexico), 170
occupations (Hungary), 115
OECD (Organization for Economic Cooperation and Development), 237
Office du Niger, 243
onchocerciasis control program (Upper Volta), 247
ORD (Regional Development Organization), 257-259

352 Index

outmigration, 226, 227, 229
  from Malaysian paddy
  farms, 225; ownership
  rights in land and, 228.
  See also migration

paddy farming, 210, 217,
    219, 227
  household income from,
  224; households, 210, 212;
  markets, 218
Pakistan, 289-293, 296-298,
    308
  literacy pyramids, 312
Palestine, 165, 166
Pao-chia control system,
    190-191
paramedical training (China),
    304
participant observers,
    policy-makers and, 322
participation
  education for, 308; political structure and, 323;
  as psychosocial need, 318-
  319, 321, 323, 329; for
  Third World stability,
  331; types of, 321
patriarchy
  in Malaysia, 227; in
  Tierra Alta, 317
Peace Corps, 322
peasants, 3, 69, 99, 186,
    210, 298, 337
people's militia (China),
    191
pest control, 246
petroleum, 273
Peul, trans-Sahelian herders, 241, 242
Philippines, 331
photovoltaics. See energy
policy-makers, microstudies
    and, 322
poor, rural
  cost effective training
  for, 299; in economic
  development, 331; education for self-reliance, 289

population, 1, 2
  control of, 69, 70; decline
  (in rural Middle East), 163;
  dynamics of, 73; equilibrium, 69, 70, 77, 102;
  growth, 9, 69, 77, 87, 102,
  209, 220, 225; movements
  (China), 197; nutrition
  and, 343; reconstruction of,
  73; regulation, 70; resource
  match and, 10; rural, 1, 2,
  163, 269; stationary, 95;
  structure, 95. See also
  poverty
potato, 43, 99, 101, 106, 107
poverty, 325, 326, 327, 329
price support policies
    (Malaysia), 227
primate settlement hierarchy,
    164
production brigade (China),
    185-205
production skills, 299
proto-industrialization, 40
psychosocial development, 321
psychosocial needs, 13, 203,
    318, 322, 323, 335, 336
psychosocial security, 11
public investment decisions,
    218, 224
public schools. See education
Punjab, 100

railroad, impact on Kahl,
    45-47
rationing (China), 197-198
receptive, dependent, as
    character type (Mexico),
    316, 318
Redfield, Robert, 5, 185, 315
refugees, 42, 49, 58-61
regional analysis, 161-163,
    180, 342
religion, 41-43, 57-59, 62-63
    320
replacement rate, 90
reproduction, 90, 317, 319
rice (Malaysia)
  consumption and imports,

221; price supports, 222-224; production, 207-231
Roman Empire, 37-39
Rorschach tests (Mexico), 320
rules, of tenure and marriage, 7
rural economy, diversified, 231
rural life (Hungary), 114, 120
rural population. *See* population
rural proletariat, 186
rural transformation, 4, 307
rural-urban linkages, 115-116

Sahel, 10, 238, 247, 248, 249, 258, 259
  drought in, 235, 236;
  health system in, 251-253
Santa Maria (Mexico), 317
Sarvodaya Shramadana Movement (Sri Lanka), 306-307
schools, 43, 57, 62, 117-118, 291, 308
  See also education
security, 143, 165, 167, 187
  as nonmaterial need, 329;
  as principle of development, 287; as psychosocial need, 318-319, 321, 323; required for Third World stability, 331
self-determination, development theories and, 295
self-reliance, 300-307, 308
  See also education
self-sufficiency, 13, 215, 218
Senegal
  animation rurale, 305-306;
  management methods in, 305
servants, *Kahars* as, 149

settlements, 163, 167, 335
  in Hungary, 119; in Iran, 168; *kampong*, 230; kin-based, 214; in Kirman Basin, 163; in Mesopotamia, 170; method of study, 164; in Ottoman empire, 165; paddy monocultures, 214; in Palestine, 165, 166; in Syria, 165. *See also* villages
sexes
  equality as psychosocial need, 319, 323; relationship between (Mexico), 317, 319
shepherds, 150
site continuity, 9, 342
social character
  development planning and, 317; economic development and, 321; exploitation and, 319; as limit to change, 322; in Mexican village, 313, 318
social conflict, 321
social organization
  in China, 186; of paddy production, 213
social science, role of, 259-262
social selection (Mexico), 316, 321
social stratification, 176
solar energy, 276, 277-284
  culture and, 280-281; in remote areas, 277; technology, 275-277
Somalia, 298
Somono fishing tribe (Mali), 242
Spessart region, 35-67
Sri Lanka, 306-307, 308
stability, humanistic principles and, 331
sterility, 91
Stone Age, 38
subsistence economy, 10, 12, 241, 254

354 Index

Sung Dynasty, 190
Swiss communes, 27

Tanzania
  education programs, 298;
  radio and multimedia
  campaigns in, 303; use of
  solar energy, 279
taxes, 194, 195, 240
technical change, 9
technical training. See
  education
technology
  agricultural, 70; failure,
  villagers and, 282-283;
  paddy farming, 229; standards for introducing, 248
Thirty Years War, 41-42
Tierra Alta (Mexico), 317
Tolna (Hungary), 109
Törbel (Switzerland), 71,
  77, 79, 99, 102
trade. See commerce
Treaty of Westphalia, 42
tribal council, 39-41
Turkey, village/agriculture
  dynamics in, 162
Turkmen
  in Anatolia, 167; fertility rates of, 172

unemployed youth (Sri Lanka),
  306
UNESCO, literacy training,
  297
urbanization, 4
urban life (Hungary), 113,
  114, 119
urban-rural differentials
  (China), 198
Urdu, 125

values, 317, 321
villagers, 8, 11, 12, 134,
  335, 337
  continuity of, 14; part-
  time, 13; relationships
  with nonvillagers, 165;
  roles, 4

villages, 8, 123, 136, 162,
  177, 248, 251
  Chinese, 185-204; completeness of, 9; continuity,
  166, 239, 343; coopera-
  tives, 303; Crulai, 86, 91;
  definitions of, 3, 6, 19,
  186-187; dependence, 167;
  development and, 238, 298,
  321, 340; Djoliba, 239-241;
  Doukolomba, 241; elective,
  11, 29-31, 335, 341; endogamous, 111; estimated
  number of, 1; exogamous,
  140; formation of, 162;
  future of, 4, 120-121, 202-
  203; global, 20; Gombad-i
  Kavus, 171; growth of, 162;
  health delivery in, 251; in
  Hungary, 116, 119; identity, 111, 343; investment
  in, 173-174; in Kahl, 35,
  343; in Karimpur, 129; in
  Kashan, 164; in Kenya, 317;
  leadership in, 317, 321;
  new selectivity in, 30;
  nonautonomous, 328; organization of, 111-112, 186,
  190, 194-195; peasant, 70,
  185; production brigade and,
  340; relationship to state,
  236; resources of, 7; roles
  in, 133, 134, 137; in Santa
  Maria, 317; school management in, 297; self-sufficient, 21, 150, 193; sites
  importance of, 144, 155;
  sizes of, 1, 111, 172, 187-
  188; strains on, 246;
  structure, 8, 12, 253; test
  of viability, 5, 119; Tierra
  Alta, 317; Törbel, 71, 77,
  79, 99, 102, 343-344; traditional, 23; tribal, 3, 38,
  167, 337; types of, 6, 21,
  239, 339; values in, 317;
  walls, 186. See also kampong
  specific villages
village viability, 9, 21, 116-

117, 123, 131, 132, 141,
145, 197, 203, 322, 335,
333, 341, 342, 344
definition of, 5; development and, 4, 238;
population structure and,
7; problems of, 5; strangers and, 23, 125; tests
of, 7, 119, 120; urban
centers and, 163
vineyards (Hungary), 112-113
vital statistics. *See* census
volunteers (Columbia), 302

wealth, limits to, 323
witch hunts, 41-42
Wolf, E. R., 185-186

women
in communes (China), 199;
managing cultivation, 227;
in Mexican villages, 317-318; role of, 227, 256,
317, 337
World Bank, 294, 298, 325,
327
World War II, 59-61

Yang, Martin, 185, 202
Yoruk pastoralists (Anatolia),
167

Zaire, 100
Zambia, 298
Zurich, 77